Dangerous Truths & Criminal Passions

Thomas DiPiero

Dangerous Truths & Criminal Passions

The Evolution of the
French Novel, 1569–1791

Stanford University Press Stanford, California 1992

Stanford University Press
Stanford, California
© 1992 by the Board of Trustees of the
Leland Stanford Junior University

Printed in the United States of America

CIP data are at the end of the book

Preface

In this study I contest the axiomatic assertion that the novel developed as a bourgeois art form. I argue instead that before it ever reflected, reproduced, or in some other fashion seemed to champion middle-class values the novel articulated the French aristocracy's hegemonic claims to natural ascendancy. French fiction confronted aesthetics with ideology in the seventeenth and eighteenth centuries, and it codified as resolutely political a literary genre that, because of its ostensible lack of a classical antecedent, remained more or less formally marginal.

In contradistinction to a great many studies of the novel, then, I locate the genre's early manifestations—and *not* its teleological origin, I should add—in the early years of the seventeenth century. During that time, rules dictating the novel's structure and subject matter defined its literary form and attendant political use. Consequently, the aim of my work is not only to sharpen the literary taxonomic systems governing the interpretation of fiction, but to understand the dialectical relationship that the novel as a discursive practice entertains with history and ideology.

My most fundamental claim in this study is that the novel developed first and foremost in France as a determinate political practice. Its aesthetic marginality provided it with an ideological malleability enabling it to represent resolutely political positions as natural and organic. In this book, I offer an account of seventeenth- and eighteenth-century French fiction as it negotiated the political concerns of dominant social groups, rearticulating the complex of moral, political, and social discourses. I argue that the debates about verisimilitude, referentiality, and literary and moral excellence surrounding early French fiction helped stake out discursive fields which in turn contributed to the formation of specific class consciousnesses.

This study is not by any means an exhaustive account either of prose fiction of the seventeenth and eighteenth centuries, or of the staggering complexities that obtain in the articulation of literary and political practice. It is, rather, an attempt to understand how specific groups naturalize their social positions by legitimating particular kinds of stories. Consequently, where previous studies of the novel identify precise narrative techniques as constituting a literary mode deemed to be self-evidently mimetic or "realistic," I attempt to identify the political forces that valorized specific narrative forms as best able to express or sustain extant social relations.

Many readers may be unfamiliar with some of the novels I cite here, particularly those dating back to the early years of the seventeenth century. Most of them, nevertheless, were popular successes in their time. Because studies of the French novel generally begin with the eighteenth century, I have not assumed that modern readers have any particular familiarity with works that antedate the publication of Madame de Lafayette's *La Princesse de Clèves*. Whenever possible, I cite current or readily available editions of the sources I treat, and in general I have provided my own translations, except in the cases of those texts I cite extensively; for these works I have relied on existing English translations.

A number of friends and colleagues have provided me with immeasurable support by listening to my ideas, reading drafts of the manuscript, arguing with me, and pretending to agree with me. For their special help I would like to thank Sharon Willis, Pat Gill, Philip Berk, Bonnie Smith, Mieke Bal, Teresa Jillson, Gerald Bond, Claudia Schaefer, Philip Lewis, Craig Owens, Richard Estell, and Jeff Hilyard. I should also thank the University of Rochester for providing support for some of the research done in Paris. An earlier version of Chapter 6 appeared in *Postmodernism Across the Ages*, ed. Bennett Schaber and William Readings (Syracuse, N.Y.: Syracuse University Press, 1991).

                                                              T. D.

Contents

Dangerous Truths & Criminal Passions

Introduction

In 1755 Bishop Armand-Pierre Jacquin published his *Entretiens sur les romans: Ouvrage moral et critique* (Dialogues on novels: Moral and critical study), a mildly petulant exposé of the political and aesthetic bankruptcy of prose fiction. Like many of his contemporaries, Jacquin believed that novels were not only useless, but detrimental to public decency as well, and he devotes most of his study to demonstrating in point-by-point fashion the snares into which novel readers are likely to fall. Disrespect of the monarch's grandeur, wanton irreligion, and a headlong plunge into moral depravity are but three that Jacquin describes. For over one hundred years, since Jean Chapelain published his "De la lecture des vieux romans" (On reading old novels) in 1646, critical treatises devoted exclusively to theoretical discussion of the French novel had raised the question of fiction's power to degrade not only virtue and truth, but the literary forms that had been empowered to serve them as well. Jacquin takes the stock critical assumption that novels would lure readers away from moral truth and appends to it an exhaustive historical account of the actual deleterious social and material effects he believes prose fiction can have. He establishes the intimate connection between the aesthetic and the political natures of the novel when he writes in his preface, "To encourage the respect of virtue, the veneration of truth, and the love of literature are at once the spirit and motive of these debates. To fulfill this obligation worthy of a citizen, nothing seemed to me more fitting than the critical examination of novels."[1] Jacquin's claim that his project is "worthy of a citizen" displays the extent to which he views the proliferation

---

[1] Jacquin, p. vii.

of novels as a threat not only to the institution of literature, but to the very social fabric of the nation.

Jacquin's work is largely derivative, in some spots patterned so closely on previous essays that it almost appears plagiarized. Asking, for example, along with Clapiers de Vauvenargues, whether fictive illusion can hold up to more than one reading,[2] he also copies Pierre-Daniel Huet's historical search for the novel's provenance, which the latter undertook in his *Lettre-traité sur l'origine des romans* (Treatise on the origin of novels).[3] If Jacquin borrowed material from previous writers, however, the thrust of his essay is both original and pugnacious. Where Huet found the Talmudic and Moslem narrative traditions to be harmless exercises in poetic mystification, for example, Jacquin condemns them as dangerous political propaganda cunningly designed to unravel the moral fiber of Western civilization. Claiming that the Roman Empire's fall was caused by the appropriation of Greek and Syrian fiction (53–55), he goes so far as to suggest that the English and the Dutch were attempting to prevail surreptitiously over France by exporting so many novels there (118–21). Jacquin's historical and theoretical explanations of the spread of prose fiction may seem exaggerated and even paranoid, but he is among the first to have explicitly addressed the social function of novels. Daring to make the connections earlier writers had only hinted at, Jacquin identifies prose fiction as a new discursive practice that so closely imitates more venerated literary forms that it appropriates their power to reproduce social reality, and so has the power to dismantle the political and moral fiber of an entire nation.

This book examines the early French novel and the series of modifications it underwent resulting from the dynamic tension between political and aesthetic domains. Jacquin's complaint that novels sullied legitimate literary forms and menaced the security of the social apparatus, although written in the eighteenth century, is emblematic of the criticisms the novel endured beginning in the middle of the seventeenth century. Such attacks will serve as the springboard for my analysis of fiction's relationship to approved literary

---

[2] Jacquin, p. 169. See also Vauvenargues, who claimed in his *Introduction à la connaissance de l'esprit humain* that "one does not reread a novel" (p. 124).

[3] First published in 1669. A very good modern edition has been prepared by Fabienne Gégou.

genres and the legitimizing authority that empowered those genres to represent sanctioned ideological positions. These attacks will also help clarify the political issues at stake in the ostensibly aesthetic critiques of fiction. From the beginning of the seventeenth century, prose fiction was a marginal literary form because, unlike the more venerated forms of tragedy, history, and the epic, it lacked an antecedent in classical antiquity. Yet, because early novels were nearly exclusively written and read by an aristocratic public, they participated in the reproduction and, indeed, in the shaping of the aristocracy's values. At once aesthetically bankrupt and ideologically sound, the early French novel articulated the contradiction between the discourses supporting the structures of power and the codification of power in a budding and still unstable literary genre. As novelists began appropriating formal characteristics of the classical genres in an attempt to legitimize prose fiction, they caused the novel to mediate between aesthetic and political ideals. The manner in which the novel inscribed and transformed ideological and aesthetic concerns will be the focus of this study.

The novel's aesthetically marginal status kept it in constant dialogue with the approved literary forms of the day. For example, when novelists began mimicking narrative devices common to the epic[4] or when critics called fiction a simple imitation of history, they underscored the intertextuality that situated the novel in a dialectical relationship to contemporary literary standards and consequently to the political power that validated and legitimized those standards. From the outset, then, the seventeenth-century novel engaged in a continual polemic with the discursive configurations of power. The clash between discursive authority, which needed to make its presence appear natural and unquestioned, and the early French novel, whose aesthetically peripheral position problematized its ideological stance, caused the novel to internalize the contradiction between the aesthetic and the political. The result is a politics of genre that puts into relief the traditional distinction between form and content: the novel appeared to reproduce social reality in the venerated tradition of historical prose, but it had no license to do so. The novel was, then, as Charles Sorel noted, only

---

[4] In fact, François Boisrobert claimed in the "Advis" to his *Histoire indienne d'Anaxandre et d'Orazie* that novels "are of the nature of the epic poem."

the image of history,[5] a verbal representation of an officially sanctioned discursive practice. It was in its imitation and appropriation of legitimate literary forms that the novel was deemed most dangerous, because critics feared it would confound its readers, stripping them of the critical capacity to distinguish fact from fiction.

The novel's early critics seemed to view its arrogation of legitimate literature's features as unacceptable because fiction was usurping the very techniques that ideologically approved forms employed in order to make their political stances appear natural and uncontrived. In short, the novel used the same techniques of realism that had been used in other forms of narrative, primarily history. In Chapter 3 I will undertake a critical investigation of the relationship between history and realism or *vraisemblance*, but I will not consider realism to be one of the defining characteristics of the early French novel. Many of the most notable studies of the early French novel find in the closing decades of the seventeenth century and the opening years of the eighteenth century a radically new genre of fiction dedicated to the plausible and psychologically motivated representation of reality.[6] With the specter of high nineteenth-century realism looming large on the horizon, many cannot resist unearthing in earlier fiction the seeds of naturalism, attempting to locate the roots underpinning what the novel was somehow inevitably to become. Vivienne Mylne, for example, seems to suggest that eighteenth-century fiction was only a dress rehearsal for nineteenth-century opening night; she remarks that "if the public and critics of the nineteenth century were prepared to discuss novels as literature, it is because a succession of eighteenth-century novels had shown that the novel could rise to the standards used for judging the literary merits of plays or poetry" (269). Georges May, whose *Le Dilemme du roman* remains one of the most erudite and critically astute works on eighteenth-century fiction, cites aesthetic and political condemnation of the novel as principally responsible for the growth of realism. He writes that "les romanciers découvrirent les merveilles du réalisme alors que

[5] Sorel, *La Bibliothèque françoise*, p. 175.
[6] See, for example, English Showalter, *The Evolution of the French Novel, 1641–1782*; Maurice Lever, *Le Roman français au XVIIe siècle*; Vivienne Mylne, *The Eighteenth-Century French Novel: Techniques of Illusion*; Georges May, *Le Dilemme du roman au XVIIIe siècle*.

leur but principal était de fuir les attaques des critiques" (247). English Showalter, alluding to May's discussion of the pressures placed on novelists to conform to the high literary standards of the day, concludes that new theories of fiction resulting from these pressures led almost inevitably to realism (193). Realism in French fiction is typically seen either as a noble but inevitable quest begun in the late seventeenth century and destined to last for over a century, or as a fortuitous accident that was bound to occur as soon as the circumstances were right. The culmination of the story, however, always seems to be the same: the works of Balzac, Flaubert, and Zola.

It has become something of a critical commonplace to label as the first modern novel a particular text from the seventeenth or eighteenth century because it attains some arbitrary threshold of ostensibly accurate character psychology or plausible narrative motivation. I am not concerned, however, with prose fiction as this sort of determinate phenomenon subordinate to the exigencies of a preexisting reality and capable only of reflecting it. Rather, it is the interaction and confrontation between novelistic discourse and other epistemological practices that will form the basis of my analysis. To consider techniques of realism as the primary force behind the growth and development of French fiction is to fall victim to the same trap that snared the early novel's critics, that of considering the form of fiction to be neutral or transparent. This is to suggest, in other words, that fiction is not based upon historically developed and socially determined convention, but that it in some way directly reproduces external or historical reality. Identifying realism as the equivalent of fiction mystifies the relationship between ideology and literary practice since the former largely dictates the conditions of the latter. Literary practice, in turn, contributes to upholding the legitimacy of ideology by causing it to appear natural. Although a significant characteristic of the early French novel, realism must not be construed as its defining characteristic since such a construct merely covers up precisely what it purports to discover: the conditions of development of the novel's hegemony in literary practice.

The term "early French novel" is one that I have more or less arbitrarily chosen to designate fiction from roughly the early decades of the seventeenth century through the Revolution. The words "fiction" and "novel" will refer in this study to any extended and imaginative prose narrative, and unless otherwise specified they will be synonymous. I have chosen the word "early" in order to avoid suggesting that there exists a categorically unequivocal source from which novels unproblematically issued forth in linear progression. To refer to the birth or beginning of the novel is to bracket the dialectical nature of genres. It is to posit the coming into being of an idealized notion of narrative representation in which the text is only an imperfect yet adequate reflection of a preexisting reality. Such an idealized conception of narrative realism invokes form not as the avatar of the literary, but as the negation or opposite of the non-literary. Put more simply, if the formal structure of narrative is merely the transparent rendering of an external reality, then what is discounted are the social and aesthetic conventions that allow literature to seem to coincide with reality itself. Thus, any attempt to isolate the first appearance of the novel generally ignores the systems, both literary and social, that occasioned its existence. Even to refer to the "emergence" of a form is problematic, as Wlad Godzich and Jeffrey Kittay have pointed out, since it is impossible to determine the composition of the ground from which difference arises.[7] Changing or developing literary forms can only be considered in relation to concurrent or existing norms. Prose narrative, especially in the seventeenth century, was so unstable and fraught with questions of authority, both political and literary, that a host of rapidly codified varieties developed concurrently, each with its own particular relationship to authority.

Because codification of literary norms evolves from an ongoing dialogue with power, literary form can never be a purely literary phenomenon. As Kevin Brownlee and Marina Scordilis Brownlee write, "genre is not in itself either a purely discursive or a purely historical fact, but rather the liminal space or point of contact which fuses a selected poetics and a particular historical moment."[8]

---

[7] "To talk of emergence raises problems by its very terms: in such change, on such shifting ground, it is difficult to know what to hold on to, for as the signifying practice that carries authority changes, the kind of authority, the kind of truth it represents changes. What will remain steadily knowable in what we sense to be the beginning of an epistemological shift?" Godzich and Kittay, *The Emergence of Prose*, p. 6.

[8] Brownlee and Scordilis Brownlee, *Romance: Generic Transformation from Chrétien de Troyes to Cervantes*, p. 5.

In this respect, genre is not so much a classificatory system as it is a response-governing one. It orders to a very large extent, although not absolutely, the production of literary discourse, and it controls to a similar extent the conditions of a given text's possible interpretations. Wedding the literary and the historical by codifying a range of suitable meanings for a particular work read by a specific group in a precise historical period, genre expresses a delimited scope of real reading practices. Because it is historically and hermeneutically governed, genre is a function and not a category. It informs and is in turn informed by the texts that make it up. In its historical constitution, genre, like the works it orders, demands to be read as an ongoing production of meaning. Because generic systems need to be read and interpreted, Adena Rosmarin writes that "genre is not a class but a classifying statement. It is therefore a text." [9]

Ross Chambers views genre as the formation of a pact between text and reader. Referring to "situational self-reflexivity," or the conditions which must be met for a reader to receive a work as an act of literary communication, he considers genre a sort of imperative mood of literature, one which issues the reader commands such as "Read me as this type of art (fiction), not that." [10] Chambers is careful to warn readers, however, not to jump too quickly to textual commands when he points out that the injunctions texts put out are part of the artistic enterprise. That is, generic or self-classificatory statements constitute a vital part of the text; readers need to be able to interpret such statements as they would any other part of the text. Chambers cautions us not to neglect the duplicity that goes into any literary work: since fiction, particularly realist fiction, must present itself as true in order to conform to the exigencies of the genre and still be appreciated as art, we must take particular care not to consider genre mere convention. We need to read a text's self-situation, including the frequent claim in fiction that the work is absolutely true, in order to understand not only how it positions itself with respect to other texts, but also where it places itself with respect to structures of authority and whence it derives its claim to truth.

In general, then, I will examine the literary devices and political

[9] Rosmarin, *The Power of Genre*, p. 46.
[10] Chambers, *Story and Situation*, p. 27.

shifts that contributed to the shaping of the early novel, and I will consider in particular the mechanisms of change, the means by which formal transformations penetrated the novel and gave rise to a genre of fiction. The handful of works I have chosen for close analysis in this book are not meant to be representative of "the novel" in general or of seventeenth- or eighteenth-century French fiction in particular. Rather, each displays a significant appropriation of the discursive devices of other signifying practices. I have chosen them not because each seems to have radically altered the course of fiction by being the first to appropriate a particular device, but because their use of particular devices can be rendered relatively apparent through detailed analysis. Most of these devices are subtle; none of them is sufficiently radical to constitute an epistemological break. On the contrary, the slow and intricate interchange between the literary and the political domains will reveal the novel to be a text nearly imperceptibly mediating between the two.

Studies of the early French or British novel have traditionally considered formal realism to be the genre's defining characteristic. Isolating a moment at which prose fiction substantially distanced itself from that of the preceding generation through authors' conscious choice to alter radically the novel's representational repertory, many critics and literary historians prefer to define the genre "novel" as fiction whose unobtrusive literary conventions afford readers a more direct and ostensibly unmediated view of their world. Different critics confront in varying ways the question of how and why the novel's conventions and iconography seemed to converge in such determinate fashion on formal realism, but in general all agree that the rising middle class had something to do with the change.

Ian Watt, whose *Rise of the Novel* has become a standard reference tool in studies of the novel, made the first sustained attempt to correlate the novel's hegemony in literary practice with the growth in strength and importance of the bourgeoisie. Watt argues that although different literary forms imitate reality in different ways, "the novel's conventions make much smaller demands on the audience than do most literary conventions; and this surely explains why the majority of readers in the last two hundred years have found in the novel the literary form which most closely satisfies their wishes for a close correspondence between life and art." [11] Watt treats the rise of the novel in England as a break with previous literary tradition, one which resulted in large part from significant changes in the reading public. Citing educational reform, inexpensive chapbooks and romances, circulating libraries, and the availability of leisure in eighteenth-century England, he points to an ever-expanding reading public whose intellectual capacities and tastes changed the direction, degree, and nature of literary consumption. In addition, the backgrounds and educations of the early influential writers, particularly Defoe and Richardson, were "such that they could hardly have hoped to appeal to the old arbiters of literary destiny" (58). Watt's theory that the novel rose as a direct result of changes in literary and socioeconomic conditions posits the genre as one that mirrors ideological concerns: since, he argues, writers wrote more or less in direct response to readers' demands and capacities, it was natural that readers unschooled in classical and medieval philosophy and rhetoric would demand as "the lowest common denominator of the novel genre" (34) formal realism.

Watt's attempt to pinpoint the rise of the novel depends on a loosely argued notion of causality and result. Once he establishes that socioeconomic factors tremendously influenced the composition of reading audiences and that authors enjoyed a relative independence from their literary past, he asserts that "society must value every individual highly enough to consider him the proper subject of its serious literature; and there must be enough variety of belief and action among ordinary people for a detailed account of them to be of interest to other ordinary people, the readers of novels" (60). Just as in the passage cited above, in which Watt claimed that novels made fewer demands on readers and hence readers came to desire a close correspondence between life and art, the logic here is somewhat loose. It is obviously not the case that reading which is not particularly taxing is necessarily realistic— folk tales and fantasy are two genres that might bear this out—and it is no more the case that only "ordinary people" read novels or that novels could in any way be considered "serious literature" in the early eighteenth century: Watt cites Joseph Addison and Richard Steele often enough to be aware of their less than tolerant atti-

---

[11] Watt, pp. 32–33.

tudes toward novels. And, as Michael McKeon has observed, Watt identifies particular narrative traits as peculiar to the novel and "simultaneously argues their intimate, analogous relation to other developments of the early modern period that extend beyond the realm of literary form." [12]

My point in offering these very basic critiques of Watt's book is not to attempt to defame one of the classic studies of the novel, but merely to point out the complex and dialectical nature of the genre. On the one hand, the novel was not considered serious literature at the time of its most dramatic rise in prominence; this, to a very large extent, contributed to its dialogic form, its interaction with other, more venerated literary forms, and its appropriation of the literary techniques prized in those forms. On the other hand, as I will argue in greater detail below, French novels of the early seventeenth century were written and read by members of the aristocracy, certainly not a group generally described as "ordinary people." Even during one of the most significant periods in its early development—the middle decades of the seventeenth century, when class conflict between aristocrats and wealthy bourgeois was heated indeed—one would be hard-pressed to refer to its readers as ordinary since they were neither common nor all of the same social stock. Thus, except for fiction of the very early years of the seventeenth century, it is difficult to label the novel as a genre properly belonging to a specific portion of the ideological spectrum. Were it simply a case of a literary form existing in social isolation and having little or no contact with a broad variety of readers, it quite clearly would not have achieved the literary predominance it continues to enjoy.

Watt devotes his attention almost exclusively to the English novel, and his elision of other novelistic traditions seems a deliberate attempt to avoid the problems they might pose for his theory. When, for example, he turns to the French novel, he claims an isomorphic analogy with the British tradition, referring to "the first great efflorescence of the genre in France which began with Balzac and Stendhal" (300). Effacing two centuries of novels in France because they were written before the Revolution of 1789, whose importance for literature he compares to the Glorious Revolution

[12] McKeon, *The Origins of the English Novel, 1600–1740*, p. 2.

of 1689 in England, Watt fails to consider historical developments in French history that, although they lacked the *éclat* of revolution, still had profound effects on social, economic, and cultural life. The legalization of the transmission of venal offices paid for in cash, the Fronde, and the growth of absolutism in France all had serious consequences on the course the French novel was to take, and we will consider each of these factors below. The point here is that it is an oversimplification to adhere to a rigid formula dictating the conditions necessary for the production of prose fiction. While the conditions giving rise to the novel may have been similar in France and England, the novel is a literary *and* a social phenomenon, and we must study it within the particular historical context in which it was produced.

I mentioned above the influential work of Vivienne Mylne, English Showalter, and Georges May in the field of the early French novel. All of these critics, like Watt before them, take as the most significant defining characteristic of the novel the genre's formal realism. Mylne opens her book with a discussion of the *ut pictura poesis* model of realism, and although she painstakingly attempts to differentiate between "realism" and "representation," her explicitly stated goal is "to show what intrinsically valuable advances in the technique of the novel came about through the efforts of eighteenth-century authors to achieve an increasingly accurate representation of life" (2). Mylne is somewhat more circumspect than Watt in her discussion of realism, pointing out that innovations in representation were not necessarily new discoveries of how to portray a slice of life more accurately. Frequently they were devices designed to protect the budding genre from critical attack. Unlike Watt, she stresses readers' initial reluctance to consider the novel "serious literature," and she demonstrates how censorship of the novel led to new kinds of novelistic representation. Like their brethren the tragedians, novelists claimed that their goal was to please and instruct their audiences, and Mylne points out that attaining this goal while simultaneously fleeing critical attack led to three basic lines of defense: justifying fiction as such, claiming that fiction could improve factual narratives, or pretending that the works were true and not novels at all. This three-pronged defense of fiction leads Mylne to discuss the intimate relationship between history and the novel in the seventeenth century. Although she points

out that most of the authors of the century's prolonged pastoral
and heroic traditions explicitly claimed to be chronicling historical
fact, she deftly eschews any discussion of the ideological ramifications of such a claim. That is, despite her incisive and exhaustive
account of the development of illusion in French fiction, Mylne
makes no attempt to demonstrate why illusion was an issue for
early French fiction. As I will show in more detail below, the imitation of reality had little to do with readers' inability to negotiate
abstruse literary convention; it was far more intimately related to
the complex of aesthetic and political condemnations the novel initially underwent. Because prose fiction had no literary antecedent
in classical antiquity, aesthetic theorists found it artistically lacking.
Novelists who tried to defend themselves from attack on aesthetic
grounds employed the defensive tactics Mylne describes, and in so
doing incurred the wrath of political authorities. If absolutists like
Richelieu and Louis XIV had not so jealously guarded their prerogative to control the dissemination and composition of "factual"
truth, and if the landed nobility had not been concerned with defending their traditional privileges against the aggressive *noblesse
de robe*, the illusion of historical fact would not have been an issue.
Competing versions of truth threatened aristocratic and noble authority, and political authorities feared that readers would be unable to distinguish between officially sanctioned historiography and
novels putting themselves forth as history.

It has become standard, then, to point out that the modern novel
is a bourgeois art form and that its rise was concurrent with the
rise in power of the bourgeoisie. A perusal of the writings of Watt,
May, Mylne, Georg Lukács, Mikhail Bakhtin, Alain Viala, or Erica
Harth, to name only some of the most notable, reveals to what
degree this assertion is generally accepted in the study of the novel
as a genre and of the French novel in particular.[13] In their critical
analyses of the novel in literary history these writers stress the novel's lack of a canon as well as the fragmentary, multi-dimensional
nature of its narration. While most other literary genres have their
roots in the traditions of classical antiquity, they point out, the
novel alone is younger than the book: its form was not codified

[13] Georg Lukács, *The Theory of the Novel*; Mikhail Bakhtin, *The Dialogic Imagination*; Alain Viala, *Naissance de l'écrivain*; Erica Harth, *Ideology and Culture in
Seventeenth-Century France*.

over a period of thousands of years, as was, for example, that of tragedy or the epic. Traditional theories of the novel have it that at the time of its rise, the bourgeoisie had not yet embraced or adopted a coherent system of representation that would express its interests. Because the modern novel emerged at roughly the same time as the bourgeoisie, then, it grew in many directions. This would account for the divergent forms prose fiction took. The declining relative strength of the nobility, particularly in the early part of the seventeenth century, and the increasing economic predominance of the bourgeoisie seem to have led to new art forms that represented a wider range of the social spectrum.

Many of these assertions have become unquestioned axioms that conceal more than they reveal. Although it is demonstrably true that the production of novels in France accelerated at the same time that the moneyed bourgeoisie extended its strength and influence beyond the venal offices to which they owed their power and into the production and commodification of culture, this does not explain why it was prose fiction, and not some other form, that correlated this new political strength. Placing two simultaneous historical developments side by side and suggesting that they demonstrate a self-evident causality is simply an exercise in mystification: one might just as well explain the stock market crash of 1929 as a result of the invention of permanent press cotton fabric. To make sense of the apparently concurrent rise of the novel and the bourgeoisie, it is necessary to investigate not only the ideology of fiction at some convenient and arbitrary moment at which both novel and bourgeoisie can be said to exist, but also the ideology of fiction as a historical process. To what ends was fiction read and used in the early seventeenth century in France? Did newly ennobled individuals read and use fiction just as the ancient nobility did? Is the novel a bourgeois invention? And, finally, can we speak of "the novel" as a unified genre with an unequivocal and unproblematic moral, aesthetic, and ideological position?

Answering these questions requires exploring three of the axiomatic assumptions inherent in the standard theory that the novel emerged at the same time as the bourgeoisie and consequently reflected bourgeois concerns. First, the bourgeoisie did not simply "emerge" and then continue on in an unproblematic and symbiotic relationship with the aristocracy. The rise in economic and ideological importance of a moneyed, non-noble group in France was a long and complex process abetted in particular by the decision to legalize the transmission of nobility conferred through the sale of offices from one generation to the next. As more and more people were ennobled in seventeenth-century France and as the balance of wealth shifted away from the hereditary aristocracy, bitter class conflict arose. Aristocratic privilege and prerogative spread out among individuals from various walks of life and with extremely diverse backgrounds and lineages. The ancient aristocracy, faced with the prospect of diminished economic and social influence, attempted to fortify its ideology by mystifying its origins and composition, claiming not economic power as its fundamental and defining feature, but an abstract and essentialistic notion of virtue and merit. Consequently, to suggest that the novel was simply a corollary or contingency of the rise of the bourgeoisie is to suggest that the bourgeoisie was or is a self-contained group enjoying complete autonomy. We need instead to investigate the development of prose fiction in France not merely as a reflection of the bourgeoisie's predominance, but rather as the articulation of the conflict between and among various social groups.

The second issue requiring clarification is the notion that the novel simply reflected bourgeois ideology. Because the rise to preeminence of a moneyed and non-noble (or newly ennobled) group was a dialectical process of class conflict involving the appropriation of aristocratic values and consequent self-legitimation, it is a gross oversimplification to infer that the bourgeoisie's ideological formation is uncomplex and absolute. It is never a simple matter to identify the ideological components of a product or system as belonging fundamentally and irreducibly to a given class; it is impossible to do so at a time when a nascent group is still in the process of distinguishing itself from another. Consequently, the novel could not have reflected exclusively bourgeois concerns. At most it could reflect the dialectical tension informing the historical emergence of a new class and the accompanying political strain. Because fiction transcribes the aesthetic, moral, and political domains of the culture in which it is produced, it registers these positions as a complex network of social and artistic concerns irreducible to the ideology of a single group. We can expect the early modern novel to represent, then, not the concerns of a single and discrete group, but the tensions and conflicts obtaining in the struggle for hegemony between two powerful social forces.

The third and final aspect requiring investigation in the standard theory of the novel's rise regards the novel's capacity or tendency merely to reflect. The assumption that the novel might reflect bourgeois ideological concerns is problematic enough given the complex composition of those concerns; that it might reflect *only* those concerns is dubious if not untenable. At the most basic level this assumption is misguided because it suggests an absolute neutrality or transparency of literary form. It implies that there exists a stock of plots, characters, and settings that are incommutably bourgeois, and that the selection and combination of those elements within a text merely translates into literary language the real world the novel ostensibly reproduces. This assumption not only grossly oversimplifies the dialectical nature of ideology but suggests, as John Frow has written, that "literary reality is immediately identical with reality itself. Or more precisely, literature is based on the iconic sign: it is natural, motivated, mirroring a sense which is independent of its interpretation." [14] In other words, to suggest that the novel mirrors or represents bourgeois ideological concerns in a transparent and immediate fashion is to find a direct and motivated adequation between world and text; it is to negate the historically determined conventions that allow a text to appear to represent the world directly. More importantly still, the assumption that the novel merely mirrors bourgeois concerns means that it can produce a textual effect no greater than the sum of its parts, thus denying it any capacity to produce meaning or yield interpretations beyond what the author intentionally put in.

If it were true that the novel merely reflected bourgeois concerns in a substantially transparent medium that directly reproduced the world for a largely passive reader, then it would be difficult to understand the aesthetic and political debates and harsh critical condemnation that surrounded the novel as early as the middle of the seventeenth century. The simple reflective nature of a purely bourgeois phenomenon should have allowed the novel to coexist unproblematically with a host of other literary forms. The presence of critical debate, however, signals a conflict in both the political

---

[14] Frow, *Marxism and Literary History*, p. 15.

and aesthetic domains, and it suggests that the novel developed through dialogic confrontation with other literary forms. It also adumbrates the novel's capacity not merely to reflect, but to produce meaning, and to extend its function beyond that of a simple mediation between reader and world and into the domain of cultural production. For in fact, the novel articulates the antagonisms and contradictions inherent in the social world. It appropriates the formal features of other literary genres and in recontextualizing them in a new ideological frame outside of the discursive structures of authority that legitimated them, it produces an alternative form of literary representation distinct from, yet contingent upon, previous modes. The novel consequently produces its own referent in manufacturing a discursive register which closely resembles previous ones but whose relationship to authority and tradition is problematized—but not abolished—by the discontinuity or break the new register occasions.[15] Particularly in the middle years of the seventeenth century—when middle-class challenges to traditional aristocratic authority increased by leaps and bounds and when new statutes dramatically changed writers' ownership of their works— the novel depicted a rising bourgeois hegemony; at the same time, the novel contributed to that hegemony by undermining structures of power and authority, primarily by appropriating in a subtle, almost imperceptible fashion the very discourses used to uphold it.

Armand-Pierre Jacquin's criticism of the novel demonstrates the almost impalpable fashion in which the genre transforms custom and is in turn transformed by it. Attributing to the novel the capacity to seduce its readers, Jacquin believes that fiction's power to destroy a society comes not from its forceful devastation of cultural practices, but rather from the slow and easy way it insinuates itself into a civilization's mores. Averring that his contemporaries, particularly women, are slaves to fashion and that novels are but one more desirable commodity (115), Jacquin goes on to point out the imperceptible manner in which fiction prevails over its unsuspect-

---

[15] Frow presents a different perspective on the manner in which the novel produces its own referent (p. 128): "This does not mean that literary texts are in some simple way 'about themselves,' but it does imply that reference to the authority of nonliterary modes of discourse is always structured by the force of reference to the literary norm."

ing victims: "Once the mind is seduced and blinded, the heart readily adopts a doctrine too fitting its passions to seem illusory; and it
is thus that we start out as feeble proselytes, but soon become formidable Masters" (213). Jacquin theorizes that novels do their
damage first by falsifying facts, giving readers inaccurate ideas or
spurious accounts of real events.[16] Once readers have been duped
into accepting counterfeit images—that is, representations not
based on historical reality or on nature—they will then lack the
critical capacity to reject the misbegotten moral the novel pro-
pounds. It is thus that they are seduced, literally led away from the
unchanging truth Jacquin is careful never to define but which he
nevertheless presumes he and his readers share. Once readers' judg-
mental capabilities are destroyed, they cease being merely led away
from the truth and take on the role of "formidable masters," champions of vice and destroyers of good.

Jacquin understood the transforming capabilities with which literature was endowed, for he believed that readers seduced by novels would no longer be content to be passive recipients of novelistic
vice. They would instead, he feared, become seducers themselves,
preaching to an ever-widening circle of victims the poison they had
assimilated. Like a virus continually replicating itself and attacking
its host, the venomous contagion novelists spread would ostensibly
lead to widespread moral debasement: "Not content to corrupt
those who read their works, authors of novels teach the deplorable
art of corrupting others. Is it not thus that youth learns to employ
all of love's ruses in order to instill a flame in another's heart?"
(337).

Jacquin's fear that novels were seducing young readers and teaching them the art of seducing others reflects a literary crisis over the
representational nature of prose narrative that had arisen nearly a
century earlier. In the years preceding and during the acrimonious
political and economic struggles of the Fronde there existed but few
varieties of prose narrative: history, pastoral romance, and heroic
fiction. Extant prose narrative relied for the most part on reproducing models of behavior that reflected readers' images of themselves,

---

[16] Some novels, Jacquin says, "impudently and under the false title of *Memoirs*
alter or augment the facts that we have often witnessed ourselves; with the greatest
malignity they discharge the venom of the blackest defamation on those whom
Heaven has placed on the throne, and to whom we owe our love and respect" (p.
290).

which means that both history and fiction translated the iconographic trappings of France's nobility into discrete allegorical pack-
ages that could be rationed out and attractively arranged in the
narrative's *récit*. Honoré d'Urfé's *L'Astrée* and François Eudes de
Mézeray's *Histoire de France* are only two examples of the manner
in which prose narrative set before readers the image of themselves
they wanted to see. D'Urfé's princely fifth-century pastoral flock
and Mézeray's perfumed and bewigged Clovis exemplify the seventeenth-century reading public's apparent desire to base historical
representation on contemporary material and social practice. In
later novels, however—and this is what troubled Jacquin—models
for emulation derived not from venerated tradition and contemporary moral and political standards, but from within the text itself.
One can understand Jacquin's fear and outrage, then, as it suddenly
became clear that moral, aesthetic, and political standards are
properly the textual products of discursive practice. The problem
was that it seemed that he and his coterie were no longer in control
of novelists and their readers; new fictive forms emerged, beginning
in the later decades of the seventeenth century, responding to readers from groups other than the aristocracy who, like their noble
counterparts, wanted to see themselves as they wanted to be.

Jacquin was primarily concerned with the novel's inveigling powers, and he believed that those seduced by novels would also be
induced to corrupt others. Jacquin's image of novels seducing readers who in turn corrupt others is, in fact, the figure informing my
analysis of early French fiction. Critics like Jacquin believed that
fiction destroyed readers' integrity, their adherence to the official
conception of truth and virtue advocated in the historical and litur-
gical writings of the day. Novels corrupt by dismantling and frag-
menting literature's ostensibly univocal claims to truth, introducing
competing theories in the process. As they do so, they collide with
the dominant ideology's discursive strategies. They remain marginal, however, because they are ambivalent toward the received
epistemological practices they appear both to appropriate and to
defy. The novels produced from the middle years of the seventeenth
century engage in the kind of seduction Jacquin named by representing a pivotal character actively engaged in the process of learning to decode the sign system of his or her society. The neophyte
courtier Mlle de Chartres, for example, gleans from her mother the

strategies for discerning the realities behind courtly appearances in Mme de Lafayette's *Princesse de Clèves*; Marivaux's Marianne apprehends from those around her the image of herself she needs to project in order to advance her social and amorous ambitions; and Sade's Justine discovers from her tormentors the advantages of relating a titillating tale. The novelistic seducers we will encounter imitate and then appropriate a discourse of power, yet they remain marginalized from the group in which they strive to attain power. At first "feeble proselytes," they become the "formidable masters" Jacquin feared in their application of what they learned; they seduce others, as we will see, precisely by using the discursive strategies of their circles in order to subvert the univocal claims to truth those strategies were meant to uphold.

In Part I we will undertake a critical investigation of the various manifestations of narrative prose in the seventeenth century in order to explore the affiliations between the structures of power and those of literature. Narrative prose, including history, occupied a pivotal position in both the inculcation and the derogation of aristocratic ideology primarily because it seemed to be able to offer an unmediated representation of reality. In the seventeenth century, whose literary life was marked by perhaps nothing so much as a rigid attention to the formal structure of genres, imaginative narrative prose fell outside of most literary classifications. Historical prose, particularly beginning with Richelieu's ministry, was the traditional vehicle for imparting ideologically charged images of France's grandeur and that of its ruling class; it served as well to legitimize contemporary political agendas by depicting the lineage of the divinely ordained monarchy. Novels, which Charles Sorel called "images of History," threatened to usurp history's privileged position of disseminating truth because they resembled the only other form of narrative prose with which readers would be familiar. They thus threatened to confound readers and tender competing versions of moral and political righteousness. The condemnation of novels, then, beginning in the middle years of the seventeenth century, arose primarily because this bastard literary form loomed forth as the destroyer of the univocality of aristocratic ideology.

Part One The Construction of a Genre

Chapter 1   The Rise of Aristocratic Fiction

Pierre Bayle published his *Dictionnaire historique et critique* in 1697, fifteen years after the *Pensées sur la Comète* (Thoughts on the comet), in which he attempted to debunk superstition and offer up a doctrine of tolerance, particularly in religious matters. Exiled from France because of his somewhat unpopular view that religion is irrational and subject to the same critiques as primitive belief in omens, he was later praised by eighteenth-century philosophers for his unwavering assault on tradition in the pursuit of truth. In the *Dictionnaire* he takes on, in the name of truth, the contemporary vogue of reading novels:

> This is a problem that gets worse every day because of the liberty taken to publish the Secret Loves, Secret History, etc. of such and such a Lord famous in history. Booksellers and authors do whatever they can to have people believe that these Secret Histories are drawn from personal diaries: well they know that the intrigues of love and other such adventures are all the more captivating when readers think they are real than when they tell themselves that they are only fabrications.[1]

Like many of his contemporaries, Bayle disapproved of fiction that imitated history, and he recognized that tales purporting to be true had a particularly seductive appeal to readers. In mocking history and reduplicating its narrative authority, however, novels seemed to be threatening history's traditional claim to truth. Bayle offers up, then, his view of the problem and suggests a compromise for novelists who insist on including historical fact in their works: "we are casting myriad shadows on true history, and I believe that we must call upon the powers to issue a rule that these new novelists

---

[1] Bayle, vol. III, p. 2091, article "Nidhard (Jean Everard)," note c.

must adopt: namely, that they write either pure history or pure fiction, or at least that they use brackets to separate one from the other, the truth from the falsehood" (III, 2091, note c).

Bayle's assault on novels and their obfuscation of the truth chronicles the culmination of an anxiety that had been brewing for the better part of a century, both in France and in England. In *The Tatler*, for example, Richard Steele condemned French memoir novels, claiming that they only glorified writers who lead undistinguished lives. "The most immediate remedy that I can apply to prevent this growing evil," he wrote, "is, That [*sic*] I do hereby give notice to all booksellers and translators whatsoever, that the word Memoir is French for a novel; and to require of them that they sell and translate it accordingly."[2] How, these critics wondered, will people be able to distinguish fact from fiction? Or, perhaps more to the point, how will readers be able to decide between or among competing versions of truth? Over seventy years earlier Jean Chapelain had noted that literature retains its appeal only when readers are able to invest it with belief, and that only believable works of art can lay claim to moral didacticism. In his letter to Favereau on Marino's *Adonis*, he wrote that "where belief is lacking, attention and sentiment lack as well; but where there is no sentiment there can be no emotion or consequently any purging or moral uplifting, which is the goal of poetry."[3] The seventeenth-century tenet that literature should uplift its readers and instruct them in the precepts of virtue while at the same time providing them pleasure was being tested by texts that offered the seductive appeal of truth without necessarily insinuating accepted images of virtuous behavior. Literature's didactic capacity had reached a critical moment heralded by the dissolution of truth's ostensible univocality. If novelists could compete with historians—whose work was generally commissioned by the king—in offering believable images of reality, then a power or authority deriving from a source other than the monarch was informing their works. Novels seemed to bear an authority and power of their own, constructed internally by the weight of their own narrative.

[2] Steele, *The Tatler*, Saturday, 22 October 1709, in Addison and Steele, *The Tatler. Complete in One Volume*, p. 186.
[3] Chapelain, p. 85.

In this chapter I will argue that prose fiction developed in seventeenth-century France as a rehearsal of the traditional aristocratic values of birth, merit, and authority, and that its early formulaic nature correlated readers' desires for social stasis. Early seventeenth-century fiction is characterized by a minimal narrative structure, by which I mean a paucity of causal sequences of events; consequently, I will show, fiction's iconography, and not its narrative composition, distinguished it as an aristocratic genre, and as the form became regularized, early notions of *vraisemblance*, which I will discuss at greater length in Chapter 2, heralded novels as the avatar of conservative ideology.[4] Because novels were written and read nearly exclusively by members of France's aristocracy, a cultural tradition developed privileging repetitive narrative forms that justified the continuing hegemony of the ruling classes. I will sketch out the development of these narrative forms below; in succeeding chapters I will show how aristocratic narrative traditions promulgated their own truth and univocality by attempting to obstruct competing traditions, consequently erecting as natural or transcendent the ideological systems they represented.

In 1559, during a brief respite in the civil war dividing France's Catholics and Protestants, Pierre Boaistuau offered up his *Histoires tragiques*, a collection of tales freely translated from Matteo Bandello's *Novelle*. Reprinted more than twenty times before the first quarter of the seventeenth century, Boaistuau's work was the first in a long series of collections of the same or similar title, and he inaugurated a new mode of fiction in France: fiction designed to consternate and appall its readers. Thematically formulaic, Boaistuau's stories deal nearly exclusively with the gruesome punishment awaiting those who transgress the bounds of legitimate authority. Often the transgression involves an adulterous love occasioned by the absence of a woman's husband. For more than sixty years after Boaistuau brought the Italian novella to France, readers delighted in the horrifying spectacle of the unfaithful or the disobedient meeting their hideous—but always justly deserved—punishment.

---

[4] *Vraisemblance* is normally translated as "verisimilitude," but because it has ramifications quite specific to seventeenth- and eighteenth-century French fiction, I will retain the use of the French word.

The opening lines of the fourth tale in Boaistuau's collection suggest something of the attraction readers may have found in these horrifying didactic tales:

> The ancient and widespread custom popular among the Piedmont gentlemen and ladies has always been to vacate the unbearably noisy, teeming cities to retire to the fields of their castles and other places of leisure, in order to get through the disagreeable parts of life with more rest and contentment than are enjoyed by those who occupy themselves with civic affairs. Said custom was so scrupulously followed before the wars disturbed the long-standing order, that barely would you have found an idle gentleman in a town; all withdrew to their rustic estates with their families, who were so well ordered that you would leave the house of a simple gentleman just as happy and edified as in some great city you would leave the house of a wise and prudent senator.[5]

Boaistuau paints the picture of a genteel nobility withdrawing from the tumultuous upheaval of war-torn towns in order to regroup in a tranquil and harmonious environment peopled by those of their own kind. Their houses, as well ordered and maintained as the members of their families, offered places of refuge and stability. A visit to the private and secluded sanctuaries was an edifying experience, one that contributed to reconstructing the sense of virtue and piety public life had quelled. Noble gentlefolk had no business in the noisy and crowded cities; indeed, they had no business at all. These people lived on country estates which their families had in some cases owned for hundreds of years, and their incomes were tied not to urban production but directly to the land. The nobleman distinguished himself from the commoner in these two fashions: first, he performed no work and engaged in no commerce, and second, he avoided towns completely to live on his ancient familial estate. Here a *gentil-homme* was free from the partisanship dividing members of the nobility; here he could cultivate an abiding and harmonious repose more conducive to the fostering of the ordered and organized society to which, by birth, he had a right.

The literary horrors that disrupted such a delectable quiescence were not-so-gentle caveats that the virtue and gentility proper to aristocrats needed to be protected from the ruthless onslaught of basely born individuals who strove to gain entry into their select

[5] Boaistuau, p. 123.

circle. In addition, it is significant that Boaistuau's tales appeared in 1559, the final year of the reign of Henri II, who had done more than any previous king to bring geographical unity to France, and who is generally considered the first genuine absolute monarch in France.[6] The popularity of Boaistuau's *Histoires tragiques* seems to correlate the attempt by France's nobility to demarcate the boundaries of their power and privilege. As they regrouped on their ancient estates away from the growing urban centralization of the monarchy, they tried to fortify their ranks against the encroachment of ambitious *arrivistes*, and their literature corroborated their anxieties: during the sixty years of popularity the various *histoires tragiques* enjoyed, the most common cause of disorder was the adulterous affair or the mismatched union involving a noble and a non-noble. Boaistuau's admonitory tales depicted the deleterious results of marriages between people of uneven social standing. In the story cited above, for example, a "valiant and noble great lord" catches his wife and a "base nocturnal ruffian" in bed together. To preserve his honor and to protect the sacred ties of marriage, he forces his wife to hang her lover and then he ensures that she will remain faithful to her husband by sealing her in the room with her lover's corpse.

The *histoires tragiques* owe a great deal, of course, to the bawdy and raucous Italian novellas, and in particular to Boccaccio, but the French tradition added to Italian ribald humor the dark specter of avenging authority united under the auspices of an angry and troubled aristocracy. Significantly, during the second thirty years of their existence, and particularly after Henri IV legitimized religious tolerance with the Edict of Nantes in 1598, the *histoires tragiques* focused particularly on maintaining the purity of noble lineage, and the punishments meted out to those who threatened the order became harsher and more bizarre.

Bishop Jean-Pierre Camus was perhaps the most widely known of all authors of *histoires tragiques*, responsible for more than fifty novels and collections of tales. Camus' tales are among the most brutally violent of all the *histoires tragiques* and he is less concerned with amusing readers than with teaching them valuable moral lessons. Unlike most of his predecessors, Camus considered

[6] See, for example, Edward John Kearns, *Ideas in Seventeenth-Century France*, especially chapter 1.

the writer's profession an expressly didactic one, harshly criticizing the "empty and chimerical tales" of his precursors whose flippant purpose "is none other than to amuse . . . by narrating illusions forged in the hollows of their brains." [7] Camus frequently began his stories with short preludes illustrating the moral of the story. The opening lines of "Les trahisons renversees" (The reversed betrayals), for example, read as follows: "No one pities the man who falls into the pit he himself has dug. Betrayal is such an odious thing that no one fails to rejoice upon seeing its punishment, and especially when stones fall on the heads of those who trouble them. Here I will present before you two such spectacles, which will show that bad advice can be good when it is pernicious to those who give it." [8] Camus ruthlessly imprecates those who form ambitious or enterprising alliances, and like his predecessors he punishes young people or covetous middle-class parents who try to increase their wealth and prestige by marrying above their station. In the fifty tales that compose Camus' *Spectacles d'horreur* this is the motif one sees most often. One of the stories, "L'infortuné mariage" (The unfortunate marriage), depicts a man who refuses to allow his daughter to marry the young bourgeois she loves; his designs for the girl are related as follows: "Her father, wanting for a son-in-law a nobleman who bore arms, and with no regard for the fine qualities of this young solicitor . . . and even though he noted the affection the young lovers shared, cruelly broke the alliance" (247–48). In another story, entitled "Le tombeau des amans" (The lovers' tomb), a young woman's father

> contrived to marry his only daughter highly and according to the pretensions that his vanity gave him; but seeing his hopes dashed by the choice her inclination had made, he was greatly troubled. He consoled himself, however, by noting that nothing irrevocable had occurred, and with the thought that he could easily lead his daughter's thoughts back to her duty, and by thinking that by proposing a more illustrious and seductive man he would make a greater impression in her heart and erase Volcace from her memory. (394)

Metrodore, the young woman in the tale, and Volcace, her true love, are separated through the marriage contract the woman's fa-

[7] Camus, *Les entretiens historiques* (Paris: Bertault, 1639), cited by Godenne, p. 41.

[8] Camus, *Les spectacles d'horreur*, p. 443.

ther arranges with a young man he deems more suitable. After an unusual series of events in which Volcace is accused of violating Metrodore's honor, the former is condemned to have his head cut off, and Metrodore swallows poison to join him in death.

The social conditions facing France's nobility in the early seventeenth century were not much different from those of the *gentilhomme* Boaistuau had described except that they were more dire. The religious wars had seriously impoverished a class used to a life of ease and leisure; perhaps more significant, however, was the institution under Henri IV of the *paulette*, a tax levied on the sale of offices that effectively legalized the transmission from one generation to the next of aristocratic status. As aristocrats saw their ranks infiltrated by wealthy commoners, the vehemence with which they guarded their ancient status increased tremendously. Camus, as if in response, closely defended the paternalistic hegemony of aristocratic privilege, offering more gruesome punishments to those who stepped out of line. "Le cœur mangé" (The eaten heart), for example, delivers not the story of an unhappy lover who languishes from a broken heart, but that of a woman who unwittingly and at the hands of the man whom her parents forced her to marry winds up literally consuming the heart of the man she truly loved. Turning up the heat—this time literally—on the punishments dealt to those who failed to respect authority, Camus attempted to excise disobedience and disrespect: "Le jeu d'enfans" (Child's play) tells the story of disobedient children who, after watching their father slit the throat of one of his cows, are so impressed with the act that they decide to imitate it. They slit their younger brother's throat and then, realizing what they have done, hide in the oven. When their mother returns home and begins preparing dinner, they are consumed by fire.

Not all early French fiction, of course, attempted to instill respect for traditional aristocratic hegemony by depicting bizarre and gruesome punishments awaiting those who would accede to higher ranks. Sentimental fiction, which was more or less historically concurrent with the *histoires tragiques*, portrayed the harmony and bliss in store for the truly noble who remained virtuous in the face of the most grueling obstacles. The action in these tales tended to be both simple and formulaic: each depicted a love interest and an obstacle preventing the lovers from being together. Writers of sen-

timental novels relied on stock characters and episodes drawn from
a rather limited pool: they emphasized not plot or character development but the simple display of sentiment. They invented episodes
that tested the young couple's love for one another as the same
accidents and bizarre coincidences separated them time and again.
Fidelity and chastity were the operative words in these works, and
they even appeared in the majority of titles. Indeed, the titles frequently included plot synopses, as if to assure readers that the work
would deliver precisely what they were looking for.[9]

The primary components of sentimental fiction included gallantry, constancy, and a neo-Platonic conception of love. Couples
in these novels displayed high-blown noble sentiment and always
distinguished the ideal love accessible only to those of their station
from base lust. In *Les Amours de Charitene et Amandus* the distinction is clarified: "When I pose the felicity of human life in love,
I mean to speak not of the evil kind, but of that which, with the
heart, soul, and mind, comforts, celebrates, and animates the senses
of man and causes him to scorn vice and follow the path of immortal virtue. I want to show beautiful lovers touched in the inner recesses of their hearts with the qualities and flames of this noble and
generous perfection."[10] This didactic story, penned by Aymar de
Veins du Coudray, is meant to instruct readers on the benefits of
noble virtue and the obduracy of vice. The attainment of pure and
true love requires the grand and exalted qualities only found among
the truly noble, and nobility in sentimental novels depends as much
on birth as it does on the more abstract quality of *gentillesse* which
separates the noble of soul from those whose lineage merely happens to be distinguished. Between five and ten sentimental novels
appeared each year in the first two decades of the seventeenth century, and elaborated in all these novels were the strength and distinction of heroes' sentiments; regardless of the adventures that
tested heroes' mettle, the same magnanimous qualities surfaced in
each.

In Jacques Corbin's *Les Amours de Philocaste*, published in 1601,

[9] Some titles from the early years of the seventeenth century include: *Les tragiques
amours du fidel' Yrion et de la belle Parithée, où se voit combien peut un'amour
honorablement et sainctement poursuivie et comme se termine celle qui a ses intentions impudiques* (1601); J. B. Dupont, *Le Miroir des dames, où les effects d'une
saincte amitié sont en vif représentés* (1605); Jacques Corbin, *Les Amours de Philocaste, ou par mille beaux et rares accidens il se voit que les variables hazards de la
fortune ne peuvent rien sur la constance de l'amour* (1601).

[10] Veins du Coudray, p. ix.

nobility, magnanimity, virtue, and above all constancy are wed in traditional sentimental format to highlight the young couple's aristocratic worthiness. Corbin's heroine is an exceptionally beautiful woman born of the noblest family: "Philocaste was the daughter of the King of England, was conceived at the epitome of honor, and born in the breast of love." [11] Philocaste is so beautiful, in fact, that as soon as she comes of age her beauty incites all of the country's noble youth to give up their aristocratic privilege of bearing arms in order to pursue her: "As soon as they saw her appear with all the dazzle that Heaven had granted her, each of the gallant knights abandoned the pursuit of Mars in order to attack the fortress of Love" (2b). Philocaste and her beau Pirame undergo a series of ritual separations caused by tempests, misunderstandings, and various ravagings, but their love always endures. More importantly, however, their respect for their parents' authority keeps them in a constant state of irritated chastity. "Thus these two loving and beloved souls, pleasurably breathing the sweet pains of Love, satisfied their appetites on the discourse of their passions, partaking every day of the same fare and mutually awaiting the hour when they could, through the consent of their parents, unite so entirely that their wills would be united." (87a–b). Philocaste and Pirame do, of course, wed in the end, having weathered all of the formulaic hardships Corbin had at his disposal. The work concludes with a moralizing apostrophe to the reader, informing him or her that "here you will learn that the constancy of love and of lovers, however much opposed by the obstacles of fortune, remains inviolate and assured, and that whosoever follows honor comes only to an honorable end" (135a–b).

In their heyday—that is, during the first two decades of the seventeenth century—the sentimental novel and *histoires tragiques* flourished: a half dozen or more were generally published each year. Most literary historians agree that the primary reason for the decline of both the sentimental novel and the *histoires tragiques* was their overly formulaic composition. Both forms tended to be short works of fiction,[12] and all of them employed the conventions noted above. Critical opinion seems to be unanimous in declaring

[11] Corbin, p. 2a. I am following standard usage in labeling "a" the first side of a two-sided leaf paginated with a single number, and "b" the reverse side.

[12] A notable exception is Sorel's *L'Orphise de Chrysante* (1623), a sentimental novel that spans over a thousand pages.

them of mediocre quality at best. Yet, the *roman sentimental* and
the *histoire tragique* did more than merely prolong the traditions
of romance and sentimental narrative exemplified by the medieval
fabliaux and the work of Marguerite de Navarre. Complicated
moral issues began to appear in fiction that had been primarily
concerned with diverting readers. The theme of resisting the temp-
tations of the flesh was the runaway hit of the era as sea voyages
and accompanying shipwrecks, abductions, and battles with infi-
dels time and again showcased noble young lovers who remained
morally pure. Although narrative situations and character types in
these novels stayed basically the same, what the sentimental novel
and the *histoire tragique* initiated was critical reflection on sentiment and moral dilemmas. In addition, they established as a common theme in fiction the problem of social standing and awareness
of one's position on the scale; they seem to have induced readers'
reflection on the plight of people whose purity of blood was being
threatened.

Sentimental novels and *histoires tragiques* reinforced the rigid social codes of the day by showing that only loves which were socially
compatible would be sanctioned, no matter how faithful or chaste
the couple. Star-crossed lovers who faced the obstacle of social in-
congruence would separate or face horrible death. Thus, for as formulaic, conventional, and homogeneous as these types of novels
tended to be, they did accurately represent one facet of reality,
namely the reality of the strict rules governing social liaison. The
unidimensionality of their plots underscored time and again this
fact of seventeenth-century life, and if sentimental novels and *histoires tragiques* did not depict people or situations as they actually
were, they did reinforce the attitudes of their aristocratic readers.
The striking similarities in the episodes that sentimental novels and
histoires tragiques related suggest that readers were less interested
in plot than in examples of noble moral rectitude. That is, with one
variable constant—the stock events sentimental novels portrayed—
sentiment and more importantly examples of upstanding noble behavior could come to the fore. Sentimental novels espoused philosophies that echoed the way nobles perceived themselves, and the
convention of portraying nobles' neo-Platonic love quickly took
hold.[13]

---

[13] Neo-Platonic conceptions of love had been in vogue since the Renaissance, in
the poetry of Maurice Scève and the Ecole Lyonnaise, as well as in the fiction of

Sentimental novels and tragic fiction were stupefyingly rigid in their adherence to established formulas, and each rehearsed some combination of the same ritualistic repertory of characters and events. There are at least two different but complementary ways to explain the formulaic nature of early seventeenth-century French fiction. We can examine the reading public from a sociological standpoint and observe that most readers were aristocratic. Writers, none of whom wrote for any appreciable sum of money, simply reproduced what readers seemed to want to read. The absence of virtually any social diversity in the reading public made this a comparatively simple task. Even if it were the case that writers were mistaken and readers only read sentimental and tragic fiction because despite its repetitive nature it was all that was available, the fiction market was not competitive. There was no coherent economic system that could allow readers' preferences to be made known, since writers had no incentive to try different forms of fiction and readers generally had no way of communicating their preferences. Although this is admittedly an extremely reductive way to account for literary production, it is important not to underestimate the hermetically closed circuit early French fiction traveled: only a few hundred copies of each new work of fiction were produced, and almost all of them were bought by aristocrats. Even if one discounts the economic aspect of the question, the fact remains that since the possibility of dissenting voices entering into the literary circuit was slim, particularly during the first two decades of the century, aristocratic attempts to canonize what was essentially their own popular culture were virtually assured success.

This socioeconomic attempt to understand the formulaic nature of sentimental and tragic fiction may account for the obduracy of formula, but it fails to explain the endurance of the particular for-

---

Marguerite de Navarre. A major breakthrough in the dissemination of Platonism and court life came in 1585 with the translation into French of Baldasare Castiglione's *Cortegiano*. Many of the principles of *Le Courtisan* that could be directly applied to sentimental novels were derived from characteristics typical of medieval courtly romance. One should "flee all ugliness of vulgar love," avoid all temptation of sins of the flesh, and consider beauty of face and body a reflection of divine goodness (pp. 615–16). Proper ladies were advised to turn a cold shoulder to conversation that was too frivolous, and never to yield to a man until she put him through rigorous trials to test his constancy and fidelity. The attractive neo-Platonic philosophies of Castiglione's work, which allowed nobles to see themselves in grand and idealized lights, seem to have been partially responsible for the codification of the conventions of sentimental fiction.

mulas elaborated above. Even Maurice Lever, in one of the finest
books on seventeenth-century fiction available, notes that each repetitive theme "crystallizes a moment of the public's sensibility,"
yet he fails to account for the public's peculiar taste.[14] If we examine
the formulas for sentimental and tragic fiction, however, it becomes
clear that both varieties play out a ritualistic separation and return.
In sentimental fiction the young lovers are separated by shipwrecks,
storms, battles, and kidnappings; in tragic fiction, similar if generally more gruesome phenomena tear the mismatched couple's
union asunder. The element that remains constant in both strains
of fiction is a return, not necessarily of the purloined lover, but of
an authority figure empowered either to sanction the union, as in
the case of sentimental fiction, or to punish the mismatch, as in the
case of tragic fiction. Early seventeenth-century category fiction re-
peats the ritual of separation and reintegration time and again and
in virtually all cases the reintegration involves reaffirming the hegemony of a strong noble lineage.

Sentimental and tragic tales of the early seventeenth century resemble one another as much as do today's mass-market romances.
As literary texts they provide little ground for interpretation, since
with few exceptions they offer practically the same characters and
the same scenarios. Like a modern romance, however, or a Marvel
Comic, they are no less valuable as cultural documents and no less
fruitful as terrains of analysis, since each genre—and precisely because they do constitute a genre, as I will argue below—can respond to difficult and varied questions if we know which questions
to pose. In their stultifying repetition, sentimental and tragic fictions rehearse the cultural anxiety of the dissolution of the aristocratic race, and the publication of each new volume reflects a new
attempt to master that anxiety. From the late sixteenth century
through the ministry of Mazarin there was a marked inflation in
the number of letters of nobility issued to commoners—in fact,
over one thousand new offices were created from the reign of Henri
IV through that of Louis XIII, each of which conferred nobility on
families wealthy enough to purchase them.[15] The repeated return
of authority in fiction, more often than not in the return of the

---

[14] See Lever, *Le Roman français au XVIIe siècle*, p. 18.

[15] See Jean-Marie Constant, *La Vie quotidienne de la noblesse française aux
XVIe–XVIIe siècles*, p. 111; and Davis Bitton, *The French Nobility in Crisis*, pp. 95,
147 n. 14.

father, brings honor back to a family—a race of aristocratic people—in danger of disgrace. In sentimental fiction, the time of separation is marked by melancholia, by a mourning of the loss of the beloved, and by an idealization and veneration of that person. Reunion brings reintegration and stability. In tragic fiction the return of the avenging father rights a usually social wrong by punishing and annihilating the intruding contaminant. In both cases a sense of happy stasis is achieved and the destabilization that fiction causes finds its cathartic relief in the mastery of the social order.[16]

Early seventeenth-century French fiction offers little or no narrative as twentieth-century readers generally conceive of it. If one were asked what, say, *Madame Bovary* is about, even the most casual reader would have little difficulty reproducing the events leading to the woman's death. Asked, however, what, for example, *Les Amours de Philocaste* is about, even the most perspicacious reader might be hard-pressed to recount some semblance of the sequence of misfortunes that precede the couple's union. For this reason, modern commentators label early seventeenth-century fiction as inaccessible to or at the very least painfully difficult for modern readers. Henri Coulet, for example, finds in these novels a fundamental "vice" born of the tendency to take literary convention to a stultifying extreme. The overuse of convention, he writes, "paralyzes and petrifies everything: the action, psychology and style."[17] Andrew Suozo registers a similar impatience with early seventeenth-century fiction when he writes that *L'Astrée* "contains enough peripheral intrigue to lose even the most impassioned reader."[18] If we read sentimental and tragic fiction from a modern perspective (and of course we have no choice), we must agree that their narratives are singularly unsatisfying: there is generally no sequence of events building one upon another in causal fashion progressing toward a climax which can be seen, in retrospect, to depend ultimately on the order of transpired events.

[16] In the early years of this century, Gustave Reynier wrote that sentimental fiction helped a troubled nobility regroup and reestablish itself as a class with shared interests: "The nobility especially, at the end of this long period of confusion and hatred, experienced the sharp need to group together to live in smooth harmony, to distance from their memory anything that could have awakened old conflicts. Intensified by the struggle, individualism began to disappear, to submit to certain rules and certain conventions. Thus was constituted a milieu which was to be favorable to the development of sentimental literature" (p. 169).

[17] Coulet, *Le Roman jusqu'à la Révolution*, vol. I, p. 141.

[18] Suozo, *The Comic Novels of Charles Sorel*, p. 22.

One must resist the temptation to consider this minimal narrative component a fault, however. It is obviously anachronistic to overlay modern models of fiction onto those belonging to another era: there is no evidence that contemporary readers found these works as dry and uninspiring as we might. Literary discourse must have some way of justifying itself, of maintaining the reader's interest, and of offering him or her reasons to continue reading. In short, literary works must have a reason for being; they must affect or in some way respond to readers' social and political identities. The tension and reintegration that early seventeenth-century French fiction rehearsed served to fulfill a social function and gave these works their point. That point, paradoxically enough, generally involved the precise phenomenon modern commentators isolate as the works' greatest flaw: their lack of narrative flow. The point early fiction seems to have had for contemporaries is easy to grasp, then, even if individual works fail to sustain our interest: the sheer repetition of types suggests that the formula, and not the narrative per se, was the element that satisfied readers, and each time noble authority predominated, their abetted anxieties proved to them that honor and virtue are not arbitrary or contingent, but natural.[19] The minimal narrative structure repudiates change and discontinuity, and provides the somewhat paradoxical illusion of continuity of historical lineage in a constant stasis of the contemporary in which nothing evolves.

For the sake of argument, I have perhaps oversimplified the composition and constitution of early seventeenth-century fiction. Although the traits I have elaborated above are evident in the vast majority of the dozens of sentimental novels and *histoires tragiques* that I consulted, several works do not fit into my model. What does one do, for example, with Camus' tale that recounts, in fewer than five pages, the accidental stoning to death of a child, the guilty father's suicide, followed by a woman who mistakenly roasts her baby to death and then hangs herself? The narrator tells us that

[19] McKeon makes similar observations on British medieval romances. He writes that "the gradual discrediting of aristocratic honor, the resolution of its tacit unity into the problematic relation of rank and virtue, birth and worth, was accompanied by the accelerated mobilization of social, intellectual, legal, and institutional fictions whose increasingly ostentatious use signaled their incapacity to serve the ideological ends for which they were designed" (p. 133). In Chapters 5 and 7, I will address the phenomenon of a breakdown disarticulating French fiction's form and the discursive political function it came to fill.

"The entire village was alarmed over such a bizarre spectacle" (*Les spectacles d'horreur*, 26), and who could blame them? More work needs to be done in this field, but the point I would like to draw from the generalizations I have already made is that what was crystallizing—slowly at first, beginning with Boaistuau, and then more rapidly in the first two decades of the seventeenth century—was a pragmatics of prose fiction. Early seventeenth-century fiction writers, in particular those who wrote *histoires tragiques*, based their works on well-known folktales or on *faits divers*, reports of various oddities or current events that circulated in oral or written form.[20] These writers gave a new form to what people already knew; they ordered and arranged their tales in such a way that they reflected aristocratic desires and anxieties and consequently, in their *dénouements*, helped shape aristocratic ideology by refining and codifying a literary form that attested to aristocratic hegemony.

Although early seventeenth-century French fiction lacked a coherent theoretical discourse capable of articulating the strategies and limitations of the form, the aristocratic reading public's use of fiction to minimalize the gap between their idealized image of themselves and their material reality provided the conditions for a new kind of literary expression. A restricted group of writers aimed its works at an equally select group of readers, bombarding them with images that through sheer force of repetition effectively became canonized. Both writers and readers normalized the stock literary conventions composing sentimental and tragic fiction, allowing to develop an early form of *vraisemblance*, that is, an aesthetically and ideologically coded style deemed suitable for shaping a literary reality fundamentally in harmony with readers' perceptions of how things ought to be. Sentimental and tragic fiction codified a narrative form for a specific group, thus providing the conditions for what was, for all practical purposes, a new literary genre.

The necessity of adhering to the rules of genre obtaining for particular forms was a literary fact of life in the 1640's and later. René Bray has provided perhaps the most complete account of the historical and philosophical roots of the obsession with rules in high

[20] Camus writes in his preface, in fact, that "you will find among the brand-new stories in these Spectacles some that have already been written, which I have gathered here" (*Les spectacles d'horreur*, "Preface").

French classicism, and more recently Henri Coulet has examined
the influence that preexisting generic conventions exerted on the
production of fiction.[21] In the early decades of the seventeenth century, however, rules of genre were not yet codified and conventionalized. Writers did not yet feel the pressure to integrate their works
into one of the tidy literary categories that would dictate to a very
large extent the style, timbre, structure, and motifs of their produc-
tions. This is, of course, particularly true of fiction, since even
though Aristotelian poetics had become the object of intense scrutiny in Italy and to a lesser extent in France during the late sixteenth
century, the ancient theorists did not include novels in their discussions; consequently fiction writers were free to experiment as they
liked. The budding genres of prose fiction, then, were unrestrained
by the categorical imperatives of high classicism. Genre in the early
years of the seventeenth century was less a trope informing the production of new works than it was a benign taxonomic system
charged merely with describing already existing works and subject
to frequent and sometimes profound modification. At most one
could say that genres of fiction in the early seventeenth century
were temporary guidelines regulating the flow of new works only
to the extent that they continued to uphold the socially and ideologically determined conventions depicting the ascendancy and natural superiority of aristocratic ideals.

Sentimental and tragic fiction established a collection of narrative
conventions for aristocratic fiction, and if they proved time and
again that aristocratic virtue and hegemony were neither arbitrary
nor contingent, but properties inherent in individual and race, it
was the pastoral novel, longer by far and psychologically more
complex, that joined a specifically aristocratic iconography to the
ideology already espoused in fiction. Pastoral fiction did not by any
means break with the traditions of fiction that preceded it. It did,
however, make explicit the aristocratic appropriation and application of linguistic artifice to literature in the service of ideologically
invested works. Honoré d'Urfé's *L'Astrée*, far and away the best-
known pastoral novel, accomplished the codification of an aristocratic language, one based on artifice, accessible only to a select
few. *L'Astrée* is imbued with the same ideological imperatives as

---

[21] Bray, *La Formation de la doctrine classique en France*; Coulet, "Un siècle, un
genre?"

sentimental and tragic fiction, but if the conventions in early fiction were becoming worn and obtrusive, d'Urfé breathed new life into them by writing a novel thousands of pages long that draws its point largely from the impenetrability to outsiders of the language of artifice.

In the second part of *L'Astrée*, Silvandre, one of the multitude of lovelorn shepherds, laments Diane's aloofness and apparent disdain for him. Settling down on the banks of the River Lignon, he decides to consult the oracle Echo, asking her what Diane's actions mean and how he should respond. Offering up the following lyric strophe, Silvandre wonders in particular what Diane's glances signify:

> Que feroit donc cet œil qui me desarme
> Par sa douceur de toute sorte d'arme,
> Et qui promet m'aymer infiniment?

> What would it do, this eye that strips me,
> By its sweetness, of any sort of arm,
> And which promises to love me infinitely?

Echo's answer is simple and direct: "*Il ment* (It lies)." [22] After a series of similar exchanges, in which Echo's response consists of a return of the lovesick poet's final syllables, Silvandre asks her: "But from whom do you know that her noble heart / Will be conquered, if I am true to her (*si je luy suis fidelle*)?" Echo's answer, of course, is that she learned the answer "*D'elle* (From her)" (II, 11). Silvandre is quite obviously providing himself with the answers he wants to hear. Whether it is his unconscious speaking or an extremely canny poetic aptitude for thinking several verses ahead and manipulating syllabic homophones, Silvandre knows that he is ultimately responsible for the good news he receives: "Although the shepherd knew that it was he himself who was responding . . . nevertheless he felt great consolation in these favorable replies . . . . " (II, 11). Still, he wants to continue believing that "these words . . . had not been pronounced by him on purpose, but through the secret intelligence of the spirit who favored him and who put the words in his mouth" (II, 11).

The play of echoes was common in the literature of the late six-

[22] d'Urfé, vol. II, p. 10.

teenth and seventeenth centuries, and it was particularly popular in
theatrical monologues as a means of foreshadowing action.[23] In
L'Astrée, however, Silvandre's echo offers only advice. Redoubling
his words and returning to the young lover his own desire, Echo
responds nevertheless in anything but an unequivocal manner.
When Silvandre asks, "Will I then never find relief?" Echo responds
with a startling "*Je mens* (I lie)" (II, 10). Evoking the unsettling
proposition that a representation which is apparently a direct reflection of a real event might be duplicitous or misleading, Silvandre's echo seems to caution him to be wary of simulacra. In fact,
all the echoes in Silvandre's *stances* consisting of a subject and verb
concern the possibility of lying or misrepresenting. Echo promises
the truth, yet she cannot be trusted to keep her promise, since the
truth in her words is fleeting and ironic. Silvandre questions each
of Echo's responses, and asks her what she means, as if to suggest
that the reflection of his speech opens up a series of interpretive
possibilities lacking in his original words. In fact, the reflection of
his own words renders them foreign and other. Because the syllables are recontextualized, they seem to have an authority the
questioner lacks. Daniella Della Valle points out that the echo in
this passage is a "reflection of the voice, equal to and at the same
time other than it."[24] Recognizing that the echo is only a verbal
artifice, Silvandre nevertheless takes pleasure in "appearances of
hope where there is no appearance of reason" (II, 10).

Silvandre's automatic responses are in many respects emblematic
of the artifice that permeates the five volumes of *L'Astrée*. At once
self-conscious and deliberately contrived, it is also deceptive and
chimerical, leading the inhabitants of Forez away from the truth.
In the second chapter of the first part of the work, for example, the
grottoes housing the Fountain of the Truth of Love, a magic mirror
in which one sees one's paramour and whether or not one's love is
requited, are fabricated surroundings "so deftly contrived to seem
natural that one's eye quite often fooled one's judgment" (I, 37).[25]

---

[23] For a detailed analysis of the use of echo in classical and modern literature, see
John Hollander, *The Figure of Echo*.

[24] Della Valle, "Le Thème et la structure de l'"echo' dans la pastorale dramatique
française au XVIIe siècle," p. 195.

[25] Jean Rousset has studied the signification of fountains in baroque literature,
and he finds that in general they suggested the fleeting truth of appearances always
in movement. See his *La Littérature de l'age baroque en France*, pp. 143–47.

Often, but not always, the inhabitants of Forez failed to recognize the human craftwork that produced this apparently natural setting. This "quite often," however, is a caveat revealing that often enough the evidence of human input, the deft arrangement of detail cunningly contrived to seem natural, was recognized and valued as a significant component in the production of social meaning at Forez. In other words, the people of Forez took pleasure in knowing that the grottoes *seemed* natural; part of their enjoyment derived from the discrepancy between the accidents of nature that produce real grottoes and the determinate work of representation that causes a given group of people in a particular historical context to consider a representation realistic. Artifice at Forez is not simply a pleasant parlor game providing the idle shepherds with something to do. Rather, it represents the excavation of a chasm between the shepherds and the previous transparency of their interpersonal relationships, a chasm they can cross only through the interpretation of others' language. In this respect *L'Astrée* depicts the fall from an unmediated understanding of sentiment and behavior to a world of mediation dominated by artifice and the necessity of interpretation.

The shepherds and nymphs at Forez attempt to untangle the web of appearances and speech that mask true feelings. They struggle to convince their paramours of their love or they strive to become worthy of their lover's passion. The four thousand pages of *L'Astrée* contain hundreds of stories, letters, verses, and judgments all devoted to proving or verifying genuine affection. Nicole Chabert has written that in their constant conversations about love "the characters of *L'Astrée* have a single mode of existence: the eternal present of their speech, which the narration of their actions never quite covers." [26] These people luxuriate in the self-conscious artifice of courtliness, yet at the same time they are reduced to a linguistic artifice to which they are not accustomed and with which they are, paradoxically, ill-equipped to deal: the artifice of the language of love. The reason behind the shepherds' exile into linguistic artifice is, in fact, the *raison d'être* of the novel: the Fountain of the Truth of Love has been rendered inaccessible. This fountain has the remarkable power to reveal the unequivocal truth about matters of love, "for he who looks into it sees there his mistress, and if he is loved he sees himself alongside her; if she loves another, he sees the

[26] Chabert, "L'Amour du discours dans *L'Astrée*," p. 395.

face of the one she loves" (I, 93). Clidaman and Guyemants, both
in love with Silvie, consult the fountain and see there only the
young woman's face, proof positive that she does not share their
passion. Distraught, Clidaman attempts to smash the fountain to
bits with his sword. When this fails, determined to render it useless,
he posts two lions and two unicorns at guard in order to make it
unavailable to others. The lions and unicorns are enchanted; the
spell will be broken only by "the blood and the death of the most
faithful lovers who ever lived in this land" (I, 282). "Thus," Leon-
ide relates, "we have lost the use of this fountain, which so success-
fully unveiled the caches of deceiving thoughts" (I, 94).

Chabert describes the people of Forez and the "eternal present of
their speech." The inaccessibility of the fountain means that henceforth no guarantor of certainty or truth is available, and lovers have
recourse only to the rigidly codified but untrustworthy domain of
courtly language. Tomantes describes their situation as follows:

> We who, up till now, have dedicated all our energies to loving well,
> and not to talking about it well (quite the contrary) to whomever
> most frequently our discretion as well as the rigour of the ladies we
> have served have completely forbidden us to speak, with great diffi-
> culty will we now be able to say that which we have so perfectly and
> so religiously observed, given that, if it is true no one must meddle in
> any trade other than the one he has learned and of which he makes
> his profession, is it not true ... that never having made any profes-
> sion other than that of loving without saying it, we will now be pre-
> vented from assuming another role and of having recourse to speech
> to verify our actions, to which we had relegated all our eloquence and
> all our conviction. (IV, 330)

The tortured paratactic construction of Tomantes' discourse eloquently states the case he is trying to make: speaking one's passion,
particularly when one has been used only to enacting it, inade-
quately reflects desire and leads to misunderstanding and deception. Chabert has unearthed a series of misunderstandings that
arise because the lovers at Forez are unable to grasp the figurative
dimension of language, confusing such things as burning one's finger and burning with desire, or misconstruing the metaphoric sense
of inscribing one's name in another's heart.[27] Accustomed to the

[27] See, for example, the following passages: "Eudoxe does not want to 'burn'
because, having already burned her finger, she imagines that it is a quite unbearable
pain" (II, 495); Silviane fails to understand how her name can be "engraved" in

unadorned truth, the people of Forez flounder in a world of signs whose dizzying instability lies in sharp relief to the fountain's pure reflection of reality. The "eternal present of their speech," to use Chabert's expression, reflects on the one hand their failure to come to terms with the uses and power of representation; constrained to circulate their language in a hermeneutically sealed world, they disperse their letters, oratory, and judgments as provisional acts awaiting the return of the fountain's power to halt the processes of signification and interpretation their speech occasions. On the other hand, the eternal present of their speech evinces an ahistorical approach to discursive practices, because no one analyzes the social construction of language at Forez—although each recognizes artifice in his or her world, none is able to excavate its function and its uses. Continually fooled by their obligatory recourse to discourse, the people in the geographically and historically sealed world of Forez are the playthings of their own speech.

Despite their subjugation to the artifice of speech, the shepherds and shepherdesses realize that they retain the power to manipulate appearances. On one level, they learn how to master the equivocal sign and make use of it in order to pique their paramours' desire. Adamas points out, for example, that "ladies who want to be loved endlessly are those who give the least satisfaction to their lovers' desire," but one must be adroit at leaving just enough hope, since "just as the lamp goes out when the oil runs out, so also desire dies when its nourishment is removed" (I, 331). On another, more complex level, the people of Forez allow the play of artifice in *L'Astrée* to extend far beyond playful aphrodisia. For as baffled as the shepherds and shepherdesses may be concerning passion and true love, the world of artifice and interpretation brought about by the inaccessibility of the Fountain of the Truth of Love in no way hinders their ability to negotiate the complex trappings associated with social class. Despite the artificiality of their pastoral garb, the people at Forez recognize each other's social position, and d'Urfé is quick to point out in his preface, which is in the form of a missive from "L'autheur à la bergere Astrée" (The author to the shepherdess As-

---

Andrimarte's heart (III, 1128); and Célidée fails to grasp how she can "shut her love up in a casket" (II, 43). Chabert's citations refer to the 1647 edition of *L'Astrée* (Paris: Augustin Courbé).

trée), that the bucolic trappings of his work are only a conceit. Addressing his title character, he writes: "You are not, any more than those who follow you, a shepherdess by necessity, like those who make their living by leading their flocks to pasture . . ." (I, 7). Astrée has freely chosen, rather, a life of leisure and tranquillity, one in which she is free from material concerns and able to devote herself entirely to contemplating the mysteries of love and the re-compenses of virtue.

The ideology of virtue in *L'Astrée* is thinly veiled in pastoral garb, however, and Galathée, one of d'Urfé's nymphs, reveals its aristo-cratic foundation when she says that "in whatever place virtue is found, it is worthy of being loved and honored, whether cloaked in bucolic attire or in the glorious purple of kings" (I, 47). Galathée's comment seems egalitarian and laudable, but the comparison is telling, particularly when the "bucolic attire" at Forez is silk and taffeta. Daughter of Forez's ruler, Galathée stresses not that anyone can love virtue, but rather that the nobly born can do so no matter what they wear. An elaborate sign system based on lineage and on the possession of a rigidly defined cultural heritage determines worth, and there are quite specific levels of cultural heritage that keep virtue and merit from being anything like egalitarian con-cepts. In *L'Astrée*, Celadon is but a simple shepherd and Galathée is a *nymphe*. Although both are people of quality, like all of d'Urfé's main characters, they recognize and perpetuate the hierarchically arranged social network: a *nymphe* outranks a shepherd, and Ce-ladon knows it. This knowledge, in part, which his own birth has bestowed upon him, contributes to his nobility: "Celadon knew who these beautiful nymphs were, and he recognized as well the respect he owed them. Although he was not accustomed to being anywhere except among his people the shepherds, his noble birth nevertheless taught him what he owed to people such as these" (I, 47).

Social standing at Forez, like the seventeenth-century model on which it is so clearly based, is inherited. Merit and rank are not merely arbitrary outcomes of birth, however; they derive as well from feudal practices, particularly as these practices were depicted in twelfth-century romance. Lindamor, for example, is nobly born and he demonstrated his merit in the traditional noble manner of bearing arms: "As soon as he was able to bear the charge of arms, urged on by this valiant instinct which presses noble courage to the most dangerous enterprises, he never missed an occasion to do battle, where he gave proof of what he was" (I, 325). More important still for the display of his nobility, however, is his courtliness: "Ever since, having returned to see Clidaman and to pay the homage he owed, he gave himself to two people: to Clidaman, as his lord, and to Galathée, as his lady . . ." (I, 325). Lindamor knows what to say and how to say it. After a tournament with Polemas, he is prudent enough to pay homage to the king and declare himself the lady Galathée's servant.

Like his character Galathée, d'Urfé emphasizes the symbolic value of pastoral garb, and he underscores the need to appreciate the artificiality of appearances in order to understand their underlying significance. In a remarkably self-conscious formulation that stresses the level of artifice active not only at Forez but in the production of the novel itself, d'Urfé writes: "I represent nothing to the eye, but only to the ear, for hearing is not a sense that touches the soul so passionately" (I, 8). D'Urfé's disclaimer is a proleptic attempt to ward off criticisms that his novel is not plausible: arguing that the work offers not so much a slice of life in the *ut pictura poesis* model of representation, but the verbal portrait of a specific signifying practice, he stresses that *L'Astrée* depicts a particular kind of language that readers are used to hearing. That language, of course, is the language of the court, and it is as densely padded with a sophisticated and self-conscious artificiality as the taffeta and silk pastoral clothing the people at Forez wear in their everyday lives.

L'Astrée depicted for its contemporary aristocratic readers an idealized image of their past, invoking a mythological feudalism in which birth and merit, military valor, and cultivated courtesy were the hallmarks of the truly noble individual. While seventeenth-century aristocrats were facing the specter of increased poverty, the novel fortified an iconography designed to display their continued preeminence by emphasizing these abstract qualities, and not material wealth. Aristocratic virtue was something one was born with; money had no purchase in the cultural capital aristocrats had accrued over the generations. The artifice in *L'Astrée*, then, was more

than a "fictionalized past [that] corresponded to the real present,"
as Erica Harth has written.[28] It was both an exclusionary device
designed to keep at a distance the rising bourgeoisie who were eager to appropriate the aristocracy's iconography, and a celebration
of a way of life headed for antiquation. Like Silvandre, who cherished the artifice of his echo's response, and Diane, who accuses
him of pretending so well that he approaches truth (II, 107), readers of L'Astrée reveled in the work's artificiality, the exaggerated
spectacle of anachronistic appearances. It was common, in fact, to
gather in salons for a reading of the novel, and enthusiastic nobles
dressed up as their favorite characters, even taking their names or
names resembling those at Forez.[29] As if to proclaim that Forez was
not a utopia or the representation of an obsolete gentility, but a
genuine social reality, aristocrats literalized the work's mythology.
They animated and vitalized d'Urfé's world, supplying the novel
with a referentiality that would attest to its truth. Minimalizing the
gap between representation and reality, they conformed to d'Urfé's
vision of their group. Harth writes that "in this world where to see
and to be seen was a chief activity, the nobility was enthralled by
the spectacle of itself. It adopted disguise in order to see itself in
disguise" (38). The referentiality they provided, however, involved
not so much a real social and historical world, but the iconography
of a particular group. In other words, novel and readers met each
other on the terrain of a shared semiotic system.

The semiotic system common to novel and readers sets forth the
ideology of virtue as aristocratic, and artifice, as d'Urfé's characters
realize, can have very real effects despite its insubstantiality. Astrée
tells Diane that "artifice never provokes such genuine passion" (III,
16), yet the inconstant Silvandre, who merely pretends to love Diane to win a wager, develops a blinding passion for her. Jean Rousset reveals the theory behind Astrée's truism when he writes that in
d'Urfé's novel "one only reaches the truth by taking the detour of
artifice" (33). Artifice in L'Astrée extends beyond the fabrication of
charming and genteel facades; it goes beyond appearances, and as-

<hr />

[28] Harth, *Ideology and Culture in Seventeenth-Century France*, p. 139.

[29] The marquise de Rambouillet, for example, whose salon was among the most
influential, was known by the name Arthénice, an anagram of her given name Cath-
érine. For more on the practice of taking names from the pastoral novels popular in
the seventeenth century, see Roger Picard's *Les Salons littéraires et la société française*, chapter 5.

sumes the role of a function marking the relationship between the real world and imaginary conceptions of it. Artifice in *L'Astrée*, like disguise in seventeenth-century salons, negotiates and reconciles the discrepancy between aspirations and reality, between, that is, desire and that which resists desire. Its purpose is less to deceive than to provide an interpretable text, a means by which readers, be they shepherds or aristocrats, can discern their relationship to reality. Jacques Ehrmann writes that artifice is nothing in itself, but that it designates "the field where the real and the imaginary meet one another, cross, and intermix." [30] Artifice, both at Forez and for *L'Astrée*'s readers, is at once calculated and inescapable. On the one hand, it is the exclusionary signifying practice by and in which members of a group recognize and identify one another and banish those who do not possess the key. On the other hand, it is the necessary product of representation, and the characters at Forez differ significantly from seventeenth-century aristocratic readers in their relationship to the inescapable alienation of verbal representation. While they muddle through deceiving appearances, struggling in vain to discover the truth behind others' words, their aristocratic counterparts appropriate the disjunction between word and deed, using it to their own ideological advantage. In short, *L'Astrée* establishes what we might properly call an ideology of artifice.

If the people at Forez know how to manipulate appearances in order to carry out a seduction, it was d'Urfé's aristocratic readers who were the real manipulators of the artifice on which his novel relies. Dressing up as his characters, making themselves the novel's ultimate referent, they also possessed the key, the code that enabled them to determine the true identities of the fictional characters they read about. Yet, however true d'Urfé's depiction of aristocratic virtue appeared to his readers, or however accurate a reflection of reality they made Forez by reproducing in their own lives the speech, manner, and dress of his characters, the fact remained that the fairy-tale portrayal of patrician gentility became more and more erroneous in the two decades separating the first and last volumes of the work (1607–27). Dire economic straits, resulting primarily from the religious wars of the sixteenth century, had left the aristocracy nearly penniless. This, coupled with an astronomically high inflation rate, brought on near total financial ruin, particularly

[30] Ehrmann, *L'Amour et l'illusion dans "L'Astrée"*, p. 76.

since most aristocrats had stable incomes based upon their land-
holdings.[31] The social front was no more encouraging to the languishing aristocracy than the economic one. Less than a century
before, François I had legalized the sale of offices conferring nobility on wealthy bourgeois, thus establishing the enmity that would
separate the *noblesse d'épée* and the *noblesse de robe* for generations to come, as the former saw their power and privilege rapidly
dwindle. Béthune de Sully, finance minister under Henri IV, aggra-
vated matters by establishing the *paulette*, an annual fee levied on
administrative posts that effectively made hereditary any nobility
granted through the purchase of *charges*, ennobling bureaucratic
posts. One must bear in mind as well that although absolute monarchy existed in France since the reign of Henri II, even Henri IV
continued to recognize the authority of the Parlement to register
royal decrees. Consequently, the aristocracy of d'Urfé's time still
had reason to consider themselves vital not only to the guidance
and well-being of the state, but to the continuing political hegemony of France in Europe. Finally, the publication of *L'Astrée*
roughly coincided with Marie de Médicis' regency (1610–17), and
regencies had generally seen aristocratic attempts to assume
power.[32] In 1614 they made just such an attempt when they pres-
sured Marie to call the Estates General. No significant changes
emerged from this convocation, but hostility between the aristocracy and the bourgeoisie was bitter; in fact, this was the last meeting of the Estates General until 1789.

The aristocracy saw themselves financially and socially bankrupt,
temperamentally as well as economically unable to assert their
predominance. Small wonder, then, that d'Urfé's contemporaries
seized the opportunity to appropriate what symbolic iconography
was remaining to them and use it to bolster both their egos and
their images. The complex hierarchies at Forez separating nymphs,
shepherds, druids, and rulers corresponded to the rigid sense of
conservative social stratification aristocrats cherished. Prizing the
structures of power, knowledge, and morality that had been in

---

[31] In 1600, for example, currency was worth roughly 20 percent of what it had
been worth one hundred years earlier. See Victor Tapié, *France in the Age of Louis
XIII and Richelieu*, pp. 10–14.

[32] On the forms of absolutism in France, see Kearns, especially chapter 1; on the
regency and the aristocracy's attempts to gain power, see Pierre-Georges Lorris, *La
Fronde*.

place since the feudal era, the aristocracy mobilized to maintain the current state of affairs. As Joseph Klaits has written, "in its vision of political and cultural life the seventeenth century was dominated by strong biases toward continuity and against change. Aristocracy, religion, classical learning, and monarchy itself were cults whose prestige derived from their lengthy lineage."[33] Maintaining this state of affairs involved in part retaining control of the discursive practices, including literature, that had the power to reflect as well as to shape ideology. *L'Astrée* constructed for aristocratic readers a parochial and fictionalized historical vision of their chivalric feudal past by appropriating and modifying the conventions of romance. Suspending all material concerns, the novel severed the relationship between social institutions and their historical foundations, thus causing to appear natural and unproblematic the aristocratic ideology it advocated. The aristocrat reading *L'Astrée*, like Silvandre listening to his echo, "knew that it was he himself who was responding," yet the pleasure the novel provided seemed to derive from this very fact. Aristocrats were in control of the production of a complex ideological artifice that could contribute to maintaining their hegemony. D'Urfé's monumental work was among the first in a series of partisan novels that inaugurated an intricate iconography depicting aristocratic values as timeless and unchanging concerns. The cultivation of gentility barely changed over the millennium separating d'Urfé's readers from the characters they read about; this, coupled with a cavalier insouciance about the material considerations of life, underscored the abstract and abiding nature of birth and merit. Madeleine Bertaud writes that in *L'Astrée* "the simplicity necessary to happiness is determined less by historical, geographical, economic, or sociological conditions than by a concerted effort: it is the duty of each to acquire a knowledge of true values,"[34] and d'Urfé's novel offered the image of historical stasis in order to cause a political vision to seem guileless and natural.

Pierre Boaistuau depicted, in his *Histoires tragiques*, noble gentlefolk who found peace and happiness by abandoning "the unbearably noisy, teeming cities to retire to the fields of their castles." What may have been imperative for the physical and emotional well-being of battle-fatigued nobility in 1559 was no less ideologi-

[33] Klaits, p. 11
[34] Bertaud, "De *L'Astrée* au *Polexandre*, pourquoi mourir?," p. 34.

cally imperative for early seventeenth-century aristocrats. The iconography of *L'Astrée*, showcasing moral excellence in a world divorced from money and material abundance, sets wealth and merit
against one another, privileging an abstract virtue attainable only
by birth and reinforcing a mythological history of the nobility that
accounts for individual excellence and collective preeminence.
D'Urfé's work elaborates a fictional and idealized genealogy in
which readers become the novel's referent. Despite or perhaps because of d'Urfé's warning not to search for a key,[35] readers continually found resemblances between his characters and the people
they knew. In fact, in 1681 Olivier Patru published an incomplete
version of the key based on conversations with d'Urfé, and even as
late as 1733 an edition appeared with the key. The referentiality
these keys provided exhorted readers to find concrete similarities
between their lives and the world the novel depicted, and the abstractions of virtue in *L'Astrée* were reified in an unequivocal treatise of conservative ideology.[36]

D'Urfé's readers attempted to establish themselves as the novel's
ultimate referent by conforming to the image of gentility the work
depicted. The adequation of signifier and signified, or more accurately of *récit* and extratextual reality, however, is not limited to a
simple resemblance between the world the novel depicts and the
one readers inhabit, particularly since such adequation only existed
because of readers' sovereign decision to bring it about. Referentiality in *L'Astrée* functions instead primarily on the level of signifying practice: it is not the events or situations the novel portrays
that ultimately made this novel the literary repository of aristocratic ideology, but its iconography and social adaptability. When
readers donned pastoral garb and appropriated bucolic names and
discourse, they legitimated d'Urfé's depiction of their class; paring
down the distance between textual and historical worlds caused the
former's ideology to appear to supplement the latter naturally. By

[35] "If you find yourself among those professional dream interpreters or mind
readers who insist that Celadon is really this man and Astrée really that woman, do
not even answer them, because well they know that they do not know what they are
saying; rather, ask those who might be misled by their fictions to consider that if
these things do not matter, I would not have taken the trouble to mask them so
diligently, and if they do matter to me, I would be quite feeble-minded to have
wanted to mask them and to have succeeded so poorly" (I, 6).
[36] For a reading of the historical and ideological impact of pastoral fiction in the
British tradition, see McKeon, pp. 212–35.

becoming the work's absent referent, they endowed it with an extratextuality to which it could refer and, ultimately, with a definitive political bias as well. Yet, as we shall now see, not all readers could identify with the work, and some in particular found its ideology outmoded and offensive. Fighting fire with fire, they attempted to undermine the force of *L'Astrée* by appropriating its iconography in the service of a different, non-aristocratic discourse.

In 1627, the year in which the final volume of d'Urfé's *L'Astrée* was published, Charles Sorel produced his *Berger extravagant*, a biting, sometimes angry parody of pastoral fiction. Borrowing principally from *L'Astrée* and Ollenix du Mont-Sacré's *Bergeries de Juliette* (1585–98), Sorel mercilessly pans contemporary fiction by depicting a bucolic buffoon who deserts his wealthy father's Parisian home to become a shepherd. Louis, who takes the name Lysis because it sounds more idyllic, procures some robes and some sheep, and takes the animals to the outskirts of Paris to graze. There he accosts a genuine shepherd and strikes up a conversation with him: "Gentle Shepherd . . . please share with me your thoughts. Are you brooding upon Clorinde's severities? How long has it been since you composed a song for her? Please, do show me some of your verses [*vers*]."[37] The shepherd, as one might expect, understands nothing of what Lysis says, and takes him for an evil spirit. Unaccustomed to Lysis' style of speech, he thinks that the phantasmal shepherd is talking about *vers de terre*—earthworms— and in his homophonic substitution displaces Lysis' speech away from the aristocratic gentility it is based on and onto the material reality of herding sheep. The cause of the misunderstanding as well as of Lysis' problem in negotiating reality can be found, Sorel intimates, in his choice of reading material. Directed by his family to the legal profession, Louis quickly tired of his studies and "instead of law books he bought only those worthless books called novels" (I, 31).

Le Berger extravagant is a protracted mockery of pastoral fiction that depicts a deluded young bourgeois who strives to live like d'Urfé's shepherds at Forez; indeed, throughout a large part of the work Lysis tries to find Forez and its inhabitants. Throughout his lifetime Sorel was rather critical of novels, in particular of those that claimed for themselves a lofty, serious purpose. In the *Biblio-*

---

[37] Sorel, *Le Berger extravagant*, vol. I, p. 40.

thèque françoise he traces the history of realistic fiction, writing that novels began to be more believable when readers tired of the emperors, kings, and princesses of medieval romance. This, he argues, is what led to the pastoral vogue: "People wanted fiction [*des Histoires feintes*] that represented human temperament as it really is, fiction that offered a candid portrait of their condition and of their nature."[38] The pastoral fiction so popular in the early years of the seventeenth century seemed to Sorel to be a somewhat odd choice for a guileless representation of reality, since everyone knew that "rustic people are generally coarse and stupid" (177). A few years later, in his *De la connoissance des bons livres* (On understanding good books), he wrote that pastoral fiction was a brief foray into realism, but that the convention of portraying the aristocracy in pastoral surroundings and clothing quickly became obtrusive.[39] Sorel makes passing reference to the flagrant immorality of poetry, fiction, or any work of literature designed exclusively for the reader's pleasure when he writes that "novels, poetry, and all entertaining works can corrupt the young or place them in danger of wasting their time" (*De la connoissance*, 65–66); yet, he is in general more concerned with readers' lack of judgment or critical awareness than he is with decreeing particular works or types of literature off limits. In other words, Sorel considered the consumption of literature in context, reflecting on the circumstances in which it was produced as well as on the social contingencies that shaped the reception and interpretation of particular texts.

Sorel was something of a literary elitist and frequently expressed his disappointment that extraliterary forces such as power and wealth had so great an influence in determining a text's worth. Daunted by readers' tendency to buy only books that were currently in vogue, he rebuked his contemporaries for allowing the whims of fashion to overshadow their aesthetic discernment: "We know that some men allow themselves to be taken with the latest fashions, however bizarre they might be; but what is truly ridicu-

---

[38] Sorel, *La Bibliothèque françoise*, p. 177.

[39] "Writers thought they could make their Artistry [*Invention*] more pleasing by relieving shepherds of their ordinary provincialism and by making them speak and act in a courtly manner. But since these sorts of tales seemed as unrealistic [*peu vraysemblable*] as those of errant knights, they finally gave us novels better adapted to men's ordinary customs, novels they tried to pass off as Images of History" (Sorel, *De la connoissance*, pp. 14–15). This critical examination of contemporary literature was initially published in 1671.

lous is their blind affection for the latest books and their rejection of any you show them that are not dated this year" (*De la connoissance*, 23). Distraught that literature was subject to the fluctuations of what had become in the 1670's a highly competitive market in books, he ruthlessly censured booksellers who discredited particular works simply because their competitors were selling them. Above all he decried the system of patronage governing the production of literature; he felt that authors only wrote what would flatter those to whom they dedicated their works in the hope of gaining financial or social rewards. Sorel dedicates a large portion of his critical writing to encouraging his readers to exercise their critical capacities; he instructs them, for example, how to approach the reading of a newly published work (*De la connoissance*, 44): "One must first of all discern whether the book in question is on a legitimate and authorized subject, and whether it is not capable of disturbing one's faith through its dangerous propositions. If it is a question of an entertaining work, one must make sure that no poison is hidden beneath an enticing lure, and that all of this does not corrupt one's morals with evil principles." Because he felt that his contemporaries demonstrated a decided deficiency of literary judgment in reading only works reflecting the latest trends, Sorel feared that their values would be poisoned by books that deftly propounded untoward values veiled beneath the veneer of harmless literary pleasure. Although many critics had expressed the opinion that comic or satiric works should be prohibited because of the licentiousness of their language and of the situations they depicted, Sorel championed the comic novel because "all their evil is on the outside; they have nothing hidden" (*De la connoissance*, 154). Sorel attempted in his literary endeavors to correct the faults he found in contemporary literature. His *Histoire comique de Francion* was designed, he writes in that novel's preface, to "show men the vices to which they are unknowingly led."[40] He uses *Le Berger extravagant* as a critique of novels and novel readers, ridiculing not only pastoral fiction but readers who, like those of the Hôtel de Rambouillet, let themselves be swept up in it.

Most of the comic and parodic force in *Le Berger extravagant* derives from the disjunctions separating various linguistic codes and from the misunderstandings that arise when pastoral and ur-

---

[40] Charles Sorel, *Histoire comique de Francion*, p. 61.

ban worlds collide. Sorel ridicules and imprecates the ideological use of artifice in the service of a particular class, the very keystone of d'Urfé's classic. Lysis yearns for the simple bucolic life he has read about, and he longs to commune with the people of Forez whose language and dress he has appropriated despite the incongruous effects this has in the modern world. Like the real shepherd who thought Lysis was talking about earthworms when in fact he was referring to the verses that adorn *L'Astrée*, virtually none of the people Lysis meets shares his semiotic codes. Conversations in which Lysis takes part are often skewed, frequently of ambiguous reference, and nearly always absurd. Because his interlocutors are in general unfamiliar with precious language, the possibilities of misapprehension are staggering. When, for example, Lysis tries to teach Carmelin how to speak like a good and noble shepherd, he professes the following: "You must always say that your mistress is ravishing." What begins as a lesson in refined language ends as a discussion of larceny when Carmelin misunderstands Lysis' use of the word *ravissante* (ravishing): "'That would certainly be true of Synope,' Carmelin answered. 'She takes everything she finds: she ravished away from me my old hat; she is as ravishing as a bird of prey or a wolf'" (I, 828). Replacing Lysis' lofty and rarefied language with a discourse steeped in corruption and dissolution, Carmelin introduces into Lysis' cultivated linguistic code the material world in which poor people steal to get by. The pastoral language of Forez was unequivocal and explicit despite its preciosity, since all its native speakers shared common cultural references; in the modern France of *Le Berger extravagant*, however, people of different socioeconomic backgrounds have quite diverse concerns, and as the two misunderstandings above show, they look for the referents in Lysis' speech in the familiar, everyday things that form their worlds.

Despite the confusion his speech and demeanor generate, Lysis appears undaunted. Whenever his words or actions produce an unforeseen befuddlement, he resorts to a literalism that throws precious language into comic relief. He attempts to explain, for example, how the three Fates can continue their toil of measuring and cutting human lives when the world's population has grown so enormous (I, 60): "They have a great basket in which there are almost as many silkworms as there are people on the earth. All the threads are pulled and arranged on a reel. The first Fate turns it to gather the threads into a skein; the second then cuts one of them with a scissors, and the third busies herself with arranging new threads to replace those cut." Whenever Lysis' precious language conflicts with the world he experiences, he attempts to resolve the contradiction not by reconsidering his language's capacity to describe or theorize, but by foreclosing its metaphorical dimensions and evoking its constative, referential function. Although many critics have debated whether Lysis' apparent inability to negotiate different registers of language means that he is insane,[41] it seems too facile to dismiss Sorel's intricate interrogation of contemporary literary practices simply by calling the principal character a madman. Such explanations for Lysis' behavior—and they are numerous and often heatedly debated—pale when his ostensible insanity begins to emerge in others. Montenor, for example, reads an explanation of why people no longer languish as they used to before they die, and his account, like Lysis' above, employs a literalization of the allegory of the three Fates: "Because the scissors with which the Fate cuts the thread of life was rusty and could only partially cut, many men were wounded and very few were killed; so I took the scissors and had them reworked at my own expense, so that now they cut so cleanly that people die right away and you no longer see them languishing" (I, 344). If Lysis is insane because he is unable to manage the commerce between literary and non-literary language, it would seem appropriate to question the sanity of readers who wade through a novel fifteen hundred pages long only to close the book feeling that Lysis' derangement explained away the

[41] See, for example, Ioan Williams, who argues that "Sorel conceives of Lysis' delusion as a simple disorder of the mind" in *The Idea of the Novel in Europe*, p. 41; Andrew G. Suozo, Jr., who contends that Lysis is merely a dupe of illusion, in *The Comic Novels of Charles Sorel*, p. 15; and Henri Coulet, who writes that "*Le Berger extravagant* is not the novel of a madman," in *Le Roman jusqu'à la Révolution*, vol. I, p. 198; Maurice Lever allows Lysis to answer the question himself, citing a passage from the 1633–34 edition, entitled *L'Anti-roman, ou l'histoire du berger Lysis* (The anti-novel, or the story of the shepherd Lysis): "Thus he confessed to Clarimond that he repented with all his heart for all that he had done, but that it was impossible for him to refrain from doing such things because even though he knew the truth, sometimes he liked to fool himself in order to fool others and thus make his adventures more remarkable" (Lever, "Le Statut de la critique dans 'Le Berger extravagant'", p. 425). It is interesting to note that the debate over Lysis' insanity begins in the novel itself, when Anselme remarks that "he wasn't quite that crazy, although he was indeed crazy" (I, 151) and Fontenay tells Lysis, "I think you are the successor of Dom Quixote de la Manche, and that you have inherited his folly" (I, 609).

work's irony and ambiguities. Such an explanation merely reflects
the contagiousness, exemplified in the novel by Montenor's story
cited above, of the very problem Sorel was grappling with: given
the necessity of using the language one is trying to attack, how can
a critic demonstrate to readers the stultifying nature of literary conventions that have outlived their utility? Sorel's solution is to highlight the tension between the highly metaphoric pastoral language
of Forez that Lysis strives to imitate and the absurdly referential
language that he finally resorts to; the novel becomes an indictment
of the precious literary tastes of the aristocracy, in particular those
of the regulars of the Hôtel de Rambouillet.[42] Sorel's intolerance of
this highly codified literary language offers a critique of the iconographic literary practices of the aristocracy, and his literary chau-
vinism contributed to the first signs of literary modernism in
France.[43]

Some of the most recent critical writing on *Le Berger extravagant*
has emphasized plot and characterization as Sorel's fundamental
tools for denouncing contemporary fiction. Jean Serroy intimates
that the novel's parodic force derives from Louis' belief that what
he reads is true,[44] and Henri Coulet suggests that the work draws
its critical power from the inadequation between the fantastic
world Lysis inhabits and the real world around him (Coulet, *Le
Roman*, 198–99). In view of Sorel's theoretical writings on the uses
and value of narrative, however, these observations are potentially
misleading. Sorel tolerates narrative prose as long as it is designed
exclusively to recount a sequence of events in unaffected language—what he calls "true or false narration into which enters
Discourse of all sorts, depending on the occasion" (*De la connoissance*, 69)—and in the *Bibliothèque françoise* he justifies the production of fiction as inherently useful to the human mind: "Just as
we have produced Letters, Orations, and other genres of imaginative Discourse [*Discours par fiction*], we have not failed to do the
same in the area of Narration, so that the human mind could have

[42] In her extremely insightful book on Sorel, Martine Debaisieux examines Sorel's
relationhip to the literary canon. She studies Sorel's literary rivalries with Ronsard
and other contemporaries, and she argues that what characterizes *Le Berger extravagant* is a "répétition et différence" that situate the writer's complex relationship
with his predecessors. See her *Procès du roman*, especially pp. 153–61.

[43] The issue of seventeenth-century literary modernism will be addressed in
greater detail in Chapters 4 and 5.

[44] Serroy, *Roman et réalité*, pp. 299–302.

material to occupy it, and so that what is not found in true things might be found in imagined things" (166–67). He approves in particular of history, the "truthful tale of the actions of public or private men, and of the succession of kingdoms" (*De la connoissance*, 75–76), but he cannot, however, abide works whose code or mode of expression competes, along with the actions described, for readers' attention. Wary of the artificiality of precious prose, he imprecates the overwrought metaphorical language of pastoral fiction and tries to wrest from it a referentiality that it is incapable of sustaining. Appropriating contemporary fiction's preciosity and conscripting it into the service of declarative language with its emphasis on extratextual referentiality, he decries all forms of narrative whose poetics involves a self-conscious awareness of language's artifice. Thus it seems more to the point to insist that it is contemporary fiction's iconography and artifice, and not its narrative structure in and of itself, that Sorel was attempting to countervail. After all, nothing that happens in *Le Berger extravagant* is impossible or for that matter particularly implausible once one accepts the initial conceit that Louis wanted to live like a fifth-century shepherd.

Sorel's disapproval of precious fiction is not limited to the offending works themselves, since he extends his derogation to readers who, as we have already seen, consume literature according to its fashionableness. Although he did recognize fiction's potential for instilling valuable moral lessons—he wrote in the preface to *Francion*, for example, that "I have to imitate the apothecaries who coat bitter pills with sugar to make them easier to swallow" (62)—he mercilessly derides those who read only what is currently in vogue, and he especially lampoons people who fail to understand the moral significance of what they read: in the preface to *Francion* he singles out readers who are "so stupid . . . that they will believe that all this is made to pass their time rather than to correct their bad habits" (61). Sorel, as one of France's first official historiographers, had a personal stake in promoting the morally edifying qualities of literature, and remaining faithful to the monarchy that supported him involved derogating forms of literature promoting causes that competed with the crown's. Thus, if *Le Berger extravagant* ridiculed the iconography and rarefied language of pastoral fiction, it was to a very large extent in order to expose as absurd and potentially immoral its underpinning ideology. Lysis behaved not according to the rules of common sense, but, like his real-world counterparts in the Hôtel de Rambouillet, according to aesthetic ideals promulgated in aristocratic art. He inhabited what Caren Greenberg has called the World of Prose, "wherein art begat art, wherein reality was no longer decipherable, but art was."[45] Greenberg writes that Louis tried to emulate what he had read in fiction and subtly became "the medium he sought to imitate." *Le Berger extravagant* blasts readers who imitate fiction and attempt to live their lives as though they are well-ordered texts subject not to the rules of legitimate political authority, but to the conventions of art that can provide them with the illusion of their own importance and viability.

Sorel was well aware of the political implications underlying pastoral fiction and the aristocratic disposition to make life imitate art. He detested the self-aggrandizement aristocratic literature seemed inevitably to lead to, and above all he despised non-nobles who sought to elevate themselves by writing works pandering to the studied and affected tastes of the aristocracy. In the preface to *Le Berger extravagant* he writes, "I can no longer bear the fact that there are men so foolish as to believe that through their novels, poetry, and other worthless works they deserve to be admitted into the ranks of the cultivated; there are so many qualities to acquire before reaching that state, that if all these men were all mixed together you would still not be able to make from them a single figure as perfect as each one believes he is." If, as tradition has it, Sorel was born in 1602, then he was only 21 years old when the first edition of the *Histoire comique de Francion* was published. By the time he was 30 years old, most of his literary output consisted of parodic or satiric gibes at contemporary letters. Except for a few brief and largely unsuccessful forays back into the field of fiction, most notably his unfinished *Polyandre* (1648), a comic novel depicting the quotidian activities of bourgeois heroes, Sorel's nonfictional prose was primarily historical and critical, but included as well a handful of scientific and philosophical treatises. Ironically, beginning with his purchase of the office of royal historiographer in 1635, Sorel's career consisted of the very social climbing through

---

[45] Greenberg, "The World of Prose and Female Self-Inscription: Scudéry's *Les Femmes illustres*," p. 37.

writing he decried. Born of solid bourgeois stock, he purchased this office in order to be more intimately associated with the scholars and noblemen of his day. His *Berger extravagant* reflects an uneasy tension inherent in the practice of writing during the early decades of the seventeenth century, particularly for the growing population of non-noble authors: inhabiting an ambiguous social and political position, they needed to write for the aristocracy, monarchy, and growing middle class, taking care to offend none and attempting to please all.

Although *Le Berger extravagant* was sharply critical of contemporary fiction, it was immensely popular with early seventeenth-century readers. Just like his character Clarimond, who wrote a sonnet entitled "Adieu à la Poësie" because, in his words, "by speaking to Poetry I wanted to pay it back in its own money and speak to it in its own language" (I, 493), Sorel spoke to the novel and its readers in their language, initiating the practice of mixing critical and literary discourses in the same work. The resulting hybrid allowed him to entertain a critical dialogue with his work that would put the unquestioned conventions of aristocratic fiction into sharp relief. He opens the second volume of *Le Berger extravagant* by noting that "I must now reveal some of the things that have held the reader in suspense" (II, 10), and then he continues laying bare the critical scaffolding supporting the fictional text. Some modern critics have balked at the procedure—radically innovative in the early seventeenth century—of Sorel's mixing of discourses in a single genre. Gabrielle Verdier, for example, calls *Le Berger extravagant* a "literary monster, a unique mixture of fiction and criticism." [46] Maurice Lever suggests that Sorel's sole purpose in writing this novel was to convince his contemporaries that pastoral fiction was empty and useless, and he concurs with Verdier that *Le Berger extravagant* belongs neither to the tradition of the *histoire comique* nor to that of pastoral fiction ("Le Statut de la critique," 421). Yet Sorel's restylization of fiction had dramatic and powerful effects on narrative prose. Abandoning the bald-faced ideological promotion of aristocratic values in fiction, he gave the novel a dialogic cast and endowed it with a sense of irony absent in earlier *histoires tragiques*, and sentimental or pastoral fiction.

In his *Roman bourgeois*, Antoine Furetière gives Sorel a taste of

[46] Verdier, *Charles Sorel*, p. 64.

his own medicine. Furetière creates a character named Charroselles, an obvious anagram of his literary rival, and he portrays him
as a grotesque pedant "who found nothing good except what he
himself did." [47] Sorel was rather unpopular among the men of letters of his day, and not merely because he criticized the contemporary literary scene: he made himself a nuisance by lambasting individual writers and by coming out publicly in opposition to nearly
everything anyone of note had written. Hortensius, the bombastic
bore in Sorel's *Francion*, is commonly held to be Guez de Balzac,
for example, and Théophraste Renaudot, the founder of *La Ga-
zette*, was severely thrashed in a series of farcical parodies Sorel
produced of the journal. [48] In addition, it seems likely that he is
the author of a tract refuting the Académie Française's official condemnation of Corneille's *Le Cid*, an act of censorship we shall address in Chapter 2, and in 1654 he published the *Discours sur
l'Académie françoise*, in which he rails against the dogmatic and
dilettantish club—a club which never, incidentally, admitted him
as a member. In this treatise, Sorel attacks Claude Vaugelas' *Remarques sur la langue françoise*, which the latter had published in
preparation for the Académie's compilation of a dictionary. Sorel
argued that the forty Academicians had no right to construe aristocratic stylistics and the language of the court as the only officially
correct version of the French language. Although Sorel might have
appeared to be an intolerant madman, he was only as mad, it appears, as his character Lysis. Both author and character confronted
the contradiction between their reality and the representation of
that reality. Despite the gibes directed at him by Furetière and others, Sorel continued in his attempt to demonstrate that aristocratic
literary conventions were no longer able or suitable to depict their
increasingly urban and middle-class milieu.

Sorel bestowed a critical dialogism upon his novels, causing them
to interrogate their own narrative procedures as well as the ideologies they advocated. In addition, he sought to daunt or embarrass
smug aristocratic readers who were interested primarily in reading
only new variations on an archaic idea: that of the vital and preem-
inent aristocracy who through an abstract virtue that they alone

[47] Furetière, *Le Roman bourgeois*, p. 1002.
[48] See Verdier, pp. 10–14; and Adam, ed., *Romanciers du XVIIe siècle*, pp. 22–
23 and 1347–48.

possessed since the feudal era nurtured France and sustained its glory and hegemony in a politically volatile climate. The concept was hundreds of years old; the iconography employed to represent it, however, underwent radical modification during the sixteenth-century religious wars and continued to develop in the sentimental fiction and *histoires tragiques* of the seventeenth century. Yet, what differentiated the fiction produced after *L'Astrée* and other pastoral fiction was a significant metamorphosis both in the reading public and in the composition of the class of people writing and selling books. In the majority of seventeenth-century novels, to use Armine Kotin Mortimer's adroit formulation, "one writes not in order to relate something new, different, striking, or strange . . . , but to tell the same old thing to like-minded people [*pour raconter le même au même*]." [49] We have seen how apt this characterization of early seventeenth-century fiction is, as aristocratic authors and readers collaborated to produce and preserve a cohesive iconographic repertory and to sustain the ideology behind it. By the 1630's, however, three new developments appeared on the social and political horizon. Taken separately, each of these developments is only marginally related to the literary sphere in general and the production of novels in particular. Together, however, they had a profound effect on the face of fiction and drastically altered its course. These three developments are the exacerbation of conflicts between the aristocracy and the growing middle class as well as of those between the aristocracy and the monarchy, a change both qualitative and quantitative in the consumption of literature, and finally and perhaps most significantly the appearance of academies in Paris.

[49] Mortimer, *La Clôture narrative*, p. 33.

Chapter 2   The Ideology of Realism in the
Early Seventeenth Century

During the second quarter of the seventeenth century, the people of
France saw profound social, political, and literary change sweep
across the country. The deaths of Louis XIII and Cardinal Richelieu
occurred within two years of one another, followed by the regency
of Anne d'Autriche and the ministry of Mazarin. Wars with Spain
and Germany had depleted the nation's budget, devastating the
poor who shouldered a disproportionately large share of the tax
burden, since the aristocracy was exempt from the *taille*. Indus-
trious men of the middle class rose to power in the Parlement of
Paris after Particelli, the Superintendent of Finance, sold twelve
new counselorships in order to increase revenues, and the government began to resemble a democracy when the Parlement constituted itself in control of fiscal policy, refusing Anne's demands to
register new taxes. The acrimonious revolts of the Fronde ravaged
Paris and the countryside from 1648 to 1653 as portions of the
nobility and the bourgeoisie, in collaboration with the Parlement,
attempted to establish a parliamentary monarchy in France and
check the growing absolutism for which Richelieu was largely responsible. The Académie Française was founded and became an
official organ of the state in 1637, effectively legitimating ideological control over literary production and in some cases outright censorship, and a proliferation of literature written by and for members of the bourgeoisie spread throughout Paris.

The year 1637 was significant for the world of letters, and not
merely because it was the year the Parlement of Paris officially registered the Académie Française. Pierre Corneille's *Le Cid* was produced for the first time, unleashing a torrent of critical debate, and

Marin Le Roy de Gomberville published the first complete edition
of his *Polexandre*, the earliest manifestation of what was to be a
major influence on the face of French fiction, namely the heroic
novel. The heroic novel, as we will see in Chapter 3, perpetuated
much of the precious imagery and language made conventional in
sentimental and pastoral fiction, yet authors and critics began to
entertain critical debates concerning the believability of fiction and
the moral and political instruction it contained. For the first time
in France, novels were compared to history, sometimes favorably
and sometimes not, but what was significant was the juxtaposition
of two frequently competing versions of narrative truth. The comparison of different forms of prose incited critical reflection on the
ideological stances adopted in history, a genre which most people
had considered virtually above reproach because it had been
handed down from the ancients. This apposition of history and
fiction had two significant results: first, it led to a critical examination of both genres and an interrogation of their differing political uses of similar narrative techniques. Second, it caused each to
appropriate narrative techniques heretofore peculiar to the other,
leading to curious new forms of fiction, in particular the *nouvelle*
and the *mémoire*, both of which gained in popularity in the later
years of the century. The critical examination of history and fiction
as well as their appropriation of narrative techniques produced
conflicting ideological stances in the two genres. As Corneille
learned from the criticism his *Cid* underwent, problematic or equivocal political slants in literary works provoked the ire of the monarchy and its bureaucratic arm, the Académie. Beginning with its
first official pronouncement on a literary work—*Les Sentimens de
L'Académie Françoise sur la tragi-comédie du Cid*, in 1638—the
Académie stringently regulated the ideological content of literature
by condemning works that conflicted with approved state policy,
and the aesthetics it endorsed helped reinforce the monarchy's absolutism.

  In this chapter I want to demonstrate that if in the early decades
of the seventeenth century the French novel adumbrated the scope
and composition of its iconography, assaying the ground in which
to plant its imagery, language, and ideology, in later years it continued the search for a coherent representational system, and displaced its focus away from language and imagery and onto narra-

tive technique. Pastoral fiction had provided the aristocracy with a living mirror—albeit a distorted one—in which readers could find idealized images of themselves and their way of life as well as an embellished history of their social class, a history that embroidered the text of medieval romance and strengthened the fabric of feudal ideology. The stories of aristocratic virtue and its seemingly natural ascendancy provided a political justification for contemporary class divisions, and as we have seen they bolstered the morale of the financially faltering aristocracy by characterizing true nobility not as an economic status, but as a moral one. Michael McKeon points out that pastoral fiction naturalized or domesticated aristocratic ideology by giving it a historical perspective and causing it to appear given and unpremeditated.[1] Where pastoral and sentimental fiction had sketched out a more or less coherent repertory of language and images, however, later novels relied on extensive authentifications of the truth they contained. Beginning in the late 1620's, authors and critics were interested not only in the material novels treated, but in the manner in which that material was arranged. *Vraisemblance* became a crucial concern in fiction, but what readers and critics considered plausible or likely in a novel depended to a very great degree, as we will see, on their political sympathies and alliances. When authors addressed the question of *vraisemblance*, primarily in the prefaces of their novels, they referred, in the early decades of the century, to the comparatively simple issue of whether or not a text articulated a plausible or even possible referent. With the inception of the Académie Française, however, the careful attention novelists began to pay to historical and cultural details in their attempt to make their novels reflect reality gave way to an attempt to have their novels shape the way reality was perceived. The Académie Française had as its ostensible mission the codification of literary convention, but the critiques it levied actually contributed to the codification of literary taste. The aristocratic iconography that had developed in sentimental, tragic, and pastoral fiction no longer merely provided the nobility with a pleasing image

---

[1] McKeon writes that "questions of virtue have an inherently narrative focus because they are concerned with genealogical succession and individual progress, with how human capacity is manifested in and through time. Before the origins of the novel these questions were mediated by the aristocratic ideology of romance, a narrative model that provided a persuasive account of private and public history alike" (pp. 212–13).

of themselves and their ancestors; literature now required a political use to be acceptable.

In 1626, Marie de Jars de Gournay eloquently attempted to argue that the primary subject of novels is love, but that this in no way meant that novels were the frivolous literary forms some critics had claimed. Rather, she maintained, they were serious bits of erudition. In the "Advis sur la nouvelle édition du Proumenoir de Monsieur de Montaigne" (Preface to the new edition of the Promenade of Monsieur de Montaigne), reprinted in her *Ombre de la damoiselle de Gournay*, she attempted to answer her critics' complaints. "Another quarrel that this season's new taste wages with this little book—or, more accurately, with all my writings, but with this one more than the others, given its novelistic nature—is that it inserts into the text some ornaments in foreign languages, and cites their authors by their names, or sometimes includes them in translation."[2] De Gournay could not understand why anyone would prohibit novelists from citing the old masters if such authorities could augment the beauty or the acumen of their works. After all, her adoptive father[3] Michel de Montaigne had freely quoted ancient authors in their original languages throughout his *Essais*, and few critics had reproached him for it. Mademoiselle de Gournay defended her own use of citation by remarking that "a good novel is just as laudable as any other sort of work" (651), and she concluded that novelists were no more licensed than other serious writers to mask the authorities who informed their thinking. Although de Gournay never enters into a critical examination of *vraisemblance*, her remarks are significant because she initiates a discussion of the novelist's relationship to tradition, and she defends her right to appropriate tradition while still retaining her own integrity and originality. She points out that Heliodorus, who often served as the model for discussions of fiction in the early years of the seventeenth century, never cited authorities in his romances, but that the Romans and those who followed them did so freely.

Mlle de Gournay also defends her work specifically and novels in general from the attack that they were not serious works of litera-

---

[2] De Gournay, p. 646.
[3] The term Mlle de Gournay uses in her *Proumenoir de Monsieur de Montaigne* is "fille d'alliance."

ture because they frequently deal with secular concerns—in particular, love. Plutarch, she points out, is a canonized author who wrote of love, and even some of the church's most austere clerics, both ancient and contemporary, dealt in matters of the heart. She reminds her readers that St. Augustine studied Virgil and wept over the fate of Dido, abandoned by the heartless Aeneas; and Camus wrote dozens of stories and novels dealing with secular love (645). De Gournay derides the "singular reason that these critics presume to have" when they forbid the reading of novels on aesthetic or moral grounds (650), yet she is keenly aware that however quirky or illogical such reasoning may be, the voice of tradition backed up by moral or political authority is difficult to silence. We will see below how a dozen years later the Académie Française resorted to this same nameless yet difficult-to-silence voice of reason in its condemnation of the *invraisemblance* of Pierre Corneille's *Le Cid* and the effects such "reason" had on fiction produced in the 1640's and 1650's. Following the politics of Richelieu and the increasingly absolutist monarchy, the Académie Française gave reason an overtly political cast and attempted to define the boundaries of the plausible in literary representation by claiming for itself absolute and exclusive authority to pronounce a text reasonable or not.

Mlle de Gournay's attempt to insert novels into the canon of serious works of literature was one of the first efforts to legitimize prose fiction as a literary genre. She defends the genre against attacks that its subject matter did not warrant critical consideration; her successors, however, needed to defend fiction against the charges that its formal structure did not meet the standards of perfection set by the ancient masters and for that reason could not be deemed worthy of attention. This issue would explode into a question of political aesthetics a dozen years after Mlle de Gournay's tract: some one hundred or so novels were published between 1626 and 1638, the year the Académie issued its *Sentimens*, and novelists were, in general, more concerned with writing works their readers would enjoy and at the same time find believable than they were with producing fiction with a serious reformative agenda. As we have seen, French fiction in the early years of the seventeenth century fostered the illusion of ideological continuity between the feudal era and the modern one; *vraisemblance* was not yet a critical concern authors faced. Instead, a work's relative transparency—

that is, the ideology informing its primary assumptions about the characters or groups of people it depicted and the sorts of activities they might engage in, as well as the political bias of the iconography the novel relied on—simply ensured its facile transmission from aristocratic author to aristocratic reader. These literary conventions appeared unobtrusive because they had been normalized for a restricted group of writers and readers and they advanced the claim that the aristocratic iconography and ideology the works bolstered were not only believable, but natural. Yet, by the end of the wave of pastoral fiction the issue of believability came to the fore, largely because of the ridicule pastoral fiction had undergone at the hands of Sorel. In 1627, for example, in the preface to his *Histoire afriquaine*, Gerzan wrote, "I have concerned myself with details that few people have observed, primarily precise geography and accurate history."[4] Gerzan, like many of his predecessors, maintained that novels must be written in a delicate language that would not offend readers, but more importantly he felt that adhering to the conventions of fiction would be pointless if one disregarded the historical and cultural details that lend an air of "vray-semblance" to a work. "I have tried to free myself from [fictive invention]," he wrote, "to ward off accusations of falsity concerning the period in which I maintain they occurred" ("Préface").

Despite Gerzan's attempt to distance himself and his work from the implausibilities of pastoral fiction, the fact remains that the story is as unbelievable and loaded with coincidences and unusual reunions as any of the works that preceded it. The story begins, as do many other novels of this period, *in medias res*: "Already the wind's violence had died down and the waves were becoming calmer" (1), and the conventional form gives way to an equally conventional plot: Cléomède and Sophonisbe are shipwrecked and they pass for brother and sister, but the existence of a diamond ring and the strange tale told by a mysterious old woman at death's door reveal that their relationship will take on a more intimate nature. There is nothing particularly African about this *Histoire afriquaine*, save for the fact that various people who speak some mythical "African language" frequently pop up just in time to overhear pertinent details that reveal hidden identities. Clarian, for example,

---

[4] Gerzan, "Préface au lecteur."

the young man who serves Floramente, Cléomède's rival, hides in a wardrobe and eavesdrops on the latter's soliloquy of misery, and then reveals that "he" is really a noblewoman disguised as a man. Clarian, whose real name is Lydiane, suffered rueful turns of fate at the hands of her evil stepmother, who forced her to let her sleep with her (Lydiane's) husband. Lydiane states with no apparent irony that because of her husband's disposition the stepmother "faced no obstacle in doing so" (I, 50). Gerzan's novel is longer by far (3 volumes and about 2,800 pages) than most of the sentimental fiction from which it draws its conventions, but its narrative is tighter and more subtly woven. Events build one upon another, sometimes with dizzying intensity, but the main intrigue is spliced with ample digressions in which, like Lydiane's tale above, characters tell their stories. For as much as Gerzan desired to write fiction that would appear true, however, he merely reduplicates accepted formulas, with the possible exceptions that the main intrigue revolves less around the love between the title characters than was normally the case in earlier sentimental fiction, and that more loyalty develops among the secondary characters, whose actions further their own interests instead of simply serving those of the principal couple.

Gerzan's desire to write fiction that would not smack of falsity was echoed a few years later by François Boisrobert, who, in perhaps one of the century's most honest and surprising authorial confessions wrote, "my only goal is to please you and to entertain you." [5] Boisrobert shamelessly admitted to his readers that it made little difference to him whether they read his work as "history or fable, as long as the reading satisfies you" ("Advis"), yet his flippant approach to the instructional value of literature becomes more serious when, like de Gournay before him, he turns to the question of how novels fit into the literary canon:

> If I wanted to hold forth, I could easily prove to you that novels which imitate epic poetry, like history, contain instruction appropriate to any state to induce the love of virtue and the abhorrence of vice—all the more so in novels since the writer aims for perfection and consequently refines the virtue of which history merely furnishes us the examples. Besides, one rarely finds a historian who is not a flatterer or a liar, since they all forget harmful truths, and they publish

[5] Boisrobert, "Advis au lecteur qui servira de préface."

obsequious lies; normally they only reveal the imperfections of others in order to curry favor with some rogue. But those who write epic poems and novels are exempt from such evil malice and this cowardly sycophancy. They describe actions not as they are, but as they ought to be [*telles qu'elles doivent estre*]. ("Advis")

Boisrobert's impatience with historians writing specifically for a particular powerful individual is no doubt a reference to bourgeois who had purchased the *charge* of royal historiographer, an office that dated back at least as far as 1558. His point, like de Gournay's, is that novels should be treated as serious literature, and despite his pretension not to be concerned with educating his readers, he tries to show that good novels are inherently more instructive than literature with an expressly didactic purpose. What constitutes a good novel in Boisrobert's eyes is one whose formal perfection aligns it with the epic, the model for lengthy narrative that the French, in their admiration of antiquity, had long revered. A good novel is better than history not only because novelists strive to imbue their works with a formal perfection the historian can never achieve, but also because fiction is abstract and can consequently represent archetypical virtues as ideal forms. That is, historians are reduced to depicting only the imperfect "*exemples*" of virtue as they are manifested in the material world; novelists, however, are free to represent loftier, more excellent examples of probity because they are not constrained by a materiality corrupting the ideational conception of virtue.

Boisrobert's pretension to be interested only in pleasing his readers drives home all the more forcefully his point that novels are more instructive than history, because he implies that a novel is naturally didactic on the one hand and politically neutral on the other. He claims that novelists are free from the limitations imposed by the necessity of representing the frequently untoward actions of real individuals, and that they are consequently exempt from the "evil malice" of pandering to the desires of their patrons. Nevertheless, he offers no political or moral touchstone to back up his notion of what actions should be depicted. For him, the expression things "as they ought to be" refers to a neo-Platonic conception of the sovereign good, and his ethics suggest an idealized and benign abstract idea of the most good for the most people.

Gerzan and Boisrobert could not agree less on the truth value of fiction, yet their theories of the novel accomplish a task that unites them philosophically. Where Gerzan had insisted on observing "precise geography and accurate history," Boisrobert begins his preface by stating, "Although I only want to pass as a simple translator here . . . and although to seem more estimable I seek out the authority of the Arabs and Indians, I assure you, reader, that you will have great difficulty convincing yourself that this tale is true" ("Advis"). Both writers, however, undertook more or less detailed descriptions of their own and their contemporaries' work. By observing the current tendencies in fiction, they were able to produce intricate accounts of the direction it was taking, and they used these descriptive prefaces as theoretical models that they would follow in their own work. When Gerzan writes that "it's crucial to treat these Loves so chastely and honestly that they could never offend even the most delicate ears, or the most righteous thoughts" ("Préface"), he is accomplishing little more than delineating the existing traditions of sentimental fiction with its insistence on rarefied sentiment and language and indicating that he has no plans to break with those traditions; however, when in the next sentence he writes that "it amounts to very little to observe all that I have just said if one does not conform novels' inventions to *vraisemblance*," he adds to description a theoretical insight that is also an aesthetic imperative. Gerzan's belief in the necessity of what he calls "vray-semblance" adjoins to the descriptive-pragmatic method of constructing novels a theoretical predilection that, because it is both historically descriptive and aesthetically prescriptive, naturalizes the new fictive form by inserting it into a recognizable critical tradition.

Gerzan is only a case in point. Throughout the 1620's and 1630's a good many fiction writers coupled their descriptive remarks on what fiction had been with their theoretical concerns about what novels needed to do and how they could do it. Sorel included an ironic theoretical diatribe on the nature of the novel in Book XI of his *Francion* in which Hortensius, the bombastic pedant, obsessively carries on about his own projected novels. Planning to complete "a novel that is better than history [*un roman qui est meilleur que les histoires*]" (426), Hortensius goes on to describe all of the novels that need to be written. Francion mocks yet encourages him, pointing out the need to stick to tradition without fearing to be innovative. Of Hortensius' relationship to the ancient masters

Francion says: "But take care not to imitate their defects or their impertinence. Imitating a man does not mean farting or coughing like him" (432). Chapelain advised of the need to write believable fiction in the "Lettre à Monsieur Favereau" and pointed out as well the maxim that "history treats things as they are and poetry as they should be [*comme elles devroient estre*]" (86). The point here is that authors were providing aesthetic rules for a budding genre that had recently formed out of an aristocratic popular tradition—a tradition, that is, whose parameters developed nearly exclusively in response to readers' tastes and desires, and which included little if any theoretical underpinning. Authors naturalized this tradition, and began to furnish it with a theoretical apparatus that would give the incipient and marginal literary form an aesthetic legitimacy. Mlle de Gournay and her successors, then, began the process not simply of describing what novels had been and what they could be but of calling for their serious consideration. No longer content to have their works considered agreeable pastimes for an idle aristocracy, writers wanted their tales to be considered literature, and the development of a cohesive theoretical discourse was the first step in that direction.

The descriptive and theoretical apparatus that fiction writers of the 1620's and 1630's attempted to erect around their works functioned as a naturalizing device whose primary goal was to eliminate the apparent artificiality of contemporary fiction. Up through the 1620's, novels had developed conventions that privileged the artificial and affected nature of stock characters and situations; fiction's limited repertory of formal components allowed it to develop the ideological foundation animating the newly formed genre's coherence and cohesiveness. In fiction written during the very early years of the seventeenth century, calculated artifice was a part of the stock of extratextual referents upon which a work could draw, and disguise, masquerade, and sartorial pretense vitalized sentimental and pastoral novels. Yet, conventionalized literary and linguistic artifice was also the thematic adhesive allowing prose fiction to jell as a literary genre for a self-selected group of writers and readers. When parodic novels like Sorel's *Berger extravagant* or Jean de Lannel's *Romant Satyrique* (1624) began to ridicule and challenge these obtrusive conventions, or when comic or burlesque novels like *Francion* or Mareschal's *Chrysolite* (1627) depicted non-noble characters, serious attempts to justify and normalize the conventions of artifice began to appear. While most writers, as we have seen, insisted that it sufficed to write believable fiction with a valuable moral lesson in order to justify their synthetic and contrived tales, writers like Gerzan offered concrete suggestions concerning what narrative techniques might help make their works seem less factitious: "It is absolutely necessary to have a lot of plots which are both often interrupted to keep the reader involved and so carefully interwoven that you cannot cut them without breaking the thread of the tale" ("Préface"). Theoretical prefaces in the novels of the 1620's and 1630's contributed to the legitimation of a genre that effectively had no history; while Gerzan tried to give it rules that would make works' narrative structure their justifying point, Boisrobert strove to align his work with the epic, thus giving it a historical legitimacy that would authorize the new fictive form. In all cases, theories of the novel attenuated the genre's ideological origins and claimed for it a self-evident and innate ability to improve and uplift the reader by offering him or her a naturalized representation of the way things ought to be. As Fancan put it in his *Tombeau des Romans*, "things seem better when they are simulated by art than when they are made by nature."[6]

Both Boisrobert and Fancan maintained that fiction is more appropriate than history to instruct readers because the latter is rooted in material reality and hence inherently defective. Some fifty years later, René Rapin was to pen a similar formulation, underscoring the Platonic conceptions of verisimilitude inherent in Boisrobert's and his coterie's excogitations. *Vraisemblance*, he wrote, serves

> to give the things that the poet says a greater air of perfection than truth itself can give, even though *vraisemblance* is only the image of truth. For truth only renders things as they are; *vraisemblance* renders them as they are supposed to be [*comme elles doivent estre*]. Truth is nearly always defective because of the mixture of the specific conditions that compose it. Nothing in the world is born which does not simultaneously distance itself from the perfection of its idea in being born. We must look for the originals and the models in *vraisemblance* and in the universal principles of things: there nothing material or particular enters in to corrupt them.[7]

[6] Cited by Coulet, *Le Roman jusqu'à la Révolution*, vol. II, p. 34.
[7] Rapin, *Réflexions sur la poétique*, p. 41.

Gerzan's early conception of *vraisemblance* as what was likely to occur in a given historical and cultural setting underwent significant modifications in the Platonic and Aristotelian conceptions of verisimilitude propounded by Boisrobert and Rapin, in which *vraisemblance* was the imperfect yet ideationally accurate copy of truth. It is important to note, however, that in the course of the nearly fifty years separating Boisrobert's (1629) and Rapin's (1675) similar conceptions of *vraisemblance*, political developments of tremendous consequence for the codification of aesthetic convention transpired, and they contributed significantly to the course prose fiction was to take. These developments, most particularly growing absolutism, the Académie's *Sentimens de L'Académie sur le Cid* reflecting that absolutism, and the political skirmishes of the Fronde, colored the perspectives of rationalism dictating what constituted an ideationally correct copy of truth. A brief examination of the *Sentimens* will reveal how *vraisemblance* came to designate not probability or plausibility in literature, but the moral and political ideals of an absolutist government.

Gerzan had indicated that literature's goal is to provide a historically and culturally accurate representation of human actions. The Académie Française, however, disputed that claim and offered its own interpretation of literary representation based on intensely reformative principles. In the opening remarks of the *Sentimens de L'Académie sur le Cid*, we read, "But before entering into the discussion of the things that come up in *Le Cid*, [the Académie] has found it necessary to state that the goal of poetry which imitates human action is not a thing yet completely determined." [8] This opening caveat establishes the ground for a discussion of literary convention modeled not on mimesis but on political utility. The Académie Française, which began as a nonpartisan group whose purpose was to discuss literary and artistic trends of the day, was primarily responsible for converting aesthetic concerns into resolutely political ones. The Académie began in 1629 as an informal gathering of friends who met once a week to discuss their common interests. By 1634, Cardinal Richelieu had afforded the group's members his protection, but not without the latter's consternation, for the members, particularly Chapelain, feared that the Cardinal's

[8] *Les Sentimens de L'Académie Françoise sur la tragi-comédie du Cid*, ed. Georges Collas, p. 5.

political agenda would interfere with their original, purely aesthetic interests. Séguier, the Keeper of the Seals, sealed the letters patent, and finally, in 1637, the Parlement of Paris registered the letters, recognizing the official foundation of the body. For whatever reluctance the group may have expressed at being made an organ of the state—and the recipients of pensions as well, it must be added—one gets a reasonably clear idea of the political line they toed, wholeheartedly or not, from the letter to Richelieu accompanying their first project: "After the great and memorable actions of the king, it is very fortunate that there are among his subjects so many men capable of reading with pleasure what we have with wonder watched executed."[9] Whatever their initial intentions, the group was supported by the king and worked in his service. The Académie worked toward the consolidation and codification of linguistic and literary convention, and if their activities contributed to the famous unities of classical theater as well as a Dictionary and a Poétique (which never saw the light of day), they were also responsible in part for the codification of taste, if we can believe Boisrobert, who remarked that the select group "gives things taste [*donne du goût aux choses*]" (La Force, 45).

Chapelain, who penned the *Sentimens de L'Académie sur le Cid*, was one of the most outspoken members of the original group, and he also claimed great concern that Richelieu's protection would destroy the camaraderie the group enjoyed. However, in 1633 he wrote his *Ode à Monseigneur le Cardinal duc de Richelieu*, which may belie his expressed concerns. Painting Richelieu as the avenging protector of truth and beauty, he casts him in a hyperbolic and mythological light that warrants citation:

> In the middle of the anguish
> That rules in the field of Mars,
> You stand guard to protect the Arts
> From adversity and servitude;
> Because of you forevermore
> From the Mountain with two sacred peaks
> Ignorance flees, and Falsehood is banished;
> Your hand which returns life to our dying states,

[9] Cited by Duc de La Force, article "Académie Française," in *Dictionnaire des lettres*, ed. Georges Grente, vol. II, p. 46.

> Which frees our allies from tyranny
> Delivers Helicon from the yoke of its tyrants.[10]

Chapelain's praise of Richelieu, written before the latter had offered his protection to the members of the first Académie, expressly links the Cardinal's aesthetic and political agendas. Aesthetic ignorance and misconceptions as well as France's foreign policy are two of the projects the Cardinal undertook, making truth and ideology interrelated concerns. The publication of the *Sentimens sur le Cid* extended the admixing of the aesthetic and the political, as the Académie, whether voluntarily or not, effectively became Richelieu's mouthpiece.[11]

It mattered little, the Académie claimed, that people enjoyed highly mimetic works and that Corneille's *Cid* was met with popular acclaim; an audience seeking only pleasure in dramatic works, they maintained, is bereft of the critical capacity to pass serious judgment on them. The Académie passed its own judgement on *Le Cid* by referring to rigidly defined notions of "le Plaisir" and "l'Utile" (the pleasing and the useful), two concerns that any legitimate work of art was supposed to manifest; in addition, they had at their disposal a wild card ready to play at any moment, and if pleasure and usefulness might harbor room for equivocation, "*la raison*" (reason), the very same *raison* de Gournay struggled against, did not. By invoking classical notions of pleasure and moderation from the Platonic and most particularly from the Aristotelian traditions, they argued that one must separate passions from reasonable pleasures:

> And according to doctrine, we might say that it does not suffice for plays to please their audience to be considered good if the pleasure they produce is not founded on reason and if they do not produce such pleasure through the channels that make it standard [*régulier*], the same channels necessary to make it beneficial. As in music and painting, one would not say that any sort of concert or painting is good, although it pleases the masses, if all the Arts' formal rules were not obeyed, and if the experts who are the true judges of art did not confirm through their approval that which the masses had given. (9)

[10] Chapelain, *Ode*, p. 15.
[11] For a rigorous and eloquently argued treatment of Richelieu's influence on the legitimation of theater in France, see Timothy Murray's *Theatrical Legitimation*, pp. 111–30.

Literary pleasure is only good—that is, correct—when it is founded on reason and when it derives from a work that adheres to the principles of art handed down from the ancients. The Académie unabashedly links form and use with aesthetic and political concerns when they maintain that the same components of a work that make it conform to artistic standards also make it "beneficial." It is easy to see how the experts' sovereign judgment and their approval quickly become their appropriation of aesthetic concerns in the service of a specific ideology when one observes how what is "beneficial" is deemed self-evident and natural. That is, the Académie fails to consider even for a moment the possibility of multiple or conflicting uses for art. Writing in the service of Richelieu and their king, they put forth a single, unequivocal combination of form and content whose utility ostensibly benefits one and all. The force of the experts' judgment and its ideological underpinning becomes apparent when one considers that the Académie based its reading of *Le Cid* principally on the work's ostensible lack of *vraisemblance*, the very same issue that had come to the fore in recent theories of fiction. Like their immediate forebears the novelists who were attempting to codify rules to make fiction seem natural and uncontrived, the Académie endeavored to efface the political nature of its artistic judgments. In order to accomplish this task, the Académie appropriated Aristotle's discussions of "good actions" from the *Poetics* and, as we will see, created a hybrid poetics that can best be described as a properly political aesthetics.

The Académie determined that Corneille's play was not "standard" because it failed to conform to their interpretation of the fundamental rules for tragedy. In particular they attacked the play because its plot was too contrived and in general they criticized the play because it was not founded on reason since it failed to respect their principles of *vraisemblance*. The Académie claims to derive its definitions of *vraisemblance* from Aristotle, and they argue that he formulated two kinds of verisimilitude. On the one hand is "le commun," which "includes the things that ordinarily happen to men according to their class, age, morals, and passions" (15), and on the other hand is "l'extraordinaire," which "embraces the things that happen rarely and outside of normal *vraisemblance*." This second type of *vraisemblance* is often called "la Fortune," they indicate, and it is acceptable as long as it arises from "a linking together of things that happen in ordinary fashion" (15). The Académie maintains that neither of these two kinds of *vraisemblance* is at work in *Le Cid*, since Chimène would never under any circumstances have married the man who murdered her father. Surprisingly, however, the Académie claims that Corneille's play contained no plot and that "one can easily guess its outcome as soon as one has watched the beginning" (13). They argue that the play's development consists of nothing but "an unexpected accident" and that the *dénouement* is nothing but another "unforeseen accident" (13). It is difficult to reconcile these last two ideas, since if the work's resolution derives from a collection of unusual series of events, it seems unlikely that one could guess its outcome from the beginning. It also seems clear that the Académie relies on an extremely restricted, sometimes rather creative, interpretation of Aristotle in order to level their condemnation of the work. Aristotle maintained that "the object of imitation is not only a complete action but such things as stir up pity and fear, and this is best achieved when the events are unexpectedly interconnected." [12] In fact, Corneille's play holds up quite well when viewed through the filter of Aristotelian poetics, and it remains to be seen what the Académie was trying to accomplish in their application of brutal interpretive force to Aristotle's *Poetics* and Corneille's *Cid*.

Aristotle maintained that tragedy is the imitation of a good action, and the examples he gives provide a reasonably clear indication of the general types of actions tragedy should represent: the wicked must not prosper, nor should the good suffer a change from prosperity to misfortune unless such a change results from a moral or intellectual fault (1452b–1453a). Aristotle is never more specific than this concerning the particular moral exempla tragedy should set, nor does he bother to qualify what kinds of people are able to undertake good actions. He is, however, quite specific when he delineates the manner in which tragedy must represent its object and it is interesting to note that Gerzan's theories of effective prose narrative derive almost directly from Aristotle's recommendations for dramatic intrigue: a complex plot involving reversal (peripeteia) is preferable to a simple plot, and unexpected events are essential to peripeteia. Contrary to what the Académie suggests in its criticism

---

[12] Aristotle, *The Poetics*, trans. G. M. A. Grube, 1452a.

of the "accidents" in *Le Cid*, Aristotle maintains that unforeseen happenings are necessary in a good tragedy as long as "they are connected with what has gone on before as the inevitable or probable outcome. It makes all the difference whether one incident is caused by another or merely follows it" (1452a). The organic integrity of a tragedy's plot is crucial, and Aristotle derides poor poets who distort the sequence of events in their plays (1451b). Although Aristotle is rarely more specific than this concerning what kinds of individuals or actions may be tragic,[13] the Académie implied that he formulated two kinds of *vraisemblance*, distinguished above. This is simply not the case. When the Académie maintains that Aristotle delineated a second kind of *vraisemblance*, namely that which consists of extraordinary events that result from a series of quotidian happenings, they are appropriating his *Poetics* for their own uses.[14] The point the Académie drew from their interpolations of Aristotle's discussion of peripeteia and probability in dramatic poetry is that a work can have a specific use, and by extending Aristotle's definitions they enabled themselves to dictate the parameters of the useful.

When Aristotle discusses believability in poetry, he normally distinguishes between the possible and the impossible. "Generally speaking," he writes, "we must judge the impossible in relation to its poetic effect, to what is morally better, or to accepted opinion. As regards poetic effect, the impossible that can be believed should be preferred to what is possible but unconvincing" (1461b). Although he makes brief reference to "what is morally better," Aristotle eschews any prescriptive discussion of what precise political ends dramatic poetry should have. The Académie, however, in a

---

[13] The tragic character should, of course, also be "famous or prosperous, like Oedipus, Thyestes, and the noted men of such noble families" (1453a).

[14] There is a passage in the *Poetics* that deals with first and second causes and the illusion of a chain of events the juxtaposition produces, but it has little if anything to do with *vraisemblance*: "When one event is followed by a second as a consequence or concomitant, men are apt to infer, when the second event happens, that the first must have happened or be happening, though the inference is false. If, then, the first event is not true but, if it were true, the second would necessarily have happened or be happening, we should establish the second if we want the first to be believed. For our mind, knowing the second to be true, falsely infers the truth of the first" (1460a). The example Aristotle provides is the meeting between Odysseus and Penelope in Book XIX of the *Odyssey*. Odysseus maintains that he is a Cretan who met Odysseus, and since he is able to indicate what he wore, Penelope wrongly assumes that his story is true.

paraphrase of this, is slightly less equivocal. "Now *vraisemblance* rather than truth is in Aristotle's doctrine the lot of epic and dramatic poetry. Since its goal is its usefulness to the listener or spectator, it much more readily uses *vraisemblance* than truth to attain this goal, and people are led to it through this instrument which does not find in them the same resistance that truth would, since truth can be so strange and unbelievable that they would consider it false and refuse to be persuaded by it" (18). Where Aristotle includes public opinion as a gauge of what is possible or likely in dramatic poetry, the Académie, as we noted above, considered most audiences incapable of making critical judgments. Aristotle's famous definition of tragedy's goal—"through pity and fear it achieves the purgation (catharsis) of such emotions" (1449b)—is supplemented to some extent in the *Politics* where he writes that vulgar people are perverted in their natural state, and so there are forms of representation that will appeal to them as well: "Every man takes pleasure in what is naturally akin to him, and we must therefore allow the performers to use this kind of *mousikê* with this kind of spectator in view" (1342a). Aristotle's discussion of tragedy never really separates the aesthetic from the moral or the political, then, since he identifies the aesthetic as a broadly cultural phenomenon: "Poetry developed in different ways according to men's characters" (*Poetics*, 1448b). He prescribes nothing for tragedy other than that it purge the audience's improper emotions and work toward the community's general moral improvement. The point here is that the Académie appropriated Aristotle for its own markedly political ends. In the passage cited above, the almost propagandistic nature of their rhetoric reveals their belief that tragedy should have specific political purposes. Tragedy has a "use" in that it is an "instrument" that "leads" people whose "resistance" will be broken down so that they will not "refuse to be persuaded." The specific nature of that political purpose becomes clear when we examine precisely which actions in *Le Cid* the Académie deemed *invraisemblables*.

Aristotle indicated that "poetry developed in different ways according to men's characters"; the Académie was quite clearly interested in causing French dramatic poetry to develop according to a specific noble character. Although some of their criticisms of *Le Cid* are based on the logic of the play's setting—they find it odd, for example, that Rodrigue is able to make his way into Chimène's bedchamber without running into any servants—most of their criticisms concerning the work's lack of *vraisemblance* derive from the claim that noble individuals would not behave as they do in *Le Cid*. Approximately one third of the 63 pages of the original manuscript is devoted to a detailed examination of the character flaws Corneille allows his personae to exhibit. That Chimène's love for Rodrigue prevails over her duty to her father (38), that Rodrigue kills the Count in a duel instead of simply overcoming him (39–40), that Elvire, a simple servant, engages in protracted discussion with the noble Count (42), and that the Infanta entertains even for a moment the possibility of marrying Rodrigue when the latter had not yet shown any signs of valor (45) are but four of the egregious affronts to noble character the Académie finds. The Académie never claims that such circumstances could never arise; they merely point out that they should not appear in a literary work meant to be useful to the public.

The Académie Française combined Aristotelian poetics with a Platonic conception of the use of poetry in the Republic to arrive at a socially controlling use for literature. In Book X of the *Republic*, Plato had argued that the only poetry admissible in the state must be that in open praise of the gods and of good men; in other varieties of poetry, "pleasure and pain will rule as monarchs in your city, instead of the law and that rational principle which is always and by all thought to be the best." [15] D. R. Clarke has recently demonstrated that the Académie Française, in particular Chapelain, d'Aubignac, and La Mesnardière, willfully misread classical poetic theory in order to prove that the poet's craft involves representing a preexisting Idea that corresponded to dogmatic political truths. "[T]he new order of the Cardinal's reformed poetics seemed bent upon relating the poet's authority to the degree in which his art made its contribution to the ideally formed order of the Cardinal's France," he writes.[16] The Académie's *Sentimens sur le Cid* harshly attacks Corneille on the grounds of *invraisemblance*, and their remarks are especially revealing when they extend beyond character

[15] Plato, *The Republic*, trans. G. M. A. Grube (Indianapolis, Ind.: Hackett, 1974), 607a.
[16] Clarke, "Corneille's Differences with the Seventeenth-Century Doctrinaires over the Moral Authority of the Poet," p. 552.

psychology and into the realm of behavior worthy of a monarch. They denounce Corneille for portraying a weak-willed monarch the survival of whose kingdom depends on a single individual (24), and they abhor the depiction of a king who pays so little attention to the wise advice of his counselors (59). In general they blame Corneille for placing on the stage the character of a king "beneath his dignity" (61).

The poet's charge, according to the Académie's liberal reading of Plato and Aristotle, is to purge harsh reality or historical truth of its inadmissible moral and political flaws and present the audience with a rarefied, Platonic vision of the ideationally correct "principles commonly accepted as best." Poets, they wrote, "must prefer *vraisemblance* to truth, and they must work on an entirely fabricated subject as long as it conforms to reason" (22). They cast *vraisemblance* in overtly political tones, and because they were the only academy officially recognized by the state, they effectively codified literary convention for all those wishing to write legitimate, publishable works. Fiction writers had begun, in the 1620's and 1630's, to construct their own theoretical apparatus around their works in an attempt to naturalize a budding, relatively unfamiliar form. Because they drew from a limited repertory of fictive conventions, they turned to the issue of *vraisemblance* both to justify their works and to uncover new narrative strategies that would minimalize the overtly stultifying and obtrusive conventions that limited their range of composition. The Académie picked up where they had left off and standardized *vraisemblance* as what was in the best interests of a growing absolutist state. The Académie's judgment concerned a tragedy, an ancient and thus legitimate literary form. Fiction, as a comparatively new and unstable genre, occupied an aesthetically marginal position, and it was not clear whether this liminal situation would place it in direct ideological contradiction with the poetics of the state machinery or whether novels would abandon the literary periphery and embrace officially sanctioned poetics.

Although it is difficult to gauge what precise effect the Académie's pronouncement had on fiction writers, there is a marked change in novelists' attitudes toward *vraisemblance* in their works after 1638. Desmaretz de Saint-Sorlin, a member of the original committee the Académie Française appointed to examine *Le Cid*, was one of the first to apply the Académie's notion of *vraisemblance* to fiction. In his *Rosane*, published in 1639, he wrote that "fictive *vraisemblance* is based on decency [*la bien-seance*] and reason, and the unadorned truth only includes the narration of human happenstance which most often is quite bizarre." [17] Desmaretz adheres to party lines in appropriating a Platonic conception of Right Reason for politically useful literature. He suggests that history fails to conform to an ideationally perfect ordering of human events and for this reason the writer's responsibility involves providing the order history lacks. *Vraisemblance* gives form to the randomness of human events, structuring narrative sequences according to a particular vision of how they should have occurred. For Desmaretz, fiction informed by the principles of reason that govern *vraisemblance* adds a corrective measure to the dry and graceless events of history, yet pure fiction is chimerical and empty when it falls short of invoking dogmatic truths. "Each must correct the other" ("Préface"), he writes, and he likens the novelist's embellishing corrections of historical truth to the parables that punctuate the New Testament, affording the novelist a similar morally instructive capacity. Fiction for Desmaretz connotes, then, not something false but something made: "Fiction must not be considered a lie, but rather the greatest effort of the mind." Fiction for Desmaretz is above all a constructive, corrective tool able to rectify readers' ideological misapprehensions. It has the power to represent "things as they were supposed to have been [*les choses comme elles ont deu estre*]."

Desmaretz rehearses the positions the Académie had taken in its *Sentimens sur le Cid*, echoing both its language and its views: relying heavily on the verb *devoir* to establish a moral imperative for fiction, he also grants fiction a persuasive function and endows it with a particular utility. The Académie had viewed tragedy as an instrument whose particular use was to lead people away from their resistance and persuade them to adopt specific ideological views. Desmaretz endows fiction with similar persuasive capacities, equating fiction with rhetorical tropes: "The most beautiful figures of Rhetoric are nothing but fictions; this shows that Fiction is necessary to move and to persuade and that the spirit is touched by it, more so than by truth itself." Passing from the general to the genre,

---

[17] Desmaretz de Saint-Sorlin, "Préface."

Desmaretz points out that rhetorical devices are nothing but constructions of language, yet he elides this general meaning of fiction as construction in favor of the more generically specific "Fiction" (with its capital F) to prove that novels serve as well as or better than truth to impart moral lessons. As long as it is rigidly controlled by rules the Académie condones, fiction and—for Desmaretz at least—its nearly synonymous counterpart *vraisemblance*, are not only tolerated but valuable as well. Fiction's power to persuade, however, only comes at the cost of awesome responsibility. Returning once again to the verb *devoir*, Desmaretz remarks that one must take seriously the task of writing novels: "It is no small enterprise to claim success in this genre of writing in which the great liberty you have to say what you like leaves you no excuse when you did not say what you should have [*quand vous n'avez pas dit ce que vous avez deu*]."

Desmaretz had contributed to the Académie's critique of *Le Cid*, yet like the members of the Académie he resists formulating a precise definition of what reasonable literature should represent. His unusual caveat expressed in the past tense—"the great liberty you have to say what you like leaves you no excuse when you did not say what you should have"—suggests that people with the temerity to produce unauthorized works should be prepared to expect the inevitable consequences from a righteous but nevertheless avenging authority. In the same year, however, Jules de La Mesnardière attempted to specify the precise parameters of literary representation. Like the Académie, La Mesnardière believed there were two kinds of *vraisemblance*, which he identifies as *ordinaire* and *rare*. *La Vraisemblance ordinaire*, he writes in his *Poétique*, "is drawn from natural qualities found in men, insofar as they have customs that they enact";[18] he goes on to specify that these qualities include "one's manner of life, the various attributes of age, nation, and fortune" (36). In contradistinction to ordinary *vraisemblance*, La Mesnardière identifies *La Vrai-semblance rare*, so named "because these events do not conform to standard appearances or order; they are extraordinary and consequently rare" (40). If La Mesnardière's definition of *Vrai-semblance rare* lacks the subtlety and finesse of the Académie's similar formulation, he does attempt to provide mate-

[18] La Mesnardière, pp. 35–36.

rial clarification. In addition to pointing out that *vraisemblance* must depend on historical and cultural considerations, he also adds a recommendation to poets on how to avoid *invraisemblance* by giving them a checklist of unsuitable literary referents:

> To maintain moral propriety, the poet must observe that one should never, unless absolutely necessary, depict a courageous young lady, or a learned woman, or a prudent valet. Although these qualities are sometimes found in this sex and in this trade, it is nevertheless true that there are few Sapphos, even fewer Amazons, and very few wise valets indeed. Thus, to put these three sorts of people with these noble qualities onto the stage would directly violate ordinary *vraisemblance* (137).

La Mesnardière, who was both a poet and the personal physician to Richelieu, had published his *Poétique* at the latter's insistence while the Académie was occupied with formulating its own definitive treatise on poetics. Despite his observation that there exist wise women and judicious servants, he claims that it is shocking to see these varieties represented. Unlike the Académie, which had attempted to articulate archetypical categories appropriate for literary representation, La Mesnardière attempts to provide a more or less exhaustive account of how particular groups or classes of people should be portrayed—he proclaims, for example, that one must never depict a faithful African, a truthful Greek, a subtle German, or, finally, an uncivil Frenchman.[19] La Mesnardière is more immediately concerned with the literary referent than he is with the broader social and ideological structures governing the production of literature, even though his *Poétique*, which privileges an aristocratic worldview, is in the same spirit as the Académie's condemnation of Corneille's *Cid*. Where the Académie had formulated the necessity of promulgating a politically correct *use* for literature, one which reinforced an ideological belief in the natural hegemony of the aristocracy in general and the absolute authority of the king in particular, La Mesnardière provides concrete advice on the particulars of that ideology. In other words, the Académie and La Mesnardière share the same views on what literature must depict, but the Académie elaborated its ideology in inductive fashion, warning authors to glean its political agenda or face censorship; La Mesnardière proceeded on the same track in inverse, deductive fashion,

---

[19] See Bray, *La Formation de la doctrine classique en France*, p. 222.

providing prospective authors with a list of suitable and unsuitable literary referents, and he showed writers how and why particular objects of representation complemented Right Reason.

The theories Desmaretz and La Mesnardière put forth concerning the suitability of particular literary representations mesh in aesthetic and political harmony with the Académie's pronouncement on Corneille's *Cid*. Where earlier writers had been concerned with defending fiction's right to exist and with the cultural and historical probability of the events their works depicted, the Académie and its mouthpieces described authors' obligations to give their works specific uses. The shift from probability to obligation in *vraisemblance*, a distinction Gérard Genette has examined at great length in Mme de Lafayette's *Princesse de Clèves* and to which we will return later, is significant for two interrelated reasons. On the one hand, the obligation to demonstrate a specific and reasonable use for works betrays a decidedly aristocratic attitude toward the consumption of literature. Maurice Lever writes that one of the reasons the novel was harshly condemned during this period of the seventeenth century was because it "offers the reader nothing but itself" (*Le Roman français au XVIIe siècle*, 27), and Jean Chapelain implicitly corroborates Lever's theory in his "De la lecture des vieux romans" (On reading old novels) when, discovered reading a novel, he claims that his sole interest lies in the contemplation of its language. "I am sure that you don't believe I have such poor taste," he writes, "to be interested in anything but the language used here, since I have robbed my affairs of the time necessary to peruse [this book]."[20] Chapelain feared that being caught *flagrante delicto* would destroy his reputation, and hoped that his friend who discovered him reading the frivolous material would not think the worse of him for it: "It's important to me that he not leave here persuaded that I have lost the taste for serious literature, since he found me engrossed in a book he considers quite awful" (164). Chapelain's comments reveal the extent to which reading novels for the sheer pleasure fiction affords was a culturally proscribed activity, and his remark that the reading of fiction took time he would otherwise have devoted to his affairs demonstrates the emphasis his social milieu placed on production, of whatever sort.

[20] Jean Chapelain, "De la lecture des vieux romans" (1646), in Fabienne Gégou's edition of Pierre-Daniel Huet's *Lettre-traité sur l'origine des romans*, p. 181.

On the other hand, when the Académie warned that literature must have a use and when fiction writers tried to adapt their works accordingly, it became clear that literature's capacity to reflect the world was being subsumed by its potential for shaping it. That is, the fact that the Académie labeled *invraisemblables* sequences in *Le Cid* that are perfectly plausible from a material point of view drives home the point that the literary text was charged with reproducing not extratextual reality in the referential sense defined above, but an ideology. The decidedly political aspect of *vraisemblance* surges forth, then, as the Académie Française and its followers attempted to cause its political vision of the world to appear natural and uncontrived. Only works that conformed to Richelieu's rigid and uncompromising absolutist doctrines earned the stamp of approval of *vraisemblance*; consequently, a properly ideological and political program mapped the domain of the authentic and the believable in literature. *Vraisemblance* ostensibly denoted a mode of writing in which texts evoked in direct and unmediated fashion the world at large and its social functioning. Following Richelieu's politics, however, the Académie dictated the rules of *vraisemblance* and made it into an organ of propaganda while surreptitiously labeling it a matter of aesthetics.[21]

During the first four decades of the seventeenth century, fiction developed along the lines of a rigidly controlled notion of artifice. In the early years, artifice served to unify aristocratic reading audiences with a moral lesson that stressed the importance of presenting a united front to the dangerous onslaught of commoners who would accede to noble status. Artifice in sentimental and pastoral fiction provided aristocratic readers with a glorified image of themselves, an image which invoked feudal privileges attesting to the ancient merit their class possessed. It was also an exclusionary device designed to ostracize those who lacked the iconographic keys required to understand the tales. Later on in the century, particularly after the official recognition of the Académie Française, artifice in the form of *vraisemblance* provided history with an ideologically corrective measure and was put into the service of monarchic absolutism. *Vraisemblance* furnished a rectifying and partisan ver-

---

[21] On the political constitution of *vraisemblance* as well as on the novel's relationship to extradiegetic elements, see Claude Duchet, "Une écriture de la socialité."

sion of Right Reason to literature, and conscripted it into the service of Richelieu's politics. It also afforded the illusion of a single, unequivocal truth whose hegemony was both self-evident and natural. The ritualistic narratives of sentimental and tragic fiction gave early novels a univocality that effectively codified convention and established a pragmatic conception of what prose fiction should be. This general pragmatic conception solidified into systematized rules as authors described and theorized their own and their contemporaries' works. With the inception of an officially sanctioned academy, novelists had to make their works conform to the authorized rules of artifice set down by the state.

Authors' theoretical discussions of their works and of the form of fiction in general marked a crucial moment in the development of French fiction because they heralded the end of what I have been calling the pragmatic conception of the genre. Marked primarily by its traditional iconography and by its evocation of established aristocratic class myths, the pragmatic conception of genre entertained few if any internal contradictions and was bereft of a theoretical discourse able to articulate its logic. *Vraisemblance* was the first formal theoretical articulation applied to fiction; it emerged as a concern when writers tried to rid their works of the obtrusive conventions popular in pastoral fiction and bestow upon them a relative transparency that would defend them against charges of falsity or inaccuracy. Significantly, *vraisemblance* was a codified narrative mode that developed precisely to efface all traces of literary convention; what it effaced, however, were the very social contradictions and antagonisms necessitating its rise. Only the presence of competing versions of truth could explain contemporaries' definition of *vraisemblance* as "things as they should be," since there would be no other way of accounting for the discrepancy between the lived and the ideal world. *Vraisemblance* appeared to be a phenomenon legitimating the aesthetic value of a work, but since such legitimating also involved political backing, the aesthetic dimension of *vraisemblance* was quite clearly subordinate to its politically reformative one.

Thus, authors' concern with *vraisemblance*, the literary mode that presented to a specific group of readers the illusion that a work offered in unmotivated and nonpartisan fashion an unmediated vision of the world, was actually a concern that literature continue to remain the property and prerogative of a privileged class. They strove to retain the hold aristocratic ideology had on fiction by attempting to efface the blatant ideological artifice underpinning its development. The development of *vraisemblance*, then, is a historically and politically determined literary mode that served to naturalize parochial representation in order to narrow the ever-widening schism separating an aristocratic ideal from elemental reality. In short, *vraisemblance* helped to reassert the ostensible adequation of ideal and real, of art and nature, while systematically eliminating any trace of political motivation.[22]

The budding theoretical discourses surrounding the production of prose fiction not only helped naturalize an ideologically invested literary form, they provided a brand new genre with an air of legitimacy as well. That is, the new theories of fiction provided writers a distance from their works, enabling them to treat them as texts meriting critical attention and as discrete objects with an aesthetic and ideological ambivalence resisting interpretation. The critical evaluation of fiction and its techniques suggested that the nascent literary form not only merited exegetical attention but could stand up to it as well as any existing genre. Theories of fiction constructed existing texts not as blatant aristocratic propaganda, then, but as ironic and ambiguous manifestations of literary expression with a problematic relationship to the world they described. As Terry Eagleton has observed, criticism and text offer each other a series of mutual reinforcements, and each makes the other appear legitimate and natural: "The literary text naturalises experience, critical practice naturalises the text, and the theories of that practice legitimate the 'naturalness' of criticism."[23] Thus, the theoretical discourses that arose in the 1620's and 1630's salvaged the aristocratic iconography that had dominated sentimental and pastoral fiction; in softening the pugnacious and self-conscious use of artifice earlier fiction had employed, novelists could retain the image of a natural

[22] See Kibédi Varga's article, "La Vraisemblance—Problèmes de terminologie, problèmes de poétique." Varga argues that although *vraisemblance* mediates between the real and the ideal, it does so ambiguously and in a fashion that admits neither history (reality) nor nature (art). He writes that "in its very ambiguity, [*vraisemblance*] strives to give this problem a response that is both realistic and idealistic" (p. 332). It is precisely the ironic ambiguity of *vraisemblance* that allowed it to maintain the illusion that works of fiction could offer unmotivated visions of the world that supported aristocratic ideology.

[23] Eagleton, *Criticism and Ideology*, p. 18.

aristocratic hegemony while still claiming to be interested only in imitating nature.

By the 1630's, prose fiction was by and large a decidedly aristocratic genre. Authors' theories of *vraisemblance* and the Académie Française's codification of verisimilitude as a resolutely political tool capped off what had been a pragmatic development of the genre and provided it with defining rules of its own. Yet, because prose fiction lacked an antecedent in classical antiquity, writers strove to give it a formal legitimacy by appropriating features of sanctioned genres. Boisrobert had labeled the novel an epic in prose, and the first manifestation of prose fiction in which we can observe the stock authors placed in this characterization is the heroic novel. The heroic novel, which became popular at the end of the 1630's, recounted the historical exploits of real or fictional characters in the remote past. Drawn from classical or French sources, these characters, like the epic heroes on which they were modeled, were quasi-divine men and women whose exploits determined the fate of entire nations. The heroic novel maintained the tradition of *vraisemblance* as a literary mode catering to the tastes and political exigencies of the French nobility, but as we will see in Chapter 3 it extended the repertory of ideologically charged iconography to include not only a work's characters and imagery, but its narrative as well. Marin le Roy de Gomberville's *Polexandre* initiated a new discursive practice for French fiction, one which according to the author had its roots in classical antiquity. *Polexandre* deftly toes the line of absolutist politics in France while continuing to glorify the role the aristocracy played in supporting the state. More significantly, however, it does so in a narrative style that attempts to ward off any interpretation that would conflict with its own ideological imperative.

Chapter 3   *Polexandre* and the Politics of
             Heroic Fiction

In his *De la connoissance des bons livres* (On understanding good
books), Charles Sorel attempted to understand the attraction that
the bellicose tales of heroic fiction had for readers. Sorel could not
bear the uncritical manner in which his contemporaries consumed
whatever novel was currently in vogue, and he blamed the proliferation of mediocre novels on the system of patronage reigning in
France. Writers only aimed to please the wealthy and powerful
people to whom they dedicated their works, he claimed, and he
believed that if they were not permitted to offer their hyperbolic
flattery in exchange for political favors, they would cease writing.
Readers, however, seemed to glean a vicarious pleasure from reading about the exploits of glorious heroes whose valor earned them
the great esteem of powerful kings who had never even met them.
Sorel believed that heroic novels allowed readers to live out their
own fantasies of feudalistic nobility: "When they see that kings and
emperors who hardly know [the heroes] give them provinces to
govern and armies to command simply because of the illustrious-
ness of their valor, all persuade themselves that soon a similar fortune will come their way, and they cherish the hope of marrying an
Infanta or of being discovered the son or grandson of kings" (*De
la connoissance*, 135). Sorel was an astute critic, and even if his
bitterness at not being recognized a great writer by his contemporaries often clouded his judgment, he was perceptive enough on this
occasion to recognize the psychological value heroic fiction had for
its readers. Generally claiming for themselves historical truth, heroic novels, like the pastoral novels that preceded them, offered to

a class of people whose political integrity was being threatened the image of historical and ideological continuity with the golden age of French aristocracy. Because they claimed for themselves verifiable historical accuracy, heroic novels alienated and exteriorized the ideological truths that pastoral fiction had proposed as the self-evident axioms available to the elite circle of readers capable of decoding its highly encrypted artifice. The heroic fiction of the 1630's and 1640's opened up a terrain of referentiality inexistent in earlier fiction by subjecting its material to potential verification and demystification. Because it seemed rooted in history, the heroic novel imparted the illusion of its own virtual objectivity, of its complete removal from any specific self-interest group. The heroic novel served up its truths as apodictic veracity accessible to readers of any social group. By virtue of its formal and narrative structure, however, it remained decidedly aristocratic.

In this chapter I will show that heroic fiction required the support of other discursive practices in order to sustain an air of legitimacy. Written during a period in which the notion of genre was harshly constraining, heroic novels appropriated features from other legitimate literary forms, in particular history and the epic, and arrogated the former's moral and political truth, and the latter's formal perfection. Epic and history had for some time been used toward political ends—d'Aubigné's *Tragiques* and Montaigne's essay on history in "Des cannibales" are only two cases in point that reveal authors' ideological biases. The heroic novel borrowed formal traits from these two venerated genres, but not without appropriating their traditional ideological predispositions as well. What resulted from fiction's arrogation of the epic's style and history's truth was an oddly hybrid novelistic genre that was ideologically apt yet aesthetically marginal; more importantly, however, the new novel form explicitly revealed the narrative construction of truth, and it suggested in the process new means for fashioning it. While it appeared to be a further encoding of literary realism, the new novel was, then, actually the formal consummation of the novel as a decidedly political literary form.

In spite of the fact that he characterizes authors of heroic novels as blatant flatterers, Sorel acknowledges that they do offer a version of historical truth. The problem he sees with their truth, however, is that it is no longer recognizable as such because "they disguise it and deform it so pitifully" (*De la connoissance*, 103). Sorel's idea of historical truth was something of an anomaly in the seventeenth century because he prized the accuracy of verifiable fact. Although authors of heroic fiction virtually always claimed that their works were historically accurate, this normally signified not that the specific events they related actually happened, but that the work contained a sententious truth about the past. The referentiality to which heroic fiction aspired was abstract and moral rather than concrete and factual. Heroic novels were most frequently set in the distant past, which allowed authors more margin to tamper with the events they depicted and thus mold their characters according to contemporary standards of heroism and, more importantly, *vraisemblance*. The novels' historical apparatuses overlaid seventeenth-century conceptions of moral excellence onto ancient or medieval cultural systems, thus implying that virtue and probity as contemporaries valued them not only derived from the great civilizations of yore, but were essentially unchanging, transhistorical truths. Heroic novels used the illusion of history to reinforce the ostensibly unmotivated standards of *vraisemblance* that the Académie Française had prescribed; this helped them obfuscate the arbitrariness of the literary convention. In her *Ibrahim ou l'Illustre Bassa* (1641), Madeleine de Scudéry candidly announces her own exploitation of the illusion of historicity in order to achieve a politically expedient *vraisemblance*. "I have . . . tried never to distance myself from [*vraisemblance*]: to that end I have observed the morals, customs, laws, religions, and inclinations of the peoples, and to give things more *vraisemblance* I have made the bases of my work historical, my principal characters famous in factual history, and the wars real."[1] Mlle de Scudéry's concern for including accurate historical and cultural details in her work recalls Gerzan's careful attention to historical accuracy. She demonstrates a keen awareness of the social function of *vraisemblance*, however, when she refuses to depict in accurate detail any error a noble might have committed: "I have even ensured that the errors committed by noblemen in my tale were caused by love or ambition, the noblest

---

[1] Scudéry, *Ibrahim*, "Préface." Although this novel is frequently attributed to Georges de Scudéry, I am taking Madeleine at her word when she refers to "mon Illustre Bassa" in the preface to *Le Grand Cyrus*.

of passions" ("Préface"). Less a revisionist form of history than a discreet effort to present a unified ideological front, heroic fiction availed itself of *vraisemblance* in order to mediate between reality and the idealized image of reality that advanced an unequivocally flattering image of France's aristocratic class.

Political concerns meshed with formal and aesthetic concerns in authors' use of *vraisemblance* in heroic fiction. Eight years after writing *Ibrahim*, Madeleine de Scudéry produced her *Artamène ou le Grand Cyrus*. In this novel, as in her first, she steadfastly maintains that the tale is historical, calling her hero "one of the greatest noblemen whose memory history preserves."[2] Mlle de Scudéry concurs with Desmaretz that unadulterated history is "dry and lacking grace," and she feels compelled to alter the truth, a truth she claims to have gathered from historical sources, in order to give the work a more perfect literary form:

> You can see that although a story [*Fable*] is not history [*une Histoire*], and that its author simply needs to adhere to what is *vraisemblable* without always telling the exact truth, nevertheless in the things that I have invented I have not strayed so far from the [ancient historians] as they have strayed from one another.... Thus, sometimes I followed one and sometimes another, depending on how they conformed to my project. ("Au lecteur")

Mlle de Scudéry carefully distinguishes "*Fable*" from "*Histoire*" as well as "*vray*" (true) from "*vraisemblable*"; writing during a period in which the monarchy jealously guarded the propagation and distribution of its representations, she judiciously eschews any untoward factual truths that might cast the throne in an unsuitable light. Her prudent distinction between truth and verisimilitude in heroic fiction brings us back to the Académie's assertion that "the goal of poetry which imitates human action is not a thing yet completely determined."

The historical accuracy of heroic fiction was never intended to be unimpeachable. More precisely a support for *vraisemblance*, it provided the illusion of referentiality novels needed in order to claim for themselves moral and political utility and fend off the criticism that they were frivolous and inconsequential pastimes, a reproach

---

[2] Scudéry, *Le Grand Cyrus*, "Au lecteur." The edition cited is the second, revised edition.

Boileau levied at Mlle de Scudéry's *Clélie*.[3] *Vraisemblance* remained, consequently, an ideological as well as a formal concern.
The claim to historical accuracy in the heroic novel lent the work
an air of legitimacy, and novelists asserted their works' historicism
on the barest of pretenses. Often they simply used figures from history as their principal characters and depicted them in circumstances in which they were known to have been involved or in
which they plausibly could have been involved. Significantly, historians did the same thing. Claiming historical accuracy for a work
of fiction was consequently problematic because no one could agree
on precisely what this meant—even deciding what constituted history was a controversial enterprise. Since at least as far back as the
sixteenth century, historical truth was a hybrid construction of religious and political ideals whose overarching purpose was to cast
French monarchs as the source and epitome of Christian devotion
and consequently as benevolent and just rulers. Beginning in the
middle of the sixteenth century the office of royal historian, a
charge that conferred nobility, was sold to ambitious men eager to
curry favor by detailing historical evidence of the French monarch's
grandeur and righteousness. The rigidly controlled system of patronage was largely responsible for history's amalgamation of fact
and verisimilitude, as Sorel, himself a royal historian, noted, and
history developed its own rules of *vraisemblance*, rules which strikingly paralleled those of fiction.

Royal historians generally went about the task of portraying their
patrons in a favorable light by interweaving stories drawn from
sacred and secular traditions. They appealed to readers' beliefs in
the unchanging truths of Christianity and wed those beliefs to
chronicles of French noble families whose power derived from their
piety and was in turn legitimated by God. Many Renaissance historians posited their rulers as a sort of first family of Christianity;
aristocratic readers affirmed their own places in the nation's political hierarchy through their own relationships to the church and to

[3] In the *Art poétique*, Chant III, lines 115–21:
Refrain from giving, as in *Clélie*,
A French character or mood to ancient Italy;
And from portraying us under Roman names,
Portraying Caton as gallant and Brutus as a dandy.
In a frivolous novel things are easily excused;
It is enough that in its whimsy fiction amuses;
Too much rigor would be out of place.

their king. François de Belleforest, for example, writing in 1568, maintained that the study of history helped lead people to their Christian salvation. The study of history is the study of the people of God, Belleforest testified, meaning of course the French. His vision of the sacred weal history provided held that only those of the proper pedigree could derive any benefit from its study.

> History is the only one of the sciences I know of that bears the name of probity, since history alone can enrich human life as much as all the other arts together; it is thus not surprising that those noble souls whose minds aspire to goodness embrace such a venerable thing, or that they devote themselves to the pursuit of what makes man just and civilized, and, when contemplated, can in its perfection use its colors to depict us with the brush of great felicity and beatitude.[4]

It was the class of *honnêtes hommes* who benefited most from the study of history, and Belleforest links contemporary aristocrats with the great men of classical and Biblical epochs. Comparing each of the kings and the men who served them to figures from classical antiquity and the Bible, Belleforest establishes a direct lineage, as Gregory of Tours had done a millennium before, from the noblemen of the ancient world to contemporary ruling families. Belleforest views history as a spiritually ennobling enterprise capable of elevating the nobly born to new heights of a neo-Platonic contemplation of truth and beauty. Endowing historiography with a moral goal and a didactic mission whose evangelical purpose mirrors that of the New Testament, he equates sacred and profane history and affirms that they are "the living portrait both of the punishment of malefactors and of the salvation of those who followed the path of virtue" ("Preface").

Belleforest's successor André Du Chesne was equally concerned with history's political mission of chronicling the piety and the grandeur of contemporary rulers. His *Antiquitez et recherches de la grandeur & majesté des Roys de France* (Monuments and researches into the grandeur and majesty of the kings of France), published in 1609, is little more than a panegyric aimed directly at his patron, Henri IV. Du Chesne's history of the French monarchy is a qualmless magnification of each French king's grandeur. Eschewing a narrative account of the succession of kings in France,

---

[4] Belleforest de Comingeois, *L'Histoire des Neuf Roys Charles*, "Preface aux lecteurs."

Du Chesne approaches his subject thematically, addressing the question of how all of the kings—usually collectively, and not individually—dealt with the issues of religion, faith, valor, power, piety, justice, clemency, and ceremony. Always speaking of the ROYS DE FRANCE as an aggregate unity, he generally chooses an issue and then illustrates how the kings reckoned with it. Godefroy, for example, went to Palestine to liberate the Holy Land and was made king of Jerusalem for his efforts, but in his magnanimity modestly turned down the offer.[5] Du Chesne's history of the French kings' greatness is such a transparent attempt to curry favor with the king that it is somewhat painful to read. His tactics consist of little more than proving the greatness of the monarchy by casting all of them in the same mold and writing an adulating chronicle of their heroic—and generally mythological—deeds of grandeur and magnanimity. Du Chesne was Henri's royal historiographer, and his shameless support of the king's absolutism demonstrates quite clearly the power patrons had over their protégés.

Not all historians, of course, manifested the same lack of subtlety as Du Chesne. Lancelot de La Popelinière, for example, writing in 1599, defined history as "a general narrative, both eloquent and judicious, of men's most notable actions, and of other incidents represented according to their times, places, causes, movements, and results."[6] La Popelinière chronicled the events of the religious wars of the sixteenth century, and unlike Du Chesne or Belleforest he stressed the historian's need to remain impartial to the material he treated. Certainly the emphasis he placed on temporal and geographical coordinates, as well as on the structures of causality that led to each of the events described, align him with more modern notions of history: La Popelinière proposed simply to tell the story implicitly intimated by the specific details and events peculiar to the period or situation at hand. He viewed his task as consisting of the straightforward arrangement of the unusual or extraordinary details obtaining in a particular set of circumstances.[7] La Popelinière

[5] Du Chesne, pp. 30–33.
[6] Lancelot de La Popelinière, *L'Histoire des histoires, avec l'idée de l'histoire accomplie* (1599), cited by Ehrard and Palmade, p. 121.
[7] La Popelinière was not alone in defining the historiographer's task as a simple and unbiased narration of the facts. Throughout the seventeenth century, different writers made the same claim for a variety of historical genres. Charles Sorel wanted his *Polyandre, histoire comique* to offer a correction, in an entertaining narrative

argues neither for the necessity of relating each and every quotidian detail—such as what people ate or the kinds of buildings they lived in—coincidental with the significant facts at hand, nor for the need to heap lavish praise on the ruler under whom he was writing. His brand of history is significant not only because it appears to correspond to modern philosophies of history, but also because it epitomizes, as we will see, the use of explanatory narrative that the heroic novel valorized.

History as La Popelinière defines it—the narration of the most notable human actions and accidents—purports to relate simply what is different from the ordinary course of daily events. Only what is strange, unusual, or different merits account, and in the deft construction of the historical narrative's plot the historian merely gives form to the past and thus renders it accessible to readers. Paul Veyne analyzes this kind of historical writing and compares the historian's activity to the grammarian's; he points out that in both historical and linguistic description only what is different or other merits attention: "A history book resembles a grammar book; the practical grammar of a foreign language does not inventory *tabula rasa* all of the language's rules, but only those that differ from the language the reader speaks." [8] Like the grammarian, the narrative historian concentrates either on what is foreign to the reader or on the particularities he or she will need to synthesize in order to grasp the systemic structure that the material implicates. Unlike the grammarian, however, who can show empirically the tangible differences between two languages, the historian must construct from a collection of abstract contingencies a palpable historical reality that readers will be able to evaluate as more or less similar to their own lived experience.

---

form, to the human faults he believed rampant in his generation. He defines an *histoire comique* as "a naive depiction of all of men's diverse dispositions, with keen censure of most of their faults," and just as in his *Francion*, which claimed a similar censoring mechanism, he believes that a simple, straightforward representation of nothing but the facts is possible (Sorel, *Polyandre*, "Advertissement aux lecteurs"). DuPlaisir, several years later, confessed, "I know of few rules for true History [*Histoire veritable*]," underscoring the fact that ostensibly naive historiography requires no rules because, unlike a literary genre whose constraining conventions dictate the subject and the strategies of its narration, historiography has no rules to fetter its narrative account of the truth (DuPlaisir, *Sentimens sur les lettres et sur l'histoire*, p. 83).

[8] Veyne, *Comment on écrit l'histoire*, p. 16.

It is precisely the historian's narrative construction of a past reality, however, that the allegation of impartiality or naïveté effaces.
In identifying unusual or significant events deserving historical attention, the historian selects and combines them to produce a
causal narrative sequence that in fiction we would designate as plot.
In fiction the narrative closure furnished by the working through
of causal narrative sequences establishes one of the fundamental
components of a work's meaning or significance. In historiography
the same type of narrative closure endows a sequence of events with
significance, but the historian must eschew all appearances that the
significance so derived is simply a product of his or her own intellect.[9] Hayden White argues that one of the unspoken axioms of
historiography is the necessity to mask the degree of narrative construction that goes into the writing in order to present as natural
and uncontrived the plot that emerges. Labeling as an "embarrassment" the plot of historical narrative, he argues that plot "has to
be presented as 'found' in the events rather than put there by narrative techniques." [10] Rather than demonstrate the degree to which
the writer retains control of the significance of the events narrated,
narrative historiography purports to alienate those events from the
writer so that they may be treated as objects of knowledge with a
self-evident import whose implications the historian reveals by providing a sequential order and an interpretation of that order.[11]

The historian's construction of a plot based upon the identification and combination of unusual or otherwise narratable events
makes history into an interpretable text of protracted change set
against a background of stasis or sameness.[12] That is, the plot the

[9] See Max Weber's *The Methodology of the Social Sciences* for a cogent discussion
of the manner in which historical narrative is informed by abstract mental constructs. Weber argues that the historian isolates specific events the sum of which is
then considered as a network of potential causal relations. Their synthesis provides
a causality that transforms reality into historical fact (pp. 165–75).

[10] White, "The Value of Narrativity in the Representation of Reality," p. 20.

[11] Robert Young has recently investigated the complex interrelationships between
history and Eurocentrism. Analyzing conceptions of history as construed in Marxist,
Foucaldian, orientalist, and postcolonialist models of history, he attempts to understand whether history which tries to understand the "Other" can extricate itself
from exercising dominance over its object. See his *White Mythologies: Writing History and the West*.

[12] See also Jameson on the textual nature of historical interpretation: "History
. . . is *not* a text, for it is fundamentally non-narrative and nonrepresentational; what
can be added, however, is the proviso that history is inaccessible to us except in
textual form, or in other words, that it can be approached only by way of prior
(re)textualization" (*The Political Unconscious*, p. 82).

historian purportedly uncovers forges a determined modification in the perceived homeostasis of current affairs. Something significant occurs that warrants analysis in the form of an explanatory narrative of causality and, since the explanatory narrative need not begin, as Veyne points out, *tabula rasa*, it accrues significance against the background of a complex of received transhistorical cultural laws.[13] The complex of cultural laws that provide relief for the historical narrative would include political and/or moral systems, against which events such as revolution or religious conflicts might be narrated, as well as technical or folk knowledge, against which histories of ideas or popular culture might be constructed. It is obviously most likely that these ostensibly unchanging cultural laws will include complex combinations of social, economic, and moral systems. In seventeenth-century French historiography, the point of narrative departure was the assumption that France was a Christian nation economically and militarily fortified by a strong aristocracy and ruled by an absolute monarch whose divine right to rule was unquestioned and self-evident.

This last assertion might appear glaringly obvious if we were describing only histories *of* the seventeenth century. In fact, however, seventeenth-century historians rarely hesitated to apply the template of their own sociocultural situations to periods dating hundreds of years before their own. François Eudes de Mézeray, to take the most obvious example, selects seventeenth-century courtly and religious sensibilities and applies them, in a manner strikingly similar to d'Urfé's, to fifth-century Gaul. In his monolithic *Histoire de France*, Mézeray describes as noble and magnanimous the wanton and murderous bandit-king Clovis, who converted to Christianity primarily as a political move in order to wed Clothilde and thus increase his power through the formation of family alliances. In Mézeray's account, Clovis delayed his marriage to Clothilde until he felt touched by the spirit of Christianity. When this happened, he exhorted his troops to convert as well, and the scene of Clovis and Clothilde's marriage as Mézeray relates it is the stuff of fairy tales:

> The Heavens were so favorable that one day as [Clothilde] and her husband were with the good prelate [Saint-Rémy], focused on the

---

[13] For a detailed account of the logic of narrative in analytic philosophy, see also Arthur C. Danto, *Narration and Knowledge*, pp. 233–56.

evangelical doctrine that he was preaching, a blinding light filled the room, from which emanated a voice that said, "Peace be with you: fear not; abide in my love." Thus the two of them, bound by the sacred knot of marriage and united even more closely by divine love, lived in continued contentment, understanding that true felicity is a gift from above.[14]

Mézeray is unable or unwilling to heed historical and cultural mandates in his account of a scene that took place twelve centuries before his own era. Instead of construing social and institutional details as part of the rudimentary touchstone against which he might construct his narrative of historical difference and significance, he opts to form a story of cultural and ideological continuity. The three volumes forming Mézeray's history of France attest to his remarkable erudition, yet he exploits the vast quantity of factual material available to him ("the truth of the things that I report is based on the best authors at my disposal, the original and ancient titles" ["Preface"]) primarily to demonstrate what his readers would already have believed: that France's absolute monarchy was divinely ordained by God himself. He concludes his chapter on Hugues Capet by describing the manifest destiny of the Capetian rise to power succored by divine intervention: "Thus in the year nine hundred eighty-eight, not so much by the will of man but by that of God . . . began the reign of Capet and that of the third race" (I, 368).

Clearly even the most dispassionate and impartial historiographers can never escape having the prejudices of their own cultural milieu penetrate their works. This is due in part to the fact that their medium of representation is fraught with social and political forces which shape and are in turn shaped by language. Historiography, like any other artistic or utilitarian application of language, articulates the writer's personal and political unconscious. While it is obviously not the case that seventeenth-century historiographers were especially susceptible to this type of biased reporting, they did need to interpret the events of the past in light of the current monarch's politics. Thus, while it is generally the historian's task to arrange his or her narrative in such a fashion that readers will agree with the interpretation of causality that he or she advances, it was

[14] Mézeray, *Histoire*, vol. I, pp. 40–41.

the more specific task of seventeenth-century royal historians to restrict the epistemological and ideological frame from within which readers could interpret the events and causes of the stories narrated. We might consequently differentiate historical/didactic narrative from its literary counterpart by focusing on the degree to which it strives to rid itself of ambivalence. While the historian attempts to persuade readers that his or her conclusions are valid, the literary writer scripts an equivocal discourse that opens itself up to multiple interpretations.

Northrop Frye has called the novel "creative history" and he argues that historiography exerted pressures on novelists to write tales that followed formal schemes set down by history.[15] Even this extremely abbreviated foray into seventeenth-century French historiography should show that historiography was also influenced by fiction. That is, it is virtually unthinkable that the tremendous popularity of novels in the first forty years of the seventeenth century did not affect the ways histories were written. The question is not, of course, simply which narrative form more greatly influenced the other. To pose the question in such a fashion is to posit one narrative form as more organically or structurally basic than the other. While seventeenth-century scholars would not have hesitated to bestow that honor on history because of its ostensibly longer cultural lineage, it is crucial to recall that both history and the novel are specific literary forms of the narrative mode, a system of representation that antedates either of these particular genres and that is not necessarily literary. In 1659, René Bary enumerated a series of different narrative forms, including judiciary, digressive or descriptive, *fabuleuse*, and prophetic. Strikingly, he does not include history, nor does he include any of the narrative forms common in the visual arts.[16] The point is that seventeenth-century scholars were well aware of the hegemony narrative enjoyed in cultural activity, but they seemed unable to recognize the general mode implicated by the various specific forms. They did not seem to acknowledge that a culture's use of narrative extends far beyond its literary practices. Narrative informs a culture's epistemology, the way it thinks about itself and the way it represents itself. Changes in cul-

---

[15] Frye, *Anatomy of Criticism*, pp. 306–7.
[16] Bary, *La Rhétorique françoise*, pp. 208–9.

tural practice produce new narrative forms and contribute to the obsolescence of current ones—the rise and fall of tragedy in Hellenistic times and the wane of the epic in the modern era are two examples in point. Although it is no doubt quite obvious, it seems important to stress that in seventeenth-century France, history and fiction, the two principal modes of narrative representation that had a stake in high culture, shared a similar cultural development. Both belonged to the aristocratic and ruling classes and both were systems of representation influenced in an overdetermined form by the reigning epistemological and ideological conditions. Although they had different theoretical uses and values, the formal rules governing their production—particularly their obsession with *vraisemblance*—were virtually indistinguishable. I will return at the end of this chapter to a detailed analysis of a historical text that clearly manifests the narrative terrain shared by history and fiction.

Although history and the novel both had a stake in high culture and were composed of virtually identical narrative devices, particularly in the 1640's and 1650's, the seventeenth century's preoccupation with genre valorized the former because of its literary lineage and cast aspersion upon the latter for its lack thereof. Seventeenth-century scholars and aestheticians failed or refused to recognize the conventional nature of historical narrative; they accepted at face value definitions of history such as La Popelinière's which construed historiography as a demystified literary mode with a verifiable referent that was alienated and exteriorized from its author. In short, they viewed history as the simple transcription of a sublimated portion of reality. In effect, although they recognized history's rhetoric, they denied its form: narrative events, they believed, simply paralleled and reproduced historical events. Bary failed to list historiography as one of the forms of narrative, an obvious omission that testifies to contemporaries' belief in historiography's apparent lack of form and convention, and the abbé DuPlaisir, several years later, supported this intuitive characterization of history as a rhetorically elegant but essentially formless genre. "I know of few rules for true History," he wrote. "It is a portrait whose features are always loved, as long as they are sincere; or at least if this essential beauty requires ornaments, it borrows them principally from exact and polished expression." [17] His-

---

[17] DuPlaisir, *Sentimens sur les lettres et sur l'histoire*, p. 86.

tory maintained an unproblematic relationship to the sanctioned literary forms of high culture principally because it had for so long been an unquestioned component in that culture. The novel's difficult relationship to high culture originated primarily because it was consumed by the same group of people who produced and consumed other forms of high culture; since it was a relative newcomer, they were not willing to admit it into the ranks of the aesthetically classic.

In the *Sentimens sur le Cid*, the Académie Française had maintained that a literary work is useless if the pleasure it produces is not based on Right Reason and if that pleasure does not arise from "the channels that make it standard, the same channels necessary to make it beneficial." We have already seen how the Académie politicized Aristotle in their determination of what constituted regularity and utility in a literary work. In the case of the novel, its aesthetically peripheral position problematized its ideological stance by setting it up in opposition to the sanctioned literary forms that had hypostatized absolutist ideology in the form of a moral and political utility. With the historical fiction of the heroic novel, authors attempted to recuperate an acceptable aesthetic and political footing by appropriating characteristics from the venerated literary forms, most particularly history and the epic.

Madeleine de Scudéry was one author who tried to apply literature's regulating rules to fiction: "Each art has its own specific rules which through sovereign means lead to the end that we set for ourselves" (*Ibrahim*, "Préface"). Like Boisrobert, Mlle de Scudéry compared fiction to the epic, and following Aristotle's advice that a well-structured narrative include series of peripeteia, she maintained that series of actions must combine to form a central, overarching narrative structure. More significantly still, Mlle de Scudéry attempted to attenuate the incongruity that her contemporaries intolerant of prose fiction perceived between the venerable genre of history and its cognate narrative form the novel. Twenty years earlier, novelists had erected a theoretical discourse around the genre in a determined effort to legitimate it. Mlle de Scudéry surpasses her predecessors in claiming not only that the novel is simply an epic in prose, but that its roots are as ancient as history's.

> I will thus tell you only that I have taken and I will always take for my unique models the immortal Heliodorus and the great d'Urfé. These are the only masters that I imitate and the only ones to be

imitated. For whosoever wanders from their route will certainly be
lost, since there is no other route that is good, and since theirs alone
is certain; theirs leads infallibly where we desire to go—I mean,
reader, to Glory. (*Le Grand Cyrus*, "Au lecteur")

Mlle de Scudéry strives to give the novel a history by tracing its
origins back to Greek romances and she ventures a contemporary
legitimation of fiction by comparing Heliodorus to d'Urfé. Following Joachim Du Bellay, who also wrote of the necessity of returning
to the ancient masters,[18] Mlle de Scudéry justifies fiction and gives
the nod to the Académie, which claimed to have relied exclusively
on Hellenistic poetics in its formulation of guidelines for contemporary literary production. In her *Ibrahim* she peremptorily solicits
the Académie's approval by mocking the style and the substance of
the *Sentimens*: "Since we can only be knowledgeable of the things
that others teach us, and since it is the lot of him who comes last
to follow those who precede him, I felt that to establish the order
of this work I had to consult the Greeks, who are our first masters"
("Préface"). The Académie had designated the Greeks as the formidable masters whose works endured the test of time and consequently served as the model for all great literary achievement. Mlle
de Scudéry and other novelists were determined to legitimate heroic
novels and to do so they began to appropriate the stylistic—and
the ideological—devices of the masters.

Marin Le Roy de Gomberville's *Polexandre*, first published in its
relatively complete form in 1637 and "Reviewed, corrected and
augmented" in 1641, illustrates how novelists began to appropriate
stylistic devices from existing literary forms while still respecting
the ideological constraints the Académie had established. The ac-

---

[18] Du Bellay exhorted authors of prose fiction to imitate the writers of antiquity;
such imitation, he argued, would lead ultimately to Glory: "I would like in passing
to address a word to those who spend their time embellishing and augmenting our
romances [*romans*] and make books out of them, books which are certainly written
in beautiful and fluid language, a language better suited to entertaining young ladies
than to writing knowledgeably. I would like, I say, to advise them to use their great
eloquence to gather the fragments of old French chronicles, and as Livy did with the
annals and other ancient Roman chronicles, build of them the entire corpus of a
beautiful history; they should intermingle their beautiful discourses and speeches in
imitation of the man I have just named, of Thucydides, Sallust, or some other approved writer, according to the genre of writing that they do. Such a work would
certainly gain them immortal glory, bestow honor on France, and serve as a great
illustration of our language" (*La Deffence et illustration de la langue francoyse*, pp.
129–31).

tion in *Polexandre* takes place in the fifteenth century, and it opens, not surprisingly, with a tempest: "A ship that seemed to triumph over the storm that had attacked it came to rest in the roadstead of this happy Isle, an isle which through a perpetual miracle sees the inexhaustible springs that water it flow from the leaves of its trees." [19] This beginning *in medias res* initiates what may be the most tortuous and labyrinthine narrative in all of French literature. *Polexandre*, like many of the sentimental novels that preceded it, is a tale of return and reintegration: the title character strives to find his way back to the Inaccessible Island, which is ruled by Queen Alcidiane for whom he has a passionate but unrequited love. Polexandre's attempts to return to the Island take him to the Americas, Africa, and all throughout Europe. Engaging in battles, duels, abductions, reunions, and pillagings, Polexandre finally regains the Inaccessible Island when a storm dashes him back to Alcidiane's domain. Disguised as a slave and assuming the name Araxez, Polexandre saves the Island from Spanish invaders and is proclaimed king by the islanders. It is then that Alcidiane recognizes her savior and, finally acknowledging her love for Polexandre, consents to marry him.

Polexandre is a prince of the most distinguished and ancient nobility, and his story is a genuine odyssey: he labors to return to the woman from whom he was separated as a young man, and his destiny, as we will see below, engulfs that of an entire nation. Gomberville took to heart Boisrobert's counsel that novels imitate the ancient epics, and he cast Polexandre in the same quasi-divine mold that the early Greeks and Romans had used, describing his hero as "the great Polexandre who seems to have descended from the Heavens to earth to rid the earth of tyranny and to exterminate all her monsters" (III, 501). Polexandre's heroism is innate and uncontested, and unlike medieval heroes such as Yvain or even seventeenth-century pastoral heroes such as Lindamor who was worthy to pay homage to Galathée only after having proved himself in battle (*L'Astrée*, I, 325), Polexandre is born a hero and consequently must fight for justice. Mark Bannister observes that the heroic novel hero's predilection for fighting aligns him more closely

---

[19] Gomberville, vol. I, pp. 1–2. Vol. V of the 1641 edition begins with p. 723, continuing the pagination of vol. IV. I will thus give page references consisting of a roman numeral indicating the volume—and not the book—of the edition of 1641.

with the classical epic hero than with the hero of medieval romance. "The hero in the romances of chivalry," he writes, "was
heroic because he had fought and won. . . . For the new hero . . .
fighting is a consequence of being a hero." [20]

Polexandre is a new hero, but he is clearly modeled on the proven
success of the classical variety. The classical epic hero did not *rise*
to prodigious heights—he was born far above the ranks of ordinary
humans, and his natural ascendancy was universally acknowledged. Although a demigod, the epic hero remains part human and
thus retains specific political ties. The heroic figures in the *Iliad*, for
example, although born of immortals, continue to represent their
native lands, and this fact contributes to providing the ancient epic
with a decidedly nationalistic cast part of whose function is to create in contemporary audiences feelings of patriotism rooted in a
golden age of the past. Like the classical epic hero, Polexandre retains a specific nationalistic character. Polexandre is Prince of the
Canaries, but the descriptions we have of him render him decidedly
French. Clearly conscious of his reading audience, Gomberville
paints his hero in all the colors of the ancient French nobility. The
Vice Roy narrates Polexandre's early days, and he tells his listeners
that Polexandre

> was born on one of the Fortunate Isles, that his ancestors' circum-
> stances were not unremarkable, and that they had always borne arms.
> Polexandre had always been naturally inclined to follow their ex-
> ample, and although he always found in his mediocre fortune enough
> not to envy greater ones, nevertheless an ardent desire to attain great-
> ness by taking the difficult route made him leave his home and seek
> out among the perils of war and of the sea satisfaction of his ambi-
> tious leanings. (II, 633–34)

The thrust of the Vice Roy's speech is clear: Polexandre is of
the highest nobility primarily because his ancestors had always
borne arms, the principal way of distinguishing a nobleman in
seventeenth-century France. Of no less significance, however, is the
fact that his wealth, although considerable, contributes less to his
nobility than does his fervent longing to maintain his renown
through the traditionally noble means of waging war.

Like a true epic hero, Polexandre rises to prodigious glory but

---

[20] Bannister, *Privileged Mortals*, p. 34.

not without undergoing preposterous tests of his mettle as a warrior, his wisdom as a councilor, and his constancy as a lover. His
final heroic deed is his crushing the Spanish invasion of Queen Alcidiane's Island, fulfilling an age-old prophecy of such a feat (V,
1268). His heroism leads all the island's inhabitants to proclaim
him their king, yet he only accedes to his exalted rank through
Alcidiane's sovereign decision to let him.

> [Alcidiane] handed him the scepter that she was holding. Polexandre
> did all that he could not to take it. But since the High Priest had
> shown him the necessity of this ceremony, and especially since Alci-
> diane had implored him to give her this last proof of his obedience,
> he was compelled to consent to his glory. Barely had he taken the
> scepter in hand when all the people began to cry, "Long live the King
> and Queen!" After these cries of joy, the music played first one hymn
> of peace and then another about this incomparable alliance. The
> High Priest completed these first ceremonies with those that united
> with indissoluble bonds Alcidiane and Polexandre. (V, 1320–21)

Polexandre, the nobly born warrior, saves Alcidiane's domain and
is richly rewarded for his efforts. Yet becoming king is not so much
a reward as it is Polexandre's natural destiny, a privilege sanctioned
by popular acclamation. When Polexandre defeats the Spaniards he
is disguised as a lowly born slave. When Alcidiane's people see him,
however, they recognize his natural, inborn nobility. "Not only the
people, but the court as well turned their eyes toward this counterfeit slave, and as he advanced a murmuring of voices attested to the
impatience or admiration of the spectators" (V, 1245). Polexandre's
heroic qualities are existentially determined: he is born a hero and
not even his disguise as a slave can mask that fact. His political and
moral rectitude surfaces in each of his actions and nothing can prevent him from attaining the height of glory to which he is naturally
destined.

Virtually all the critical writing on the heroic novel suggests that
in heroic fiction writers attempted to depict members of the aristocracy in a glorifying light that would return to them their aggrandized image of themselves. Madeleine Bertaud believes that while
pastoral fiction was a primarily feminine and domestic genre in
which quasi-divine heroines helped men attain the summit of neo-
Platonic mysticism, *Polexandre* is a mature, virile work whose
global dimensions correspond to the bellicose tastes of a France

now at war.[21] Bannister concurs that conflict informed the new direction fiction was taking, but for him it was domestic and not foreign conflict that changed the face of the novel. He argues that the epic features assigned to the heroic novel's principal characters are the same as those the *noblesse d'épée* had always claimed as its own, but he contends that "since Richelieu's propagandists were busily pointing out that the aristocratic ideals were a well-worn myth with little relevance to the contemporary world, the novel can be seen to be representing an anti-absolutist position" (63). Marlies Mueller offers the most persuasive synthesis of aristocratic and royal politics when she attempts to demonstrate that if *Polexandre* perpetuated aristocratic class-myths, it also judiciously acknowledged absolutist politics. Mueller rightly contends that the political nature of *Polexandre*'s fairy-tale ending in which Polexandre becomes king but only by obeying Alcidiane's command to do so accomplishes an aristocratic behest to Louis that he remain a strong monarch but that he recognize the contribution the aristocracy made to the construction and protection of the state.[22]

Each of these three critics holds to a greater or lesser extent to what we might call the reflection theory of literature, which maintains that literary works reflect and reproduce specific contemporary values. While this theory is obviously always true to some degree, it fails to account for cultural change and it construes the literary text as the unproductive parasite of its culture. If the text had only this derivative and ancillary function, it would be difficult to account for the vehemence with which particular works or genres are frequently met. In other words, if the literary text had only a reflective capacity, it would be quite simple to dismiss unpopular or untoward works merely by discounting their truth value. Yet it is precisely because specific problematic texts question the stability of a culture's truth and demonstrate its discursive and relativistic nature that they cannot be so easily dismissed. By selecting and recombining elements from its own and other genres' history—in particular the narrative devices and iconography of history and the epic, as well as the use of digressions borrowed from pastoral and sentimental fiction—the heroic novel interrogated the axiomatic and unchanging truths contemporaries accepted and it

---

[21] Bertaud, *L'Astrée et Polexandre*, chapters VI and IX.
[22] Mueller, *Les Idées politiques dans le roman héroïque de 1630 à 1670*, p. 33.

developed a new narrative mode for producing truth. This is by no means to suggest that the heroic novel was a revolutionary form—in fact it was quite conservative. However, as we will now see, it developed a narrative style radically restricting interpretive possibility and it consummated the heretofore pragmatic development of the novel by appropriating rules from other genres and formalizing their use in prose fiction.

Polexandre is a novel of over 4,000 pages, and as in much of the fiction that preceded it the principal narrative thread—Polexandre's quest for the Inaccessible Island and Queen Alcidiane—occupies only a small portion of the work. Interwoven stories of secondary characters' lives, which are in turn frequently interrupted by digressions concerning other characters, occupy the greatest part of Gomberville's novel. The use of intercalated narratives and the beginning *in medias res*, however, are only two features that link *Polexandre* to its immediate predecessors. Gomberville did not hesitate to employ the stock narrative and iconographic conventions from sentimental and pastoral fiction. One of the first adventures in which Polexandre engages is his search for Bajazet, the man who had stolen Alcidiane's portrait from him. While the tradition of heroes crossing great distances for the love of a woman they had seen only in portraits dates back to medieval romance, Gomberville uses the motif to establish a tie with Greek epic: he creates a heroine who is so beautiful that, going Helen of Troy one better, even a picture of her face can launch myriad ships. When one of Polexandre's soldiers sees Alcidiane's portrait, he cries out, "There, there is the fatal countenance that caused all the labors we have suffered and which will cause all the perils we have yet to risk" (I, 125).

Gomberville employs many of the stock literary devices available to fiction writers that had already begun to appear archaic or to come under ridicule. The portrait that drives men wild, for example, had already been ruthlessly imprecated by Sorel in his *Francion*.[23] The grottoes at Forez, whose artifice d'Urfé had described as "so deftly contrived to seem natural that one's eye quite often fooled one's judgment" (*L'Astrée*, I, 37), have their *trompe-l'œil* effect matched at the pirates' fortress, which is "a place that nature and art had equally fortified" (*Polexandre*, I, 162); the fortress is

[23] Francion and Nays both fall in love with portraits. In one scene, Nays, looking at Francion's portrait, pronounces the following hyperbolic diatribe:

"a locale that one might justly call the masterpiece of the mind and of the strength of man" (I, 173), and it contains a ceiling consisting of "a concave mirror made of several large panels of Venice glass so industriously placed one next to the other that, through a miracle of perspective, you would think that you were under an extremely high vault" (I, 177–78). *Polexandre* deftly plays human artifice and organic nature off one another.[24] Where the folks at Forez reveled in the artificiality of their world, however, and had recourse to speech primarily because the guarantor of truth and unequivocation—the Fontaine de la Vérité d'Amour—had been rendered inaccessible to them, in Polexandre's universe people continually strive to demystify the artifice surrounding them. In the pirates' lair, for example, it is always clear to what extent human craftwork has embellished nature, whereas at Forez, as we have seen, human craftwork imitated nature so well that the eye could not discern the difference.

When in *Polexandre* the distinction between appearances and reality is not clear, an explanation is warranted, and explanations generally take the form of long narratives that secondary characters inject into the work's *récit*. These narrative explanations order the heroic characters' universe; even Bajazet's army of pirates is a well-disciplined and organized group whose members are called upon to narrate. When Bajazet's senior pirate soldiers are promoted to the rank of captain, Bajazet tells them that their advancement is not yet complete: "Our laws demand that you give us a summary of your life before we give you these last marks of the command to which you have legitimately been called" (I, 428). Not just anyone

---

"'I have been really foolish up until now to love a painting,' she thought to herself. 'Then I found out that the man I loved without ever having seen him had many fewer perfections than people said. Now I can no longer be fooled. I see before my eyes an object worthy of admiration. He is a seigneur of note, of excellent physiognomy, endowed with a fine mind, and what I consider more important, he is of excessive affection—so that I will have no trouble winning him over, as I would have with Floriande.'

While Nays was entertaining such thoughts, Francion was having his own, which centered on loving her eternally as the most perfect lady he had ever known" (*Francion*, p. 356).

[24] Gomberville may, in fact, have had his predecessor d'Urfé in mind. Bertaud has pointed out that Gomberville was an avid reader of *L'Astrée*—the young Gomberville produced, at twenty-five years of age, a continuation of d'Urfé's unfinished novel. See her "De *L'Astrée* au *Polexandre*, pourquoi mourir?," pp. 47–48.

can be a pirate captain—the position is sufficiently prestigious and important to merit a complete background check.

Nothing could be more natural in Polexandre's fifteenth-century world than the long, explanatory narrative, and often those who express the desire to hear an elucidative story are judged for that very reason to be distinguished. When Polexandre (who is in disguise) hears Almaïde's tale relating the death of the beautiful Iphidamante (who is really his brother disguised as a woman), he presses the man for more details. "Almaïde was far from imagining that the man who was speaking to him was Polexandre. He did not reflect much on his agitation, but rather attributed it to that impatient and imprudent curiosity that extraordinary events cause in the most solid and the most circumspect minds" (III, 501). Almaïde considers Polexandre's curiosity perfectly natural, and after only the briefest reflection he agrees to tell his story.

Explanatory narratives often illustrate the true nobility of the frequently disguised characters portrayed in them. Although Mueller's astute political reading of *Polexandre* reveals the attraction heroic fiction may have had for a threatened aristocracy, it fails to distinguish between pastoral romance and the genre of fiction that superseded it: aristocrats had been painting glorified images of themselves in novels since the sentimental fiction of the early seventeenth century and in romance since the twelfth century, and her analysis neglects to account for the specificity of heroic fiction. I want to suggest that the heroic novel differed significantly from its predecessors in more ways than just a change of disguise from shepherds' to warriors' garb. *Polexandre*, with its near wholesale appropriation of characteristics from the ancient epics, dramatically altered the way aristocrats depicted the nature and vitality of their caste: because of the Académie's recent politicization of literary convention and aesthetics, writers who were constrained to produce ideologically approved works arrogated to themselves a classical form and infused it with contemporary partisan ideals. "Epics are systems of political myths," Gilbert Cuthbertson has written,[25] and the formal devices Gomberville appropriated from epic literature contributed to the further codification of seven-

[25] Cuthbertson, *Political Myth and the Epic*, p. 42.

teenth-century fiction as an aristocratic genre. However, as we will
now see, in arrogating the epic's formal and stylistic features, Gomberville also adopted the unequivocal nationalism of the ancient
texts. Thus, the novel continued to develop along class lines, and
since the political utility it prescribed coincided with the Académie's and Richelieu's views on verisimilitude, it remained, at least
for the time being, an unproblematic genre.

It is a commonly held critical tradition that the *Iliad* originated
from stories told of the trade wars between the people of the Troad
and the Achaeans, or from tales of an early Viking invasion of
Greece.[26] Although it seems implausible that over hundreds of years
of narrational embellishment a single, specific historical event remained intact and uncontaminated by details of other incidents, it
is quite likely that some sort of political strife incited storytellers to
select and combine details of valorous actions and embroider them
into a tale of heroic valor. Regardless of which particular historical
details might have motivated the construction of epic narrative, it
seems safe to characterize the classical genre in part as a representation of one cultural group's political and geographical integrity
threatened by the encroachment of a foreign or alien group. More
than a mere articulation of national boundaries, however, early epics helped form and maintain cultural identities. Both the *Iliad* and
the *Aeneid* depict the host culture's formation of a national identity
and its resistance to outside corruption. Epics commonly portray
tales of ritualistic bride-stealing, disguise and recognition, and long
voyages to the homeland; they help solidify feelings of nationalism
and cultural identity. Helen of Troy, for example, wife of the Spar-
tan king Menelaus and arguably the most famous objectified
woman in history, metonymically represents the precariousness of
the Greek culture's ability to retain and control the reproduction of
its cultural identity, and she incites the development of a new type
of cultural hero.[27] In the course of the war over her repossession,
Achilles emerges as a new brand of cultural hero, one who has
rejected the archaic individualistic warrior ethic in favor of a more

[26] See James Nohrnberg's "The *Iliad*"; Richmond Lattimore's preface to his translation of the *Iliad*; and Albert Lord's *The Singer of Tales*, chapter IX.

[27] Cuthbertson argues, for example, that Paris' choice to abduct Helen and forgo
fame or power in war signals the institutionalization of new and reformed cultural
values. "When Paris rejects the traditional values of society, the whole of archaic
Greece is plunged into war," he writes (p. 47).

compassionate, cooperative, and pluralistic ethos. The motifs of disguise and exposure and the return to the homeland, particularly evident in Homer's *Odyssey* and Virgil's *Aeneid*, further develop the notion of a national identity by playing benign depictions of the familiar and recognizable off of the generally malevolent and threatening representations of alien invasions and the malaise of deracination.

Quasi-divine heroes pondered their own mortality and potential oblivion in the *Iliad* and the *Aeneid*, brooding over the question of whether a long but undistinguished life was preferable to a short but glorious one; seventeenth-century French aristocrats faced the potential extinction of their coterie at the hands of both ambitious bourgeois who sought to supplant them and a jealous monarch who attempted to undo them. The heroic Odysseus wandered for years before returning home to his wife, and Polexandre suffered involuntary separation from the woman he loved; like Odysseus' story, Polexandre's includes myriad shipwrecks and impromptu voyages. The return and reintegration that both the ancient and the seventeenth-century texts depict imply a xenophobic longing for a nationalistic identity in which radical otherness loses its power to impinge on the hero's identity. Each of these admittedly superficial resemblances between the ancient, revered epics and Gomberville's novel reveals that whether or not he consciously imitated epic style (and the facts point to just such a deliberate imitation) the decidedly political nature of early nationalistic epics surfaced in his work.

One of the characteristics of epic literature in general and of the *Odyssey* in particular is the narration of past experiences and the construction of a heroic persona. George Lord has demonstrated that Odysseus' construction of fictional personalities at crucial moments serves as a mechanism both for self-defense and for testing the various people he comes across. He argues that Odysseus possesses a "polytropic" self whose protean personality allows him to assume a collective identity, and that his return to the hearth marks an evolution from heroic warrior to fully developed culture hero.[28] I would argue that it is in the construction of a narrative self that *Polexandre* most closely resembles the classical epic tradition, since

[28] Lord, *Trials of the Self*, pp. 18, 23.

not only does the hero attain, through the judicious use and appropriation of narrative, the status of general equivalent of the collective social body, but he also asserts a definitive nationalistic and
ideological use for narrative. Classical epics had been concerned
with constructing a national identity for often radically disparate
social groups forced to unite in a single, culturally diverse nation.
Both the *Iliad* and the *Aeneid* narrate the formation of a collective
social body in the distant past. Gomberville's *Polexandre* represents
a similar attempt to unite a social group headed for antiquation
and dispersion, but its prudent appropriation of politically sanctioned narrative forms helps further codify the conventions of the
budding novelistic form, asserting the control France's aristocracy
maintained on the genre.

In *Polexandre* there is a determined effort to account for every
detail of the past and to integrate each action into a larger scheme
whose narrative significance can become immediately apparent. *Polexandre* effectively reverses *L'Astrée*'s pastoral aesthetic of controlled and ennobling artifice, and represents the end of illusion and
the instantiation of an immediate lucidity achieved through the explanatory narrative. Where deliberately contrived artifice had occupied a significant portion of pastoral fiction, the characters in
Polexandre demand a lucid understanding of each event that befalls
them. These people are not content to discuss the inconstancy of
the heart or the means to convince a paramour how much he or
she is truly loved: they want to understand their world but, as we
will see, they have a quite particular way of understanding it. To
that end, they construct narratives that not only display their ancient nobility, but demystify the apparent randomness of the world
and reveal the natural order into which their lives fit.

Demystification is the driving principle in Polexandre's world and
people's ability to spin an engaging and illuminating tale is as ennobling as their curiosity to hear one. Characters often compete
with one another to demonstrate their own talents as storytellers,
and their proximity to important figures can confer high status. An
old islander engaged to tell what he knows of Polexandre willingly
obliges his listeners, "and to show that he knew how to tell a story,
he so skillfully combined the adventures that Zelmatide, and even
the Vice Roy, despite his chagrin and loss of heart, received great
pleasure" (II, 406–7). Because the ability to relate an engaging and

elucidating narrative can confer status, the Vice Roy, upon the islander's conclusion, picks up the thread of the narrative and demonstrates his own superior knowledge. "What you know about this
is barely enough to merit consideration" (II, 407), he boasts, and
spins out his own extremely long and well informed tale of Polexandre's origins. Characters frequently crop up who pronounce mysterious and troubling admonitions, but their interlocutors know
that they must wait to hear the complete story from an appropriate,
socially sanctioned narrator. "Flee this desirable enemy [Polex-
andre] and come learn things which, without such a fatal meeting,
would scarcely seem believable," an unknown old woman tells Almanzaïre. Although the latter is completely mystified ("Almanzaïre
understood nothing of the old woman's speech" [III, 190]), she fails
to demand an explanation, and waits to get the story from Alma-
trée, who, though dying and perhaps unable to deliver the complete
tale, is nevertheless culturally prescribed to narrate.

Telling relevant and interesting stories, however, never suffices in
and of itself to confer honor. It is a culturally determined activity
bestowing prestige only upon those whose birth and situation make
them already worthy. When a foreign ship captain is asked to clarify some of the details in Zabaïm's tale, he begins in the customary
way: "The captain, following the unhappy custom of those who
come from far away, did not want to leave out even the most insignificant detail in his voyage; he was about to begin a terribly boring
tale when Zabaïm ordered him to respond succinctly to his two
questions" (III, 337–38). The intolerance with which the captain's
attempt to narrate is met reveals that the explanatory narrative is
the privileged property of a specific cultural group; ownership depends on nationality and above all on class.

This is not to suggest, of course, that only nobles tell stories in
Polexandre. Frequently characters of questionable birth or origin,
like the captain noted above, are called upon to tell stories whose
informational content is crucial to the noble characters. When this
is the case, a valorized character generally appropriates the tale and
translates it into terms with which the other noble characters can
identify. The novel's first long intercalated tale is the story of Almanzor's suicide over Alcidiane's indifference to him. Significantly,
it is Almanzor's mute servant who delivers this tale, in writing, and
his lack of a voice represents his disenfranchisement from the he-

roic theater in which he has only a cameo appearance. Two volumes later Polexandre appropriates the mute's tale in a significantly abridged version but retains its affect for his listeners. Paring down an 80-page tale to less than three pages, Polexandre reintegrates the mute's story into the discursive framework of his own life story, relating only those aspects that he can show have a particular significance for both the present and the future. His quest for Queen Alcidiane becomes the overarching narrative that structures the lives and worldviews of each and every individual he encounters as each of them relates stories that will eventually be shown, in retrospect, to have led to his becoming king. When he finishes his recounting of the mute's tale his listeners understand the world better and the significance it has for their lives:

> Almanzaïre sighed several times while Polexandre was telling this tale, and when he had finished, she said, directing her eyes toward heaven, "Almighty God, you have shown us your justice in the death of the child of corruption; now let your mercy shine forth in the recognition of the child of grace. The crime is punished; allow the criminals to recognize one another and let things finally get back on the course you have set for them, after such great disorder." (III, 188)

In his appropriation and condensation of the mute's tale, Polexandre gives his own life a narrative sense. Almanzaïre recognizes that sense, for she knows the narrative conventions, and immediately apprehends the inherent meaning that must inevitably result from previous acts. Life for these people has innate significance, and they seem to believe that it is only a matter of time before the plot gets back on track and plays itself out to its ultimate narrative closure.

The cultural and class specificity of the explanatory narratives establishes the epistemological conditions and limitations in Polexandre's world. Characters who recount past events make those events accessible to their listeners, to be sure. More importantly, however, the existence of a sanctioned mode of telling and the privilege of narrating that particular individuals enjoy show that the past and the sense that it has for the present and the future can be structured according to a specific worldview. Characters who produce or appropriate explanatory narratives overlay series of narrative fragments and, like the historian, they "find" the plot the entire complex contains. In addition, they construct their tales in such a way that not only does the plot seem self-evident, but so too does the reasoning they provide to explain the moral and political causality behind the events. Characters with the privilege to narrate thus guarantee the truth and interpretation of their tales. The captain cited above is not permitted to spin a long tale; all that he may contribute is a brief response to two precise questions. Zabaïm controls the sense and the affect of the captain's tale and it is up to him to establish the significance of the story for the current situation and for the people involved.

For as long and disjointed as many of the intercalated stories in *Polexandre* might appear, the point is that it is not the simple capacity to keep telling that is revered, but the aptitude for revealing the profound and inherent sense each action has for the world as this restricted and privileged group of inhabitants understands it. Cultural and class differences not only pass unrecognized but are banished from the scene. Each valorized narrative is part of a systematic attempt to reveal more of the world's deep structures, and characters seem to believe that it is only a matter of time and the passing of words before everything falls into place and a perfect epistemological transparency establishes itself. Indeed, the continual desire for increased narrative acquisition suggests that what the inhabitants of Polexandre's world are seeking is the very end of epistemology itself: they pursue an immediate adequation between knowledge and its object. The end of the story would be the end of knowledge's somewhat limited charge merely of constructing its object in favor of addressing it directly. Each narrative detail, each unmasking of a character in disguise, each interpretation of an individual's motives furthers the illusion that an immediate lucidity is imminent. That lucidity comes about at the work's end when Polexandre is recognized by all as Alcidiane's rightful king and explanatory narratives become superfluous: "I knew that you planned to justify all that you have done," Alcidiane tells Polexandre. "But there is no need for that. The absolute Power who has complete control over our lives is your justification" (V, 1304).

Characters' construction of an overarching narrative that orders each of the actions in *Polexandre* suggests that they structure their lives according to the principles of *vraisemblance*. Their intercalated narratives bestow on the existing world order an increasingly restricted structure that molds their reality in the resolutely heroic light of contemporary fiction. Edward Turk, in the most erudite and useful study on *Polexandre* we have available, writes that the novel's intercalated narratives restore ordered reflection to series of instinctive and impulsive acts. He characterizes the work as "an adventure novel whose most basic rhythmic pattern is the quick encounter with brute realities requiring extended explanations in the form of stories of limited reliability." [29] Although Turk provides examples of what he considers unreliable intercalated narratives, in general they do not involve factual inaccuracy but omitted details that emerge later after the initial telling. The tales seem unreliable, I would argue, only to the extent that they are generally fragments, or more accurately metonyms, of the complete story. Turk points out that the characters in *Polexandre* "are primarily speakers and auditors, and only secondarily people concerned with nonverbal activities" (33), which, I think, underscores the significance that providing narrative structure has for the construction of *vraisemblance* in the characters' lives. In short, the people in Polexandre's milieu continually attempt to inhabit not a world but a text; they want to be characters in a story based on seventeenth-century ideological and aesthetic discourses.

People cause themselves to be cast as characters in Polexandre's story in order to take part in the construction of a single and unequivocal discourse charged with articulating reality. That discourse provides the illusion, at the work's end, that verisimilar narrative can be coincidental with its referent if narrators respect the epistemological and political conditions of narrating. When, finally, explanatory narratives become redundant and Polexandre accedes to the throne, his empowerment is seen to be divinely ordained ("The absolute Power who has complete control over our lives is your justification") just as were the circumstances leading to Polexandre's landing on the Inaccessible Island—a storm tossed him there when all attempts to navigate to the locale proved futile (V, 1071). The novel's intercalated narratives progressively illuminate Polexandre's natural destiny as legitimate ruler, and the unambiguous ending suggests that the tales, while useful for elucidating the conditions of knowing in Polexandre's world, are fundamentally

---

[29] Turk, *Baroque Fiction-Making*, p. 45. Turk's book has two indispensable appendixes containing a brief plot sketch of *Polexandre* and a detailed outline of the novel's intercalated narratives.

superfluous because in any event everyone knew the final outcome: Polexandre's crowning as king. That is, the intercalated stories in *Polexandre* seem able only to illustrate the inevitable. At the end of the novel Polexandre's inexorable and divinely ordained empowerment is described:

> [God] sends storms, he uncovers reefs, and causes shipwrecks, so that a great king, having lost all marks of his dignity, effectively becomes a slave, and in this unfortunate condition wanders incessantly in the deserts of Africa. . . . God only made Polexandre a slave to show that His decrees are absolute, and at the same time to prepare for him a straight and wide road that might easily lead him to the auspicious abode, an abode where neither labors nor vigils nor searches would ever have led him. (V, 1268–69)

This final explanatory narrative provides the work's narrative closure. Each ostensible obstacle was imbued with a profound and inherent significance, and what appeared to be an obstacle was, in fact, a necessary step toward return and reintegration.

Gomberville refers to *Polexandre* as a "Political and moral story [*histoire Politique & Morale*]" in the preface to the work's third volume. We can use this characterization to reconcile an allegorical reading of the novel which, like Mueller's, considers the work an extended reflection of the aristocracy's relationship to the monarchy, with a politically aesthetic reading that gives the novel not just a reflecting but a formative capacity. If, as Mueller suggests, Gomberville's aristocratic reading audience found in *Polexandre* a glamorous reflection of their indispensability to the monarchy and to the state as well as an acknowledgment that they helped protect French royalty, they also needed to acknowledge the depiction of the absolutist monarchy that the novel tenaciously maintains. It seems singularly unsatisfying in this complex work that interrogates the conditions of knowledge and their relationship to privileged or valorized narrative modes merely to suggest that it reflects aristocratic psychology or ideology. *Polexandre* reveals that the way a culture understands itself is directly linked to the manners of narrating it has at its disposal; more significantly, the novel shows that modes of narrative are hierarchically arranged and that tellers take a position in that hierarchy. A speaker's discursive authority— and hence the validity attached to his or her tale—depends ultimately on his or her social and cultural situation. Thus, I would argue, *Polexandre* not only reflected contemporary ideology, but helped shape it in the work's careful hierarchization of narrative and ideological modes.

Furthermore, the ampersand uniting "Politique" with "Morale" in Gomberville's description of the work ensconces *Polexandre* in the tradition of *vraisemblance* that the Académie Française had inaugurated and that writers like Desmaretz and La Mesnardière had continued. That is, Gomberville claims for his work a moral utility that is complemented by an ideological practicality, and the ideological imperative he causes his work to articulate is the protection and glorification of the French monarchy. Dedicating his work in the preface to the first volume to Louis, Gomberville intends Polexandre's exploits to reflect the moral and political rectitude of the king. "When I read that for the general welfare of the world [Polexandre] brings terror and death to the realm of the tyrants and then declares himself the universal Protector of oppressed innocence . . . I cannot help but believe either that Polexandre is Louis the Just or that he is another of his manifestations [*ou que c'est un autre luy-mesme*]" (I, "Au Roy").

Finally, Gomberville's appropriation of the formal features of the epic hypostatizes the pragmatic development of the novel as an aristocratic genre by codifying its overt political stances within the language of an aesthetic discourse. Polexandre's heroic deeds and his natural and inevitable rise to power not only allegorize Louis' absolutism, but they do so in a mock historical narrative which, because it is set in the distant past, effectively prevents a reassessment of the values the work privileges.[30] That is, the work's explanatory narratives that principal, valorized characters either relate or appropriate from others establish the work's epistemological framework; all action reveals itself to have contributed to Polexandre's final glory, and there is no knowledge but that which pertains to the title character's eventual empowerment. Thus, the conditions of knowledge relate only to Polexandre's rise to the throne. The work's explanatory narratives provide a retrospective yet unequivocal and immutable justification of absolutism; they are the metonyms of the unironic and univocal discourse that aristocratic

[30] See Mikhail Bakhtin, "Epic and Novel," in *The Dialogic Imagination*, pp. 19–24, for a discussion of temporality in the epic and the novel. Bakhtin's theories of the epic and the novel will be readdressed in the following chapter.

fiction had been erecting since its inception in sentimental novels. *Polexandre*, with its insistence on exegesis and demystification and its wholesale appropriation of the formal features of the classical epic, reified the unsystematic and pragmatic conventions of earlier aristocratic fiction. It conventionalized them into a codified novelistic language whose aesthetic ideology promulgated a utilitarian *vraisemblance* concerned with articulating and promoting the dominant classes' political interests.

Gomberville's attempt to construct an unironic and univocal novelistic language depends on demonstrating a direct adequation between representation and referent. The attempt to demystify appearances to establish the epistemological and ideological framework of novelistic discourse is no more apparent than in his theoretical discussions of the work's goals. In the preface to the third volume, he theorizes the need to construct an unequivocal form of narrative:

> I know that there is nothing so pure which, through an ingenious corruption at the hands of evildoers, cannot be made impure; nor is there anything so innocent which, through a fearful timidity, imbeciles cannot make into a subject of scandal and an occasion of sin. This is why in giving to the public a book that can be diversely interpreted, I felt the need to consider these two sorts of sicknesses and to work with incessant care on equally dangerous sorts of wounds. In order not to make a mistake in such a delicate and important operation, I consulted the examples of the best centuries and the practice of the most excellent masters, and by an excess of good fortune, I encountered for both of these spiritual sicknesses remedies that have been judged foolproof by oracles that have never been wrong. (III, "Preface")

Attempting in proleptic fashion to foreclose the untoward interpretations of political rivals, Gomberville endeavors to attain an unequivocal adequation of representation and referent, an endeavor he continues in the "Advertissement aux honnestes gens" (Preface to honorable people) concluding the work in which he debunks the mysteries surrounding some of the more fantastic scenes.[31] Gom-

---

[31] For example, Gomberville demystifies the location of the Inaccessible Island by attempting to provide it with real geographical coordinates: "I will say that Alcidiane's isle must be the famous Isle of Felicity that Diodorus Siculus described at the end of the third book of his tale. He tells us the wonderful adventure in which a Greek merchant named Iambole was blown to this happy island. . . . If Iambole's

berville claims to imitate the ancient masters and his unequivocal
novelistic discourse strives to eradicate the possibility of conflicting
interpretations.

Gomberville codified an aristocratic discourse of fiction by implicitly following Boisrobert's advice to cast novels in the form of
epics. Claiming, as did most of his successors, to imitate the ancient
masters as well as to base his work in historical fact, he propounded an unequivocally ideological form of fiction that attempted to ward off any interpretation which might compete with
the principles and the spirit of the Académie's politicized version of
vraisemblance. Adhering to the stylistic and literary conventions of
a sanctioned literary form dating back to antiquity, he helped legitimize the novel form by inserting it into literary history and giving
it a past. Both Gomberville and Mlle de Scudéry, as we saw above,
refer back to the masters whose works served as paradigms for
infallible literary excellence. Both writers strove to imitate those
formidable masters in order to achieve the literary legitimacy the
classics enjoyed. In order to achieve ideological legitimacy, however, they heeded the Académie's definition of *vraisemblance*. The
novelistic discourse they consequently promulgated effectively became the discourse of the master, the aesthetically and ideologically
codified fictive form put forth as unequivocal and unironic; the discourse of the master is not subject to interpretation, as Gomberville
implicitly claims, unless such interpretation shares the epistemology of the work to which it is applied. The heroic novel, then,
capped off the process of defining the new genre of fiction by borrowing formal rules from existing genres and subjecting them to
the ideological constraints of contemporary literary practice. Putting an end to the precious artifice of early fiction, authors attempted to demonstrate that if their works were not entirely fac-
tually accurate, the adequation they did achieve between representation and referent was cultural—that is, moral and political—
rather than literal.[32]

---

miraculous island is not in fact the Inaccessible Island, it is at least its keen representation" (V, 1339–41).

[32] Bannister makes a similar claim for the use of history in heroic novels. He
argues that the respect afforded history among the nobility, in particular the *noblesse
de robe*, derived from the fact that history was charged with depicting not so much
factual truth but moral truth. "History was seen as a series of memorable incidents
to be studied in isolation rather than as a continuum," he writes, "and consequently

However much heroic fiction appropriated the stylistic and sua-
sive devices of historiography and the epic, novels remained a marginal literary genre—Chapelain's embarrassment at being discovered reading a work of fiction, recounted in his "De la lecture des
vieux romans," manifests this. Writing to Gondi, Cardinal de Retz,
Chapelain documents the frivolity with which novels were generally associated when he describes the work in question as one "you
have no doubt heard about but which you have most likely never
been tempted to read" (164). Yet however marginal novels remained, it is striking to note the degree to which history and fiction
resembled one another in the middle years of the seventeenth century. Fiction writers sought shelter in the license that the illusion of
historical truth could afford them; it is equally true, however, that
historians gleaned from novelists many of the techniques of *vraisemblance* they required to assure their works' smooth and unproblematic reception. Royal historians, most of whom purchased
the office in part to increase their prestige and influence, needed the
illusion of truth in order to demonstrate their own proximity to the
king and involvement in affairs of the state.[33] The relative preponderance of fictional narrative and aristocratic readers' near wholesale acceptance of it contributed to altering the narrative mode
most likely to appeal to those readers. While royal historians
needed to convey their intimate knowledge of state secrets, they
could only do so if their works were read; this accounts, in part,
for history's appropriation of the tactics of fiction that readers
found pleasing. The heroic novel's implication that narrative could,
under specific conditions, reproduce reality directly in an unmediated and unequivocal fashion was appropriated by historians
who needed a similar claim in order to appeal both to their readers
and to their patron. While history and fiction reinforced and legitimated one another and resembled each other more and more,
both depended on what Thomas Pavel has called an inference system allowing readers to relate narrative events to historical ones.[34]
That is, works in both genres needed to appear *vraisemblable*, manifesting an intimate relationship to the moral and ideological sys-

---

tended to be anecdotal in its presentation: the historian aimed to build up a picture,
using a variety of factual, or at least generally accredited, data, to produce the desired edifying effect" (*Privileged Mortals*, pp. 91–92).

[33] See Harth, *Ideology and Culture*, pp. 135–39.

[34] Thomas Pavel, *Fictional Worlds*, p. 17.

tems of the day, but they also required a direct line to a touchstone of factual accuracy that would keep them from collapsing into speculative philosophical works or political or moral treatises. The intuitive difference between history and fiction—that of their relationship to referentially verifiable fact—disappeared, and this had a paradoxically legitimating and destabilizing effect on the novel. While some believed that the novel's use of verifiable fact might make it a more palatable didactic tool, others feared that the lack of distinction between the two genres would make truth itself obsolete. A brief return to the work of François Eudes de Mézeray will illustrate the radically new conception of narrative that resulted from the rapprochement of history and fiction.

Mézeray's fairy-tale rendition of Clovis and Clothilde's wedding is only one of dozens of examples of the historian's attempt to make his voluminous history of France more *vraisemblable*. Throughout the first volume of the *Histoire de France*, France's early kings witness almost daily the astonishing and miraculous signs from heaven that their rule is divinely countenanced. Frequently the signs recall the ancient epics, particularly the *Aeneid*. When Clovis sets off to fight the Arians, for example, his army cannot find a way to cross the river barring their path; then "without being chased, a deer ran out of the nearby forest and showed him the best place to cross" (I, 35). Charlemagne receives the most frequent signs of divine intervention in the form of miracles that recall Biblical traditions. Faced once with a crippling drought, he and his army happen upon a ravine that in the absence of any rain suddenly fills itself with enough water to sustain the troops (I, 165). Charles' death, however, occasions the most astonishing miracles:

> For three years the sun was obscured by several eclipses, and for eight days one could see in the sun a black spot; the bridge he had built over the Rhine near Mayence burned in three hours, and the palace at Aix shook, causing the beams and the floorboards in the chamber to creak as though they were about to break; the chapel where he was buried was struck by lightning, and even the inscription inside the chapel bearing the name of this prince who had built it was erased by a bolt of lightning at the juncture of the words *Princeps Carolus*. (I, 202–3)

Mézeray's frequent descriptions of the supernatural signs that either revealed to the early French kings the action they should take or sanctioned their decisions with marks of approval bring to mind Herodotus' repeated reports of oracular prophecy. In Herodotus' *Histories* leaders consult the oracles at every turn to decide upon a course of action, yet the oracles are always ironic and misleading. One might recall Croesus, who consulted the oracle before beginning a huge military campaign and learned that he would bring down a great kingdom. That kingdom, of course, was his own.[35] Unlike Herodotus, however, Mézeray avoids any trace of irony; it would seem counterproductive for him to reveal, as his classical ancestor had, the possibility of equivocation in language. Heroic fiction had begun to demystify the artifice popular in pastoral fiction and to create the illusion of a master discourse, a direct adequation between narrative and its referent eschewing interpretation. Mézeray works to restrict reader interpretation in his history to achieve a similarly unequivocal discourse.

The second and third volumes of Mézeray's work rely less on the presence of divine intervention to demonstrate the ascendancy of French absolutism, and depend more on the spectacle of noble splendor and might. Narrative descriptions in the last two volumes of the work closely resemble the style of heroic fiction and Mézeray seems to have borrowed from Gomberville and the Scudérys the tools for describing battles and constructing portraits. His description of François I and Henry of England is particularly striking, and it merits citing at length:

> The two kings met in the agreed upon site, each mounted on a Spanish horse and accompanied by innumerable nobles. . . . Because they had brought with them the most beautiful women from their estates, each one attractively dressed, and the most beautiful Nobility ever assembled, an extravagance of riches from the two kingdoms was laid out on display: so much so that, according to DuBellay, they brought their forests, fields, and mills on their people's shoulders, and the richest fabrics seemed common there; the assembly has, in fact, since been called the Camp of Golden Cloth. . . . The kings . . . jousted for ten or twelve days, to the universal delight of the spectators. After spending a long time deciding whether to admire the pomp, the gold and jewels shining from all quarters, the address and gallantry of so many brave knights, or the superb beauty of the ladies watching from the gallery, the spectators cast their attention on the countenances and actions of these two great kings. (II, 404)

[35] Herodotus, *The Histories*, pp. 58–80.

The display of such military prowess must have been quite a sight. More arresting still, it seems to me, would have been the sight of forests, fields, and mills borne on the shoulders of the kings' subjects. Yet for all of this Mézeray doggedly persists in the notion that his narrative is a believable tale strictly adhering to the traditional principles of *vraisemblance*. One can easily mark Mézeray's belief in the verisimilitude of his tale by noting the passages in which he explicitly and self-consciously deviates from *vraisemblance*. When he describes the famine during the reign of Philippe I, for example, he relates the accompanying natural disasters: eclipses, firestorms and meteor showers, flaming clouds of butterflies, and crosses mysteriously appearing on the clothing of many Christians. He closes this bizarre litany of prodigious occurrences with a disclaimer that reveals his conviction in the verisimilitude of all that he has related thus far: "I am omitting several other marvels because they are not *vray-semblable*, although it is possible that they are true" (I, 420).

We need to keep in mind the important distinction between verisimilitude and truth that Mézeray is careful to maintain when we evaluate the degree to which his narrative style keeps to contemporary standards of *vraisemblance*. It may be belaboring the point a bit, but it is important to underscore the social and political, as opposed to the factual, exigencies of seventeenth-century *vraisemblance*. Boisrobert had already referred to historians' "harmful truths" ("Advis"), and Desmaretz had observed that "the truth of history all by itself is dry and lacking grace" ("Préface"); these comments show that history needed to embellish the truth in order to present an acceptably complimentary image of the king. The historian, just as much as the novelist, was writing for a specific social and political group interested in the essentially transhistorical truth of its own hegemony and ascendancy. The historian's work was complicated by the fact that he received his pension from the king and thus needed to compose his narrative in such a way that royal flaws or miscreant behavior could be seen as virtues serving the best interests of the people. Mézeray concludes his monumental work with the peace treaty of Vervins signed in 1598; he reminds his readers of this lofty purpose and underscores the ultimately political truth that his history was charged with reproducing:

Thus a long and cruel war, which for thirty-nine years had rent France with the furor of civil and foreign arms, finally ceded to a profound and happy peace. During that time of peace the king applied himself with a marvelous kindness and with careful ministrations rarely found in kings to repairing the ruins of his state; he reestablished in no time at all justice, security, and abundance, and earned for himself the title of the Great. And well he deserved it, since A PEOPLE'S FELICITY IS THE TRUE GREATNESS OF A SOVEREIGN. (III, 1232)

In 1598 the tensions between the monarchy and the aristocracy were just beginning. In 1651, however, the year these lines were published, the acrimonious events of the Fronde were at fever pitch. The final sententious truth with which Mézeray closes his 3,000-page history reveals the work's point: that the accurate and exhaustive account of France's past is less important than elaborating, in this period of tremendous strife, the grandeur and justice of Louis XIV, Mézeray's king and patron. Although Mézeray's history of France concludes at the beginning of the seventeenth century and thus does not detail the events of the Fronde, it is easy to view his historical account of the French monarchy, particularly in light of its closing paragraph, as a revisionist attempt to recast the throne as the defense and bulwark of the nation, the very image the mutinous nobles had attempted to appropriate for themselves. Mézeray related the immediate steps the king undertook to restore the physical and political well-being of the nation after the treaty of Vervins, effectively effacing all traces of a struggle. Projecting to readers during a time of intense political struggle this antebellum image of political harmony as well as the sententious truth that subjects' happiness is the grandeur of their monarch can only be viewed as the most blatant form of propaganda.

Or as the most refined form of *vraisemblance*. The very undecidability of this truthful representation of politics or this political representation of truth points to an unmitigated contamination of ideology and aesthetics. The heroic novel and historiography had evolved in such a way that there was virtually no formal way to distinguish between them: they took similar subject matter, told their stories in the same cadences and using the same narrative devices, and they both reported characters' speech in direct discourse, a device historians had been using since Thucydides. In addition, since both history and fiction in the seventeenth century were produced by and largely for members of the ruling class, they encoded their ideological concerns in a similar manner. In both narrative forms, causality was expressed in terms of existing, valorized narrative structures, and in both forms causal narratives were designed to valorize the dominant ideological configuration. In short, the lack of distinction between the two forms of narrative arose for two principal reasons. On the one hand, history had long been the form of narrative charged with representing reality, and since reality had no discernible form it only made sense that history should not, either. To establish specific formal constraints any more specific than La Popelinière's general characterization of history as the narration of the most notable human actions would be to acknowledge and make explicit the historian's license to invent whatever he pleased. Although the system of patronage in seventeenth-century France did, in fact, give such a license to historians, the point was that the historian had to supply the appearance of neutrality and objectivity.

On the other hand, since novelists needed to shelter themselves from the criticism that their works were mere frivolities with no inherent moral or didactic value, the illusion of historical truth gave them an air of legitimacy. The narrative style that developed in heroic fiction, best exemplified in Gomberville's *Polexandre*, appropriated history's claim to clear, objective truth by constructing it directly in a narrative style that would admit little conflicting interpretation. Authors freely built complex historical worlds based on contemporary notions of truth and then used the intercalated narrative to imbricate narrative fragments in such a way that not only would the plot seem self-evident, but so too would characters' interpretations of the moral and political causality behind the events. If the plots in heroic novels were "found," to use White's characterization of the embarrassment of history, the causality behind such plots was always constructed to give the appearance of having been divinely ordained.

Heroic fiction gave history the narrative tools it needed to embellish the truth and acquire a more formal perfection, thus augmenting the grandeur of the patron to whom it was dedicated. History provided fiction with an alienated referential object and hence its own air of legitimacy. Both forms relied heavily on *vraisemblance*, but we might hazard here a new definition of *vraisemblance* as it was conceived in the middle decades of the seventeenth century. As opposed to history-like or even "realistic," *vraisemblance* was an intensely politicized version of the old aphorism "suspension of disbelief." It signaled the narrative composition of a tale that readers could believe, but it was so intricately encoded for a specific ideology that stories departing from the narrative causality of aristocratic hegemony that sentimental, pastoral, and heroic fiction had established would seem fantastic. In other words, however formally plausible a work might be, if its implicit or explicit narrative causality was not based on aristocratic or noble ascendancy, it was found to be *invraisemblable*. Works that depicted bizarre coincidences or wildly unlikely events were believable as long as the motive for such events derived from innate noble virtue. Many of Mézeray's accounts of royal splendor or divine intervention can test a reader's patience; several of them are pure hogwash. They are, nevertheless, rarely obtrusive enough to impede a reader's ability to follow the tale, and they always demonstrate the monarchy's inherent justice and splendor. The same is true of Gomberville's descriptions of Polexandre's valor.

There is, thus, little in the way of formal characteristics that can help us understand the difference between seventeenth-century history and fiction. Both used ostensible facts to support the moral truths they tendered, and both constructed expressive narrative causalities—that is, allegorical reflections of a larger, overarching structure—that would restrict the possibility of interpretation conflicting with their own ideological stances.[36] In addition, both construed *vraisemblance* to designate not "realism" as we as moderns understand it, but a believability based on contemporary sententious moral and political truths. Erica Harth attempts to describe how *vraisemblance* served both history and fiction, and like many she finds its nature paradoxical:

> Both true and fictional narrative needed the moral support of verisimilitude. In history, it padded truth so as to present an acceptable image of the great; in fiction, it helped to strengthen the illusion of truth by imitating history. For both, it provided decorum in the tradition of classical antiquity: reflections, *sententiae*, *harangues*, and so

[36] I am borrowing the term "expressive causality" from Fredric Jameson's modification of Louis Althusser's notion. I will return to the concept in Chapter 4.

on—all the paraphernalia of morality which justified the utility of
history but added to it the embellishments of fiction, and modified
the pleasure of fiction in the direction of historical utility. The paradoxical nature of verisimilitude is such that it can support either fact
or fable. (146)

There is, I have argued, no real paradox in *vraisemblance*'s capacity
to support either history or fiction. *Vraisemblance* was simply an
ideologically valorized narrative mode that could buttress a variety
of genres. It connoted not necessarily what was believable in narrative, but what was appropriate. In fact, to search for a fundamental difference between fictional and historical *vraisemblance* is to
misconstrue the sense of the word, particularly in light of the fact
that *vraisemblance* not only obtained for the practically identical
genres of history and fiction, but for tragedy as well.[37] It is only our
modern notion that history and fiction differ quite radically, namely
in the presence or absence of a verifiable external referent, that
causes us to search for a difference in seventeenth-century narrative
modes.

The heroic novel brought to an end what I have called the pragmatic development of early modern French fiction by assigning
rules and paradigms to the young literary form. Early manifestations of French prose fiction tendered formulaic stories of minimal
causal narrative sequence; the ritualistic nature of tragic and sentimental fiction suggests that their popularity stemmed from their

---

[37] Corneille, for example, learned the hard way how important the mode was for
tragedy. Ten years after the debacle of his *Cid* he wrote in the preface to *Héraclius*:
"Here is an audacious charge on history, from which you will recognize nothing in
this tragedy except the order of the succession of emperors" (Pierre Corneille, *Héraclius*, "Au lecteur," p. 439). Corneille continues, describing why he altered historical fact: "I will not take the trouble to justify the license I have taken: the result
justifies it enough, and the examples from the ancients that I reported in *Rodogune*
seem to legitimate it sufficiently; but to speak plainly, I would not advise anyone to
take it as an example. That would be quite a risk, and one is not always successful;
and in a project of this nature, what a happy success causes to pass for inventive
courage, an unhappy one makes seem ridiculously fearful."
Similarly, Racine argues in the preface to *Iphigénie* that there exists a cultural
continuity between the ancient Greeks and contemporary Parisians allowing his
work to be not only believed but appreciated for its emotional intensity as well: "I
recognized with pleasure, through the effect produced on our theater by everything
I imitated either in Homer or Euripides, that good sense and reason have been the
same in all centuries. Parisian taste is the same as that of Athens. My audience was
moved by the same things that brought tears to the eyes of the wisest people of
Greece" (Jean Racine, *Iphigénie*, "Préface," p. 133).

rehearsal and subsequent subdual of the anxieties of aristocratic obsolescence. Early seventeenth-century fiction had no codified rules. In their place it had a complex of obdurate formulas, monotonous plots, and prosaic characters that authors appropriated in a stultifying series of works that seem, for better or for worse, to have responded to readers' demands for social validation. More complex pastoral fiction developed beginning in the second decade of the century, and if authors borrowed their plots and characters from existing fiction and medieval romance, the narratives they developed adhered less rigidly to previous models. D'Urfé introduced highly encrypted artifice into fiction; his aristocratic readers made themselves the referents of his work by decoding and imitating his iconography. Pastoral fiction mystified the tools and mechanics of social domination, making them accessible only to those who possessed the cultural key. If *L'Astrée*'s characters struggled through the ambiguities and ironies of symbolic communication, its readers reveled in the transparency of its ideology which heralded a historical continuity with feudal times in an unevolving narrative of noble probity.

In the 1620's and 1630's, writers began to distance themselves from their craft and to construct descriptive and prescriptive analyses of fiction. Criticism and theory helped naturalize the young genre, and by alienating authors from their works they mitigated the obtrusively aristocratic iconography that had permeated fiction for almost a century. Authors were concerned with adhering to temporal and geographic coordinates; weary of the implausibility and anachronisms of their forebears' works, they developed a working notion of *vraisemblance* that was modified and conventionalized, in official form, by the Académie Française. Beginning in the 1640's, literary works needed to be not only formally regular, but ideologically correct.

With Gomberville's *Polexandre*, the move to regularize the novel was complete. Gomberville attempted a formal legitimation of the novel by appropriating techniques from two of the literary genres the Académie prized, history and the epic. More significant than his effort to imitate the ancient masters, however, was his attempt to control in rigid fashion readers' interpretation of the work. Gomberville aimed at constructing a master discourse, one of unequivocal and unironic dimensions, by borrowing the epic's national protectionism and history's claim to veracity. He strove to assure the unambiguous transmission of his moral and political truth by building a complex narrative sequence—practically unheard of in earlier works—and then linking that sequence to an explanation of its causality. The imbrication of event and interpretation was designed to allow readers into the text with no way out other than through the interpretation Gomberville had designed.

Chapter 4 The Alienation and
            Commodification of the Novel

In the preceding chapters I have emphasized the thematic and semantic components of seventeenth-century fiction that provided
the genre with enough ideological coherence to stabilize its form. I
have labeled the early modern novel an aristocratic genre, identifying the features that gave it its particular ideological thrust. Tales
of imperiled family status and avenged nobility highlighted early
tragic fiction, and the return and reintegration of traditional aristocratic values graced sentimental novels. *L'Astrée* linked contemporary cultural practices with medieval feudal systems and legitimated readers' aggrandized self-images by allowing them to become the work's external referents. The semantic conception of
genre that this thematic analysis of early modern French fiction
inspires supports the inveterate notion of genre as a relay or contract between writer and reader; one of the primary functions of
such a relay or contract is to specify the range of acceptable interpretations for a given work.[1] A complex of recurrent narrative patterns aligns readers' responses to texts and fixes them in a more or
less stable configuration informing not only how a particular genre
is to be received, but also the genre's relationship to existing literary
practices. Marcelin Pleynet has called the implicit or explicit spec-
ification of a work's genre its "master word" (*maître mot*), and he
argues that this master word often reduces a work to an interpretive practice that allows it to produce as well as to be produced by

[1] For variations on the idea of genre as a relay or contract between writer and
reader, one of whose fundamental purposes is to delimit possible interpretations, see
Jameson's "Magical Narratives" in *The Political Unconscious*, pp. 103–50; and
Tzvetan Todorov, *Introduction à la littérature fantastique*, pp. 10–23.

its generic category.[2] The semantic theory of genre can be a powerful tool for analyzing the hermeneutic imperatives texts issue their readers; it is equally valuable for increasing our understanding of how works construct their own reading audiences by tendering referential hooks directed at specific groups. Nevertheless, traditional genre criticism frequently finds itself in the awkward situation of explaining its taxonomic classifications as a function of their constituent elements, and individual texts as a function of the overarching literary forms under whose aegis they were produced. If genres and their component works mutually determine one another's identity, it is difficult to explain the rise of new genres or the situations of texts that do not readily lend themselves to classificatory statements.

In order to explain the development of new genres or the mutation of existing ones, we need to consider them historically and dialectically in their interaction with other forms of representation. I have so far been concerned with articulating the early modern novel as an aristocratic literary form, and I have shown how early seventeenth-century fiction was politically aligned with the conservative ideology of France's aristocracy. What remains to be seen, however, is why prose fiction in particular served to express the aristocracy's political and ideological concerns, and how an upwardly mobile middle class later succeeded in appropriating fiction for its own ideological ends. In short, we need to consider form, the novel's aesthetic malleability, as a necessary precondition of its rise to literary hegemony. Consequently, in this chapter I will consider the relationship between the novel's form and its early ideological mission. If we look closely at the history of prose narrative in France, we perceive a complex interaction among various signifying practices; this interaction forms the basis of what Pleynet and others have called a genre's intertextuality. This intertextuality will afford a glimpse of why prose fiction encoded conservative aristocratic concerns in the early years of the seventeenth century, and how the bourgeoisie appropriated the genre for its own ends.

We might justifiably identify tragic and sentimental fiction as continuations of earlier fiction, in particular the work of François Rabelais, Marguerite de Navarre, or Miguel de Cervantes. Each of

[2] Pleynet, "La Poésie doit avoir pour but . . . ," pp. 95–100.

these writers produced lengthy narratives in prose involving complex and extended plots loosely based on a causal sequence of events, and all of them make rather bold claims about the truth of their tales. Rabelais concludes the "Prologue de l'auteur" of his *Pantagruel* (1532) with the brutal admonition: "And like Sodom and Gomorrah may you fall into a pit of sulphur and fire if you do not steadfastly believe all that I tell you in the present *Chronicle!*" [3] Marguerite de Navarre is far less strident in asserting the relationship that the tales in her *Heptaméron* (1560) have to verifiable truth; she merely insinuates as much in the prologue and in the guise of her character Parlamente, who proposes the project of telling tales like those in Boccaccio's *Decameron*. Parlamente, however, specifies that none of her friends "will write any tale that is not verifiable truth," and she also submits that each person "will tell some story that he has seen or heard from a trustworthy man." [4] Finally, Cervantes avers in the first paragraph of *Don Quixote* (1605) that "it will be enough not to stray a hair's breadth from the truth in telling [the story]." [5] Although each of these writers cedes to a higher authority in his or her assertion of truth—Rabelais refers his reader to God, Marguerite de Navarre yields to the authority of the nobleman's word, and Cervantes stakes his faith in the veracity of the traditional tales underpinning his work—there is nothing at issue in verifying the truth of these tales, nothing, that is, more than the individual writer's license to narrate. None of these writers makes any explicit or implicit reference to the cultural use to which the truth of his or her narrative might be put; at best we might consider Cervantes' critique of *Amadis of Gaul* and other works from the romance tradition a debilitated caveat that such tales had outlived their unspecified and imprecise use. In other words, whatever critical or reformative thrust we might identify in these writers is limited to discrediting precurrent or contemporary literary practices without specifying anything to take their place.

To the objection that it is not self-evident that all literary works need to create for themselves a critical discourse specifying their cultural use, I would reply with cautious assent. Works that readily identify themselves as belonging to a particular existing genre have

---

[3] Rabelais, vol. I, p. 219.
[4] Marguerite de Navarre, pp. 9, 10.
[5] Cervantes, p. 25.

had that work done for them in the historical and dialectical development of the literary class to which they belong. It is difficult, however, not to view as in some way subversive, critical, or liberatory those texts which eschew traditional generic classification. This last category of works explicitly or implicitly reveals the inadequacy of existing literary forms to communicate the specific cultural, literary, or political truths obtaining at the moment of their production. Revealing such inadequacy, however, is only the first step toward elaborating an alternative truth. Unless the work can construct for itself a delimited pool of readers for whom this alternative truth pertains, its demystification of the conventionality of previous truths amounts to little more than the reappropriation for itself of the target discursive practice's tricks. Mikhail Bakhtin elegantly states this argument in his analysis of Rabelais, in which he argues that parody and satire amount to very little if nothing is erected in the place of the institutions a work attempts to demolish.

> Turning away from language (by means of language, of course), discrediting any direct or unmediated intentionality and expressive excess (any "weighty" seriousness) that might adhere in ideological discourse, presuming that all language is conventional and false, maliciously inadequate to reality—all this achieves in Rabelais almost the maximum purity possible in prose. But the truth that might oppose such falsity receives almost no direct intentional and verbal expression in Rabelais, it does not receive its *own* word—it reverberates only in the parodic and unmasking accents in which the lie is present.[6]

To the semantic encoding of a literary genre, then, which establishes the new cultural truths obtaining in a given historical moment and the specific group for which they pertain, we must add the syntactic encoding which delineates the signifying practices charged with communicating those truths. To put it in simpler, more traditional terms, we need to understand the relationship between a genre's form and its content. I have argued at length that prose fiction in the early seventeenth century was an essentially aristocratic genre and I have detailed the conditions that gave rise to the need for a new set of cultural truths validating contemporary aristocratic ideology. It is now essential to investigate briefly why prose fiction evolved as the literary form best suited for communi-

[6] Bakhtin, p. 309.

cating those truths. The discussion to follow of this extremely complex issue will be necessarily concise; I merely want to suggest some of the reasons why prose fiction, and not some other literary form, developed at a crucial juncture in France's social history to communicate one political group's concerns and to reformulate those concerns into an ostensibly transhistorical truth.

The anonymous author of *Clorinde* (1654) went against the grain of the accepted practice in fiction of claiming to imitate the ancient masters in his or her bold statement that "antiquity itself has left nothing that can equal us."[7] This writer was quite enamored of contemporary fiction's apparent ability to imitate the real world in language devoid of convention. Contemporary novels, he or she claimed, "imitate so well what ordinarily happens in life that you might say they uncover a portrait of all men, where each one sees and recognizes himself" ("A Lysis"). In 1654, largely because of the process we observed in the preceding chapter in which fiction appropriated the formal rules of officially sanctioned genres, the novel was becoming a naturalized literary form whose conventions, through repetition, no longer obtruded into works' semantic and narrative structures. The only convention readers seemed able to identify in prose narrative—whether history or fiction—was *vraisemblance*, but as we have seen *vraisemblance* was a narrative mode encoded for moral truth rather than factual reality. DuPlaisir remarked that "*vraisemblance* consists of saying only what is morally believable" (*Sentimens sur les lettres*, 96); consequently fiction, like history, seemed to have no genre-specific conventions. As the author of *Clorinde* points out, contemporary fiction surpassed the works of the ancient masters because it seemed able to imitate nature in a more direct and unobtrusive fashion.

The narrative styles common to both history and fiction caused quite a bit of consternation on both aesthetic and moral fronts. Religious authorities like the abbé Pierre de Villiers and Pierre Nicole feared that the indistinction between verisimilar texts and those charged with imparting transhistorical religious and cultural truths would corrupt readers. Villiers believed that novels, in their imitation of truth, were evil works: "All the little novels and all the little histories are not simply hostile to the purity of sentiment and

[7] *Clorinde*, "A Lysis."

morals. These sorts of books spoil the mind even more than the heart." [8] Villiers cites the case of one Mme D who, impassioned by the dross emanating from the publisher Barbin (who was Villiers' publisher as well!), lost her judgment and became "incapable of partaking of a good thing since she only has taste for the bad" (248). Nicole, one of the most learned theologians of Port-Royal, attacked Desmaretz for having criticized Jansenism, and he attempted to undermine Desmaretz's criticism by assaulting his credibility as a writer. Nicole assailed Desmaretz's novels and called him a "public poisoner"; he wrote that the sort of works Desmaretz was writing were contrary to Christianity. Novels disguised as truth insinuated themselves into readers' hearts and minds, he wrote, and the falsification of truth was the novelist's gravest sin: "The more careful he was to cover with a veil of respectability the criminal passions he describes, the more dangerous and able to corrupt simple and innocent souls he made his works." [9]

In 1667, when Nicole wrote this critique, mimetic discourse was undergoing a formal and a political crisis: different literary forms were competing to be the vehicle of stable, transhistorical truth. Since the Académie's judgment on the *Cid*, tragedy had begun to encode traditional aristocratic values tempered by monarchic absolutism, and Christianity appeared on the stage in Corneille's *Polyeucte* in 1642. Yet, with the proliferation of fiction and history, works purporting to relate referential reality were competing with those charged with depicting moral and political truth. In other words, mimetic discourse ostensibly capable of seamlessly describing how things were or had been collided with aesthetic forms conventionally encoded to transmit the values of France's religious and political authorities. Before the proliferation of fiction claiming for itself the accuracy of history, officially commissioned historiography assumed the burden of chronicling reality while remaining within the confines of truth and *vraisemblance* that other literary forms respected. New partisan forms of prose, however, contested the univocality of royal historiography. Factual reality and moral and political truth became ambiguously enmeshed. No one would ever have confused the contemporary truth tragedy related with the political reality historiography asserted; their formal differences en-

---

[8] Villiers, *Réflexions sur les défauts d'autruy*, p. 247.
[9] Nicole, *Les Imaginaires et les Visionnaires*, p. 253.

coded their specific didactic purposes. With the advent of popular prose fiction, however, the possibility of competing versions of reality put into question the univocality of truth.

Since the Middle Ages, prose was seen as the literary form best able to relate referential reality. Unencumbered by formal considerations that intruded on the way they treated their material, prose writers asserted their own greater claim to representational accuracy. In the opening lines of the prose *Guillaume d'Orange*, for example, the author writes that "history, which never lies, will tell the tale in this book, if God grants me the grace to translate old rhyme into prose. For . . . language is more pleasing in prose than in rhyme—so say those whom it pleases and who would like it to be such." [10] There are several ways to account for the rise of prose as the language of truth in medieval France. Henry Chaytor suggests that the advance of education in France demystified the air of awe and reverence surrounding the national epics; people no longer felt constrained by tradition simply to accept the fantastic worlds described in the *chansons de geste*, and those who sought to tease out the factual truth of the tales began to transcribe them into prose. In addition, he argues, the increase in literacy and the rise of lyric poetry made the assonance of national epics obsolete: rhymed verse and prose became more fundamentally opposed literary forms. Readers interested in other national literatures but lacking the linguistic skills to read texts in the originals had to content themselves with translations which were not, by and large, rendered in their original verse forms but in prose.[11] Prose provided writers a newfound freedom, allowing them to cast off the constraints of traditional verse forms; they seemed able to devote themselves more directly to their material.[12]

Wlad Godzich and Jeffrey Kittay extend the analysis of prose's ability to communicate the truth by observing that not only does prose appear less encumbered and more transparent than verse, but it developed new techniques of precision to make up for the visual

---

[10] Cited by Doutrepont, p. 380.

[11] Chaytor, *From Script to Print*, pp. 83–115.

[12] See also Doutrepont: "Men do not willingly read a long poem in verse when they only want to know the *story*. Now, this is the state of mind of certain amateurs of literature in the fifteenth century. They follow the *story* more easily when it is rid of an ornamentation which, however poetic it is, is no less encumbering" (pp. 394–95).

cues *jongleurs* communicated in the performance of most popular literature. In particular they note in prose a more precise punctuality and causality than in verse. Complex syntactic subordination arose in prose, they argue, largely because of the performer's absence. While the *jongleur* could mimic the voices of his actants, for example, there is no non-diacritical agent in prose capable of doing this. "[Prose] cannot orient a represented action around itself," they write. "It has no voice and cannot mime. Its stake in the visible and the audible is smaller." [13] Godzich and Kittay point out that many medieval epics had a dual structure that mirrored the tension between traditional and contemporary values; the writing down of these epics and the radical change in form that accompanied transcription seem to have been a way of domesticating the tension by fixing it for contemporaries or successors who might have been better able to synthesize them. [14]

Godzich and Kittay's most powerful analysis of the significance of the transcription of verse into prose, however, occurs in their discussion of prose history. Although they agree with Chaytor that prose seemed less encumbered by form and consequently better able to relate the unmitigated truth, they postulate that prose's ostensible formlessness is only an illusion—its use and formal significance had to be codified through practice. Prose is a specific and precise literary form that emerged when conceptions of truth changed; new human truths can only be communicated in new literary forms unencumbered by the historical and cultural baggage of existing forms. Commenting on the adoption of prose in historical documents, Godzich and Kittay write: "When truth changes, there is a lack of synchronicity between the signifying practice and its message: a lag is sensed between what is then seen as a new content versus an old form. Attention is called to a form–content distinction, which was irrelevant up to that point" (144). The semantic development of aristocratic fiction I elaborated above,

[13] Godzich and Kittay, *The Emergence of Prose*, p. 39.
[14] See also William W. Ryding, *Structure in Medieval Narrative*. Ryding argues that the diptych and cyclic narratives popular in the *chansons de geste* seem clumsy or inadequate to modern readers who are more accustomed to more directly causal narrative sequences. He postulates that dual or cyclic narratives not only reflect but help sustain the tensions between traditional and modern values. These tensions were, in part, resolved, he argues, by the tendency in many of the epic cycles to amplify or continue their basic narrative structures.

which encoded prose fiction as decidedly aristocratic, was reinforced by its formal or syntactic relationship to referential reality: asserting in the early years of the seventeenth century the truth of aristocratic virtue and hegemony, writers needed a literary form that was marked to depict reality, but not yet codified to relate a specific ideological point of view.

Prose narrative, which imposed a new form on the culturally valorized heroes and events of ancient epics, seemed in its apparent removal of the metric and verse forms characteristic of epic merely to jettison an antiquated form. In fact, however, aristocratic prose fiction retained, as we have already seen, many of the political and nationalistic features of the epic. The epic hero's truth remained in heroic fiction, but not in the form that had codified him as a specifically Hellenistic or Roman cultural figure. The qualities of grandeur, magnanimity, constancy, and piety were transformed and reappropriated through the imposition of a new literary form— prose fiction—into their seventeenth-century French equivalents.[15] The "lack of synchronicity" between form and content that Godzich and Kittay identify when truth changes and no longer finds its expression in existing literary forms disappeared; form and content as well as factual reality and cultural truth once again seem to coincide in a stable literary form manifesting no encumbering, obtrusive conventions.

Finally, when prose fiction appropriated historiography's illusion of referentiality, it gained for itself history's syntactically and semantically structured facility for creating ontologically valid worlds. As Paul Veyne pointed out, history need not describe its object beginning *tabula rasa*; the conventions of historiography are such that it requires fewer textual markers informing readers of the relationships they must infer between the primary ontology of the real world with which they are familiar and the secondary ontology created by narrative. It is, in fact, the historian's project to minimize the difference between primary and secondary ontology in order to induce readers to reflect not on the narrative that he or she constructs, but on the expressive causality that his or her narrative

---

[15] On the ambiguous nature of early seventeenth-century concepts of heroism, see André Stegmann, "L'Ambiguïté du concept héroïque dans la littérature morale en France sous Louis XIII."

advances. Constructing a narrative reality is less important than explaining the complex interrelationships that obtain within the already existing world, and the historian must proceed as though the narrative in his or her account is a fundamentally natural one. The heroic novel, as the most fully developed form of the early modern novel, imitated contemporary historiography by expressing causality in terms of existing, valorized narrative structures, and it endorsed the current ideological configuration. Thomas Pavel writes that the reader of fiction constructs sets of possible truths based on the predication of characters and events that the narrative fabricates, and then he or she attempts to integrate them into the larger set of actual truths. This process is abetted by collections of "decoding relations" or "inference systems" that relate textual practices to cultural ones.[16] The fully developed form of early modern fiction appropriated the apparent formlessness and unmediated relationship to reality prose assumed, and it actuated a new discursive practice adept at relating contemporary cultural truths whose expressive causality exhibited the monologic stability of a master discourse.

I have borrowed the term "expressive causality" from Fredric Jameson's reworking of an idea Louis Althusser advanced concerning the relationship of elements in a structure to the totality of that structure. Althusser distinguishes two sorts of causality: the first is the transitive variety, issued forth from Descartes and perhaps best illustrated in the domino chain model. The second, involving Leibnitz's theory of expression and governing most of Hegelian philosophy, posits for each and every structure an interior essence phenomenally reflected by each of its elements. Althusser writes that this model of causality "supposed a certain nature of the totality, precisely this nature of a 'spiritual' whole, in which each element is expressive of the entire totality, as 'pars totalis.'"[17] An expressive

---

[16] *Fictional Worlds*, pp. 17, 43–48, 60. Pavel argues that the correspondence between possible truths and actual truths is a convention no different from rhyme or rhythmic patterns in poetry or the number of acts in tragedies. The strength of his argument derives from his refusal to posit fiction and reality as diametrically opposed entities. He argues, for example, that although one may theorize fiction by relating it to an overarching theory of being and truth, it is more productive and revealing to analyze it from the point of view of readers' understanding and use of fiction once they enter the fictional world and relinquish their relationship to external reality (p. 16).

[17] Althusser, *Lire le capital*, p. 168.

causality reflects the a priori essentialism of a structuring totality in its vertical relationship to each of its constitutive elements. The fundamental nature of the whole, given in advance or determined by means ulterior to it, provides an overarching sense informing the particular meaning or significance of its parts. Jameson argues (*The Political Unconscious*, 28) that expressive causality translates into interpretive allegories "in which a sequence of historical events or texts and artifacts is rewritten in terms of some deeper, under-lying and more 'fundamental' narrative" which becomes the key indexing the sense of the text.[18] In heroic fiction, the expressive causality to which I have been alluding is the abstract merit and virtue of France's hereditary aristocracy in its role as the bulwark of the nation and the guardian of high culture. The expressive caus-ality of aristocratic fiction emanated from specific hermeneutic methodologies which in turn resulted from seventeenth-century cultural practice, to be sure—this is how canonical or exegetical traditions pass from one generation to the next. More crucially, however, the expressive causality so produced, which bracketed conflicting ideological interpretations in favor of the monologic voice of cultural unity, actively obstructed competing theories and put forth as transcendent truth what was in fact a mark of domi-nation.[19]

The stability and univocality of a monologic master discourse are difficult or impossible to fathom outside of a specific historical con-text and a determined political intentionality. That is, few modern readers would accept the proposition that a given text has one and only one possible interpretation. Seventeenth-century readers, how-ever, generally had access to the early modern novel—and I am referring here especially to heroic fiction—only in its self-defined context as a didactic work celebrating the virtue and importance of the aristocracy and the power and glory of an absolute monarchy. While Ross Chambers reminds us that "one should not allow one's own mode of reading to be exclusively determined . . . by the ide-ology of art to which the text happens to subscribe" (*Story and*

---

[18] Robert Young provides a detailed critique of notions of causality as they are construed in Jameson's and Althusser's works. See his *White Mythologies*, pp. 97–109.

[19] For a very good discussion of the means by which hermeneutic traditions con-struct truths and oppress competing versions, see John Brenkman, *Culture and Domination*, especially chapter 2.

Situation, 27), seventeenth-century readers inhabited a world in which modes of reading were rigidly controlled by the rise of academicism and other discursive practices indexed to govern their responses. Louis XIV, for example, built the entire physical and iconographic edifice of his court at Versailles to evince his control of the nation's political and representational systems. The physical arrangement of the gardens, the allegorical fountains, and indeed each statue held a symbolic meaning whose key Louis alone possessed.[20] Louis went so far as to convert the aristocracy, whose traditional privilege of bearing arms he effectively abrogated by forming a professional army, into spectator-participants whose function at the court was to contribute to and be witness of the king's splendor. Thus, while it is clearly not the case that authors of heroic fiction succeeded in constructing narratives that assented to a single interpretive response, the conjunction of rigidly controlled semiotic practices helped create a hospitable context in which the desired response could more easily come to the fore.[21]

The stability of the early modern novel's master discourse found its corollary in the seventeenth century's search for a steady and unified national language. François de Malherbe, official poet to Henri IV, undertook the purification of the French language first by ridding it of Latinisms and then by proscribing neologisms, dialectal variations, and any ambiguities prohibiting a general, broad-based comprehension of the language. In his letters to Peiresc he prescribes methods to improve poetic diction and form.[22] In 1647, Claude Favre de Vaugelas, an original member of the Académie Française, wrote his *Remarques sur la langue françoise*, in which he transcribed the Académie's decisions concerning grammar, vocabulary, and usage. Concerning this last he described the necessity

[20] See Jean-Marie Apostolidès, *Le roi-machine*, especially pp. 50–60; and Harth, *Ideology and Culture*, pp. 250–55.

[21] Susan Suleiman describes a similar historical and political situation for the nineteenth-century *roman à thèse*: "If a story is to be read as having a single specific meaning, it must either be interpreted in a consistent and unambiguous way by the teller, *or* it must exist within a context that invests it with intentionality. Now this context is none other than another text (or a set of other texts), in relation to which the story presents itself as a variant or an illustration—or, more generally, which can be 'read into' the story. What we have here, then, is a particular kind of intertextuality" (*Authoritarian Fictions*, p. 43).

[22] See, for example, a letter dating from August 1621 in which Malherbe criticizes the use of Latin in contemporary verse and offers corrections for a more cogent use of the language (Malherbe, *Œuvres*, p. 725).

of finding a unified linguistic practice that would serve as a model for the spoken language. In the preface to his work he demonstrates the ideological nature of the project when he writes: "It is one of the principles of our language that when the court speaks one way and the town another, one must follow the court. . . . The court's usage must prevail over the other without having to provide a reason."[23] A brief exchange in Molière's *Précieuses ridicules* underscores and satirizes the exclusivity of court language and its intimate relationship to the language of heroic fiction:

> *Marotte*: Here is a footman asks if you are at home, and says his master is coming to see you.
> *Magdelon*: Learn, you dunce, to express yourself a little less vulgarly. Say, here is a necessary evil inquiring if it is commodious for you to become visible.
> *Marotte*: I do not understand Latin, and have not learned philosophy out of *Cyrus*, as you have done.[24]

Early modern French fiction, the most fully developed form of which is the heroic novel, developed at a time during which political, moral, aesthetic, and even linguistic authorities struggled to secure the stability of the discursive practices within their purviews. For a limited period the restricted literary practices of high classicism and the unyielding politics of absolutism that Louis XIV inherited from Richelieu suggested that a politically expedient literature of immutability and univocality was accessible. Prose fiction seemed especially appropriate for underwriting a discourse of political and representational stability because authors appropriated much of their material from the Greek and Roman masters, and because the literary forms they imitated supported the partisan construction of ostensibly natural truth in the service of a restricted group of people. The discursive stability of prose fiction, however, was comparatively short-lived; novelists began to test language's capacity to deliver an unequivocal master discourse whose expressive causality dictated the conditions of its representation. Before we consider the conditions giving rise to fiction that put into question the fundamental features of the heroic novel, however, a brief

[23] Cited by von Wartburg, p. 172.
[24] Molière, *Les précieuses ridicules*, in *Œuvres complètes*, vol. I, p. 201. English translation, *The High-Brow Ladies*, in the New American Library edition (New York: Modern Library, n.d.), pp. 23–24.

examination of two theories of the novel from a syntactic point of view is in order. Georg Lukács and Mikhail Bakhtin consider the novel's ostensible closure and completion, as well as the language used to construct a univocal master discourse of interpretive stability. Their theories of the novel will shed a great deal of light on the political and aesthetic ambiguity that I consider an essential feature of the modern French novel.

Georg Lukács, in his *Theory of the Novel*, distinguishes between the "integrated" world of the epic, in which the destinies of the hero and of the community were one and the same, and the "alienated" civilizations that characterize the world of the novel. While epic heroes represent the ideological points of view of an entire community, heroes in the novel are characterized by their own particular problems and destinies: they stand apart from their society. The alienation Lukács describes is a form of distancing; it is a way of giving the hero a particular point of view or system of beliefs that separates him or her both from the views of the reading audience and from the literary and rhetorical devices this audience had come to expect. In the "integrated" civilization of the Greeks, life was based, Lukács avers, on totality. The totality of Greek life was rounded from within—that is, it was harmonious and complete within itself. Meaning was "ready-made and ever-present." [25] Basing his critique of classical Greek literature on a Platonic notion of Form and Idea, Lukács writes:

> Totality as the formative prime reality of every individual phenomenon implies that something closed within itself can be completed; completed because everything occurs within it, nothing is excluded from it and nothing points at a higher reality outside it; completed because everything within it ripens to its own perfection and, by attaining itself, submits to limitation. Totality of being is possible only where everything is already homogeneous before it has been contained by forms; where forms are not a constraint but only the becoming conscious. (34)

The world of the epic Lukács constructs is one of totality in that he views Hellenic civilization as homogeneous, the representation of which is complete in itself and subject to no higher reality existing outside itself. The imposition of form through the production of

[25] Lukács, p. 3.

epic is not, in Lukács' view, constraining in the way that representation in Plato's view is. For Plato any imitation or representation, in particular poetic representation, is only one of appearances and never one of reality. The imposition of physical, articulated forms divorces things from their Ideal Form or reality.[26] In Lukács' world of the epic the imposition of form does not limit or constrain. The giving of form, rather than inserting an unbridgeable chasm between things represented and their Ideal Form, merely allows these things to be perceived. In other words, there is no significant difference between the represented world of the epic which gives listeners a means to imagine the heroic deeds of their ancestors, and the ideal form of the Hellenic civilizations so represented. Nothing significant is lost in the translation from deed to epic representation.

There has been, in recent years, a great deal of criticism concerning Lukács' work and the political and philosophical implications of his thought. Paul de Man, Fredric Jameson, Agnes Heller and J. M. Bernstein, for example, each point out that Lukács constructed his own version of the Greek world in order to juxtapose to it the world of the novel.[27] Each of these writers has his or her own criticism to offer on Lukács' discussion of the novel: de Man comments that he has a "deliberate tendency to substitute general and abstract systems for concrete examples" (52), and Jameson complains of metaphysical traits in Lukács' writing. Whatever the criticisms offered may be, however, each of the writers named above seems to agree that, whether he stated it or not, Lukács was not so much offering a typology of the novel form as he was describing a novelistic practice. The practice Lukács describes involves the imposition of form—the particular mode of representation the novelistic text employs—as a wedge inserting between the world depicted and the reader of the work a particular ideological view through which all events are filtered.

The ideological opposition Lukács establishes between epic and novel is significant for our discussion of seventeenth-century fiction not only because the seventeenth-century heroic novel was frequently compared to the epic: the ideological differences that con-

---

[26] Plato, *The Republic*, 601c.

[27] Paul de Man, *Blindness and Insight*, pp. 51–59; Fredric Jameson, *Marxism and Form*, pp. 160–82; Agnes Heller, *Lukács Reappraised*, especially pp. 68–69; J. M. Bernstein, *The Philosophy of the Novel*, especially pp. 72–78.

cern us here between the early modern and the modern novel closely parallel the distinctions Lukács makes between integrated and alienated civilizations. In the introductory paragraph to the chapter entitled "The Inner Form of the Novel," he writes:

> In a novel, totality can be systematised only in abstract terms, which is why any system that could be established in the novel—a system being, after the final disappearance of the organic, the only possible form of a rounded totality—had to be one of abstract concepts and thereby not directly suitable for aesthetic form-giving. Such abstract systematisation is, it is true, the ultimate basis of the entire structure, but in the created reality of the novel all that becomes visible is the distance separating the systematisation from concrete life: a systematisation which emphasises the conventionality of the objective world and the interiority of the subjective one. (70)

Lukács claims here that unlike the epic which *reproduced* an integrated civilization of always-evident meaning, the novel can only *represent* a totality or, perhaps more exactly, the *suggestion* of a totality. The novel's representation, its "created reality," is not the totality of a hero's and a community's life and destiny, but a self-consciousness, an awareness of its own process of systematization. What the novel renders visible is not a slice of life, but the schism or gap between reality and the representation of reality. Unlike the epic's more or less transparent representation that reproduces for the audience a complete world without internal contradiction, novelistic representation is opaque in that in depicting a bit of reality it also makes apparent the particular point of view informing its depiction. Novelistic representation, then, always comes up short. The novel, according to Lukács, gives distinct form—ideological point of view—and is consequently constraining because it closes the door on the supposed totality of the epic for which form is the "becoming conscious." Epic representation depicts both the totality of the lived experience of its hero and that of its community, but unlike the novel, it also reproduces that totality in a univocal point of view.

One might argue, of course, that any system of representation, epic, novelistic, or otherwise, is doomed to fragmentation owing to the process of representation itself. But Lukács is not so much concerned with general problems of representation as he is with the ideology of form. The entire basis of his discussion of the differences between the epic and the novel rests on the premise that there is no significant ideological difference between epic representation and the world on which it was modeled. If no representation can ever depict the totality of its object, Lukács gives the epic the advantage over the novel because he finds no ideological conflict between author, hero, and audience: this is its "rounded totality." The "created reality" of the novel exposes its ideological point of view in the process of creation. Because novels are produced in eras and in societies with conflicting class interests, their systems of representation are informed by a particular ideological slant. In short, the novel is politically fragmented; the point of view in the novel is a specific one, representing not that of an entire community but one of a particular individual or group.

Addressing the same issues but writing in less essentialistic terms, Mikhail Bakhtin characterizes the tradition of the epic as a sacrosanct one in which completion or integration do not exist a priori, but have to be constructed for the audience through a skillful manipulation of language. The four essays of *The Dialogic Imagination* deal with different elements of the novel's form, and, like Lukács, Bakhtin bases a significant portion of his discussion of the novel on a comparison with the epic. Fundamental to his comparisons in each essay is an examination of the manipulations of language in the novel, manipulations Bakhtin believes were not available to the authors of the ancient epics.

Language in the epic, Bakhtin writes, "is not separable from its subject, for an absolute fusion of subject matter and spatial-temporal aspects with valorized (hierarchical) ones is characteristic of semantics in the epic" (17). Where Lukács' and Bakhtin's theories coincide is in their belief in the integral nature of the epic: both view the epic as a form in which the same point of view is shared by all. But Bakhtin differs significantly from Lukács in that he explains the homogeneity of point of view not by referring to some abstract notion of completion or ever-present meaning, but by examining the use of language. The fusion of the epic's language, subject matter, and spatial-temporal aspects establishes an audience identification with the epic hero and his world such that "point of view and evaluation are fused with the subject into one inseparable whole" (17). Because epic events always take place in the distant past, they form an untouchable world, one that is complete and unchangeable. Audiences have no choice but "to accept the epic world with reverence" (17). The completion of the epic world in Bakhtin's view is not a given; it has none of the metaphysical characteristics of teleological completion that Lukács assigns it, but it is complete insofar as its distance in the past renders it untouchable and immutable. Fusion of language and subject matter in the epic directs audience reaction.

Events in the epic take place in the distant past, and because the time separating events from their narration is so great, Bakhtin points out that these events become valorized and canonized. A community tradition arises through the telling of the lives and times of great heroes, and golden ages of glory are constructed from which members of the audience have sprung. Only great and glorious deeds occurred in the past, the epic tradition suggests, and all great and glorious deeds occurred only in the past. The discourse in which such deeds are recounted is thus codified by tradition, and in order to maintain the respect commanded by community ancestors responsible for the founding of the audience's way of life, epic discourse displays a deep piety toward its subject matter. Epic discourse is built around a tradition of maintaining and guaranteeing the community's commonly held reverence for its ancestors, and such a discourse must attempt to exclude the possibility of alternate interpretations.

By contrast, Bakhtin views novelistic language as characterized by "stylistic three-dimensionality"; it is composed of a broad spectrum of language from the colloquial to the formal, the irreverent to the sacred. Use of language in the novel is not restricted, as Bakhtin suggests it is in the epic, to the function of capturing audience attention in order to direct it to the pious veneration of hero and event the epic demands. In the epic the poet's speech is highly formalized, ordered by the cadence of meter and rhyme; it is marked by frequent repetition of formulas and epithets. It is an all-encompassing, homogeneous literary language. This is not the case with narration in the novel. Bakhtin writes that

> the novel can be defined as a diversity of social speech types (sometimes even diversity of languages) and a diversity of individual voices, artistically organized. . . . The novel orchestrates all its themes, the totality of the world of objects and ideas depicted and expressed in it, by means of the social diversity of speech types and by the differing

individual voices that flourish under such conditions. Authorial
speech, the speeches of narrators, inserted genres, the speech of characters are merely those fundamental compositional unities with
whose help heteroglossia can enter the novel. (262–63)

By considering various types of speech to be "fundamental compositional unities," Bakhtin suggests that novelistic discourse not
only represents *by means of* language, but it also represents *language*.[28] This means that novelistic language is poetic, at least in
the sense the structuralists understood the term, since it emphasizes
not only its referent but the language used to describe it. Bakhtin
in fact calls novelistic discourse poetic, but indicates that the novel's
poetics do not coincide with traditionally official or "high" poetic
genres (269). The novel's alienation, then, arises both from the distance it establishes between itself and official culture, and from its
heteroglossia, the confrontation of differing strata of language that
provides the contexts in which the novel may be read. Heteroglossia removes the possibility of a univocal language or master narrative; it substitutes for the primacy of secure referential meaning
fragmented, contextual signification.

It is not my intention here to reduce Bakhtin's and Lukács' complex theories of the novel to the single issue of fragmentation and
alienation. I do want to stress, however, that the alienated, linguis-
tically complicated novelistic narration they describe provides a
convenient way to begin looking at the fiction that developed in
France after the demise of the heroic novel. The political and representational stability of heroic fiction was relatively short-lived.
One of the reasons for its demise was that the form's ideological
expediency was undercut by its aesthetic marginality, and this discrepancy between form and content contributed to a crisis in representation marking the later years of the century. From a purely
formal point of view, the fusion of ruling-class truth with a non-
classical literary physiognomy produced a tension in fiction that
was never quite resolved. Readers seemed unable to appraise prose
fiction *as* prose fiction; its lack of a classical critical tradition meant
that it could only be evaluated in terms of something else, most
often the genres from which it borrowed its formal features. This
formal instability provoked reconsideration of language's capacity

---

[28] We will return to the notion of novels directly representing language in Chapters 6 and 7.

to deliver the truth and a distrust of the literary forms that had always been associated with truth. Charles Perrault, for example, cast suspicion on the venerable institution of history by comparing the historian's techniques to the novelist's. Novelists, he wrote,

> are the masters both of facts and of words, but this is not the case with true stories (*histoires veritables*) in which one must present things as they are and in the manner in which one was able to learn about them. If the historian recovered a speech, let him transcribe it as he found it; if he only learned its substance, let him only transcribe the substance, and let him refrain from amusing himself in having me admire his keen talent for eloquence when my only desire is to know the truth.[29]

A discussion concerning Thucydides provoked the above diatribe, and in particular the two interlocutors were discussing the ancient historian's technique of inventing long speeches for historical figures. Recent prose fiction that included direct discourse in dialogue format cast suspicion on the time-honored tradition in historiography of putting words in the mouths of famous figures. The novel's seamless appropriation of the unquestioned and axiomatic techniques of historiography was largely responsible for advancing the disquieting proposition that history was no more true than fiction (II, 90).

The formal collision of fiction and historiography was only one of the motivations leading to the destabilization of heroic fiction's univocal truth. The writer's relationship to his patron and to his work, as well as the economic rights he enjoyed over it, contributed to a very large extent to refashioning the discursive practices of fiction. I have already pointed out that royal historiographers could not keep from fashioning their works in a manner that would please their patrons. Most writers, in fact, even those without official court appointments, depended on the generosity of a wealthy and powerful patron to sustain and support them. Jean Bertaut, official court poet under Henri IV, wrote the following verses to Louis XIII on the event of his coronation:

> . . . know that the years devour all things
> Except the sacred labors of a great writer;

[29] Perrault, *Parallele des anciens et des modernes*, vol. II, pp. 89–90.

That the sword is nameless which owes nothing to the
  book;
And that to acquire the honor of living forever
If the one does not speak, the other battles in vain.[30]

For many writers, glorifying a patron was one road to self-
glorification; for many others the money they received supplemented their marginal incomes.[31] In the second and third quarters
of the seventeenth century many writers had a number of patrons,
and maintaining credibility among protectors with often vastly di-
verging political and financial interests entailed producing deftly
duplicitous works. Mézeray's work, particularly in its numerous,
restyled editions, exemplifies how the most gifted writers used duplicity and equivocation to their advantage. Mézeray, as noted
above, was a royal historiographer who received a pension from
the king for his voluminous *Histoire de France*. In 1668 he published an *Abrégé chronologique de l'histoire de France* (Chronolog-
ical abridgment of the Histoire de France), in which he criticized
fiscal policy. Colbert, minister of finance, was not pleased with the
way Mézeray peppered the *Abrégé* with subtle insinuations concerning the injustice of the current tax structure. One example relates the decision under Charles IX to raise taxes despite the
church's concern: "For the clergy was alarmed, but permitted the
tax increase of four décimes in six years, and the third estate five
sous per *muid* on all wines entering into closed cities. This tax has
continued to rise from that time up until the present." [32] Colbert
accused Mézeray of sensationalism, claiming that criticizing fiscal
policy was a cheap trick designed to please the public. After he
threatened to withdraw Mézeray's pension, the historian made the

[30] Cited by Leiner, p. 161.
[31] On the complex relationship among patrons and clients in the seventeenth century, see Sharon Kettering, *Patrons, Brokers and Clients in Seventeenth-Century
France*, pp. 184–230.
[32] Mézeray, *Abrégé chronologique de l'histoire de France*, vol. V, p. 45. Other
examples abound, particularly in the second volume. "The King [Philippe le Bel]
had hard and pitiless ministers bent on extracting the last cent. The most powerful
of all was Enguerrand le Portier, seigneur de Marigny, who, in levying great taxes
for his master, did not forget to fill his own coffers and to give his own family more
land, offices and feudal concessions than a faithful and disinterested servant ought
to take. Thus the people had to suffer extreme persecution" (II, 799).

corrections the minister demanded and published another edition in 1672.

Few writers were exempt from the uncertainties of having to please more than one patron. Some, like Gomberville, whose noble origins were somewhat dubious, dedicated their works to the most powerful people of their time. Gomberville dedicates four of the five volumes of *Polexandre* to different people: the king, Richelieu, Chancellor Séguier, and the mareschal Schomberg. In addition, he seems not at all hesitant to contradict himself in his dedications. In the first volume he says that Polexandre's glory is really the king's: "Polexandre would not consider himself the legitimate possessor of his glory if he did not pay homage to Your Majesty, and if he did not recognize the miracles of your life as the first authors of the great actions he performed" (I, "Au Roy"). In the volume dedicated to Richelieu, Gomberville tells the Cardinal that "if you deign to glance [upon my book], I am convinced that you will recognize yourself each time you see Polexandre" (II, "A Monseigneur le Minentissime Cardinal duc de Richelieu"). These two dedications are, of course, only nominally contradictory. The king and Richelieu shared the same political philosophies and goals, and Gomberville's dedications rehearse the formulaic and hyperbolic *discours obligé* of the period.

Many writers, however, found themselves in the position of needing to offer their works to powerful men of quite conflicting political philosophies, or of attacking an individual only to have to write in his service later on. Cyrano de Bergerac attacked Mazarin in his *Ministre d'Etat, flambé* (The ruined minister of state), a pamphlet that Alain Viala argues was the model for all the ensuing *mazarinades*, pamphlets attacking Mazarin and his politics; after losing all his support at the end of the Fronde, however, he found himself in the situation of having to contradict himself. His *Lettre contre les Frondeurs* (Letter against the Frondeurs) gainsays each of his previous positions.[33] Viala has unearthed a host of political pamphlets consisting of contradicting political positions, and he attributes much of the shifting of political alliances to the vicissitudes of patronage. One pamphlet, *Le Point de l'Ovalle*, supported Condé in his efforts to deliver the people from the tyranny of the

[33] See Viala, *Naissance de l'écrivain*, p. 60.

monarchy. "Justice is not with the king but with the royalty," the pamphlet specifies (Viala, 66), and it comes out early in favor of Condé. By the end of the pamphlet, however, there is a call to massive revolution and for the ruin of all noblemen: "It is clear that the great nobles are only great because we carry them on our shoulders: we only have to shake them up to strew the earth with them" (Viala, 68). Viala reads the conflicting statements in this pamphlet, which begins by supporting Condé and winds up, only a few pages later, calling for the destruction of *all* nobility, as reflective of the duplicity that the contemporary system of *mécénat*, or patronage, implicitly supported. In a period distinguished by nothing so much as the intersection of conflicting alliances, all writers, from those of heroic fiction to those of the brief but inflammatory *mazarinades*, learned to mark their works with an ironic duplicity in which they encoded multiple, often conflicting significations. "In their formulaic speech," Viala writes, "[writers] introduce equivocation and distortions which show how they undergo constraint without subscribing to it (*comment ils subissent la contrainte sans y adhérer*)" (68).

Writers' duplicity played itself out on many fronts, and the equivocal handling of political issues that resulted from having to deal with different protectors became even more delicate in the third quarter of the seventeenth century. Up until the 1650's, books required a *Privilège du Roi* in order to be printed. Ostensibly granted to allow writers to draw some financial benefit from the sale of their works, the *privilège* in fact empowered booksellers to exploit writers by purchasing their works at a flat fee and then drawing as much income from them as they could. Some writers, however, were granted a *privilège général*, which covered any and all of their works. Because the standard *Privilège du Roi* specified the bookseller licensed to distribute the book, the *privilège général* gave writers a bargaining chip: they were in a better position to negotiate with booksellers because their works belonged to them more fully than they ever before had.[34] The consequences of this developing literary propriety were rather dramatic, and they substan-

---

[34] See Viala, pp. 98–105; and H-J. Martin, *Livre, pouvoirs, et société à Paris au XVIIe siècle*. For more detailed information concerning payment and other benefits of authorship, see Harth, *Ideology and Culture*, pp. 162–75; and Pottinger, *The French Book Trade in the Ancien Régime, 1500–1791*, especially chapter V.

tially changed both the way writers implicitly addressed their audiences and the way their works were received. Sorel found the
growing commodification of literature abhorrent and argued that
the individual merits of literary works were subservient to the marketing practices of booksellers eager to turn a profit: "The jealousy
and malice sometimes exhibited among merchants lead them to dis-
credit as much as they can the books their competitors sell, in order
better to sell their own: let us believe that the reputation of a good
book and that of its author finally surmount all these obstacles"
(*De la connoissance*, 28). Boileau as well regretted the passing of
the era when people wrote not for profit but for truth and glory
(*L'art poétique*, Chant IV, lines 125–32):

> Work for glory, and never let a sordid profit
> Be the object of an illustrious writer.
> I know that a noble mind can, without shame and without
>   crime
> Draw from its work a legitimate tribute;
> But I cannot bear these renowned authors
> Who, turned away from glory and hungry for money,
> Put their Apollo to work for a bookseller
> And make of a divine art a mercenary trade.

Self-appointed aestheticians expected to find corruption of literary standards in works that sold for a profit, but they generally did
not consider the change that literary propriety effected in the manner writers addressed and consequently constructed their reading
audiences. Before the Fronde, the number of wealthy patrons who
sustained writers through financial sponsorship was fairly large
and included the most influential members of the French aristocracy. After the Fronde, Mazarin continued, in somewhat reduced
and restricted form, the system of royal patronage that Richelieu
had instituted. Beginning in the 1660's, the number of royal gratifications extended to authors of literary works declined sharply: by
1675, the number of gratifications paid out to men of letters was
reduced by 75 percent, in spite of the fact that until 1672 the
amount of money spent on all gratifications increased steadily.[35]
More and more writers depended on the income they received from
the sale of their works, and while most could not live on this re-

[35] See Harth, pp. 158–62.

muneration alone, a few—like Corneille, Racine, Scarron, and La Calprenède—had incomes enabling them to live quite comfortably. Viala points out that in the second and third quarters of the century most successful writers depended on both royal gratifications and income derived from the sale of their works, and after the Fronde in particular ambitious writers needed to frequent salons and academies in order to be known by their publics. In addition, they depended on the moneys that the sale of their works provided as well as on gifts from protectors and royal gratifications (110–13, 163).

The necessity of appealing to several groups of readers and addressing each of their collective concerns meant that heroic fiction's master discourse of univocality had run its course. Writers could no longer assume that their readers shared a common political vision, nor could they suppose that they had similar or even equal educations or had access to the same cultural capital. By the second half of the seventeenth century, writers were in the position of having to construct their own reading audiences, and this took the form of indicating, in more or less subtle fashion, what readers needed to know in order to understand the work. In Chapter 6, I will show in detail how Mme de Lafayette adroitly accomplished this difficult task by introducing an apprentice reader—the Princess of Clèves—whose assimilation of interpretive strategies helped guide readers unfamiliar with the work's iconography through the job of decoding its somewhat hermetic narrative.[36] In the second half of the seventeenth century the axiom that literature should both please and instruct its audience was still accepted; it was not always clear, however, who stood to learn what. Wealthy bourgeois

---

[36] Tristan l'Hermite's *Page disgracié* (1643) is in this respect a forerunner of *La Princesse de Clèves*. Tristan's main character and narrator learns at an early age that "appearances are deceiving," and part of the page's apprenticeship consists in learning and repeating stories. He seduces his mistress by repeating to her what he had read in *L'Astrée*: "Everyone knows that this is one of the most cultivated and pleasing novels ever to see the light of day, and that its famous author obtained a marvelous reputation from it. I spoke about it with my mistress every day for five or six hours without her ears becoming tired, nor those of her confidante either, and this was a charm that I used to put her mother and one of her confidantes to sleep, in order that they would not be able to pay heed to the furtive glances we exchanged or to the words we whispered in one another's ears" (pp. 69, 146–47). The page, however, in some respects resembles Sorel's Lysis, since a large part of his adolescence was spent reading novels: "Reading novels had made me haughty and intolerant; when I had some insignificant dispute with my friends, I imagined that I had to win the day with a great struggle and that I was one of Homer's heroes, or at least some errant knight, or one of the knights of the Round Table" (p. 81).

composed an ever-increasing portion of reading audiences, but aristocrats still held the majority. Prose fiction in the 1660's began addressing readers from a broader range of the social spectrum, and the result was an ambivalent and equivocal form of narrative that needed to address aristocrats and bourgeois as though each group were the targeted audience. Prose fiction was no longer able to construct a master discourse that would attempt rigidly to control readers' responses through the imposition of an expressive narrative causality dictating the context in which the work should be read. Philosophical and ideological truths were changing, to use Godzich and Kittay's formulation, and the form of fiction had to change as well in order to express the multivalent concerns of a heterogeneous reading public.

The novels that I will consider in the second part of this book contest the univocality and stability aristocratic fiction tried to construct. Literary production in the second half of the seventeenth century was considerably complicated by economic forces which controlled to a very large extent the way writers addressed their audiences. Private and public patronage of the arts led to conflicts of interest among benefactors and writers developed duplicitous styles in order to solicit and placate potential patrons. Heroic fiction, which represented the semantic and syntactic culmination of the various genres of aristocratic fiction, could no longer unproblematically construct heroes who unequivocally represented the collective reading audience to whom the works were directed. The epic distance Lukács and Bakhtin identify as principally responsible for construing the air of awe and veneration surrounding a community's heroic past began to crumble as new political agendas emerged requiring fresh ideological representatives. The modern novel, a form I will more fully define in the following chapter, retained the syntactic features of aristocratic fiction: since prose narrative was identified with the seamless representation of reality and since prose fiction in particular had not yet developed a tradition lengthy enough to have encoded an unassailable depiction of a specific ideological point of view, writers appropriated it as the form best suited to contest the ostensible stability of language and partisan representation. They learned to adapt it to suit the needs and tastes of an expanding reading audience, and writers in the later years of the century deftly incorporated the techniques of the masters from the century's early years. Equivocation and ambiguity replaced the monologic stability of earlier fiction, however, inaugurating a tradition of fiction that put itself forth as both the avatar of tradition and the emblem of evolution.

Part Two   **The Development of the Modern Novel**

Chapter 5   *Le Roman bourgeois* and the Modern Novel

Two very similar parodic novels that ridiculed and contested the claim to hegemony that the heroic novel had made in the field of fiction appeared within a year of one another. Antoine Furetière's *Roman bourgeois*, a well-known tale of bourgeois life in Paris, appeared in 1666, the year after Jacques Alluis published his seldom-read *L'Escole d'amour ou les heros docteurs* (The school of love, or the doctor heroes). Both novels purport to detail the lives of ordinary people from urban surroundings. Both as well define their characters in part by emphasizing the differences between them and the folk who inhabited the heroic fiction of the previous generation. Furetière's *Roman bourgeois* and Alluis' *Escole d'amour* mock the conventions of aristocratic fiction by revealing its inability to negotiate the complexities of contemporary metropolitan life. Heroic fiction was equipped with a literary orthodoxy that selected reading audiences by tendering language, images, and truths with which they could identify; it did not have the means at its disposal to depict the realities of bourgeois existence. *Le Roman bourgeois* and *L'Escole d'amour* challenge the putative monologism of earlier fiction by disputing the possibility of a master discourse, the language of an abiding representational reliability capable of reproducing in unmediated fashion the world at large or of restricting interpretation to a specific, ideologically invested point of view.

L'Escole d'amour offers up the story of two young lovers of imprecise but apparently bourgeois origin who unexpectedly find themselves in the Pays des Romans (Land of Novels), a world whose inhabitants have included the likes of King Arthur, Lancelot du Lac, Percival, the Knights of the Round Table, Amadis de Gaule, and various shepherds and shepherdesses. Dorise and Alidor, the young couple, whimsically reflect on the sights and people they encounter on their voyage through the Pays des Romans, and early on in the novel Dorise tells Alidor that "the world almost always believes things to be other than they really are."[1] This subtle caveat on the discrepancies between representation and reality informs the skepticism but ultimate acceptance with which these people greet the world. These lovers distrust the ability of representational systems to offer a reliable model of the way things really are. Perhaps surprisingly, their skepticism extends to one another's language as well. Early in their travels Dorise asks Alidor for proof of his love; he recites a somewhat insipid poem designed to demonstrate his passion for her. "If, as I believe," Dorise tells him when he is finished, "you are the author of this beautiful precept of love, it seems to me that you will have more trouble persuading me to believe it than you had composing it" (3–4). The novel thus starts us off on unfamiliar territory: where her predecessors would have accepted with glee their lovers' poetic proof of passion, Dorise contests the trustworthiness of her paramour's language. She does not doubt his love; she merely questions the capacity of his standardized formulas to represent with any degree of specificity his particular feelings for her.

Alluis' early interrogation of conventionalized language's ability to attain any sort of representational specificity quickly turns into a derogation of the literary form he finds primarily responsible for the bland regularization of literature. Dorise and Alidor enter the Ville des Romans—the City of Novels—which is populated by a host of characters from recent heroic novels. The people of the Ville des Romans "are people of the most eminent quality—they are extremely honorable [genereux]" (22). Their exceptional traits, however, are soon put to a rigorous test of logic that the conventional language of heroic fiction was not designed to support: although the people of the Ville des Romans greet Dorise and Alidor with all of the courtesy their station in life allows, they are unable to offer them any sort of material comfort, as the following passage illustrates. "All these heroes and their ladies dine miserably and do not treat their guests splendidly: they are so accustomed to living

---

[1] Alluis, p. 3.

badly, either at war with soldiers, unknown in some enemy land, or as the prisoners of some cruel pirates, that now it does not inconvenience them in the least; in fact, they cannot abandon their unfortunate life, however miserable it may be" (22). Alluis reflects on the consequences of the heroic lifestyle and presents his characters with a band of heroes who resemble nothing so much as faded movie queens: they exist solely on the basis of their past merits, and nothing but the dim memory of their reputations sustains them. Pushing the logic of their situation one step further, Alluis informs us that one of the fundamental rules of this country is that fighting is prohibited "both because they have already fought so much in their youth, and because their combat would be useless, since with the exceptional strength and address each one has, it would be impossible for any to gain the advantage over another. What could Polexandre win from Pharamond?" (22). This is a country inhabited only by people each of whom is the best in the activities all of them practice. The grammatical logic of the superlative quickly breaks down when these transcendentally superior individuals are drawn together.

Like Sorel before him, Alluis subjects the language of contemporary fiction to its own internal logic and discovers it to be both ridiculous and unable to adapt to situations beyond the scope of its own immediate linguistic constructions. Heroic fiction turns out to be so tightly bound to its contextual markers specifying how and by whom it should be read that it cannot support divergent interpretations. Any attempt at an original or unenlightened reading of a heroic novel will simply reveal the work's unmitigated subordination to its arbitrary conventions. Alluis challenges heroic fiction's capacity to withstand interpretation uninformed by the iconographic traditions composing the genre: the novel's subtitle, in fact (*les heros docteurs*), couples heroism and erudition.

Alluis offers his own ironic instruction designed to teach the conventions of heroic fiction to the uninformed. After Alidor and Dorise come across a giant and Alidor somewhat blithely slays him, they chance upon the rustic Lysis, who tells of his love for Climene. What follows is the School of Love, in two parts, from which the novel draws its name. Sixteen lessons addressed to "les Amants" (suitors) cover such topics as the declaration of love, the lover's duties, remedies for jealousy, and the best time to make love. Eight lessons for "les belles" (the beloved) concern themselves with distinguishing between male and female love and then with teaching women how to get a man to fall in love with them. The most fundamental lesson for women dictates that they should never declare themselves first; the reason is

> That a heart acquired without pain is scorned,
> That such a conquest
> Accomplished without headaches
> Is an overly facile happiness. (126)

Alluis' School of Love frequently mixes the lofty and precious language of heroic fiction with the indecorous or earthy language of the rising middle class. The lesson seems clear: the middle class can be instructed in the traditional iconography of heroic love as long as the people are taught in their own language. Once they acquire the erudition required for decoding the complex systems of *bienséance* and *vraisemblance*, they can compete with the best of heroic figures which, in light of the life they lead in the Ville des Romans, is not saying much. After Alidor and Dorise learn their lessons, he is revealed to be the son of Cleopatra and she the daughter of Clélie, two of the most notable figures in the heroic tradition.

Alluis' novel serves as something of a model for most of the novels I will consider in the rest of this book in that it establishes the parameters of a specific, valorized discursive practice and then goes about the task of instructing characters as well as potential readers how to accede to that discourse. In light of the radically changing relationships between writers and their audiences, and the increase in non-aristocratic readers in the 1660's, the establishment of such parameters was crucial. Authors needed to take a more active role in defining their own reading audiences and they needed as well to take care not to alienate any potential book buyers. Alluis goes so far as to suggest that his book belongs to a new literary form; at least, he indicates, it fails to fall into any of the literary categories previously established:

> Concerning the bourgeois privilege that I give my hero in the City of Novels, let people not believe that vanity obliges me to do so, nor that I want to have this book pass for a completed novel. I know well that if it is too long for a novella, it is too short for a novel, and that in any case it cannot pass for half a novel or for a novella and a half.

> But I feel that I could well give this bourgeois privilege to my hero, after so many people have given the privilege of immortality to their heroes, who perhaps were of no better family than mine. ("Au Lecteur")

In his hesitation to place his work in one of the existing literary classes, Alluis suggests that readers whose needs or interests were not addressed by existing categories of fiction might find something of value here. In addition, he defends his right to write for a bourgeois audience and he questions the ancestral integrity of previous works of fiction.

L'Escole d'amour demystifies the conventions of aristocratic fiction, particularly the heroic novel, by making them appear both less lofty and more easily accessible to non-noble readers. The work is, however, fraught with a double-edged irony that fails both to establish the desirability of acceding to the discursive practices of aristocratic fiction and to locate the specific interest of this new form of fiction. On the one hand there is something less than gracious in the ease with which readers who learn Alluis' lessons can ostensibly attain mastery of heroic fiction's conventions; the questionable allure of something so easily gained reminds one of the joke, "I would never join a club that would have someone like me as a member." In addition, Alluis presents heroic fiction and its characters in such a ridiculous light that even if it did seem easy to be initiated into their ranks it hardly seemed worth the trouble. On the other hand Alluis argues in his preface that his novel is unlike any other work of fiction currently on the market; those who felt drawn to it might be glad to learn that it was written for them. But to whom, specifically, was this book addressed? In its unabashed ridicule of aristocratic tradition and manipulative patronizing of the bourgeoisie, it seemed to have succeeded in alienating any potential readers. Alluis appears indeed to have created a form of fiction unlike any other, but the value and use of this new form are not immediately apparent.

Antoine Furetière's *Roman bourgeois* is a similar but somewhat more successful attempt to parody existing literary forms and provide a viable alternative to heroic fiction. In the opening lines of the novel the narrator announces his rather poetic project: "I sing of the loves and adventures of several bourgeois of Paris, of one and the other sex. And what makes this marvelous indeed is that I sing of these things, and I do not know music." [2] These inaugural sentences establish the sardonic tone that Furetière maintains throughout the two books composing his novel. The very first words of the work imitate the opening of the *Aeneid* and place the novel in the heroic tradition of fiction that had been popular in France for the preceding twenty-five years. In the same breath, however, the narrator destroys this lofty pretense by including bourgeois among his subjects. As if this were not enough to confound any aristocratic members of his audience and delight the bourgeois, he continues his subversion of the heroic form in the following sentence by deliberately misconstruing the poetic sense of the verb *chanter* (to sing). Continually conscious of the noble, heroic literary traditions his century had established and revered, Furetière wafted gibe after pointed gibe at the stifling conventions of portraying only members of the nobility in a style that had come to be identified with them as well as at those who put stock in these conventions.

Le Roman bourgeois is a relatively short novel set in the Place Maubert and peopled by lawyers, merchants, courtiers, and a host of other characters drawn for the most part from Paris' middle class. Divided into two books, it details first the courtship and eventual marriage of two young people of bourgeois stock and then, in the second book, the story of Charroselles (an anagram of Charles Sorel), the unsuccessful and often ridiculed writer who courts Collantine, a dyed-in-the-wool litigant. There is no obvious connection between the two parts, save that the people depicted are all bourgeois, and Furetière in fact warns readers not to try to find any relationship between the two books. The novel is primarily concerned with presenting a mirthful image of contemporary middle-class people, and it opens with a description of bourgeois values. Javotte, one of the first book's principal characters, is collecting alms in church: "He who gave the greatest amount was deemed the most in love, and the girl who gathered the most money was considered the most beautiful. As in older times, when to sustain the love of a beautiful mistress the knightly proof was to present oneself with lance in hand and take on all comers, likewise the bourgeois proof was to have one's mistress canvass with cup in hand and take on all suitors" (906). Furetière adroitly appropriates the

[2] Furetière, *Le Roman bourgeois*, p. 903.

conventions of romance and heroic fiction, and he gives them a decidedly bourgeois turn by marrying beauty and amorousness with venality. A man's ostentatious spending and a woman's ability to shake men down for money are characteristics prized in this parish; these valued mercenary traits are translated, in Furetière's bourgeois universe, into the more traditionally valorized sentiments of gallantry and beauty.

Throughout *Le Roman bourgeois* middle-class characteristics and attitudes are translated in similar fashion into heroic or noble features. Javotte laments her inability to engage in the elegant conversation characteristic of upper-class women, for example, and complains of not having access to "their book where they get all that" (1004). Pancrace, who is courting her, gives her a copy of *L'Astrée* and other popular novels, with the result that "by dint of studying night and day she learned so much in a short time, and became the greatest conversationalist and the most flirtatious girl in the neighborhood" (1007).[3] Social climbing and the attempt to appear more cultivated than they really are constitute most of the characters' activities, and usually with predictably ridiculous results. Furetière's characters, like Sorel's in *Le Berger extravagant*, frequently misconstrue highly encoded figurative or professional language, and they try to derive from it a literal, referential meaning. Belastre, for example, a bourgeois who purchased a charge in order to become a seigneur, hears a colleague refer to the Law of the Twelve Tables. "Truly (Belastre interrupted him), these Romans must have really dined well!" (1050). High social standing in *Le Roman bourgeois* continually revolves around an ironic appropriation of aristocratic values by characters who fail to understand the class they try so desperately to imitate. Many of Furetière's characters are recently ennobled *robins* who, because they belong to the *noblesse de robe*, lead dual existences whose complexities they are not fully able to master. Nicodème, for example, is "an amphibious man who in the morning was a solicitor and in the evening a courtier; in the morning he wore the robe of the Palace to plead or to listen, and in the evening he wore the *canons* and gold festoons to court the ladies" (907).

---

[3] Nicodème, one of the novel's many lawyers, accomplishes his own education in a similar manner: he is described as a man who "had paid his court directly in Cyrus and Clélie" (p. 911).

Furetière's novel is a protracted attempt to negotiate the changing social status of an upwardly mobile middle class, and the "amphibious" characteristics typical of the *noblesse de robe* abound. As both Kathleen Wine and Philip Stewart have pointed out, even the title of Furetière's work is amphibious in its deliberately oxymoronic construction: coupling the genre *roman* with the social group *bourgeois* is an absurd rapprochement that contemporary readers would have found at the very least curious.[4] Stewart labels the association of these two almost mutually exclusive terms "an alliance of the ridiculous with the sublime" (33), and Wine argues that it produces a tension that is never quite resolved in the novel (50). What had been depicted in *romans* were the adventures of noble individuals; the tension Wine identifies is not only the coupling of what had traditionally been an aristocratic genre with bourgeois subject matter, but the violation of the accompanying aesthetic rules governing novelistic composition as well. Wine views Furetière's work as a scathing critique of the seventeenth-century novel, writing that "fundamental to this critique is the consideration of romanesque literature as a body governed by certain absolute laws" (52). She attempts to demonstrate that Furetière's primary concern in *Le Roman bourgeois* is to ridicule the premise that novels should be subject to guidelines regulating their production. She reads the narrator's relationship to the reader as one founded on their mutual awareness of the conventions established in fiction, primarily the heroic novel, and as one founded on the ongoing attempt to demonstrate the absurdity of observing these conventions. *Le Roman bourgeois* achieves its parodic force by smugly conforming to the conventions of aristocratic fiction and either self-consciously explaining why they are inappropriate for a particular situation or adhering to them to the letter with predictably ridiculous results. The amphibious nature of many of its characters permeates the novel's structure as it attempts both to heed and to repudiate heroic fiction's conventions.

Furetière keeps his readers aware of the conventions of fiction by making frequent reference to reader expectations, noting that it is within his power to subvert them completely,[5] or, perhaps more

---

[4] Kathleen Wine, "Furetière's *Roman bourgeois*: The Triumph of Process"; Philip Stewart, *Rereadings: Eight Early French Novels*. See also Maurice Laugaa, "Pour une poétique de la négation."

[5] For example: "Do not expect me to describe her here, as one customarily does on these occasions" (p. 906).

frequently, remarking on the conventions of the novel that make some of its elements so predictable that they do not need to be described:

> If you are so curious to know how to reveal passion, I'll show you several ways found in *Amadis*, *L'Astrée*, *Cyrus*, and in all the other novels, which I have neither the time nor the inclination to copy or to rob, like most authors who have used the inventions of their predecessors. . . . You will only note that it's always the same thing, and just as you know the refrain of a song when you see the first word followed by "etc.," all you need know now is that our marquis was in love with Lucrèce, etc. You can guess or augment easily enough what he says to her or what he could say to touch her. (936)

Furetière asserts a guild-like solidarity with his predecessors whose inventions for relating lovers' professions of passion he refuses to plagiarize but he distances himself later on from the archaic system of publishing in which "a merchant would buy [the book] by the page" (1032). More significantly, however, he repudiates the conventions of heroic fiction that standardized aesthetic response, pointing out that merely indicating the marquis' love for Lucrèce provides readers with enough information to imagine the details of his declaration. There exists throughout *Le Roman bourgeois* a tension between the accurate representation of reality and the codified conventions of fiction that relied heavily on *vraisemblance* and consequently on readers' access to an accumulation of cultural capital iconographically associated with the aristocracy.[6] Furetière believes that readers are familiar enough with the world he is describing to be able to fill in their own details that do not advance the story. This presumption implicitly casts aspersions on the convention of *vraisemblance* so crucial in earlier fiction because it suggests that readers need not have access to the aristocratic cultural capital informing that fiction; all they require is an intuitive understanding of how the world functions. While the tight correspondence between the primary ontological world and the world the fiction creates suggests a nascent realism in the modern sense of the term, we should resist the temptation to apply this term to an early modern novel. The significance of the analogy between empirical and fictional worlds in *Le Roman bourgeois* lies more properly in the repudiation of the hermetic conventions that had traditionally mediated between the two.

[6] On the concept of cultural capital, see Bourdieu, *La Distinction*, chapter one.

What seems to frustrate Furetière is readers' tacit acceptance of the conventions of fiction, conventions designed not to make the production of fiction more economical and inventive, but to make it standardized. Furetière repeatedly reminds us that he can write like everybody else, but if he did we would not have an accurate portrayal of how things really are. He avoids the extravagance of writing like his contemporaries, reminding us that he had promised us "a true story" and that truth simply does not fit into the neat models aesthetic conventions have proposed for it. Furetière disdains the apparent mania for the categorization of reality, and he sees the heroic novels so much in vogue in his day as the prime culprits. Authors of heroic and pastoral fiction had theorized about the nature and goals of fiction in the prefaces to their works, as cited in the previous chapters, and their prefaces helped codify the conventions of fiction as an aristocratic and partisan genre. Furetière expresses over and over again his desire to break free from the established models, and his disdain for theoretical prefaces is summed up, paradoxically, at the very end of *Le Roman bourgeois* in a description of a four-volume work entitled *Somme dedicatoire* (Dedicatory compendium) that is nothing but preface and the examination of the premise of prefaces. The first two chapters of volume one of the *Somme* are summarized as follows:

VOLUME ONE

Chapter 1—Of the dedication in general, and of its good or bad qualities.

Chapter 2—If the dedication is absolutely necessary in a book. Question decided in favor of the negative, against the opinion of several authors both ancient and modern. (1086)

It takes four volumes, or so much reading material that "we would have trouble dealing with [it] in twelve sittings," to analyze the question of the preface. Nothing, finally, is decided about the nature of novels' representation; the only issue resolved is that the praise and flattery one often sees in prefaces should be sold at a high price.

The price of praise in literary works is one of the main issues of Furetière's *Somme dedicatoire* and it raises the issue of the "amphibious" nature of the writer in the 1660's. Furetière's concern with the production of literature divorced from the influence of wealthy patrons leads him to question all of the possible conflicts of interest a writer might have. Chapter 10 of the work's fourth volume, for example, discusses this burning matter: "If women, whom one often flatters for nothing and who think that all manner of praise is by right their due, must pay just as men do for the compliments authors pay them in their books or in their dedicatory epistles" (1092). Following the table of contents of the *Somme dedicatoire* is a price list of various works of praise an author might include in his or her work. An epic poem in alexandrine verse, for example, is worth 2,000 livres, and a simple sonnet, 3 livres. Other chapters of the *Somme* treat complex legal concerns such as whether a patron who is not satisfied with the work he or she commissioned can return it for a full refund, and whether one can sue a patron for nonpayment. All told, however, it is concluded that the richest patrons are not always the best, for they sometimes fall victim to a "sudden paralysis in the hands when it is time to pay up" (1088). The most valuable patrons are those who keep up their end of the bargain and pay the agreed-upon sum for the delivery of the contracted work.

The amphibious nature of the writer in the later years of the seventeenth century is addressed most explicitly in the "Advertissement du libraire au lecteur" (Publisher's preface to the reader) preceding Book One. The conceit, of course, is that here it is the publisher, and not the author, addressing the reader, but Furetière confounds the artistic and commercial natures of writing by putting these words in the "publisher's" mouth:

> You will perhaps say that I am speaking not as a publisher but as an author. The truth is that all that I have said was extracted from a long preface that the author himself put in the front of the book. But unfortunately, since it was written long ago by a man who had fun composing it in his youth, it was subject to all of the things that can happen to the first few pages of an old manuscript. . . . I had the things I considered too old removed, and I had a few new things added to bring it up to date. If you find it to your liking, I'll do the same for what follows, and I'll give it to you, if you are kind enough to pay for it. (902)

In his prefatory remarks Furetière confounds the intuitive distinction between artist and salesman, and writing and marketing become ineluctably fused in one and the same process. The seventeenth-century systems of patronage and bartering of literary works induced authors to adopt a deftly duplicitous voice; their books needed to flatter the wealthy and incite them to pay for a dedication and yet still appeal to a broad reading public. This amphibious and duplicitous voice, born of the need to tread lightly around specific or localized ideological engagement, introduced into fiction a new discursive practice. This new discursive practice repudiated the truths ostensibly mirrored in but ultimately constructed by the putative referentiality of heroic fiction in its claim to historical accuracy. As Furetière's narrator continually demonstrates, the truth of his tale lies only in the telling, and it is well within his power to subvert our expectations, to skip descriptions that we can supply for ourselves, or, as in the passage cited above, simply to present to us as true whatever we are amenable to pay for. In short, he is a supplier who gleefully hawks his merchandise to readers as long as they are willing to buy it.

The development of the modern literary marketplace in which authors tried to appeal to patrons as well as purchasers of their works helped lead to a commodification of culture. Works of fiction that could no longer address the ideological concerns of a single, restricted group were alienated from both writers and readers; consequently, no unilaterally constructed group could lay hegemonic claim to the truths they contained. *Le Roman bourgeois* helped precipitate the antiquation of heroic fiction's values by interrogating its pretension to referentiality and by uncovering the ideological construction inherent in the transhistorical truths it purported to reflect. Furetière's renunciation of earlier fiction's claim proceeds first by appropriating and interrogating contemporary discursive practices. That is, before his narrator can introduce the move of demonstrating the sterility and ultimate oppressiveness of a conventionalized language ostensibly answerable to a preexisting reality, he must take hold of it and put it to service in a context for which it was not designed. In *Le Roman bourgeois* classical and neoclassical language strain against a referentiality—the urban scenarios of middle-class Paris—completely alien to their original functions. Furetière's juxtaposition of traditional language with a startlingly new and inappropriate subject matter devalues the dominant discursive practice by showing simultaneously its capacity and its inability to express unfamiliar realities: the neoclassical language with which Furetière opens his novel ("I sing of the loves and adventures of several bourgeois of Paris, of one and the other sex") is capable of *denoting* the Place Maubert, but this highly conventional form of discourse had as its very specific use the construction of an ideological truth which did not obtain in bourgeois Paris. Consequently there is a disjunction between this language's ability to represent a particular reality and the affective analytical domain that inheres in that language. In other words, Furetière chooses a form of language that is not suited for expressing his subject matter because it is too intimately associated with the ideological truths inhering in aristocratic fiction; the tension in *Le Roman bourgeois* arises from the fact that the neoclassical language of heroic fiction with its claim to historicity and referentiality mystifies or occults its own creation of the values and truths it purports merely to relate. By emphasizing the ideological overdetermination of heroic fiction's conventions, Furetière implicitly contests their denotative dimension and reveals the extent to which truth is not a form of collective and unequivocal community property but a constructed relation inhering in representation.[7] The neoclassical language that Furetière takes to task offers its users the ostensible integration Lukács found obtaining in ancient epic, an integration providing the illusion of an adequation between language, world, and knowledge in which discourse simply enunciates in objective fashion the world at large and its truths.

Like his forebears, Furetière imitates the ancient masters, yet his imitation quickly becomes appropriation when he allows the disjunction separating the referential and the analytico-ideological domains to take hold. After stating his program to sing of the lives and adventures of several Parisian bourgeois, he continues in mock-heroic form:

> And what makes this marvelous indeed is that I sing of these things, and I do not know music. But since a novel is nothing but poetry in prose, I would be beginning poorly if I did not follow the example of my masters and include a proper prologue: for since Virgil sang of

[7] Timothy J. Reiss observes in *The Discourse of Modernism* that the fundamental assumption in neoclassical language is that "the proper *use* of language will not only *give* us [the] object in a gradual accumulation of detail . . . but will also *analyze* it in the very form of its syntactic organization. Moreover that syntax not only analyzes the world but also presents . . . the mental judgment taken to be coincident with that process of analysis in syntax" (pp. 41–42).

Aeneas and his arms, and Tasso . . . distinguished his work with can-
tos, their successors, who were no better musicians than I, have all
repeated the same song and have all begun on the same note. (903)

Furetière's parody of the *Aeneid* in his opening sentence as well as
his later references to Virgil and Tasso are not-so-subtle digs at the
discursive conventions his contemporaries employed as part of
their attempt to license and legitimate their works. Boisrobert had
argued that a novel is nothing more than an epic in prose, and
Furetière exposes the absurdity of attempting to reproduce the sociopolitical truth of an antiquated literary genre in a radically new
form. Averring that his contemporaries who struggled to translate
the ideological integrity of the epic into narrative prose and still
retain the adequation of language, world, and knowledge that
characterized it were no better artists than he, Furetière evinces the
disjunction between language and its political and empirical referent. He shows that epic language is simply unsuitable for rendering
contemporary bourgeois society: it expresses either an absurdly inappropriate literalness illustrated by the misconstrual of poetic
singing, or it overlays an antiquated value system onto the contemporary world. Furetière's narrator is aware of the tradition and the
language that contemporary convention demands he employ, but
he also feigns ignorance of their significance. That is, although he
can imitate the letter of classical language and open his work in the
style of Virgil (the *Aeneid* begins, of course, "Arma virumque
cano" [I sing of arms and of a man]), the narrator is unable to
reproduce the spirit of the epic. He misconstrues the sense of the
Latin word *cano* ("I do not know music") and implies either that
he knows nothing at all about music, or that he does not know the
music for the song he is about to sing. That is, he is going to play
by ear and improvise as he goes, ignoring any literary precedent or
tradition.[8]

In addition to contesting the referential capacity of heroic fiction's language, Furetière establishes a narrator of indeterminate
voice whose identity is unclear and problematic. The novel begins
with the personal pronoun "I" and thus predicates a discrete nar-

___

[8] The point, in fact, is driven home even more forcefully in the following statement: "I do not want to make poetic fictions, or skin the eel by its tail—that is,
begin my story with the end—like all those gentlemen who think they're so smooth
finding the marvelous and the surprising when they tell a tale that way" (p. 903).

rational voice whose peculiar relationship to the work's subject matter is in contradistinction to the homogeneous and univocal voice of heroic narrators. Although Furetière's narrator opens the work with a series of literary platitudes that gauge his literary capital and consequently license him to narrate—he starts off with reference to the Muses, avers along with his predecessors that a novel is a prose poem,[9] indicates the necessity of imitating the ancient masters, and inserts his own work within the tradition of canonical authors such as Virgil and Tasso—he asserts his individual and decidedly unconventional voice by misconstruing traditional classical literary language. Whether his misconstrual is intentional matters less than his failure to engage with the spirit of classical literature; what remains is the empty shell of a discursive practice, a practice that the narrator deactivates by stripping it of its power to represent the concerns of a collective social body and inducting it into the service of a distorted individual practice. The narrator's individualistic use of classical literary language inaugurates him into a relationship with his reader that they both need to negotiate: he by asserting his rhetorical and discursive construction of a virtual reader, and the novel's real reader by contending with and decoding the narrator's disfigured classical literary language.

The narrator localizes his and his reader's negotiation of their relationship in the series of self-conscious allusions to narrational authority that punctuate the novel. As cited above, he makes frequent and detailed reference to his capacity to adhere to or subvert readers' expectations, thus inferring a well-educated reader capable of not only grasping his allusions but also of understanding the significance of the subversion taking place. Furetière's narrator retains a bantering familiarity with his reader, and on at least one occasion he interjects a performative apostrophe that both addresses the reader and comments on the address taking place: "If the proverb 'Like master like servant' is true, then you can judge (my dear reader, whom I have not, it seems to me, addressed in some time) who will be master" (1047–48). Furetière's narrator is, in effect, little more than a voice occupying the discursive position such an apostrophe suggests. That is, his "I" exists in opposition

[9] See also Perrault's *Parallèle des anciens et des modernes*: "Since the comedies in prose are just as much dramatic poems as comedies in verse, why would not stories in prose be poems just like those told in verse?" (III, 148).

to the "you" of his reader; it is a voice capable of addressing, but in possessing no identity of its own, it is individuated only through its otherness to the reader as well as to the narrating voice of classical literary language that it demands readers recognize.[10] Furetière's narrator causes his readers to identify with him solely on the basis of his own particular and unconventional use of classical literary language and style. Forcing them to recognize the differences between existing modes of fiction and his own invention, he highlights not the ostensible referentiality and transhistorical truths aristocratic fiction had valorized, but the construction of contingent truths whose reality inheres in his own practices of representation.[11]

The opening lines of the "Advertissement du libraire au lecteur," in fact, detail Furetière's concern with the means, as opposed to the ends, of representation. In this preface to his novel, Furetière advances the belief, generally associated with modernist theories of representation, that a text's capacity to construct its referent is of more critical interest than any denotative capacity we might attribute to it. Comparing his work to a portrait, he writes: "Just as an excellent portrait demands our admiration, even though we may have none for the person portrayed, likewise one can say that well-written fictions that use borrowed names make a greater impression on our minds than real names and true adventures could ever do" (901). Here we are close to the beliefs of Fancan or Rapin, cited in Chapter 2, that a contrived representation is generally more ideationally preferable to works of nature. Furetière differs radically from his predecessors and contemporaries who held this view, however, in his elision of *vraisemblance* as a necessary mediator between reader and referent. Evoking none of the truisms or formulas implicit in other forms of fiction, formulas designed to control and direct reader response to a morally or politically useful interpretation, Furetière eschews literary representation with a built-in response. *Le Roman bourgeois* attacks the idea that the

[10] J. A. G. Tans argues that the narrator in *Le Roman bourgeois* acquires a specific identity only by imposing itself as narrative *instance* and that it is a nearly pure pretext situating itself only in opposition to heroic fiction. See his "Un Sterne français: Antoine Furetière, la fonction du *Roman bourgeois*" (pp. 281–83).

[11] Jean Nagle has advanced the proposition that the second book of *Le Roman bourgeois* contains a latent referentiality that documents Furetière's career as a magistrate. See his "Furetière entre la magistrature et les bénéfices: Autour du Livre Second du *Roman bourgeois*."

discursive practices earlier or contemporary authors had deployed in their novels could in any way naively attain the world they sought to represent; the separation between language and reality asserts itself in Furetière's novel, leading to the suggestion—quite radical for the period—that literary language is little more than a collection of arbitrary conventions underpinning the ideological hegemony of a specific powerful group.

To claim, as I have done, that *Le Roman bourgeois* repudiates aristocratic conventions of fiction by contesting their claim to referentiality and consequently their moral and ideological programs is not tantamount to arguing that Furetière advocates a specifically bourgeois literature or political agenda. After all, authors like Cervantes, Rabelais, Scarron, or even Sorel satirized existing literary practices and stable notions of truth without erecting any genuinely systematic alternatives in their place. In adding to his critique of traditional discursive practices the description of bourgeois Paris, however, Furetière not only disarticulates fiction's form from its established content, but he duplicitously disguises the subject of his specific attack. That is, unlike his parodying predecessors who took on particular literary forms, practices, or even works, Furetière makes it difficult for us to determine whether he is ridiculing the novel's conventions and discursive practices or its traditional subject matter. His obtrusively interrupting narrator makes it quite plain, through his use of neoclassical language to describe vulgar people and activities, that he conceives of a separation between form and content, particularly since he so ruthlessly ridicules his bourgeois subjects: Furetière thus makes explicit the fundamental contradiction between prose fiction as it was traditionally conceived and representations of the bourgeoisie.[12] The novel proposes no answers, then, but instead creates tensions and poses questions concerning the nature of representation and the localization of political or moral truth within representation. *Le Roman bourgeois* cloaks itself in the *robin*'s mantle, the bourgeois' frock, and the noble's *canon*; it refuses all attempts to be categorized aesthetically

---

[12] Antoine Adam writes that although he was born of solid bourgeois stock, Furetière nevertheless unmercifully imprecated his own social milieu and heartlessly ridiculed the people who composed it. Remarking that the seventeenth-century bourgeoisie was composed of both archaic and modern styles of life, Adam argues that Furetière "portrayed characters of both types, and all of them, or just about, are ridiculous and foolish" (*Romanciers du XVIIe siècle*, p. 46).

or politically. Furetière's amphibious characters who wear the magistrate's robe in the morning and the courtier's velvet in the evening
always appear ridiculous because they are never comfortable no
matter what they don. These characters hypostatize the tension inhering throughout the novel: given that traditional discursive practices are cloaked in aristocratic sensibilities, how can one write a
novel about the bourgeoisie without its seeming ridiculous?

The work's last paragraph shows why an answer to this question
is impossible. In Furetière's amphibious world, answers and conclusions are forever deferred. This is because his narrator's highly individualistic use of language eschews any claim of attaining an adequation of representation and referent, a claim heroic fiction had
staked in its construction of a master discourse whose expressive
causality aimed at restricting interpretation to a specific ideological
one. *Le Roman bourgeois* concludes with Charroselles and Collantine continuing their passion for litigation even after they are married; in the work's last paragraph the narrator proposes a parable
to suggest a way of conceiving an ending for a seemingly intermin-
able process:

> In the land of fairies there were two special animals: one was an en-
> chanted dog, which had the gift of catching any beast it was let loose
> upon, and the other was an enchanted hare, which had the opposing
> gift of never being caught by whatever dog was pursuing it. Chance
> had it one day that the enchanted dog was let loose on the enchanted
> hare. Everyone wondered which of the two gifts would prevail,
> whether the dog would catch the hare, or the hare would escape from
> the dog, as it was written in the destiny of each. The resolution of
> this difficulty is that they are still running. It is just the same with the
> trials of Collantine and Charroselles: they have always pleaded cases
> in court and they continue to do so; they will plead as long as it
> pleases God to allow them to live. (1104)

The novel does not conclude, then—it simply stops. Furetière had
promised to tell his readers "what the outcome of the trials was"
(1104), but he is unable to describe the outcome because it lies
outside the physical and expositional confines of the book. The
real-world ramifications of the fictional world he has created logically extend beyond the boundaries of the novel, but whatever geographically or temporally distanced consequences his story implies
have no bearing on his tale. Consequently the litigation's outcome,
like that of nearly all of the actions or events in the novel, is sus-

pended indefinitely and retranslated into a mechanistic process privileging not the referent but the play of representation.[13] Furetière thus evinces a near total disregard for empirical referentiality, and he privileges the representational moment of language, providing his readers with specific details only when it is "necessary to the story" (907). He confesses an inability to report characters' conversations at which he was not present,[14] and he reveals that when he does report intimate conversations "I put some of my own invention into them" (936). The practice of fiction that his mechanistic privileging of process over product helped establish, then, is one that relies on empirical referentiality only in order to distance itself from the rigorous conventionality of *vraisemblance* in heroic novels. That is, there exists a bourgeois, urban world never accounted for in previous works of fiction, and if Furetière refers to it the effect is not to put it on equal footing with the idealized world heroic fiction described. Rather, by destabilizing the ideological relationship between neoclassical language and its traditional aristocratic truth, he demonstrates that fiction, particularly in its newly commodified form and in its complex relationship to patrons and the literary marketplace, depicts not enduring transhistorical truths but merely contingent and relational ones.[15]

On the stage, Molière offered a similar subversion of referential language in his *Dom Juan* (1665). Molière's Dom Juan is a master of duplicitous language. He has learned to manipulate the conventional language of *politesse* to the point that it prohibits communication, as M. Dimanche, his creditor, learns ("he is so courteous and he pays me so many compliments that I couldn't ask him for

---

[13] Wine, in fact, argues that "in his critique of the novel, Furetière shows that as the creation of novels becomes more mechanical, the process itself takes over, generating endless works" (p. 60).

[14] "Unfortunately for our story, Lucrèce had no confidante, and the marquis had no squire, with whom they could share their more intimate conversations. These are things that heroes and heroines have always had. How else can one know their adventures? How can one know what goes on in their conversations, how can one know their secret thoughts? How can one have a copy of their poetry and love letters, and of all the things necessary to build a plot? Our couple was not of the standing to have such confidants, and thus I learned nothing of them that did not appear in public" (p. 936).

[15] Laugaa offers a similar formulation in his "Pour une poétique de la négation": "The title introduces and represents a logical game which exceeds the restricted signification of its project: bourgeois parody as foreclosure, in the city, of heroic passions and adventures; it is a foreclosure as well of truth and of the real, by its expulsion out of the enclosure of the powers of imagination" (p. 527).

money").[16] Relatively recent work on *Dom Juan* has shown, with the support of speech-act theory, that much of Dom Juan's language of seduction eschews referentiality and depends ultimately on language's capacity for self-reflexivity. Shoshana Felman argues that Dom Juan seduces women by promising to marry them; his *promise* appears to refer to an extralinguistic reality, but in fact it is an utterance that refers ultimately only to itself: the utterance creates a pact but denotes nothing outside of the speech situation in which it is pronounced.[17] Similarly, Claude Reichler contends that Dom Juan only "borrows" signifiers from denotative discourse in order to give his interlocutors what they want to hear. Dom Juan is the master of the speech situation because his words cleave designation from signification, the latter referring primarily to the play of signifiers within a system of representation.[18]

Molière's play was a popular success, but it met with harsh critical disapproval. The title character's blasphemy and moral depravity were so offensive that the play ran for less than a month. *Dom Juan* and *Le Roman bourgeois*, each in its own fashion, repudiate the relationship between language and realistic or verifiable representation. In both works a single discursive agent—the title character in *Dom Juan* and the narrator in *Le Roman bourgeois*—establishes his own distinctive and decidedly unconventional use of language primarily by placing it in opposition to received models of discourse. Resembling the standardized language they reject, these individualistic uses of language call for specific and conventional responses, but they ridicule or reject those responses when they are forthcoming. They derive their power by offering their real or virtual interlocutors merely the illusion of what they expect; their discourse, however, undermines the simple relationship between language and referent and turns on itself, transforming a denotative object into a dynamic process.

Alluis' and Furetière's works mark a radical change in the novel's discursive practices, a change that came about contemporaneously with modifications in the political, ideological, and aesthetic domains in seventeenth-century France. The seventeenth century saw

---

[16] Molière, *Dom Juan ou le Festin de Pierre*, in *Œuvres complètes*, vol. I, p. 761.
[17] Felman, *Le Scandale du corps parlant*, especially pp. 39–40.
[18] Reichler, *La Diabolie*, especially pp. 45–50.

a significant economic transition from feudalism to capitalism.[19]
Manufacturing displaced production by artisans, and distribution
of manufactured goods increased tremendously thanks to the
highly developed system of maritime trade. A number of manufacturing or commercial entrepreneurs amassed considerable fortunes,
and they gained substantial political power during the reign of
Louis XIV, effectively completing the process begun under the
sixteenth-century system of venality of offices, in which hereditary
privilege began to cede its authority to wealth. These economic and
political changes led inevitably to ideological ones, and the commodification of culture began to displace the bequeathing of culture, as powerful bourgeois sought aesthetic validation of their contributions and their worth. They not only commissioned works of
art but they purchased those which, particularly after the Fronde,
responded to their tastes. Aristocratic cultural capital, which had
been passed from generation to generation without substantial
modification of its ideological composition, failed to communicate
the political values of the rising economic class.[20] Consequently,
artists, particularly writers who had gained greater control over the
sale of their works, appropriated and modified traditional forms to
suit the new consumers' interests and needs. In fiction in particular,
ideological form and denotative content entered into contradiction
with one another, provoking a crisis in representation which was
met, as I have argued, by a destabilization of contemporary fiction's
discursive practices.

The destabilization of language to which I have been referring in
the works of Alluis, Furetière, and Molière consisted of an interrogation of referentiality, as I have noted above, but this does not,
of course, deny language its constative function. Rather, all three
writers demonstrated that referentiality is an elusive linguistic
property that frequently masks an insidious ideological function.
The individualistic yet authoritative languages of Dom Juan or of
Furetière's narrator challenge the received notions of a commonly
held linguistic referentiality capable of revealing an adequation be-

[19] In addition to the historians already cited, see G. N. Clark, *The Seventeenth
Century*; and R. J. Holton, *The Transition from Feudalism to Capitalism*, especially
pp. 173–76 and 192–97.
[20] I will discuss the specific composition of what I am here referring to as "the
political values of the rising economic class" at greater length in Chapter 7.

tween truth and its materially present avatars. Their language denotes or evokes an extralinguistic presence, of course, but it also accomplishes a signifying task in the process, thus negating the possibility of being judged true or false: Dom Juan's preferred linguistic model is the performative, as Felman has shown, and as an act that ostensibly engages him in a commitment—the promise to marry—it cannot be judged to be true or false, only to be in good or bad faith.[21] It denotes nothing save the linguistic utterance itself. Likewise, Furetière's narrator repeatedly negates the referential authority of heroic fiction by asserting his own authority to subvert readers' expectations and to apply the specific ideologically valorized language of aristocratic neoclassicism to bourgeois subjects. His language ceases, finally, to refer beyond the confines of the book and implodes at the work's end in an unremitting collision of signifiers incapable of describing the outcome of the tale he himself has constructed.

Alluis' *Escole d'amour* and Furetière's *Roman bourgeois* unabashedly place themselves in direct opposition to the heroic fiction of the day, and it is through their opposition to existing practices of fiction that they articulate their own aesthetic principles. *L'Escole d'amour* and *Le Roman bourgeois* subvert aristocratic aesthetics, but they do not construct an alternative poetics of bourgeois fiction isomorphically analogous but politically opposite to the heroic novel. Rather, in their opposition to existing fiction they erect a new model of interpretation based not on an exegetical decoding of enduring iconography in order to arrive at a standardized version of truth, but on compounding ambiguities in a duplicitous voice addressing readers of diverse backgrounds, interests, and political affinities. To accomplish this, both novels teach their readers new strategies to add to their interpretive repertories. Alluis' novel introduces its principal characters, as well as any unenlightened readers, to the somewhat hermetic text of heroic conventions in the "Escole d'amour pour les Amants" (School of Love for suitors) and the "Escole d'amour pour les belles" (School of love for the beloved), in which, as noted above, students learn to decipher the discursive codes of aristocratic courting. Furetière continually enjoins his readers to break free of the constraining conventions to

---

[21] See also J. L. Austin, *How to Do Things with Words*, especially pp. 10–11.

which they have become accustomed, and he proffers a work with little narrative integrity; ending his novel with a tale whose conclusion is forever deferred, he privileges not the product, but the process of narrative, the means by which social meaning encoded as *vraisemblance* takes shape. Repudiating the stability and integrity of heroic fiction's ostensibly unequivocal discourse, a stability their predecessors had tried to develop by appropriating the practices of the ancient masters, Furetière and Alluis disarticulated the contrived univocality of the master's voice and exposed the ideology of its form.

It is now possible to offer a definition of the modern novel as it appeared from the late seventeenth century onward. Beginning roughly in the 1660's, fiction began to privilege signification over signifying and it no longer originated from a single, apparently stable ideological base. As the two examples above show, novelists abandoned pastoral and heroic mythology which constructed readers and their class myths as the ultimate referents of their works; they formulated an alternative aesthetic and discursive practice of fiction by placing their works in opposition to the received models. Because this alternative form of fiction consisted principally of negating an existing practice, the new novel privileged a dynamic *process* of constructing sense over the established static *form* from which readers extracted a more or less predetermined meaning. Radical changes in cultural participation resulting from a dramatic influx of wealthy and powerful bourgeois patrons and purchasers, combined with new laws governing the sale and circulation of literary works, led to literary works of ambivalent ideology. The modern novel no longer offered readers the illusion of ready-made meanings inhering in works that they could simply process in order to have their self-images confirmed for them. Eschewing the socially charged and highly codified *vraisemblance* that had marked earlier novels as the organ of conservative aristocratic ideology, the modern novel originated principally as a genre of negation. Nevertheless, in its earliest manifestations it achieved its own positive signification from the tension it produced by pitting a traditionally aristocratic form against urban bourgeois subject matter, consequently exposing the socially constructed nature of the ostensibly natural relationship between the world and novels' depiction of it. The modern novel in France made its earliest appearance, then, as a contestatory interrogation of the repertory of conventions that existing fiction was employing. Implicitly political in its use of bourgeois subjects to expose contemporary novels' limitations, it nonetheless retained a significant degree of ideological uncertainty, since its derision of middle-class content tempered its repudiation of aristocratic form. Not until the eighteenth century, as I will argue below, did the modern French novel less equivocally advocate specifically bourgeois concerns. As Bourdieu has argued for cultural forms in general, and as Harth maintains for seventeenth-century ones in particular, disenfranchised or marginal political groups frequently adopt the cultural icons belonging to the dominant class. Because there was no coherent repertory of bourgeois iconography ready to evoke middle-class ideological concerns, novelists learned to articulate those concerns by appropriating and distorting aristocratic symbolic forms, putting a hegemonic form into the service of a marginal process.

Prose fiction was ideally suited to respond to bourgeois' aesthetic and ideological needs and interests for two principal reasons: on the one hand, the novel was a comparatively new genre in France, and authors were able to seize its protean form in order to use it for a variety of purposes. On the other hand, writers adopted the novel form precisely *because* it had developed as an aristocratic tool. The ability that aristocratic fiction had assumed to mimic history and describe the world in an ostensibly unmediated fashion contributed to making the novel the form best suited to transcribe bourgeois ideology because novelists could translate its allegedly unembellished representation of reality into a celebration of middle-class truths. One of the modern novel's most powerful tools for undermining the hegemony of aristocratic fiction lay in its discursive ability to construct alternative models of interpretation, display how those models operated in opposition to received exegetical standards, and then demonstrate to readers the processes by which they might accede to the new interpretive practice. More powerful still, however, was the modern novel's ideological and formal duplicity, the guileful manner in which it repudiated existing practices while appearing to conform, on the face of things, to existing literary practices. As Fabien Sfez has phrased it, "the novel is subversive not in that it introduces a new kind of reading, but in that it is an unveiling of the functioning of the reading of any text."[22]

Neither Alluis' *L'Escole d'amour* nor Furetière's *Roman bourgeois* was a great success in its day. Alluis' novel barely saw the light of day, and Furetière's only began to find its reading audience in the early eighteenth century. While Tans suggests that particularly in Furetière's case this was because the novelist boldly contradicted the normative and essentialistic aesthetic of the time, I would argue that the reasons for literary failure are both more subtle and more complex. Both these "bourgeois" novels explicitly confronted the reigning aristocratic aesthetic and positioned themselves in opposition to it. Their emphasis on the mechanistic process of signification over the static concept of form nullified the dominant conception of literary form as an essentially transparent device. They revealed the disjunction between text and truth, and disclosed the conventional nature of literary language, emphasizing the normative function of contemporary discursive practices. The development of a bourgeois aesthetic in seventeenth-century fiction began as a negation of aristocratic poetics and consequently it entered into intertextual dialogue with received models. As a result, modern, bourgeois fiction not only began to evince an extreme self-consciousness on the level of its relationship to contemporary literary standards, but it entered into dialogue with the discursive registers of power as well.[23] The duplicity of novelists who earned substantial portions of their income from both patrons and purchasers of their works, two groups with frequently conflicting interests, initiated a literary modernism predicated on language's capacity not to reproduce referentially valid worlds, but to fabricate new conventions that suppress denotation in order to privilege the construction of meaning.

The literary modernism I have identified in the third quarter of the seventeenth century was a historically determined, diachronic

---

[22] Sfez, "Le Roman polylexique du XVIIe siècle," p. 52.

[23] See also Frow, who makes a similar argument for intertextuality in general: "Intertextuality is always in the first place a relation to the literary canon (the 'specifically literary' function and authority of an element) and only *through* this a relation to the general discursive field. This does not mean that literary texts are in some simple way 'about themselves,' but it does imply that reference to the authority of nonliterary modes of discourse is always structured by the force of reference to the literary norm" (*Marxism and Literary History*, p. 128).

phenomenon that initially arose as a critique of reigning and synchronous aesthetic practices. The institutionalization of aesthetics by the Académie Française and the political legitimation of those aesthetics in an increasingly absolutist state established a formidable ideological amalgamation of theory and practice. New regulations governing writers' relationships to their works contributed to a commodification of the literary text; a dramatic rise in literacy meant that more people drawn from a wider range of the social spectrum had access to and were purchasing literary works.[24] Finally, ideological conflict, marked in particular by hosts of wealthy bourgeois assuming political power in domains traditionally belonging to the aristocracy, led to the creation of a literary expression whose political orientation, if not expressly middle class, was at the very least undecidable. Perry Anderson has written that these three phenomena—academicism, the emergence of mass consumption, and the potential of social unrest—are the three factors contributing to the aesthetic apparatus of modernism. The conjunction of these three phenomena, he argues, helps establish a dominant aesthetic against which a new discursive practice can articulate itself by appropriating and modifying suitable elements.[25] The literary modernism of seventeenth-century fiction embraced an aesthetic and political ambivalence that made use of existing conventional language and fictive devices to expose the novel's formal and ideological constraints. Its aesthetic and political marginality gave it the means to ridicule both bourgeois and aristocratic subjects and allowed it to exist alongside sanctioned literary forms as a problematic yet sufferable fictive mode.

Different thinkers have elaborated series of definitions of literary or discursive modernism, and the philosophies informing their thinking range from Lukács' neo-Hegelianism to John Frow's Marxism. Common to most discussions, however, is an analysis of the breakdown of traditional aesthetic authority and of the relationship between the objectified measurement of reality and the

---

[24] On the rise of literacy in France, see Chartier, Compere, and Julia, *L'Education en France du XVIe au XVIIIe siècle*; Mandrou, *Des humanistes aux hommes de sciences*, especially pp. 107–20; Stone, *The Crisis of the Aristocracy*, pp. 303–31; and Martin, *Livre, pouvoirs, et société à Paris au XVIIe siècle*.

[25] Anderson, "Modernism and Revolution," pp. 324–25.

subjective, anti-aesthetic destabilization of truth.[26] The modernist text presents itself as individualistic and contingent; it strives to lay bare the enunciating subject and repudiate the belief that although discourse seems unimpeachable because it corresponds to received notions of truth, it is, nevertheless, a historically determined convention that achieved its status as truth through a series of obfuscations of specific ideological origin.[27] Although few historians of the novel identify the late seventeenth century as a period in which the characteristics of modernism—normally associated with the late nineteenth and early twentieth centuries—punctuated dominant aesthetic practices, it seems clear that the tension obtaining between bourgeois' participation in political life and their alienation from cultural life contributed to producing a new discursive mode.

It is important at this juncture to delineate the features composing the novels I will from this point on be referring to as "modern" and to justify this nomenclature as well as to locate critical precedents for it. When I refer to the modern French novel, I am above all addressing a specific discursive practice inhering in a work that might in other contexts be identified as traditionally neoclassic. Madame de Lafayette's *Princesse de Clèves*, for example, a work written by a noblewoman and presumably directed at an aristocratic audience, employs the expressive causality of heroic fiction in its appropriation of historical fact as the basis for its plot. Madame de Lafayette's narrator addresses readers in a manner that suggests they are familiar with court life, as we will see in Chapter 6, and the total lack of metaphor restricts interpretation to what is seemly at the court. The novel constructs an expressive causality dictating reader response primarily through the use of model interpretations that readers are enjoined to imitate, models that occur

[26] See in particular Matei Calinescu, *Five Faces of Modernity*; Michael Levenson, *A Genealogy of Modernism*; and David Hayman, *Re-Forming the Narrative: Toward a Mechanics of Modernist Fiction*.

[27] Reiss states the case quite succinctly: "The production of discourse, its objects, and its relations by the *I* of enunciation that originated it, in secret, in power, and with the complicity of a knowing elite, was gradually occulted: discourse became the common, transparent, and objective property of all, while the enunciating *I* was hypostatized as individual will. Discourse was infallible because it corresponded to 'common sense,' while will could control it only with the assent of all potential users" (p. 360).

in what are most often referred to as "digressions" in the work. Despite the formal appearance of adhering to neoclassical models of fiction, however, I will argue that the novel privileges not the denotation of an ideological truth, but the connotative process by which discourse constructs meaning. This is the fundamental characteristic of the modern novel: it is composed of a discourse that reveals itself to be the result of specific, politically informed practices whose meaning does not inhere in words but is rather constructed through the confrontation of conflicting ideological positions.

There are, of course, differing conceptions of what constitutes the modern novel. Two in particular, because they are so fundamentally opposite, can help clarify what is at stake in the novel's new discursive practice. Marthe Robert discusses two kinds of modernity in fiction, identifying the first as the continuing search for their own meaning that texts such as *Don Quixote* evince and the second as the representation of bourgeois concerns. *Robinson Crusoe* is an example of the latter in its depiction of "the tendencies of the mercantile middle class which emerged from the English Revolution." [28] Robert maintains that novels always remain highly ambivalent and ironic because they oscillate between depicting their own representational systems, as in *Don Quixote*, and reflecting aspects of the empirical world, as in *Robinson Crusoe*. Novels, she argues, demand that readers both recognize and ignore the degree to which their truths are discursively constructed. This, she avers, forms the basis of their irresolution: "Fictional illusion can be achieved in two ways: either the author acts *as if* there were no such thing, and the book is then said to be realistic, naturalistic or simply true to life; or else he can stress the *as if*, which is always his main ulterior motive" (35). Novels are inherently subversive in Robert's schema because they are above all calls for change.

> "Faire un roman" is to express a desire for change which can be satisfied in one of two ways: either by altering *what is*, or by altering *who one is* through an alliance with someone above one's standing. However, both solutions are a rejection of empirical reality for a personal dream presumed to be attainable by dint of deceit and charm.

[28] Marthe Robert, *Origins of the Novel*, p. 19 n. 1.

The conquest of a world thus deceived and charmed can only be achieved once its hierarchies have been rejected. (17)

Robert locates the origin of the modern novel in a representational indeterminacy that vacillates between privileging its own discursive construction of meaning and the social reality of the world it putatively describes. The novel resists favoring either its own construction of meaning or its reflection of real social conditions, a resistance at the very core of its modernism, and it is consequently, Robert argues, undeniably progressive in its attitudes toward social change.

Lennard Davis agrees that *Don Quixote* and *Robinson Crusoe* are crucial texts in the development of the modern novel, but the conclusions he reaches could not differ more radically from Robert's. Concurring that the power of the novelist's illusion distinguishes Cervantes' work while the depiction of bourgeois practices, particularly as they concern property, marks Defoe's novel, Davis nevertheless argues that novels are not inherently subversive but conservative.[29] Davis maintains that the modern novel originated as a literary discourse which for a variety of political and aesthetic reasons needed to remain ambivalent toward its own invention and reproduction of meaning. Novelists who claimed their works were true initiated the familiar framed narratives of early fiction, and this pretext "created a mode of literary creation and fabrication which is obsessively bound up with speculations on the capacity of narrative to carry a purely factual or purely fictional message" (*Factual Fictions*, 24). Although he believes that the ambivalent relationship the novel entertains with factual and fictional reality is part of its peculiar aesthetic, he strenuously argues against Robert the question of the novel's capacity to change:

[29] In *Factual Fictions*, Davis writes that "in Cervantes' novel, while some characters are involved in fabrications or are the dupes of fabrications, the reader never is. In Defoe's narrative, however, the butt of the major fabrication is the reader him- or herself who is involved in the con game ostensibly perpetrated by the author who maintains that the novel is not fiction but fact" (p. 21); in *Resisting Novels* he writes that "the point at which the novel diverges from earlier forms, theoretically speaking, is the point at which objects are included and described outside of an exterior, fixed system of meaning such as that provided by allegory. The new system of meaning by which objects are inscribed is the more ambiguous one of ideological meaning" (p. 58).

Novel reading as a social behavior helps prevent change. . . . Like any complex social formation, novels are highly ambivalent in their messages. . . . Novels can offer in their heroes and stories various kinds of opposition to stasis and power, but at the same time it would seem that the formal elements of the novel add up to a social formation that resists change. . . . For the large mass of people, reading novels is an activity that prevents or inhibits social action as do so many leisure activities in a consumer society. (*Resisting Novels*, 17–18)

Davis elaborates the ways in which novels prevent people from engaging in social action and he argues that because readers involuntarily identify with characters and their situations they re-enact their scenarios in conditions akin to a psychoanalytic one. That is, Davis cites Freud in "Remembering, Repeating and Working-Through" and points out that analysands repeat emotionally painful situations under conditions of acute resistance in order to avoid confronting their unconscious directly.[30] The novel-reading situation is analogous to the analytic one, Davis maintains, in that novels have repetitious plots that nearly always involve the protagonist's dramatic change at the work's end; this repetitive structure, Davis writes, "provides a false or surrogate example of change that might satisfy any external need or desire for change" (*Resisting Novels*, 19).

It should be clear by now that I agree with Davis about the conservative ideology of fiction, at least as far as the aristocratic fiction of the seventeenth century is concerned. However, I am equally persuaded by Robert, particularly with respect to eighteenth-century novels. The crucial concept here, however, belongs to Davis, who isolates resistance as the key to understanding the political nature of fiction. Although separation between premodern and modern fiction as I have defined it does not fall conveniently on the year 1700, I would argue that there is little resistance fiction as Davis has described it prior to the third quarter of the seventeenth century precisely because novels were principally conservative works of literature designed to maintain aristocratic hegemony. By the end of the seventeenth century, however, the changes in the publishing industry I have described, coupled with radical modifications in the system of royal patronage, all but forced novelists to adopt a polit-

---

[30] This essay is in vol. 12 of Freud's *Complete Psychological Works: Standard Edition*, trans. and ed. J. Strachey (New York: Norton, 1976), pp. 147–56.

ically ambiguous position that translated, later in the eighteenth century, into a progressive movement of exposure and reform.

In the following chapters I will explore the manner in which seventeenth- and eighteenth-century novels erect and hypostatize the proposition that literary meaning does not inhere as an objectified textual product but occurs, rather, through the collision of contradictory reified discursive practices. As I intend to demonstrate, these novels propose alternative reading strategies that contradict traditional aesthetics, and they do so in both their thematic and their structural dimensions. Significantly, a great number of these novels employ similar narrative techniques in order to deploy the constructivist discourse of modernism. Quite often we find problematic principal characters whose distinctive and frequently antipathetic behavior sets them off from the community at large. These marginalized characters are frequently neophytes who need to learn the sign system obtaining in their group, and only by learning to manipulate the discourse privileged in their world do they succeed in integrating themselves into their societies. Marivaux's Jacob in *Le Paysan parvenu* (1736) and his Marianne in *La Vie de Marianne* (1731–41) are folk of base or indeterminate origin who learn to thrive in polite Parisian society. Similarly, Diderot's Suzanne Simonin masters the discourse of seduction in order to induce the kindly marquis de Croismare to come to her aid in *La Religieuse* (written 1760). One of the most distinctive characteristics of the modern novel's principal characters is their striking aptitude for deception; once they learn to imitate the discursive practices of the circles they need to enter or contain, they reproduce them with enviable acumen and transform their initially marginal positions into situations of significant power or control.

Chapter 6 A Discourse of One's Own: *La Princesse de Clèves*

At the age of nineteen, Marie-Madeleine Pioche de La Vergne, later to become Madame de Lafayette, wrote to Gilles Ménage, one of the regulars of the Hôtel de Rambouillet: "I am so convinced that love is such a bothersome thing that I am happy that my friends and I are exempt from it."[1] Twenty-five years later she wrote a novel depicting the aggravations of love at the court of Henri II in which the protagonist, driven to desperation, makes a startling confession. *La Princesse de Clèves* has incited an enormous amount of critical commentary, most of which deals with this confession and the plausibility of the tale. Mme de Clèves' behavior shocked and appalled seventeenth-century readers because no one found it believable that the central figure of a work of fiction would ever behave in such an unprecedented way.

Mme de Lafayette seems to have realized that readers might object to some of the more unconventional aspects of her work. In an often cited letter to Lescheraine, she wrote: "What I find most striking [about *La Princesse de Clèves*] is that it is a perfect imitation of the world of the court and of the manner in which people live there. There is nothing novelistic [*romanesque*] or elevated about it; thus, it's not a novel; it's more aptly a memoir, and people say that that was its title, but it was changed."[2] Having written this letter during a heated debate over the novel's *invraisemblance* and before she acknowledged authorship, Mme de Lafayette claims not that the work is *vraisemblable*, but that it accurately transcribes the reality

[1] Letter of 18 September 1653, in *Correspondance de Madame de Lafayette*, ed. André Beaunier, vol. I, p. 34.
[2] Letter of 13 April 1678, in *Correspondance*, vol. II, p. 63.

of Henri's court. Her remarks recall Furetière's strategies for writing *Le Roman bourgeois*: she equates an accurate transcription of reality ("a perfect imitation of the world of the court") with the absence of earlier fiction's stylization ("There is nothing novelistic or elevated about it") and following Furetière's lead in not calling *Le Roman bourgeois* a novel because of the term's connotations she agrees that labeling *La Princesse de Clèves* a novel might be misleading ("thus, it's not a novel").

Yet, the author of *La Princesse de Clèves* goes beyond simply stating that her work is not a novel because it is realistic. She calls it a perfect imitation of the world of the court. It is one thing to claim that a representation accurately depicts the way things were or could have been in a given historical setting; it is quite another to claim that a text perfectly imitates a world. A perfect imitation suggests that the imitation and the model it represents are indistinguishable, a problematic concept for literary mimesis, since there is obviously no inherently mimetic relationship between a collection of words on a page and the world beyond the page's borders. Only readers' tacit agreement to consider a text mimetic or realistic can guarantee that relationship, and a particular group of readers will only agree that a text is mimetic if it displays characteristics found in forerunning texts deemed realistic or in current mimetic works of different forms or genres. Since it can never imitate its model directly, narrative depends on codified tradition to be considered realistic. Narrative provides, as Gérard Genette has written, only the illusion of mimesis, and it depends on the unstable and continually varying relationship between author and reader. Unlike other forms of mimesis—sculpture, for example, or theater—the novel cannot show or depict its referent directly. A *récit*'s relationship to its *histoire* is always at one level removed from a direct mimesis; consequently the degree of fidelity readers find in narrative mimesis is purely a matter of convention. Genette writes that narrative can only ever offer the illusion of mimesis "for this unique and sufficient reason: narration . . . is a fact of language, and language signifies without imitating. Unless, of course, the object signified (narrated) is itself language." [3]

In order to understand how *La Princesse de Clèves* perfectly imi-

[3] Genette, *Figures III*, p. 185.

tates the "world of the court and . . . the manner in which people live there," we need to explore how Mme de Lafayette depicts the daily activities at the court of Henri II, where courtiers constantly engage in discovering others' secrets while safeguarding their own. It will become clear that the world of the court is a textual one structured by a specific discursive practice at which courtiers must become adept: they need to interpret others' behavior in order to discern and understand their motives. By exploring the discursive practices of the court and the use Mme de Lafayette's novel makes of them, we will see that *La Princesse de Clèves* is in fact a perfect imitation of this world, primarily because one of the principal narrated objects is, in fact, language.

La Princesse de Clèves depicts Henri's court as a hermetically sealed community distinguished by the production and interpretation of ambiguous signs. Characters negotiate their way through this community by confronting its complex discourse and constructing narratives; they erect an epistemological framework that provides the contexts and limits of knowledge at the court and assigns them places within that framework. Henri's courtiers construct a narrative understanding of their world and are in turn constructed by the places they hold in that world. Their stories, which all conform to the same general model of court life, have an expressive causality based on seventeenth-century standards of *vraisemblance*: each tale that courtiers tell expresses, as we will see, the overarching narrative and ideological structure of their restricted circle. By depicting a principal character whose behavior violates all convention, however, the novel explores the limits of *vraisemblance* and expressive causality. Mme de Clèves struggles to decode behavior at the court by applying the interpretive strategies she gleans from others. Because her predicament differs quite radically from received models, however, her attempt to imitate courtly discourse fails.

Like its principal character, *La Princesse de Clèves* appropriates a discursive practice—the *vraisemblance* of earlier historical fiction—and tests the limits of its applicability. It represents to its readers characters engaged in the process of interpreting discourse from within the confines of established conventional practice, and it shows this practice break down when confronted with situations it was not designed to reckon with. In this respect, then, *La Princesse de Clèves* dismantles one of the fundamental constructions of aristocratic fiction: its expressive narrative causality linked to the rhetorically restricted interpretation of events. As we saw in Chapter 3, Gomberville's *Polexandre* directs its readers to arrive at the rather circumscribed conclusion that aristocratic virtue and valor naturally predominate; one of its mechanisms for doing so is the appropriation of explanatory narratives that retrospectively demonstrate the profound and inherent significance each episode had for the final, expected outcome. *La Princesse de Clèves* makes similar use of the explanatory narrative, but it undoes the certainty that Gomberville's narrative causality imposed, highlighting instead the construction of literary meaning and the potential for misinterpretation.

In its disassembling of contemporary narrative modes, *La Princesse de Clèves* resembles Furetière's *Roman bourgeois*. Both works investigate conventionalized language's validity and its capacity for representing subjects outside the rigidly defined borders of its ideological domain. Unlike *Le Roman bourgeois*, however, *La Princesse de Clèves* depicts highborn subjects in the stylistic and narrative modes of aristocratic fiction. Rather than ridiculing the conventions from which it ultimately distances itself, *La Princesse de Clèves* explicitly portrays a literary commonplace of aristocratic fiction—the love affair between two extraordinarily beautiful and noble individuals in a fairy-tale patrician setting—and then systematically reveals convention's limitations by showing it break down in the very environment in which it was designed to thrive. Moreover, Mme de Lafayette's novel expressly represents the conventions of *vraisemblance* by depicting characters actively abiding by them in their own interpretations. Her problematic protagonist, however, fails to learn the conventions adequately and defies others to understand her behavior in terms of these narrative paradigms. *La Princesse de Clèves* thus represents the world of the court, but more importantly it reproduces in objectified fashion the discursive practices that make it up. Bakhtin characterized the novel as a genre "made up of the images of 'languages,' styles and consciousnesses that are concrete and inseparable from language. Language in the novel not only represents, but itself serves as the object of representation" (49). It will become clear that *La Princesse de Clèves* isolates and objectifies contemporary *vraisemblance* and consequently suggests alternative discursive strategies for fiction.

The publication of *La Princesse de Clèves* triggered a heated debate about the outrageous confession that the Princess makes to her husband that she loves another man. Most readers found her confession *invraisemblable*, but it was not because they found it inconceivable that a woman would make such a confession; rather, it was because there was no precedent for such a thing in fiction.[4] Significantly, readers' responses to Mme de Clèves' confession matched those of the novels' characters: even the Princess realizes how extraordinary her action is. After Mme la Dauphine tells her that an unidentified woman in love with M. de Nemours confessed everything to her husband, Mme de Clèves, who knows that the story is true because she is the woman in question, answers: "I don't think all this sounds very probable, Madame, and I should like to know who told it to you?"[5] Mme de Clèves' remark underscores the crucial distinction courtiers make between what is plausible or likely at the court, and what actually occurs there, and it shows the extent to which generalized narrative principles inform the way courtiers conceive of their relationship to their society. Courtiers turn all their experiences into narratives, and the Princess herself, as Dalia Judovitz has observed, experiences her own life as "a story rather than an event."[6] This brief episode in the novel hypostatizes the contemporary critical and aesthetic debates that distinguished factual accuracy from *vraisemblance* as the literary

---

[4] Roger de Rabutin, comte de Bussy, who was imprisoned in the Bastille for his *Histoire amoureuse des Gaules* (Amatory history of the Gauls), a collection of libelous portraits of contemporary courtiers, remarked that the author of *La Princesse de Clèves* deliberately tried to flout convention: "Madame de Clèves' confession to her husband is bizarre and could only happen in a true story. But when someone invents a story, it is absurd to give the heroine such an unusual sensibility. The author, in so doing, clearly tried more not to resemble other novels than to follow the rules of good sense" (letter of 26 June 1678, cited by Geneviève Mouligneau, *Madame de Lafayette romancière?*, p. 47).

[5] Mme de Lafayette, *The Princesse de Clèves*, trans. Nancy Mitford, p. 143 [p. 345]. All references to *La Princesse de Clèves* are to this edition, and henceforth page references will be given parenthetically in the text. For the convenience of readers more familiar with the work in French, I will include in brackets the corresponding page numbers for *La Princesse de Clèves* in the readily available Classiques Garnier edition of Madame de Lafayette's *Romans et nouvelles*.

[6] Judovitz, "The Aesthetics of Implausibility: *La Princesse de Clèves*," p. 1051.

mode that depicted to a specific group of readers a parochial version of the way things ought to be. The range of actions in which people engage is relatively restricted at the court, normally to those activities that might advance one politically; no woman had ever confessed such a thing to her husband, and such a confession was in this circle *invraisemblable* not because it seemed impossible, but because as a purely personal or private affair it would serve no social or political function. The *vraisemblance* of internal court narratives—that is, as the courtiers themselves perceive and interpret them—consequently depends on the concept of expressive causality elaborated in Chapter 3 in which each narrative element or episode expresses, often in overdetermined form, the inner essence of the entire structure. Courtiers perceive a master narrative, an abstract code that structures all their attempts to understand their world, and they strive to structure all narrative episodes according to the master code.

As we have seen, the plots of aristocratic fiction were also restricted to what was deemed politically and morally useful. Since the Académie's politicization of *vraisemblance* in 1638, literary discourse had become but one manifestation of an overarching social, political, and economic discourse of upper-class hegemony; the aesthetic object became an expressive signifier designed to render directly the signified both of aristocratic superiority and of political absolutism, a denominative phenomenon that reached its epitome in fiction during the era of the heroic novel. When Mme de Clèves characterizes her own confession as *invraisemblable*, she establishes the intimate connection between narrative signifier and signified—between, that is, *histoire* and *récit*—in contemporary fiction: a work's narrative content and enunciating discourse must share a common code—*vraisemblance*—that restricts the interpretation of possible narrative episodes to received paradigms.[7] Narrative episodes or events that fail to express the politics of *vraisemblance*—at the court, the attempt to ingratiate oneself with powerful individuals, or at the level of the work's *récit* the rendering of upper-class political hegemony—seem unrealistic because they conflict with seventeenth-century master narratives that dic-

---

[7] Gérard Genette defines *histoire* as "the signified or content (even if this content turns out to be in this case of a weak dramatic intensity of a factual nature)" and *récit* as "the signifier, *énoncé*, discourse or narrative text itself" (*Figures III*, p. 72).

tate a function or a political use for all works of art. The discursive convergence of *histoire* and *récit* had been aristocratic fiction's cachet: marking no difference between the language of its characters and that of its narrators, earlier seventeenth-century fiction had erected a hegemonic interpretive framework that valorized the pretensions of France's nobility. Restrictions on language and subject matter in fiction—*vraisemblance*—were motivated not by aesthetic concerns properly speaking, but by ideological ones. Plausibility was governed by political utility.

That the restrictions placed on fiction have motivations other than the adequate representation of reality became explicit the month following publication of Mme de Lafayette's novel. The *Extraordinaire du Mercure Galant*, a sort of *New Yorker* of seventeenth-century Paris, asked readers whether a confession like the Princess's was ill-advised:

> PROPOSED QUESTION
>
> I would like to ask whether a virtuous woman, who has all the esteem possible for her perfectly honorable husband, and who for all that evinces a passion for a man that through all sorts of means she strives to stifle; I would like to ask, I say, if this woman, who wants to retire to a place where she will not be exposed to this man who she knows loves her without his knowing that she loves him, and who cannot oblige her husband to consent to this retreat without telling him what she is trying to flee, should reveal her passion to her husband or keep it silent at the risk of the constant struggle she will be obliged to wage because of the unavoidable occasions she will have to see this man, from whom she has no other way to distance herself than the revelation in question.[8]

Readers' reactions to the Question, published later in the same year, were mixed. Opinion on the matter was evenly divided between those who felt that the unusual situation called for an admission, and those who felt that such an avowal should never be made under any circumstances. The Question's wording, however, although clearly inspired by *La Princesse de Clèves*, asks not if a woman in a novel should do such a thing, but whether a real woman ought to behave in this way. Mme de Clèves' confession is clearly not, then, empirically inconceivable, even by contemporary

[8] *L'Extraordinaire du Mercure Galant* (Apr. 1678), pp. 299–300.

standards. However, its manifest *invraisemblance* encodes it as an action that should not occur in a literary work.

But how does a specific conception of verisimilitude become commonly accepted in a given culture? How can people be certain that their narrative apprehensions of the world will correspond to others'? Any narrator needs to set out with a collection of presumptions about what his or her audience knows or takes for granted; this is why historical narrative, for example, need not describe in minute detail every excruciatingly precise aspect of the culture it relates and can concentrate instead only on the differences that give it its significance. Plausibility is therefore contextually and culturally determined within a specific group's narrative traditions. I plan to show that in *La Princesse de Clèves* Mme de Lafayette painstakingly coaches her readers in the principles of plausibility and verisimilitude accepted at the court of Henri II by establishing the background against which all actions are juxtaposed. Then, with the aid of the frequently criticized digressions, she brings to light the models according to which courtiers narrate and interpret their world, and she tests the applicability of these models for contemporary fiction.

The background for all of the action in *La Princesse de Clèves* is the highly complex court of Henri II, in which the one thing that can be taken for granted is that virtually all people are involved in behavior they need to disguise.

> The Court gravitated round ambition and love, the chief occupations of men and women alike, for there were so many factions and intrigues, and the women played so large a part in them, that love was always mixed with self-interest, and self-interest with love. Nobody was tranquil or indifferent—everybody was busily trying to better their position by pleasing, by helping, or by hindering somebody else; boredom and idleness were unknown, the occupations of the day were pleasure and plots. (41) [252]

Courtiers have to become adept at interpreting the equivocal speech and actions of their associates. Since most actions are undertaken with a vested interest in mind, people at the court must discern the likely reason for which a given person would engage in a particular activity or utter a particular sentence. Although the range of possible reasons is large, it is finite: given that everyone "was busily trying to better their position by pleasing, by helping, or by hindering somebody else," one need only determine the various permutations and combinations of a given court activity. Consequently, courtiers have a sense of what kinds of motives are likely to provoke the outward behavior they see and they can react appropriately. Thus, there exists a *vraisemblance* at the court that helps people read others. Conversely, those who are engaged in an intrigue need to disguise their activities as much as possible to prevent others from learning the truth behind their own appearances. They need, in other words, to project contextually plausible pretenses to keep themselves from being accurately read.

Courtiers' reactions to events at the court consequently bear a striking resemblance to readers' responses to a text. Given a particular set of denotative raw material—that is, a collection of signs— they need to decode this material in order to construct a meaning behind the facade, a meaning that may or may not reflect a courtly reality but which does in either case help them negotiate court semiotics. One's ability to read the signs of the court depends on one's past reading experience and the attentiveness with which one has listened to explanatory narratives. The neophyte Princess, for example, makes a casual remark to her mother concerning the apparently tight relationship between the queen and M. le connétable, only to be cut short by her mother, Mme de Chartres: "Yes, indeed, that is very far from being the case" (54) [264]. What follows is a lengthy digression in which Mme de Chartres reveals the history of the queen's hatred for the constable.

The digressions into events of the past in *La Princesse de Clèves*, although one of the things most frequently criticized in the articles of the *Mercure Galant* and Jean-Antoine de Charnes' contemporary criticism of the novel,[9] establish norms of behavior. Contemporaries familiar with the historical world Mme de Lafayette depicts viewed the digressions as inessential to the novel's action. Jean-Henri Valincour, in his *Lettres à Madame la Marquise * * * sur le sujet de La Princesse de Clèves*, published just after Mme de Lafayette's novel, finds the digressions distracting: "I had trouble understanding the relationship between what [Mme de Chartres] tells [her daughter] about Madame de Valentinois, about Madame

---

[9] De Charnes, *Conversations sur la critique de La Princesse de Clèves*.

d'Etampes, about the death of the Dauphin, and the story of *La Princesse de Clèves*. It seems to me that in works of this sort one should suffer nothing but that which is necessary to the plot."[10] Valincour bases his criticisms of the digressions into the past that punctuate the narration of *La Princesse de Clèves* on the readerly urge to get on with the story. Since he can see no relationship between the tales courtiers spin and the unraveling of the apparent main plot interest—the love triangle in which the Princess finds herself—he considers them dispensable. This is a far cry from readers' reactions to heroic fiction which just a generation earlier had employed exactly the same types of digressions as a means both of making up for inadequacies in the third-person narrator's omniscience and of filling out the psychological construction of particular characters. Valincour, in his impatience to get on with the story, recalls Furetière's narrator in *Le Roman bourgeois* who wanted to dispense with the pat descriptions of characters with which readers were overly familiar in order to let the action of the work take hold.

These so-called digressions, however, are absolutely indispensable for this novel if it is ever to be a "perfect imitation of the world of the court and of the manner in which people live there." Like maxims which help set standards of behavior at the court,[11] the digressions show how specific individuals go about the task of distinguishing appearances from reality. The digressions function as explanatory narratives with a bivalent elucidative function. On the one hand these narratives provide crucial background information that may be essential for deciphering the current state of affairs. On the other hand they provide a model of interpretive practice that demonstrates the level of inferential sophistication required in order to function smoothly at the court. The explanatory narratives offer inexperienced court interpreters examples to emulate by laying bare the courtly decoding practice.

[10] Valincour, p. 98.
[11] John D. Lyons claims that there are fifty-two utterances in *La Princesse de Clèves* that can be considered maxims pertaining specifically to courtly behavior; he calls the maxims in the narration "a repertory of models of human conduct." He argues that Madame de Lafayette creates a dynamic of exceptional behavior and that the energy of the narrative comes from the failure of what is experienced to coincide with what is said about experience. See his article, "Narrative, Interpretation and Paradox: *La Princesse de Clèves*."

The digressions in the narration of *La Princesse de Clèves* serve, then, to establish in the diegetic register of the novel's internal narratives an object of imitation for the inexperienced. Those unfamiliar with the rigors of interpreting equivocal actions or ambiguous appearances learn to read the text of the court by imitating the reading processes exposed in the narrations of experienced courtiers. Thus, diegesis in the internal narratives becomes an object or model for mimesis. Analytical narrations which show how a given interpretation of a courtly situation was produced serve as models to be imitated. They help the uninitiated learn.

Four protracted explanatory narratives punctuate the *récit* of *La Princesse de Clèves*. Each reveals its narrator's mastery both of court history and of court interpretive theory. In his long narration to his wife recounting Sancerre's unhappy love affair with the widowed Mme de Tournon, for example, M. de Clèves situates the beginning of his story at the theater:

> One evening, when there was to be a play at the Louvre, we were all waiting until the King and Madame de Valentinois should come for it to begin, when we were told that Madame de Valentinois was unwell and that the King would not be coming. Everybody guessed that this indisposition of the Duchess was really some squabble with the King. Of course we all knew how dreadfully jealous he had been of M. de Brissac while he was at Court, but it was now several days since he had gone back to Piedmont, so we could not imagine what this was all about. (73) [281]

No one knows whether Mme de Valentinois was really taken ill. What is significant is the explanatory narrative courtiers constructed once they heard of her illness. First they test the verisimilitude of the claim to determine whether it holds up under the plausibility criterion. A likely cause is suggested, in this case a rift with the king, and then back-up evidence is applied. Yes, the king was jealous of the maréchal de Brissac, but Brissac was no longer at the court; consequently, something else must be the matter. What is almost amusing is the degree to which courtiers are carried away with their own narrative formation. Since Brissac is no longer at the court, it is determined that the king's jealousy is not the cause of the squabble, yet no one is willing to dismiss the interpretation that there was some sort of dispute between the king and Mme de Valentinois. In other words, the duchess's illness is replaced, near the end of the explanation, with an argument as the real reason behind the couple's absence. Since feigned illness is the most frequently employed excuse, no one considers even for a moment that the woman might really be sick. That might be true, but it would not, in these circumstances, be *vraisemblable*.

When the Princess attempts to mimic Mme de Valentinois and feign illness, however, she needs back-up support from her mother because her story, given visible evidence, is not plausible. The Princess does not want to go to the maréchal de Saint-André's ball for fear of letting Nemours know that she loves him. Her mother, seeing her obstinacy, "said in that case she must pretend to be ill in order to have an excuse for not going" (64) [273]. Her mother *told* her what to do and the Princess does it, but not very convincingly:

> You are looking so beautiful I find it hard to believe that you have been ill. I believe that when M. de Condé told us what M. de Nemours thinks about parties he put it into your head that by going to his ball you would be conferring a favour on the Marshal, and that this must be your reason for not going.
> Madame de Clèves blushed when she realized that Madame la Dauphine had made this lucky guess in front of M. de Nemours. (65) [273]

Mme la Dauphine is a clever reader. Even though the Princess deliberately came to the court "dressed rather carelessly" (64) [273], her face registers no signs of illness. Mme la Dauphine then correctly assumes that an ulterior motive prevented the Princess from attending the ball and that it involved her desire that M. de Nemours not know her feelings for him. The Princess blushes at Mme la Dauphine's astuteness, for she has easily guessed the real and in this case *vraisemblable* reason behind her unsuccessful feigning. The Princess's failure to provoke the desired response results from the fact that she did just what her mother told her, but only on the most superficial level. She displayed the most fundamental signs of illness, coming to the court "dressed rather carelessly," but failed to reproduce any of the subtleties that make for a convincing appearance. The *vraisemblance* of her not wanting to send a man a gallant message outweighs the potential veracity of her claim to be ill.

The Princess's failed attempt to reproduce the appearances that might lend an air of plausibility to her claim of illness characterizes her problematic relationship to the court's discursive practice. She imitates the enunciating register of this discourse, but falls short of replicating its effect; experienced courtiers consequently perceive a gap separating what she says from what she does. The Princess's inability to reproduce court discourse and appearances in convincing fashion results in part from her lack of experience: she is the only person of her generation portrayed at the court, and it is consequently difficult to determine to what extent her naïveté informs her clumsiness.

Another, more crucial factor animates her ineptness, however, and we can easily chart its significance in her development: the Princess's mother strives to inculcate in her daughter austere principles of virtue, principles that might have obtained for an earlier generation, but which are out of place and even incapacitating at the current court. Mme de Chartres, for a variety of reasons that will become apparent, attempts to make her daughter a unique example among the court's figures, and she scrupulously governs her daughter's thoughts and deeds. Endeavoring to make her daughter an exceptional woman, she severely restricts her ability to function at the court. She succeeds in rendering her daughter unique, however, and the first level on which her uniqueness appears is the semiotic one.

Mlle de Chartres' mother recognizes in her daughter the potential for excellence. Not content, however, to let the girl's stunning beauty and coveted wealth provide for her a life of merely ordinary distinction, she pushes her daughter to become truly exceptional and unique. Seeing personally to the young lady's moral and courtly education, she hopes to show her "the particular glamour that attaches to noble birth when there is also virtue" (36–37) [248]. Mme de Chartres seeks to preserve her daughter from the corrupting forces of the court by inculcating in her the love of virtue and, in addition, by cultivating between her and her daughter a friendship that will induce her daughter to confide in her.

> [There] was a discreetly exciting atmosphere which made this Court an agreeable place to live in, though not without its dangers for a young girl. Madame de Chartres was perfectly well aware of these dangers, and her preoccupation was how best to guard her daughter against them. She begged her, not as a mother but rather as a friend, to confide in her whenever words of love were spoken, promising her

guidance and support in matters which are often embarrassing when one is young. (42) [253]

Mme de Chartres' concern for her daughter's welfare in the highly volatile atmosphere of the court seems laudable enough. Offering her daughter the wisdom normally only acquired through years of experience at the agitated and dangerous court, she makes a deal with Mlle de Chartres, the terms of which are something like, "If you tell me the propositions men make to you, I promise to help you through the rough spots."

Mme de Chartres thus seems to be the ideal mother, taking the time to educate her daughter on matters most other mothers leave to chance. The threat gallantry poses to young women is a universal concern among mothers whose daughters are about to debut at the court, yet only Mme de Chartres concerns herself with warning her daughter about gallantry's pitfalls:

> Most mothers think that they can best protect young people by never speaking of love in their presence, but Madame de Chartres had different ideas; she often described it to her daughter, minimizing none of its charm, so that the girl should more readily understand what she told her of its dangers. She told her that men were not very sincere, not very faithful, and not above deceit; she spoke of the unhappiness that love affairs can bring to a family, and then, on the other hand, she showed her the life of a good woman, happy, serene. (36) [248]

Mme de Chartres knows that the complexities of the court should never be underestimated. Although the narrator indicates that "the Court gravitated round ambition and love" and that "everybody was busily trying to better their position by pleasing, by helping, or by hindering somebody else," Mme de Chartres plants in her daughter's mind even before she ever sees it for herself an image of impossibly complex behavior at the court. Mme de Chartres shows her daughter through vivid portraits the court's dangers, and she narrates men's infidelity in order to make the girl see the benefits of virtue. The litany of terms describing processes of representation in the above passage has led Marianne Hirsch to state that in her education of her daughter Mme de Chartres attempts "to substitute the narrative for the forbidden experience." [12] Ostensibly desiring

[12] Hirsch, "A Mother's Discourse: Incorporation and Repetition in *La Princesse de Clèves*," p. 75.

to preserve her daughter from the traps of gallantry and unfaithful men, she succeeds instead, as her daughter's behavior will show, in diminishing the Princess's capacity to judge and interpret for herself.

As if to show Mlle de Chartres how much she needs her mother, Mme de Chartres sends the girl off alone, before her first official court appearance, to select her jewels. While she is making her choice in the Italian merchant's shop, M. de Clèves arrives and is so taken with her beauty that he cannot contain his reaction. Mlle de Chartres, without her mother at her side, "seeing the state into which she had thrown him, could not help blushing" (37) [249]. Apparently some of the instruction her mother gave her rubbed off, for she does manage to extend to him the gesture of civility propriety demanded for "a man of quality." Recognizing people of quality, however, is not the same thing as being able to deal with them. Despite all of the lessons her mother gave her concerning court behavior—or perhaps because of them—Mlle de Chartres finds herself embarrassed in front of this man of obviously considerable merit. Unable to remain under M. de Clèves' gaze, she rushes off, and if her beauty was what first caught his eye, her unconventional behavior convinced him that he had to find out who she was: "He noticed that, whereas most young people enjoy seeing the effects of their beauty upon others, it only embarrassed her, and he felt that he was hastening her departure" (38) [249]. Mlle de Chartres' first experience with a gentleman of the court foreshadows those that are to come: without her mother's strong guiding presence, she falls to pieces when she has to interact in society.

Before she brings her daughter to the court, Mme de Chartres offers her verbal portraits of all that she is about to see, and, offering to be her friend, promises to help her through the tangles of courtly behavior if only her daughter confides to her all of the *galanteries* men speak to her. Hirsch sees in the relationship between the Princess and her mother "a bond of sincerity and honesty" (75) and in the latter's education of her daughter on the passionate intrigues that go on at the court an attempt to replace experience with narrative. Her reading of Mme de Lafayette's novel is informed by feminist theories of female identity, based to a large extent on Luce Irigaray's and Nancy Chodorow's views on women's relationships to their mothers. Hirsch's reading of *La Princesse de Clèves* centers less on the novel's love triangle and more on the relationship between mother and daughter as it informs the Princess's subsequent dealings with people at the court. Although she admits that the heroine of the novel is trapped in repetitions "which ultimately preclude development and progression" (75), she believes that the outcome of the story—the Princess's self-seclusion in a convent—represents an uncompromising victory for this woman who refuses to be the feminine erotic object in a world dominated by the male ego and libido. Much of Hirsch's analysis of *La Princesse de Clèves* centers around the fact that Mme de Chartres creates in her daughter "the potential for absolute uniqueness" (74), since she attempts to couple with the girl's beauty and wealth the principles of virtue. As we will see, however, her contention that the bond between mother and daughter is one of "sincerity and honesty" is questionable. Moreover, Mme de Chartres not only creates the *potential* for absolute uniqueness in her daughter, but she denies the possibility that the girl will ever be even remotely like anybody else.

Like Hirsch, I consider the Princess's relationship to her mother to be of paramount importance. I want to emphasize not the benevolent nature of the mother/daughter bond, however, but the debilitating effects it has on Mme de Clèves. After Mme de Chartres promises her daughter to help her understand the complexities of the court, she gives her this cryptic bit of advice: "If you judge by appearances in this place . . . you will go on making mistakes, for things here are seldom what they seem" (55) [265]. This statement both reconfirms to her daughter the necessity of consulting her mother on matters of courtly interpretation, and it underscores the worth of the help Mme de Clèves gets in return for confiding in her mother. The mother had initially promised her help; now, however, she reveals with this statement not only her capacity for helping her daughter, but her interpretive hegemony on matters pertaining to the court. That is, she knows when appearances and reality do not coincide ("things here are seldom what they seem"), but in failing to give her daughter a way to distinguish between the two she leaves the girl forever uncertain about whether her own readings get to the heart of the matter or only appear to do so.

Mme de Chartres' statement concerning truth and appearances at the court informs Hirsch's observation that the mother substitutes narrative for forbidden experiences. Mme de Chartres replaces showing with telling in the education of her daughter, and this is the germ of all of the Princess's problems: her mother never gives her examples of what she must do or what she must avoid. The Princess becomes enslaved to her mother's apparent interpretive mastery of the court. Mme de Chartres continually spouts what can only appear to the Princess as apocryphal promises of happiness that will come her way if she follows to the letter all the advice given her, yet for all the instruction she gives her daughter on things *not* to do at the court she never provides her with any useful counsel on what she *should* do. Mme de Chartres only presents her daughter with a list of interdictions, and if the girl avoids all of the forbidden experiences, then what is left is virtue. In other words, all of the instruction the Princess receives concerning virtue and how to attain desired states of happiness involves, basically, not doing anything at all. Each bit of advice Mme de Chartres gives her daughter, both that concerning not getting involved in any gallantries and that regarding not being too quick to judge by appearances, sends her the message that the good woman is passive and silent, and that if she remains so the life of *tranquillité* the virtuous woman deserves will be hers.

In *La Princesse de Clèves* it is the Princess's struggle to be a virtuous woman and escape the dangers of a love triangle that forms the narrative interest of the work. Were not the bond between mother and daughter so tight there would not be much of a story, for it is Mme de Chartres' concern for herself that incites her to keep her daughter's behavior in line. Whatever else the bond between Mme de Chartres and her daughter may be, it does not seem particularly appropriate to call it one of sincerity and honesty, as Hirsch does. Mme de Chartres comes up short of being totally sincere with her daughter, and her honesty is belied when she sacrifices her professed wish to find her daughter a husband, one who will love her and whom Mlle de Chartres can love in return, for a stronger desire: that of revenge. When the chevalier de Guise begins his short-lived campaign to win Mlle de Chartres' hand, the scheme is immediately nipped in the bud by his brother who bears a lifelong grudge against the vidame de Chartres, the young lady's uncle. Mme de Chartres, incensed that a family with less wealth than hers would refuse permission for an alliance, makes it known publicly that she would never consider such an arrangement. She then directs her energies to finding a distinguished family into which to marry her daughter, but she scraps her earlier plan of setting her up in an emotionally satisfying marriage. Her pride is injured by the Guise clan, and "such was her indignation that she now had a mind to marry her daughter to somebody whose rank would put her above those who thought themselves too good for her" (43) [254].

Mme de Chartres uses her daughter first as a sort of social weapon, by making her so virtuous that she is above all other courtiers, and then as a tool for revenge against families that had slighted her. The girl's unprecedented perfection is meant to show all how inferior they are: "Madame de Chartres, by her own care for the proprieties combined with her daughter's goodness, managed to give the impression that here indeed was somebody quite out of reach" (50) [260]. By the time she marries the girl off to M. de Clèves, she has succeeded in making her a wonderful status symbol, but not a very effective courtier. The Princess's near total dependency on her mother for knowing how to behave and react at the court is manifested in the incompetent and often blundering way she deals with court goings-on.

The episode that perhaps best illustrates the mother's imposition of an interpretive mode on her daughter is the one dealing with the purloined letter that allegedly fell from M. de Nemours' pocket. The queen, who has always been curious about the affairs of M. de Nemours, gives the letter to Mme de Clèves and tells her that it belongs to Nemours. Mme de Clèves reads the letter and believes that it is addressed to Nemours, even though nothing in the letter suffices to identify its author or its addressee. Any number of plausible stories could be constructed around it by varying the identities of sender and recipient. Yet, Mme de Clèves constructs a story of Nemours' string of mistresses, all of whom he is cheating on, and she concludes that the discretion Nemours had been showing her, even after Mme de Clèves had inadvertently shown him signs of her love for him, was merely "due to his passion for this other woman and a fear of displeasing her" (106) [311].

Mme de Clèves constructs her own explanatory narrative, expecting the worst and finding it when she mistakes Nemours' genuine discretion for duplicity. Given the predisposition her mother has planted in her for this sort of interpretation, however, her conclusion is not surprising. Mme de Clèves expects Nemours to be fickle in his love relationships: during her pre-court education her mother "told her that men were not very sincere, not very faithful, and not above deceit." The Princess has assimilated a model of courtly behavior and interpersonal relationships, including men's incapacity for fidelity, but it is based solely on matching all she sees and hears with the repertory of narratives her mother has provided her.[13] She never performs analysis by analogy. In following to the letter her mother's advice, Mme de Clèves is incapable of all but the most literal interpretations. After reading the letter and reflecting on Nemours' despicable behavior, her thoughts race to her mother's words on men's infidelity: "She went on, torturing herself with every fancy which could increase her despair, with self-reproaches and with memories of her mother's advice. . . . The torture she was suffering, even if it drove her to extremities, was nothing to the knowledge that M. de Nemours loved another while she had disclosed her love for him" (106) [311].

Mme de Clèves accepts as truth everything her mother tells her. This is reasonably unproblematic when her mother narrates court history or explains court appearances, but when Mme de Chartres narrates her daughter's feelings and emotions, Mme de Clèves accepts these stories as well, and attempts to adapt her behavior to her mother's narrative account of her life. It is, for example, Mme de Chartres who reveals to the Princess her feelings for Nemours:

> She was agitated beyond words, her mother having now opened her eyes to the fact that M. de Nemours was much more to her than it was right for him to be. She saw only too clearly that her feelings for him were exactly those which the Prince de Clèves had so often besought her to have for him; she was bitterly ashamed to think that she could have such feelings for one who was not her husband. Also she was wounded to the quick that M. de Nemours should be making use of her to further his affair with the Dauphine. This thought decided her to tell Madame de Chartres her secret. (66–67) [275]

In this single moment Mme de Clèves apprehends her mother's narrative encapsulation of her life: that she loves Nemours, that the love she feels for him is of the same kind her husband wanted her

---

[13] Judovitz makes a similar observation: "[Mme de Clèves], like the reader, has to rely on the images of the world presented to her either by her mother or others. Her perception only mirrors pre-existing images and narratives" (p. 1040).

to feel for him alone, and that Nemours is using her to get to the Dauphine. Mme de Chartres had known all along about her daughter's love for the man and in fact is the first to articulate Mme de Clèves' feelings. On her death bed she tells her what to do about them: "You stand on the edge of a precipice and can only hold back by making a superhuman effort. You must solemnly reflect upon your duty, both to your husband and yourself, remembering that you stand to lose the reputation you have built up and which I have so much desired for you. Be brave my darling, be strong and leave this Court. Force your husband to take you away" (69) [277–78]. After this little speech, Mme de Chartres refuses any further dialogue with her daughter, offering her only a silence that typifies her behavior when she cannot support the platitudes constituting her advice with concrete examples of how to carry it out. Her last words to her daughter warn her that she will be lost at court without her mother, curiously reiterating the first lesson she taught the girl when she sent her off alone to select her jewels.

To the Princess, Mme de Chartres appears to have mastered courtly interpretation. She seems always to know precisely who is doing what, and she can always penetrate the opaque veil of appearances to get to the reality they hide. Mme de Clèves is frustrated, however, because her mother never tells all that she knows: "'If I had a complaint,' said the Princess, 'it would be that you never tell me enough, either about the past or the present'" (54) [264]. Mme de Clèves perceives her mother's mastery of courtly equivocation, and furthermore she suspects her mother of withholding from her vital information.[14] Mme de Clèves thus construes her mother not only as the repository of secure and unequivocal interpretation, but as the cache of historical sources that endow court narratives with meaning and bestow on them a situational significance. She invests her mother with the power to articulate the expressive causality of the court and of her own life, and because of the circumstances of her upbringing and her interaction at the

---

[14] After Mme de Chartres tells the long story of the stormy relationship between the queen and M. le connétable, the following mother/daughter exchange occurs:
"Madame de Chartres then added, 'Perhaps you think I have told you more of these things than you wanted to know.'
'That,' replied Madame de Clèves, 'is the last complaint I am likely to make, and were I not afraid of being importunate, I should ask about many circumstances of which I am ignorant'" (60) [269].

court she accepts the proposition her mother's advice implies: that there exists a single, comprehensive, and stable interpretation that can present readers of the court with its unequivocal reality.

As Peggy Kamuf has pointed out, Mme de Chartres' narration of court experiences to her daughter "gives her a position comparable to that of the omniscient narrator."[15] The omniscient narrator knows the whole story and is totally other because he or she is removed from the action and is consequently able to comment on it disinterestedly. It is the narrator, of course, whose language constructs a work's plot and characters. Mme de Chartres constitutes herself as master, both in her pretension to deliver the truth behind the appearances of the courtly text and in the pact she makes with her daughter always to listen to her stories and help her through the rough spots. She seems completely detached from the court's intrigues. Not stymied by the complexity of appearances, she seems, rather, to be in control of them. The master position she occupies is the control she exercises which her daughter attempts to imitate. Her mastery, however, remains an inaccessible object of imperfect imitation because the mother/daughter pact is decidedly one-sided. Although Mme de Clèves confides everything to her mother, the latter seems always to withhold crucial information or advice that the former requires in order to interpret the court and to keep herself from being read. The economy of their relationship, which began with the mother's using the daughter as a status symbol, fails to circulate evenly and flows instead primarily from Mme de Clèves to her mother. Consequently, the mastery of appearances and virtue that Mme de Clèves strives to imitate and appropriate from her mother remains a mysterious phenomenon the subtleties of which Mme de Chartres appears always to withhold.

Although Judovitz, Hirsch, and others have noticed Mme de Chartres' narrative influence on her daughter and Mme de Clèves' tendency to experience her own life as a narrative, no readers of *La Princesse de Clèves* seem to have taken into account the fact that Mme de Chartres only has access to her daughter's life through the latter's narrative construction of it. As noted above, Mme de Chartres insists that her daughter confide in her all of the *galanteries* men speak to her. More crucial still is the fact that Mme de

[15] Kamuf, *Fictions of Feminine Desire*, p. 71.

Chartres is totally removed from the court: in only one episode—cited above, in which she helps her daughter feign illness—does she participate in court events. She relies nearly exclusively on her daughter's narration of court events, and her ensuing interpretation of Mme de Clève's behavior draws not on the particulars of her situation but on traditional court *vraisemblance*. That is, although Mme de Chartres painstakingly educated her daughter to be unlike any other woman at the court, conventional wisdom concerning plausible activity at the court informs each of her readings of Mme de Clèves' thoughts and deeds. Mme de Chartres thus allows the master narrative of the court, which dictates that all people there get involved in intrigues and adulterous affairs, to influence the story she constructs of Mme de Clèves' life and consequently the advice she gives her. However exceptional and unique the Princess may be, then, because she strives to imitate her mother's mastery of the court, a mastery based on conventionalized narrative, she is ineluctably drawn into the very situation her mother strenuously attempted to keep her away from. In short, by the time Mme de Clèves' narrative passes into her mother's hands and back to her, it is stripped of its particular significance and standardized to conform to the general rules of court *vraisemblance*.

Mme de Chartres' interpretive superiority and the power it gives her over her daughter are thus largely responsible for the Princess's love for Nemours. Mme de Chartres' story of Mme de Clèves' love for Nemours incites the daughter to produce more material for interpretation (it "decided her to tell Madame de Chartres her secret") and after her mother's death, when the Princess finds herself alone, she lacks an adequate interlocutor to whom she can narrate her experiences and from whom she can learn their interpretation. Her courtly development is consequently arrested. Her mother suspends the story of her life with the Princess hanging on the edge of a precipice, and this is where she remains for the rest of the novel. Mme de Chartres' last words to her daughter—"try and remember all I have told you" (70) [278]—inscribe her continued influence on her and speak to her from beyond the grave as the Princess strives to remain virtuous and unique as well as to seek out another person who seems to have mastered court interpretation and appearances.

It is M. de Nemours who calls forth from the Princess the resistant and exceptional virtue her mother constructed for her, and it is he who displays the discursive mastery of the court she continually strives to achieve. On the one hand, her affiliation with him is unique at the court in that she seems to be the only woman not to have had an affair with him, at least according to Mme la Dauphine, who remarks that "the title [of mistress] was shared by so many ladies that had they all been absent the attendance [at the ball] would have been rather thin" (63) [272]. Mme de Clèves' resistance to Nemours consequently continues to constitute her as exceptional and unique. Over and over again the Princess sees various examples in her life of how unlike other women she is; she notices it, and others do, too.[16] And, it is precisely because of her wish or need to be unique that the Princess cannot allow herself to become involved with Nemours, even after her husband's death: Mme de Clèves fears being reduced over time to the lot of other women—that is, to sameness.

On the other hand, Mme de Clèves is fascinated with Nemours' apparent mastery of all situations: "She saw him always greatly surpassing all the others and always master of the conversation wherever he was . . .; before long he had made a deep impression on her heart" (53, translation modified) [263].[17] In addition to being at all times master of the situation, M. de Nemours has the gift of projecting appearances that mask reality in order to keep himself from being read. When the court is discussing the recent predictions an astrologer made concerning various members of the king's entourage, for example, Nemours whispers to Mme de Clèves a gallantry that reveals his love for her. Mme la Dauphine spies a secret conversation going on and she asks M. de Nemours what he said; he replies with a banal generalization. "A man with

[16] The following exchanges exemplify the Princess's uniqueness at the court: "It's your fault for giving him the letter. No other woman in the world runs to her husband with all the things she knows" (123) [327]; "Madame de Chartres argued for a while with her daughter, who she really thought was being quite unusual" (64, trans. modified) [273]; "But there could not be another story like mine, no other woman would be capable of such a thing! It cannot have been invented or imagined by chance, nobody but me has ever conceived of such a thing" (147) [349].

[17] The following description of the Princess's behavior underscores Nemours' interpretive mastery: "However much she sought to avoid his eye, to speak less with him than with others, she gave herself away by something in her first movement, and the Prince felt certain that she was not indifferent to him. A man with less penetration might not have noticed anything" (92) [298].

less presence of mind would have been taken off his guard by this remark" (91) [297], and he pulls off a response that both satisfies the queen and leaves Mme de Clèves with no doubt that he is in love with her. Able to hide his true feelings and reactions when it would be dangerous to reveal them, Nemours possesses such great self-control that he can dominate most situations at the court.[18] The Princess is irresistibly drawn to Nemours both because of his ability to project plausible yet deceiving appearances and because he knows how to make himself "master of the conversation wherever he was." That she is drawn to him and yet continually resists him validates her as uniquely virtuous.

Mme de Clèves remains, however, "on the edge of a precipice": if she cannot resolve either to avoid Nemours completely or to have an affair with him, neither can she enjoy the *tranquillité* derived from loving her husband and being loved by him, the state of bliss her mother narrated to her. She never displays to her husband the passion he desired in her and, as the Princess tells Nemours after her husband's death, her remaining aloof to M. de Clèves is what kept him in love with her: "Does any man preserve his original passion? . . . There was perhaps one man and one man only capable of remaining in love with his wife, and that was M. de Clèves. It was my bad luck that this brought me no happiness—possibly this passion of his would not have continued so strong if I had requited it" (189–90) [387]. Mme de Clèves kept her husband in love with her by never loving him in return. Nemours' passion was unbridled for similar reasons. In a somewhat perverse but perfectly comprehensible way, given her mother's tales of men's infidelity, Mme de Clèves preserves men's love for her and consequently her control over them by withholding from them what they desire most.

Mme de Chartres provided her daughter with a narrative image of the court ostensibly structured to protect the girl from danger, but since the mother only had access to her daughter's life through the latter's discursive representation of it, the interpretations she returned were steeped in local *vraisemblance*. Mme de Chartres

---

[18] Alain Niderst argues in *La Princesse de Clèves: Le roman paradoxal* that the ability to hide one's true feelings leads to the power to control others: "Dissimulation is thus always admirable. It signifies mastery of self. It permits mastery over others. It allows one to escape any dependence" (p. 58).

carefully depicted for her daughter court intrigue, interpersonal relationships, and even her daughter's personal feelings, but her unexpected death prevented her from reaching the end of the story.
Mme de Chartres' narrative authority governed virtually every aspect of Mme de Clèves' life, and its sudden withdrawal left her "on
the edge of a precipice" of narrative climax: she provided her
daughter with her life's narrative exposition, but was unable to
round out the tale with narrative closure. Consequently, since she
fails to apprehend her mother's version of the master narrative's
end, Mme de Clèves prolongs the narrative indefinitely, and she
does so by perpetuating men's desire for her. Since by her own admission she cannot reach the *dénouement* of her mother's tale,
which is "the one line of conduct which can make a woman happy,
that is to say, loving her husband and being loved by him" (37)
[248], Mme de Clèves holds the two men in her life in thrall by
projecting to each the image the other desires: to Nemours she is
the dutiful and unreachable wife, and to her husband she is the
passionate lover capable of the most violent emotions, only not for
him. Their sempiternal desire for her keeps M. de Clèves and M.
de Nemours enthralled, and each expects from this exceptional
woman behavior that conventional court *vraisemblance* would dictate. Their pleasure, however, is thwarted because Mme de Clèves
cannot allow the narrative to wind down to one of two possible
climaxes of equal but ideologically opposed verisimilitude: living
happily ever after with her husband or having an affair with Nemours.[19]

After her husband's death, Mme de Clèves' opportunity to have
a storybook happiness is forever foreclosed. She will never love her
husband and be loved by him—her mother's rendition of "the one

[19] Failing to recognize the minimal separation between her appearances and her
reality, for example, ultimately leads to M. de Clèves' death: when the *gentilhomme*
whom he has sent to spy on his wife returns to report any clandestine meetings she
may have had with Nemours, M. de Clèves refuses to hear him out:

"'I see how it is but I cannot bear you to tell me.'

'I have no proof of anything,' replied the gentleman, 'though M. de Nemours did
go into the forest garden two nights running and then the day after went to Coulommiers with Madame de Mercœur.'

'Enough,' said M. de Clèves, dismissing him with a gesture, 'that is all I want to
know'" (174) [372].

M. de Clèves does, of course, need further clarification, because Mme de Clèves
did not even see Nemours at Coulommiers. Nevertheless, "he succumbed that very
night to a high fever" (174) [373] and he dies, never quite understanding that, because his wife is truly exceptional, interpreting her actions and appearances according to received models is not only unwise, but it may be fatal.

line of conduct which can make a woman happy"—and she cannot be happy with Nemours because she cannot trust him not to have an affair and consequently fracture her unique identity. Forcefully ejected from the life her mother strove to manufacture for her, Mme de Clèves retires to a convent and lives the rest of her life in seclusion. Here the narrativization of her life ends and she ceases to be a player in a drama over whose script she has no control. When Nemours comes to see her, the messenger to whom he speaks tells him that "Madame de Clèves had not only forbidden her to bring any message from him but even to give her any account of their conversation" (197–98) [394]. Escaping at long last the narrativization of her life, which is where all her troubles began, the Princess takes authorial responsibility and writes her own ending. The novel's last words, however, describe the somewhat ambiguous significance this well-ordered life conveys: "Indeed her life which was not a long one, provided inimitable examples of virtue" (198, translation modified) [395]. Even Mme de Clèves' death is inscribed in the narrative structure her mother had plotted. If she could not attain happiness, which was, after all, a secondary consideration in Mme de Chartres' plan to make her daughter outshine all that was glamorous at the court, she was at least capable of remaining exceptional in her abiding yet ultimately pointless virtue.

Mme de Clèves paradoxically deceived others by unconventionally avoiding duplicity and allowing her words and actions to express in unequivocal fashion precisely what she felt and thought. The novel's last sentence communicates not only her distinctiveness, but the complete lack of expressive causality the narrativization of her life bears. Her "inimitable examples," be they of virtue or of any other trait, fail to close off the work precisely because they cannot be repeated. Inimitable examples serve no moral or political didactic function; they cannot restrict interpretation, as the morals of previous historical fiction had tried to do, to an unequivocal celebration of a specific ideology. Consequently, both virtue and the preeminence of *vraisemblance* remain marginal in this work. The novel closes with the depiction of an ambivalent virtue—ambivalent because it is unrepeatable and, moreover, because the Princess attained it somewhat accidentally—as well as that of a dysfunctional interpretive practice—court *vraisemblance*—that can no longer adequately privilege a particular narrative point of view because it cannot negotiate the difference between reality and representation. In other words, the traditional distinction between truth and verisimilitude breaks down in this novel; fiction is consequently unable to prescribe a specific moral or political lesson because it cannot distinguish between the expressive causality that had been the hallmark of *vraisemblance* and the simple accidents of everyday life that compose reality. In the absence of a highly developed structuring apparatus of description able to show unequivocally that each episode of a work self-evidently expressed a specific and obvious ideological truth, the interpretation of fiction is thrown open to a broad spectrum of readers with differing political allegiances and alliances.

La Princesse de Clèves contests the received models of narrative interpretation by hypostatizing, in the figure of Mme de Chartres, an archaic mode of reading. Traditional exegesis conceived the interpretive process as a relatively simple act of decoding the material that constituted a text. However hermetic a text might appear, diligent analysis could ostensibly arrive at its final signified or meaning by unpacking a work's rhetorical structure and laying bare the sense it contained. Fabien Sfez writes that interpretation was viewed in the seventeenth century as the isomorphically inverse process of writing: "Writing marks a signified in a signifying system," he writes. "Reading uncovers the signified through the signifier."[20] Such a model of interpretation served contemporary views of literature's didactic or politically useful function because it sought to control the meaning readers could extract from a text—a master code governed the interpretive process, and literature afforded no surprises because it foreclosed competing or conflicting analyses. Philosophical or moral treatises as well as narrative or theatrical works afforded standardized views of contemporary social reality because only works based on conventionalized *vraisemblance* received a *Privilège du Roi*.

Mme de Clèves reifies a nascent contradiction in interpretive pro-

[20] Sfez, "Le Roman polylexique du XVIIe siècle," p. 56. In a similar vein, Claude Reichler notes that "in the seventeenth century, signifying relations were not conceived of as essentially vertical: the horizontal dimension of the exchange is taken into consideration, both by the recognition of an equivalence between diverse 'signs'—for example, the sureness of the communication. This semiology, the trace of which we find in numerous texts, is always applied to organize the exchange according to a model that tends toward the analytic: on the linguistic level, as we know, usage is strictly codified and ambiguities are eschewed" (p. 13).

cesses, that between the expressive causality of earlier fiction in which texts seemed to possess an inner essence reflected or expressed by each of their constituent elements, and the motivated verisimilitude of budding fiction. In the latter form of fiction, aptly described by Genette,[21] textual maxims theorize or justify characters' behavior. In motivated verisimilitude, *vraisemblance* is not so much an intuitive collection of existing and externalized moral and political principles that must be brought to bear on a work, but an understanding of sequences of events whose logic follows from psychological and physiological rubrics actuated by the unfolding of the plot. In *La Princesse de Clèves*, Mme de Clèves lives her own life as the vicarious narrative expression of her mother's expectations. She conforms to her mother's ostensibly omniscient knowledge of her feelings and actions, and narrating to her mother the events of each passing day, she accepts her mother's interpretation of those events with the result that despite the particularities of her own situation she ineluctably conforms to what is expected of her. After her mother's death, however, Mme de Clèves possesses no stable, unequivocal interpretation of her life and resorts to a prolonged seduction of her husband and M. de Nemours as a means of forever deferring the expected narrative climax. Her final withdrawal from the court seems less an unmitigated victory for the young woman than an inexorable ending to a tale that fails to resolve itself in a conclusive and satisfying *dénouement*, and instead simply winds down and stops.

Mme de Clèves does, finally, write her own story by leaving the court and consequently the pages of a textualized world whose limited narrative repertory dictates an extremely restricted set of possible narrative outcomes.[22] Her escape from the constraining parameters of courtly behavior represents an evasion of the expressive causality of aristocratic *vraisemblance*: the irreplicable nature of her behavior on which the work closes not only fails to conform to any of the models of conduct recounted in the court's explanatory narratives, but it falls short of conveying any potential didactic message to the novel's readers precisely because of its uniqueness.

---

[21] Genette, "Vraisemblance et motivation," in *Figures II*.

[22] Both Sylvère Lotringer, in "La Structuration romanesque," and Nancy K. Miller, in "Emphasis Added: Plots and Plausibilities in Women's Fiction," argue that Mme de Clèves' flight from the court is a move to preserve the erotics of her current situation.

Mme de Clèves' actions are thus *invraisemblable* with respect both to the internal narrative practices as they are observed at the court, and to the external, homogenizing conventions of contemporary fiction. In this respect, then, the Princess's withdrawal from the court represents a victory, but it is a victory over the constraining conventions of narrative structure as the defining limit of epistemological and political practice. Her unprecedented escape from the court heralds a departure from the master narrative of aristocratic fiction, and it ushers in a subtle resistance, the manifestations of which would grow stronger throughout the eighteenth century, to moral and political hegemony buttressed by the control of the production and interpretation of narrative.

La Princesse de Clèves conforms, on the formal level of structural appearances, to the conventions of historical fiction as it was construed in the middle decades of the seventeenth century, but Mme de Lafayette's novel helped initiate resistance to the master code of hegemonic narrative by objectifying and criticizing contemporary interpretive practice. Although the novel demands that its readers be familiar with contemporary *vraisemblance* both in order to follow the explanatory narratives within the work's *récit* and to recognize the tradition into which the text inserts itself, it ultimately distances itself from that tradition by externalizing *vraisemblance* and transforming it from a useful interpretive model into a problematic and impeding discourse. It exhibits the restrictions that contemporary notions of verisimilar expressive causality placed on narrative by depicting the crucial scene of the Princess's confession along with its interpretation in the form of the court's reactions. The reified analysis of Mme de Clèves' actions becomes, like the actions themselves, an object of representation; the novel incorporates the discursive practices which normally function to elucidate behavior into its repertory of depicted objects.

In this respect, then, *La Princesse de Clèves* offers a compelling example of narrative mimesis as Genette described it precisely because at least one of the text's signified objects (*"objet narré"*) is itself language—the discursive and interpretive practice of the court. *La Princesse de Clèves* depicts language, but more importantly it reifies an already stabilizing mode of reading and offers it up as a spectacle for analysis, just as the title character is a continual object of visual analysis in her own circle. *La Princesse de*

Clèves lays bare the scaffolding supporting contemporary *vrai-semblance*, and displays it as an object of analysis while at the same time entreating readers to contextualize it within the frame of plausible narrative motivations that would explain Mme de Clèves' decision to leave the court. Two competing theories of narrative realism, then, exist in this novel: that of the explanatory narratives told within the novel, narratives that adhere to a rigidly defined notion of expressive causality and seventeenth-century standards of *vraisemblance*, and that of contextually based considerations of possible or plausible actions that conform not to preconceived standards, but to psychological and social motivation.[23]

In reifying the interpretive practices of her generation, Mme de Lafayette dissociated *histoire* from *récit* and consequently initiated a critical examination of the master narrative codes that had informed aristocratic fiction. *La Princesse de Clèves* separates narrative from the affective response that seventeenth-century heroic and historical fiction had traditionally demanded from its readers. While on its surface the novel resembles traditional aristocratic fiction,[24] it differs significantly from conventional heroic and historical fiction in the use it makes of artifice and deception. The Scudérys, Gomberville, and La Calprenède wrote novels that depended on artifice as a means of identifying their readers. Aristocratic readers possessed a cultural capital that distinguished them from the less nobly born, and they conscripted that capital into the service of the cryptanalysis that constituted the reading of fiction. In *La Princesse de Clèves*, however, nothing is hidden and no information is encoded save that which is ultimately elucidated in the work's explanatory narratives. To read *La Princesse de Clèves* requires no

---

[23] Miller argues that "the plots of women's literature are not about 'life' and solutions in any therapeutic sense, nor should they be. They are about the plots of literature itself, about the constraints the maxim places on rendering a female life in fiction. Mme de Lafayette quietly ... italicize[s] by the demaximization of [her] heroine['s] text the difficulty of curing plot of life, and life of certain plots" ("Emphasis Added," p. 46).

[24] Pierre Bayle, for example, argued that *La Princesse de Clèves* was just like other heroic fiction and he found that Mme de Clèves resembled other heroines, all of whom were generally described as inimitable or unique; he objected that she, like they, was too individualistic to be believable. Maintaining that no woman like Mme de Clèves existed in France, he made a provocative promise: "If there were such a woman, I promise that I would go see her, even if I had to travel four hundred leagues on foot" (Pierre Bayle, *Objection*, cited by Laugaa, *Lectures de Madame de Lafayette*, p. 114).

specialized training in the verbal artifice that constituted the world of the court because the crucial analytic processes determining membership are laid bare. The only deception operating in Mme de Lafayette's novel is the Princess's unwitting seduction of her husband and M. de Nemours, a paradoxical seduction that exists only because no one expects the young woman to say and do exactly what she feels. In this respect, then, *La Princesse de Clèves* appropriates the seduction its principal character undertakes: misprizing the historical and cultural significance of conventional narrative codes, it staves off narrative closure based on received models of interpretation, and concludes only when it can effect an ending based upon its own individualistic logic.

La Princesse de Clèves seduces its readers by projecting the deceiving image of the sort of work they would be accustomed to reading. Erecting a discourse of putative stability in the form of Mme de Chartres' master narratives, the novel continually searches out similar unequivocal positions only to subvert the link between aesthetics and ideology when it confers on the Princess herself the last word on analytical authority, and only after she leaves the court: "The passions and entanglements of the world now appeared to her as they would to people with higher and more detached vision" (196) [393]. Final elucidative authority is reserved for the young woman who remained dispossessed of traditional aristocratic interpretive processes; her dispassionate comprehension of the court is completely divorced from the politics that animate it.[25] *La Princesse de Clèves* was thus a subversive novel in the seventeenth century because it exposed the link between aesthetics and ideology by revealing that narrative forms deemed pleasing and

[25] Shoshana Felman has argued that narrative authority functions to initiate a transferential process similar to that operating in psychoanalysis. Readers construe narrators as omnipotent and omniscient beings who in turn invest their audiences as addressees of their unconsciouses. Narrative knowledge or stability in Felman's argument bears an importance that pales in comparison to the activating mechanism of the text itself. See her "Henry James: Madness and Interpretation." Gilbert Chaitlin applies Felman's argument to early French fiction, in particular *La Princesse de Clèves*, in order to argue that "Mme. de Lafayette articulated a new kind of narrative situation in which the act of narrating became more than a ritual or the transmission of a content; transitive narration became an event, an activity that constitutes the subjectivity of the participants. For some two hundred years thereafter, the major thrust of the French novel was to explore the relationships that narration defines among speaking and listening subjects, desire, and the law" (p. 298).

regular were ineluctably linked to the political and epistemological discourses that valorized them.

Most of the novels that preceded *La Princesse de Clèves* undertook to foreclose the potential for competing interpretations by constructing in their enunciative registers the specific reading their audiences were supposed to infer. Based on the premise that individual narrative episodes reflected the inner essence of a particular work, the valorized interpretations suggested that a stable and unequivocal meaning inhered in fiction and that readers could extract it through informed processing of its iconography and artifice. The fiction that antedated *La Princesse de Clèves* eschewed any suggestion of deception or dissimulation: produced by and for members of a restricted social group, it was designed to uphold the conspicuous superiority of the aristocracy. *La Princesse de Clèves*, however, helped inaugurate a poetics of deception in prose fiction. Interrogating the intimate connection between political and aesthetic discourse, the novel rejects out of hand the overwrought conventions of contemporary fiction and it indicts their inability to negotiate narrative descriptions not based in a narrowly defined political arena. It accomplishes its rejection by depicting an apprentice reader who fails to master the reigning descriptive conventions and unwittingly seduces two of its experts, only to escape herself unscathed from the vicious circle of interpretive hegemony.

Mme de Lafayette's exposure of aristocratic fiction's conventions is of a more subtle nature than Furetière's sarcastic and scathing denunciation. Her depiction of an apprentice reader and potential producer of ambiguous signs reveals not only the archaic and inappropriate nature of received models of interpretation, but the staggering potentials for misreading and deception that inhere in even the most putatively unequivocal discourse. More crucially, however, she disengages the interpretation of fiction from the web of aristocratic hegemony and makes it accessible to a broad reading public with little or no access to the cultural capital constituting upper-class taste. As readers follow Mme de Clèves' courtly education, receiving along with her the historical and analytical lessons of the explanatory narratives, they glean all the information necessary to understand both the cabalistic nature of the court and the reasons behind the Princess's seductions and her ultimate withdrawal from the court. *La Princesse de Clèves* provides disenfranchised readers with the key required for its interpretation.

In Chapter 4, I argued that changes in the laws and practices of the publishing industry were largely responsible for broadening the constituency of reading audiences. The sale of books became a more profitable enterprise for writers and printers alike, and authors and publishers consequently sought to increase their sales by including as potential customers a broader portion of the social spectrum. Michael Moriarty has recently shown that the aesthetic ideals composing the generalized notion of *goût* (taste) were undergoing a rapid metamorphosis in the 1670's, and he argues that social barriers no longer exclusively determined the constituency of reading publics. He contends that during the 1670's, truth, reason, and good sense, which had only a generation or so earlier been the property of the privileged classes, were accessible to all; they no longer marked the exclusionary hegemony of the aristocracy. Good literary taste, particularly in the theoretical writings of Boileau, whose *Art poétique* preceded *La Princesse de Clèves* by only four years, involved recognizing "the exceptional, privileged status of particular utterances, texts, authors, not of poets and poetry, even ancient poetry, in general." [26] The identification of the privileged status of specific articulations, works, or writers clearly involves an ideological move valorizing a particular political agenda. However, it is crucial to note the changing definition of taste in the seventeenth century: in high French classicism, good taste consisted of the appreciation of a venerated and reified corpus of classical works whose availability, both physical and cultural, was restricted to an elite group. In the later years of the seventeenth century, however, good taste consisted in esteeming a less circumscribed corpus of works valued not as objects of cultural capital but as expressions of social values. The change is subtle yet critical. It monitors the decisive shift from aristocratic hegemony in the aesthetic domain to an enfranchisement of previously marginalized groups, groups who had been barred from possession of cultural capital, yet who were educated enough to participate in the specifically literary celebration of social values.

[26] Moriarty, *Taste and Ideology in Seventeenth-Century France*, p. 182.

In d'Urfé's time, aristocratic readers held the iconographic keys required for the interpretation of pastoral fiction. Nobles gathered in salons and, dressed as their favorite characters, they reenacted scenarios from *L'Astrée*. What may have been an amusing pastime in early seventeenth-century salons evolved into a political fact of life for the aristocrats who formed the heart of the court of Louis XIV. Particularly after he moved his court to Versailles in 1682, Louis XIV wrested cultural control from the aristocracy and constituted himself as the source from which emanated not only all political authority, but aesthetic and iconographic power as well. Louis kept his entourage of courtiers constant spectators in the exhibition of his grandeur.[27] Elaborate dinners and marvelous spectacles replete with curious and wondrous machines constituted court life at Versailles. Each spectacle had its own allegorical theme and each element in the spectacle bore a frequently arcane and hermetic signifying relationship to that theme, to which Louis and his favorites alone possessed the key. Nobles' extravagant lifestyles, centering around expensive entertainment and its paraphernalia, kept most of them in constant debt; eager to please their king in the hope of receiving financial reward, courtiers lived in near total dependency on their king.[28] The upshot of this financial and iconographic dependency on the king was a cultural absolutism that constituted a split in the French nation separating those, nearly exclusively aristocrats, who understood and participated in the royal allegories, and those artisans responsible for producing their material base. As Jean-Marie Apostolidès has argued, under Louis XIV all intellectual and artistic production served the state; original genius or creativity had to be put in service of the king. Artistic and intellectual labor thus constituted an ambiguous zone equalizing

[27] George Rudé discusses the distribution of political power between aristocracy and monarchy and its relationship in the struggle for control of the state. See his *Europe in the Eighteenth Century*, especially pp. 175–82.

[28] Saint-Simon wrote that Louis XIV "knew that he did not have ... enough favors to distribute to make a continued effort. He substituted jealousy, the hope that little preferences and distinctions bring about; no one was more ingenious than he in inventing these sorts of things" (cited by Levron, p. 52). In *Les Cérémonies de l'information dans la France du XVIe au XVIIIe siècle*, Michèle Fogel writes that "there was nothing ceremonial in France save that which cultivated the monarch's self-consciousness and that of the 'honorable and familial society' that he chose, the circle of the court of which he is the center, model and explicit master, and which spreads outward in discrete channels.... This self-consciousness of absolutism grows knowing that all resistances ... failed" (pp. 241–42).

the class differences between noble and bourgeois producers while at the same time creating an unbridgeable chasm between lofty creative work and the vile physical labor of the artisan.[29] Under Louis XIV specialized armies were formed and nobles were consequently dispossessed of the traditional privilege to bear arms. Thus, divorced from their traditional prerogatives, Louis' aristocrats became a spectator class who shared in the state's iconographic autorepresentation; cut off from any real power, they participated in the illusion that their authority, prestige, and relationship to their king formed an uninterrupted continuum from the feudal era.[30]

Louis XIV mobilized a complex network of people drawn from all walks of life to participate in the production of the illusion, one based largely on ostentatious consumption, that his grandeur was timeless and natural. Ironically, the ahistorical image of royal splendor he sought to reproduce depended to an enormous extent on social relationships of production and exchange, relationships whose presence he sought to efface. During the 1670's and 1680's, however, dire financial straits led to the curtailment of gratifications paid out to historians and other court-appointed writers and artists. Erica Harth has shown that during the 1660's and early 1670's the crown paid out between 83,000 and 100,000 livres annually to writers, scientists, historians and various other *érudits*. By 1683, however, that sum had fallen to only 32,000 livres.[31] Disenfranchised chroniclers and historians turned to the production of a new narrative form, the secret history or *nouvelle*, which allowed them to appear to participate in the ideological reproduction of the state apparatus. Their participation, however, had the effect of exposing the stitches in an otherwise seamless representation of royal splendor. The popular *nouvelles*, which DuPlaisir argued "should

---

[29] Apostolidès, *Le roi-machine*, pp. 21–38.

[30] Apostolidès remarks: "Through the play of emblems, [the discourse of representation] shows the relay position which is thenceforth that of the nobility: forming the circle of the court, the nobility refracts in all directions the solar image of the sovereign placed in its center" (pp. 45–46).

[31] See Harth, *Ideology and Culture*, especially pp. 156–63, for an excellent analysis of how financial exigencies caused by increased military spending in the seventeenth century affected royal patronage of arts and sciences. Harth argues that after the decline of royal patronage of historians, "the ranks of a new ideological army were forming. The splendor of the Sun King shone not in *histoires de France*, but in the châteaux, gardens, fountains, and machinery of lavish spectacles that were to eternalize his reign. Louis wisely chose to glorify himself in the silent impersonality of stone and marble rather than in the human voice of history" (p. 161).

not take for their subjects actions which are too old, and I might add to this that they should not take place too far away," [32] chronicled the secret lives of some of France's most famous figures, and their frequently ignoble and sordid depictions of these figures assured their authors' popular and financial success.[33] The secret histories that the *nouvelles* exposed rendered both historical and contingent the rise to power of specific individuals, thus destroying the illusion of intrinsic and harmonious virtue and majesty that Louis' iconography sought to inspire.

César de Saint-Réal, Courtilz de Sandraz, and Edme Boursault were among the most prominent authors of the new historical fictions. While these authors claimed absolute veracity for the factual details their works contained, they were somewhat more circumspect about the personal details they added, the very details that made them so popular. Saint-Réal's *Dom Carlos* (1672) brought to the forefront historical elements that in previous generations only served to justify the telling of the tale. In his preface Saint-Réal writes:

> Having discovered in several sources the particularities of their stories [i.e., of D. Carlos and Elizabeth of France], the author deemed it necessary to communicate them to the public, because they justify the memory of this Princess, and they show that there was no guilt on her part. Even if she only uncovered the conspiracy we will see described here, she deserves her share of renown, since it is certainly true that without her the Prince of Navarre would never have become the greatest king in the world, nor, what is more, the ancestor of Louis XIV.[34]

Saint-Réal is interested primarily in setting the facts straight. He wants to expose the causal sequence behind Louis' coming to power, and he wants to do it in a work of fiction. Although the stories of D. Carlos' love for Elizabeth, along with those of the jealousy of Philippe II and the imprisonment of D. Carlos by his father, were welll-known legends at the time of the work's publication, Saint-Réal cites all his historical sources, including Bran-

---

[32] DuPlaisir, *Sentimens sur les lettres*, p. 93.

[33] Charles Sorel, in the *Bibliothèque françoise*, characterized the *nouvelle* by writing, "We began . . . to understand what things deemed *vraisemblable* were, through the little narrations that came into fashion and which were called *nouvelles*. You might compare them to the true stories of adventures peculiar to men" (p. 178).

[34] Saint-Réal, "Avis."

tôme, Mathieu, and Mézeray. His novel threw fiction open to a
wider reading audience: no longer the domain of the aristocracy,
historicized fiction was open to outsiders, both writers and readers,
who dealt with people who were famous not simply because they
were aristocratic, but because they played crucial roles in national
or international politics. Fiction no longer celebrated the glorious
loves and passions that underscored the aristocracy's splendor and
strength of character. Now love was a weakness and the *nouvelle*
aimed at showing all the secrets and seaminess love relations could
harbor.

Not all authors of historical fiction were as straitlaced as Saint-
Réal. Courtilz de Sandraz claims that his *Mémoires de M.L.C.D.R.*
(1687) are true, but he makes no lofty pretense of the educational
worth of his project: "I believe . . . that the principal reason why
M. le CDR wrote was not so much the desire to show his part in
secret affairs, but to make others circumspect and judicious
through his example. . . . Nevertheless, if these Memoirs are not so
useful as I imagine, they are still quite curious. You will read things
here . . . that have never before been written."[35] Courtilz's curiosi-
ties evoke Boursault and his theoretical preface to *Le Prince de
Condé* (1681). Boursault, like so many of his contemporaries, argued that the historical background of his tale was true, but that
its real interest lay in the fictionalized accounts of illustrious
people's lives.

> Although this little work contains enough historical circumstance to
> convince people that it is entirely true, I would like, if possible, to
> amuse my readers without abusing them, and warn them of the trap
> they will fall into if they believe every incident they read here. You
> can consider each portrayal of war to be true, but I do not guarantee
> the truth of the accounts in which love plays a part. Strictly speaking,
> this is really just a novel to which I am lending famous names in order
> to guarantee it a favorable reception, since people are more interested

[35] Sandraz, "Preface." Courtilz's narrator opens with a rather bawdy account of
his own birth: "Between the towns of Paris and Etampes . . . is a château called
Olinville that was once a royal house. . . . My father once left his home to see the
master of the house, who was a relative of his, and he brought my mother, who was
four and a half months pregnant. They were staying at the nearby home of a gentleman named Grigni. The coachman, having got drunk, discharged his water over the
entryway of the château d'Olinville, even though it was the prettiest roadway in the
world. Although my father had been expecting to have a good time in this house,
this accident brought about a great affliction; for my mother was wounded and
delivered the following day, and died two days later" (pp. 1–2).

in the adventures of a prince they know than in those of a hero they do not.[36]

Courtilz's and Boursault's theories of the genre constitute the *nouvelle* as a curious literary form operating in the interstices between fiction and history. Bearing a close formal resemblance to the historical narratives of heroic fiction, the late seventeenth-century *nouvelle* was nevertheless ideologically opposed to its forebear in that it most often trivialized or overtly ridiculed the achievements of the French monarchy. Breaking the fundamental rule of royal iconographic representation which according to Apostolidès consisted in never revealing that "the man of the court is a creation of history and not an essence" (54), the *nouvelle* articulated the historical construction of images of grandeur by reveling in the seamier sides of monarchic splendor.

The *nouvelle* appropriated the formal techniques of historical fiction, which included placing illustrious characters in a grandiose setting of tremendous national consequence, but unlike *La Princesse de Clèves* or any of the megalithic historical romances of the 1660's, it included real individuals as its heroes. According to Marie-Thérèse Hipp, the primary distinctions between the *nouvelle* and the giant novels of the previous generation concerned "its more circumscribed dimensions and, in general, the unity of its action."[37] History was a backdrop in the *nouvelle* and the *mémoire*, two forms of fiction that, despite authors' and critics' claims to the contrary, seem particularly difficult to distinguish; it served primarily to justify the existence of the fiction the author related.[38] That is, writers protected themselves from the critical attack that they were poisoning the minds of the young with lies by claiming that their works were factual and hence benign. Late seventeenth-century historical fiction constituted ideological resistance to the standardized and homogenizing cultural unification of Louis' court, then, because it revealed the historical and material origins and limitations

---

[36] Boursault, "Le libraire au lecteur."

[37] Marie-Thérèse Hipp, *Mythes et réalités: Enquête sur le roman et les mémoires (1660–1700)*, p. 52.

[38] See Godenne, *Histoire de la nouvelle française aux XVIIe et XVIIIe siecles*, pp. 80–84; and Stewart, *Imitation and Illusion in the French Memoir-Novel, 1700–1750*: "If the writer is skillful enough to create literal illusion, the question of verisimilitude or 'realism' was never raised: historicity was a shield against all charges which could be leveled against the novel" (p. 6).

of the king's power; in addition, it threw open to politically disenfranchised groups the production of iconography normally reserved for the crown and its intimates, and made that iconography available, through the sale of fiction, to a wide range of the social spectrum.[39]

Fiction in the third and fourth quarters of the seventeenth century emphasized the private rather than the public aspect of historical characters' lives, and it stressed the relative accessibility of the characters it portrayed. The conjunction of an increased marketing of books with the expansion of reading publics to include wealthy and educated members of the bourgeoisie seems largely responsible for these changes, and particularly for the incidence of seduction and deception in fiction. Authors in the later seventeenth century came largely from the lesser nobility or the *noblesse de robe*, and they consequently enjoyed solid educations;[40] their ambiguous social position, coupled with the need to address an ill-defined reading audience, caused them to articulate ambivalent or duplicitous aesthetic ideologies. Since it was no longer possible to court an exclusively aristocratic clientele with fiction designed to reaffirm what they already knew or believed, authors needed to invoke multiple and often conflicting political stances in their works. The expressive narrative causality of heroic and historical fiction, in which a work's *récit* and *histoire* colluded in offering up narrative episodes that metonymically expressed the tale's political essence, gave way to stories of deception and seduction. Characters misrepresenting themselves and attempting to lead others astray fit the new ambiguous political agenda for fiction because authors could exploit them for a binary didactic end that would proclaim a different moral truth for different readers: noble readers might heed the warning this fiction issued about middle-class upstarts who attempted to usurp their traditional positions of ascendancy and au-

[39] Harth writes that "the *nouvelle* told a story that was counterhistory, a pastiche of alternative news. One day the story would achieve independence from official history and would assume responsibility for its condition as fiction. Nobles had emulated royalty in the trompe l'œil history of the *roman*. Bourgeois literature in its very beginnings adopted the preexisting mold of trompe l'œil, for bourgeois in their turn wanted to emulate nobles" (pp. 178–79).

[40] For a thorough discussion of the social origins of authors in the seventeenth century, see Henri-Jean Martin, *Livre, pouvoirs, et société à Paris au XVIIe siècle*, particularly vol. II, pp. 907–16, where he discusses the concept of author in Paris from 1665 to 1702.

thority, and bourgeois readers could learn, as Mme de Clèves did, the contrived nature of the elaborate sign systems they would have to penetrate in order to accede to the ranks of power and privilege.[41]

An early critique of deceptive or seductive fiction reveals that what many critics feared in late seventeenth-century fiction was precisely this equivocal moral and political stance. Pierre Nicole attacked novels for this very reason as early as 1667. This passage, often quoted out of its context, is part of a lengthy diatribe against Desmaretz, who had recently criticized the premises of Jansenism. Although in part an *ad hominem* attack, Nicole's remarks concerning fiction's seductive capabilities are revealing, and the argument merits quotation in full:

> Everyone knows that [Desmaretz's] first profession was writing novels and plays, and that this is where he began to make himself known in the world. These qualities, which are not entirely honorable in the judgment of respectable people, are quite horrible in light of the principles of Christianity and the teachings of the Gospel. A novelist [*faiseur de Romans*] and a playwright is a public poisoner, not of the body, but of the soul of the faithful, and he is guilty of an infinity of spiritual homicides that he caused either directly or indirectly through his pernicious works. The more careful he was to cover with a veil of respectability the criminal passions he describes, the more dangerous and able to corrupt simple and innocent souls he made his works.[42]

Nicole's frontal attack against Desmaretz is also an implicit assault on contemporary fiction which, unlike its progenitors, failed to express an unequivocal ideological intent. Laden with a polysemantic richness absent from pastoral and heroic novels, fiction in the later years of the seventeenth century supported multiple and conflicting

[41] The abbé DuPlaisir hypothesized a didactic purpose for fiction along similar lines in 1683. DuPlaisir maintained that the instruction works contain must be self-evident for different groups of readers and that they should not need to exert any particular effort to seize it: "These sorts of stories, like theatrical works, are themselves a school of edification; their conclusions must always contain a moral, and this moral must be plainly evident, and not require a great deal of penetration and education on the part of the reader" (pp. 182–83). Similarly, La Mothe le Vayer argued that the attraction of novels lies in their ability to show readers what they want to see. He wrote that the appeal of fiction depends on the human instinct which wants to know "what is indefinite and without limit, like fables, because they have that in common with our minds, whose activity is not restricted because its nature is infinite" (*Considérations sur l'éloquence françoise de ce temps*, in *Œuvres*, vol. I, p. 465).

[42] Nicole, *Les Imaginaires et les Visionnaires*, p. 253.

ideological stances. Moral and political authorities—beginning with Nicole and continuing on into the eighteenth century, as we will see in the following chapters—worried that novels would cause readers to stray from the truths that officially sanctioned works promulgated, perverting their ethics and their politics and rendering obsolete the unequivocal master's voice that traditional literature had constituted through its careful construction of *vraisemblance*.

Mme de Lafayette explored the limits of contemporary fiction's discursive strategies in her *Princesse de Clèves*, but it is important to keep in mind that to disclose limits is not necessarily to undo them. *La Princesse de Clèves* was a subversive work in the seventeenth century primarily because it tested the bounds of fiction while appearing to abide by nearly all the rules historical novels had prized. It seduced its readers into seeing an apparent regularity of form and overlooking its dismantling of the most basic premise of aristocratic fiction: that interpretation requires possession of an ideological and iconographic key based on acquisition of a cultural capital normally available only to members of privileged classes. If Mme de Lafayette failed to escape completely the traditional discursive space of seventeenth-century fiction because of her need to use the very terms and conventions her novel criticized, she did sketch out a new zone of fiction based on the deceptive iconographic sign. She contested the stability of referential and conventional causal discourse, and proposed a model that demanded readers' interpretation based not on tradition, but on the mechanics of deception and seduction the work promulgated. Novels that privileged a specific mode of seduction based upon the apparent stability of the signifying practice that its characters valorized appeared with greater frequency after publication of *La Princesse de Clèves*, and became the norm in the eighteenth century. Prévost's *Manon Lescaut*, Marivaux's *Vie de Marianne*, Diderot's *La Religieuse*, Crébillon's *Egarements du cour et de l'esprit*, and Restif's *Paysanne pervertie* are but five novels among dozens that depict apprentice readers who absorb and later manipulate the complex discursive strategies valorized in their social milieus. These works portray extremely canny heroes and heroines who appropriate dominant narrative modes and put them to use for their personal reward. They succeed to a greater or lesser extent, as I will demonstrate in the following chapters, because the victims of their seductions indiscriminately overinvest in a putatively unequivocal discourse of power whose conventions they fail to recognize as such.

During the greater part of the eighteenth century prose fiction continued to suffer charges of moral and artistic illegitimacy. Many of
the same issues that opponents and champions of fiction had raised
in the seventeenth century continued to surface in novels and theoretical debates in the eighteenth century, in particular the novel's
status as a literary genre, its relationship to truth and to history,
and its didactic function. In addition, the master discourse of aristocratic hegemony that authors such as Furetière and Madame de
Lafayette had slyly challenged underwent a significant metamorphosis: no longer the ostensible guarantor of unequivocal meaning,
the master's voice in eighteenth-century fiction ventriloquized stability but spoke ironically.

In this and the following chapters I will investigate the novel's
renunciation of a stable, unequivocal interpretation ostensibly accessible in the last exegetical instance to those in possession of the
requisite key or cultural capital. By the beginning of the eighteenth
century, the expressive causality marking the political investment
in heroic fiction had effectively disappeared, for reasons outlined
above. Nevertheless, a number of eighteenth-century novelists continued to exploit the figure of a master discourse underlying the
equivocation of the novel's *récit* by employing a narrative irony that
affords readers the illusion that the work's origins and deceptions
are demystified for them. As we will see, these novelists frequently
mobilize the distinction between the duplicity of a cunning seduction and the stability of a received moral truth, ostensibly in order
to highlight their works' didactic righteousness. Writers as diverse
as Prévost and Sade refer their readers to precepts of virtue no less

abstract than those underpinning seventeenth-century aristocratic fiction but significantly more general in their claim to moral validity for all people at all points on the social spectrum. I will argue that eighteenth-century novels—in particular novels of seduction—tend to depict the unstable and duplicitous language and behavior of a socially marginal protagonist who is portrayed either learning the discursive structure of his or her world or duplicitously manipulating others with those structures. In both cases the novel's readers are enjoined to recognize their own interpretive superiority, since the complex social and narrative mechanisms underpinning protagonists' behavior appear ironically demystified. What remains to be seen, however, is how eighteenth-century novels undermine the very process of demystification that they undertake.

Eighteenth-century novelists mobilized the displacements that complex narratives effect both in order to undermine convention and to suggest alternative reading strategies. *La Princesse de Clèves* had challenged aristocratic fiction's conventions by underscoring the incompatibility between aristocratic virtue and narrative. Mme de Chartres' advice to her daughter consisted only of prohibitions, from which we might infer that the virtuous urbane woman was both inactive and invisible, obviously not a particularly suitable subject for the elaboration of engaging tales. Mme de Clèves' story bears telling only because she diverges from the sameness of quotidian court activity. *La Princesse de Clèves* incorporates its main character's narrative divergence into its enunciation, effectively demonstrating that activities deemed *invraisemblable* on the level of the work's *histoire* might take on crucial significance for its *récit*. Because the actions the novel depicts are quintessentially mundane in this locale in which adultery, betrayal, and deceit are facts of life, the Princess's refusal to engage in them marks her as locally *invraisemblable*. Out of step with the interpretive and discursive practices of her world, Mme de Clèves serves as a model for the work's readers by introducing new and unconventional exegetical models. The cliché of female initiation and the bizarre narrative twists to which it can lead in fiction consequently established new formal features for novelists to exploit as they turned their attention away from the exhausted and antiquated conventions of a monologically partisan fiction and erected new, more politically ambivalent conventions.

Female characters who strayed from the narrow paths of virtue

peopled an enormous number of eighteenth-century novels in both
France and England. Manon Lescaut and Moll Flanders are two
examples that offer themselves most readily, but others abound:
Aphra Behn's Silvia, in her *Love Letters between a Nobleman and
his Sister*; Henrietta, in Penelope Austin's *The Life and Adventures
of the Lady Lucy*; Eliza Haywood's Emanuella, in *Rash Resolve*;
Miss Milner, in *A Simple Story* by Elizabeth Inchbald; the marquis
de Sade's Justine; Restif's Ursule, in his *Paysanne pervertie*; Laclos'
Présidente de Tourvel and Cécile Volange; and, of course, Richardson's Clarissa. These women either choose a life of debauchery or
have their virtue commandeered. Their often titillating stories place
them in both the active and the passive roles of complex seductions,
and they engage in numerous illegal or immoral actions; in any
event, their actions or situations are generally exceptional enough
to merit narrating. In most eighteenth-century novels whose main
characters are female, the plot revolves around the woman's
struggle to maintain her virtue or the extraordinary things she does
once she has given it up.

I will return below to a more detailed discussion of the female
protagonist in eighteenth-century fiction and the specific form of
virtue—namely, the strict regulation of her desire and her sexuality—that characterized novels' ostensible didactic aims. What we
will need to consider is the relationship between new and problematic conceptions of virtue—conceptions based less on birth and abstract notions of merit or worth than on property and value—and
the female protagonist who seems to represent the epitome of both
morality and depravity. Moreover, we need to theorize the novel's
rising hegemony in eighteenth-century literary practice and the increasingly participatory role it assigned its readers in the production and promotion of alternative models of truth. To do so, we
need to understand why competing ideologies, especially after the
death of Louis XIV, found the novel a particularly hospitable vehicle for the promulgation of models of virtue based implicitly or
explicitly on notions of property and value. Examining eighteenth-
century novelists' and theorists' conceptions of prose fiction will
demonstrate that this marginally legitimate form could easily propound—as a result of its marginality—models of moral truth that
challenged the aristocratic hegemony of the previous century.

In order to chronicle eighteenth-century fiction's rejection of the political aesthetics of the previous century and its promulgation of an alternative, no less politically invested poetics, we need to begin once again with the question of *vraisemblance*. As we have seen, *vraisemblance* in seventeenth-century fiction generally consisted of conforming to received notions of what could or should happen in a given situation, and then providing great globalizing narratives able to cast virtually any event as an attestation of aristocratic virtue and of the class's indispensability to the survival of the French nation. By the late seventeenth century, however, novelists began to reject traditional narrative paradigms and construct their own maxims to justify their characters' behavior, a phenomenon about which Genette and Geoffrey Bennington have theorized.[1] Narratives no longer needed to reflect aristocratic and absolutist politics in an expressive causality formed through the overdetermined ideology of each event in a sequence. In fact, novelists and historians alike began to distrust overarching narrative structures that encompassed and merged the specific and fragmentary in order to create a homogeneous and seamless cultural unity. Bussy, for example, criticized historians who relied on eyewitness accounts of particular events to construct a narrative understanding of an entire moment:

> These gentlemen the historians do not doubt that any man in combat incontestably knows everything that is going on: nevertheless, they must realize that this man may have been in the rear guard, where he did not even see the enemy. Even if he had been on the front line he perhaps saw nothing more than what was directly in front of him, especially since he would have needed to remain level-headed enough to see clearly what he did see and to make a faithful report of it. As far as what went on elsewhere, he would not have been able to say anything except what others told him, which could be false.[2]

Clearly we have come a long way since the cautious and menacing theoretical musings of the likes of Desmaretz and La Mesnardière

[1] Bennington argues in *Sententiousness and the Novel* that eighteenth-century novels rely on maxims as much as did seventeenth-century works, with the single but crucial difference that later novels induced maxims instead of relying on previously existing ones. "The maxim is no longer so much a starting point," he writes, "as a result, the end of a narrative rather than a beginning. And the result is not final (even if it erases the traces of the narrative which produces it); it cannot be invoked dogmatically as absolute truth" (p. 26).

[2] Bussy, *Les Mémoires de Messire Roger de Rabutin, Comte de Bussy*, vol. III, p. 28.

concerning the necessity of adorning the truth with well-chosen embellishments in order to make the moral lesson of history more palatable.[3] Bussy's skepticism about globalizing historical narratives that concern themselves more with promulgating a generalized and approved truth at the expense of specific facts correlates the nascent trend in fiction to disregard stultifying literary conventions and construct instead tales that adhere to their own internal logic and have their own specific truths to communicate.

The distrust of broad, globalizing narratives that subsumed the particular under the standardizing guise of the general contributed to the demise of the formulaic stories that marked heroic novels. The dramatic increase in the number of people reading novels and their vastly differing social alliances made fiction's celebration of aristocratic merit and virtue obsolete. Nevertheless, novelists continued to require both an aesthetic standard and a moral touchstone—or at least the illusion of both—to underpin their works in order to escape unremitting charges like Nicole's that their works were immoral and should consequently be banned. Like their seventeenth-century forebears, proponents of the novel in the eighteenth century intimated that their defense of the genre emanated from purely aesthetic concerns. A brief synopsis of their arguments, however, will demonstrate that the poetics of fiction in the eighteenth century was no less political than it was during the reign of the heroic novel.

One of the earliest eighteenth-century theoretical tracts on the legitimacy of prose fiction is André-Michel Ramsay's preface to Fénelon's *Télémaque*. First published in 1717, Ramsay's "Discours de la Poesie epique et de l'excellence du poeme de Telemaque" (Treatise on epic poetry and on the excellence of the poem about Telemachus) justifies Fénelon's work as an epic, and considers the moral utility of fiction. Like Boisrobert, who almost a century earlier had claimed that novels are simply epics in prose, Ramsay attempts to legitimate the novel by associating it with a classical antecedent.

---

[3] La Mesnardière's advice to writers concerning their subtle manipulation of the truth reveals the seventeenth-century preoccupation with embellishing the truth to make it conform more closely to official ideology: "Even though truth is always to be revered, *vraisemblance* can nevertheless be more important; and falsehood which is *vraisemblable* must be esteemed more than the bizarre, prodigious, or unbelievable truth: provided that . . . the tale one is relating is not the Holy Scriptures, which must always appear in their totality or not appear at all" (p. 34).

Unlike Boisrobert, however, Ramsay attempts a formal definition of the ancient genre, and molds it in such a way that the definition might easily refer to contemporary fiction as well. An epic, he writes, is "a tale told by a poet to excite admiration and inspire the love of virtue by depicting the acts of a hero favored by the heavens who performs a great deed in spite of all the obstacles that oppose him."[4] Ramsay extends his characterization of the epic by noting that "the action must be great, one, integral, fantastic, and of a specific duration" (ix), and by remarking that "in the epic we do not seek the astonishing plots of modern novels" (xviii). Ramsay's definition of the epic is a determined effort to legitimate prose fiction by allying it with the formal features the Académie Française had established for theater just ten years after Boisrobert's similar attempt to grant the novel legitimacy. That is, he ascribes to the novel the necessity of adhering to the celebrated *trois unités* of French classical theater, and he warns that a novel should contain no extraordinary peripeteia for which the work itself has not prepared readers.

Bruzen de La Martinière and Jean-Baptiste d'Argens also voice their approval of novels by noting the characteristics they share with epic. Argens provides a simple formal definition of the novel that links it to the venerated classical genre: "The novel, in imitation of the epic poem, makes use of long episodes, some of which run the entire course of the work."[5] La Martinière maintained that while the novel must maintain a formal resemblance to the epic, it alone has the liberty to depict less venerable subjects. In novels, he writes, "the rules of the epic poem should . . . be observed, but with this difference: the subject must be very different. The epic's subject must be noble, heroic, and instructive."[6] La Martinière omits any description of what sorts of subjects novels should contain; since he notes that the novel's subject matter must differ radically from the epic's, however, we can deduce that the lofty material characteristic of heroic fiction is not necessarily appropriate to contemporary prose fiction. His definition of the genre is purely formal, containing no reference to a moral or political function: "We call

[4] Ramsay, p. ix.
[5] d'Argens, *Lectures amusantes*, p. 12.
[6] La Martinière, *Introduction générale à l'étude des sciences et des belles lettres en faveur des personnes qui ne savent que le François*, p. 178.

novels those works in which the author worries little about historical accuracy, chooses a subject wholly or partially fabricated, and
ornaments it with all the episodes he deems proper to excite and
maintain the reader's interest, up until the final *dénouement*" (176).

These early eighteenth-century justifications of fiction from the
point of view of its formal features are interesting principally because they are nearly exact replicas of similar attempts made to
legitimate the genre almost a century earlier. As we have seen, the
novel's critics feared that since the genre seemed to replicate the
formal features of history, readers would be unable to distinguish
this politically legitimate genre which unabashedly glorified the
monarchy from its imitator. Prose fiction was consequently considered not poetic or imaginative, but fraudulent. After the death of
Louis XIV, however, which precipitated the decline of undisputed
absolutism in France, prose fiction boasting a formal cohesiveness
and a cautious approval of monarchic politics appeared less sedi-
tious. The publication of *Télémaque* and eighteen years later Ramsay's defense of it ideally illustrate the conjunction of formal and
political concerns facing the novel and the changing climate surrounding them at the beginning of the century. In 1699, when Fénelon's work was first published, the implicit critiques of the government of Louis XIV earned the writer public disgrace and cost
him his preceptorate of the duc de Bourgogne. Ramsay's defense of
the work in 1717, however, appeared during the Regency; the specifically political advice to the young duke concerns the benefits of
a benevolent monarchy and the dangers to a kingdom in which a
king assumes too much power. One passage in particular sums up
Fénelon's political philosophy quite nicely, when Mentor advises:

> Remember that countries in which the sovereign's domination is more
> absolute are those whose sovereigns are less powerful. They take
> everything and ruin it, and they alone possess the state. But the entire
> state languishes: the fields lie fallow and almost deserted, the towns
> dwindle every day, and trade dries up. The king, who cannot be king
> all alone, and who is only great because of his people, destroys him-
> self little by little through the imperceptible annihilation of the people
> from whom he draws his wealth and power.[7]

When Fénelon wrote these words in 1699 they were viewed as a
treacherous attack against the state and consequently inappro-

---

[7] Fénelon, *Télémaque*, Book X, p. 349.

priate, if not dangerous, for a work of literature. Eighteen years later, however, attitudes during the Regency toward absolutism had drastically changed. Ambitious nobles sought once again to have their contributions to the nation valorized and monarchic authority tempered. Economically powerful bourgeois sought the freedom to expand the sphere and scope of their investments. Consequently, Ramsay could pen his "Discours de la Poesie epique et de l'excellence du poeme de Telemaque" without fear of reprisal; he could praise this work, in fact, as both formally and politically correct.

Although most of the attempts to legitimize novels from a formal perspective appeared in the early years of the eighteenth century, novelists and critics alike addressed the question of fiction's formal structure throughout the century; most often, they combined aesthetic and philosophical debates to argue that novels served a general—if frequently extremely abstract—moral purpose. Aubert de la Chesnaye Desbois noted that novels most often inspired untoward passions in readers and corrupted their morals. However, he grudgingly admits that some novels can be beneficial: "Novels, when they are well written and when they conform to the rules that good sense has had to prescribe, are far from being the school for libertinism; rather, they show virtue crowned and vice punished." [8] Jean Formey, in his *Conseils pour former une Bibliothèque peu nombreuse mais choisie* (Advice for assembling a small but select library), is more specific about how novels achieve this lofty moral purpose. Like his predecessors in the seventeenth century, Formey likens prose fiction to historiography. Acknowledging that only the latter is a legitimate literary form, Formey hastens to point out that the metaphor of legitimacy is apt in this situation because illegitimate forms of art, like illegitimate children, frequently surpass their licit counterparts: "We could say that novelists are to historians what bastards are to legitimate children. But, to soften the comparison, I would add that . . . experience teaches us that bastards are often more clever, have more charm, and are frequently better endowed with the gifts of nature than are legitimate children." [9] Like a large portion of its reading audience, the novel could not trace its ancestry back several generations to locate any noble progenitor. Nevertheless, this did not prevent it from serving a valued social

[8] Chesnaye Desbois, *Lettres amusantes et critiques sur les romans en general*, "Première lettre," p. 20.

[9] Formey, pp. 40–41.

purpose. Formey's metaphor of illegitimacy to describe the novel aligns it with eighteenth-century bourgeois readers who were filling more and more of France's legal and administrative positions while lacking the pedigree of the ancient nobility. Paradoxically, the novel's formal illegitimacy—that is, its break with the perceived continuity of literary history—allowed it to convey moral truths more appropriate for its growing population of readers.

The novel's reading audience expanded by leaps and bounds in the eighteenth century, primarily because of the influence of literary salons, academies, and a newly defined aristocracy whose influence on French political and cultural life derived from direct input in administrative and legislative matters. If the reduction in gratifications to royal historians and men of letters dramatically altered the seventeenth-century literary scene, the death of Louis XIV and the ensuing Regency had a no less profound effect on cultural life in general and literary output in particular in the eighteenth century. Within days of Louis' death on 1 September 1715, Versailles became a veritable ghost town as courtiers stumbled over one another returning to Paris. The salons of Mme de Lambert and Mme de Tencin soon replaced the court as the intellectual and artistic centers of the capital. The polished and glamorous aristocrats of the *noblesse d'épée* had been Versailles' shining stars; in the salons, however, a somewhat more popularly egalitarian spirit reigned. Frequently sharing little in common except a considerable amount of leisure time, the constituency of eighteenth-century salons consisted of wealthy aristocrats, to be sure, but it was most likely also to include men and women drawn from the *noblesse de robe*, the clergy, and other factions of Paris' more affluent population. In addition, each salon had its resident writers on whom the reigning *maîtresse* doted; salon regulars paid them court as a tribute to their hostesses. Wealth and political influence might suffice to gain one admission into a popular salon, but a sharp mind and a facility for glib conversation were required if one wanted to shine.[10]

Catherine de Vivonne, the marquise de Rambouillet, had assembled the first intellectual and urbane salon in her famous *Chambre bleue* on the rue Saint Thomas du Louvre. From 1608 until 1665 the marquise received the most notable figures of her

[10] See Marguerite Glotz and Madeleine Maire, *Salons du XVIIIe siècle*, especially pp. 16–41.

time; it was in her *hôtel* that she and her circle reenacted the most colorful scenes from d'Urfé's *Astrée,* and where the nonrational, sentimental aspects of human feeling and perception took hold as a crucial force that needed to be reckoned with as much as did logic and reason. Carolyn Lougee argues that in the early salons "a revised epistemology which emphasized the value of human feelings made non-rational woman the repository of sentiment."[11] Lougee traces the romantic emphasis on feeling and intuition to the early salons, and argues that the impugning of physical force and heroic masculinity contributed to the valorization of sweetness and delicacy that constituted *bienséance,* an abstraction that would lead, later on in the century, to the codification of courtly language. It was in the salons of Mlle de Montpensier, Mme de Sablé, and Mme de Sévigné that La Fontaine, La Bruyère, and La Rochefoucauld introduced their fables and maxims which dictated to such a great extent the limits and conditions of *vraisemblance.*[12] The eighteenth-century salon, heir to the refinement of manners and language regulated in the previous century, cultivated the new epistemology to which Lougee refers. The disintegration of the court at Versailles and the ensuing erosion of moral standards based exclusively on aristocratic values led to a more socially egalitarian epistemology in which a *bel esprit* could shine regardless of the social class to which it belonged.

As salon regulars refined the codes of *bienséance* and repudiated the heroic exploits that characterized the aristocratic ideology of the seventeenth century, there developed a concomitant skepticism toward the great globalizing narratives of historiography I mentioned above. The skepticism toward history that Bussy demonstrated was a phenomenon that preoccupied not only salon regulars but the minds of European historians in general.[13] Particularly during the years 1715–22 and before Louis XV reestablished the court at Versailles, the issue of a historical truth divorced from conventionalized and partisan conceptions of reality fascinated intellec-

---

[11] Lougee, *Le Paradis des Femmes,* p. 31.

[12] See Picard, *Les Salons littéraires et la société française,* pp. 101–17.

[13] "Already doubt is on the inside, in the very consciousness of historians," writes Paul Hazard in his *Crise de la conscience européenne.* "For they are humanists, but late ones, and they are aware of their delay. A lingering doubt gnaws at them; even when triumphant their minds cannot rest, and even while singing before the public their songs of bravado, they worry: *Quid est veritas?*" (p. 30).

tuals and salon regulars alike. No longer constrained to articulate the restricted notion of moral and political order that had dominated during the reign of Louis XIV, writers who had got their first taste of intellectual freedom when their pensions were withdrawn at the end of the seventeenth century found a new liberty to explore polemical issues in the less coercive intellectual environment of the salons. The unyielding plasticity of highly self-conscious seventeenth-century fiction, whose unremitting construction of conspicuous artifice reinforced the ideological hegemony of those in possession of its key, ceded to a fiction that addressed matters more directly related to life and the experience of reality. It is no easy matter, however, to account for the subtle social transformations that caused readers both to identify with concerns more intimately related to a material experience of reality, and to locate in that experience of reality more specifically middle-class concerns. We need to consider the mutual influence that the displacement of France's intellectual center from the court to the capital and the increasing socioeconomic power of the bourgeoisie had on one another.

The death of Louis XIV and the subsequent dissolution of the court at Versailles contributed to transferring France's intellectual center to Paris, the nation's commercial and bureaucratic hub. Salons became the heart of artistic and philosophic activity, and the likes of Voltaire and Montesquieu tested their works on salon regulars; theatrical representations and readings of new works were also a common occurrence. Even after the majority of Louis XV and the reconstitution of the court, Paris and its salons remained the focal point of intellectual life. Louis XV did not share his great grandfather's exuberance for lavish spectacle and conspicuous display of wealth in celebration of monarchic grandeur; consequently he did not promote an elaborate network of royal patronage of arts and letters as had Louis XIV. Jean-François Solnon claims, in fact, that Louis XV and his successor effectively halted the practice of royal patronage of the arts and literature in France.[14] Solnon argues that because Louis XV had all but abolished the practice of *mé-*

---

[14] See Solnon, *La Cour de France*, especially pp. 469–72. Solnon argues that Louis XV not only remained largely indifferent to the promotion of the arts and literature, but scorned writers who strove to accede to a "royauté littéraire" by flattering their king.

cénat (patronage), writers turned to the salons of Paris in order to find not only approval for their works, but monetary remuneration as well.

Daniel Roche maintains, however, that the practice of *mécénat* was alive and well throughout the reign of Louis XV, but that it evolved significantly from the days of Louis XIV. Literary patronage and official historiography, he argues, served the interests of the absolutist state during the reign of Louis XIV. After 1715, however, the system of *mécénat* allowed writers to produce works without obligation to their patron. Roche claims that artists and writers were encouraged simply to deliver work of superior quality; those works no longer served merely to glorify the patrons for whom they were created, but to procure for their makers both financial reward and the prestige of belonging to an artistic elite. Thus, Roche notes, the system of *mécénat* consecrated the autonomy of the individual artist or writer by transforming his work into an object whose value was no longer limited to the use the patron could derive from it. Its worth included an exchange value when a genuine market for literary and artistic works developed.[15] As the specific merits of particular writers, painters, sculptors, or architects became recognized, the creation of art and literature entered into a legitimizing relationship based no longer on absolutist ideology, but on the operation of a less restricted market. That market constituted the writer and the artist as agents of cultural production in eighteenth-century France.

I argued in Chapter 5 that the influx of the bourgeoisie among the ranks of literary patrons caused a significant shift in the practices of *mécénat* in the seventeenth century, a shift which ultimately led to a greater aesthetic and political duplicity on the part of published authors. Because patrons representing the *robins* and the bourgeoisie aspired to the station of the ancient landed nobility, they encouraged writers whose services they had engaged to produce works employing the iconography and subject matter tradi-

---

[15] Roche, *Les Républicains des lettres*, p. 260. In a more complicated economic formulation, Roche writes, "the patron inscribes himself in the complex history of the contradiction or of the alliance of use value and exchange value as much as in that of surplus value. The history of patronage can neither separate nor oppose the realities of economics and the imagination of reality which is manifested in discourse and in works. Representations are inherent to realities; one cannot know the one except through the other" (p. 256).

tionally associated with "high" or aristocratic culture. The duplicity implicit in these works consequently concerned the degree to which readers' interpretations were directed to a specific, partisan reading. Little tolerance for divergence from received forms, however, restricted the range of duplicity in literary works to a contestation of referentiality and the stability of language; what resulted was a literary modernism that mobilized irony and ambivalent ideological affiliations. There was little opportunity in late seventeenth-century modernism to venture beyond the confutation of traditional discursive models. With the disintegration of a rigidly absolutist hold on literature's iconography after 1715, however, writers as agents of cultural production faced a broad marketplace whose field was delineated principally by the dissemination of the salons previously mentioned and by the proliferation of academies. The number of academies in France and especially in Paris grew greatly in the eighteenth century; because membership in royal academies could be denied to anyone "who is not pleasing to Monsieur the Protector, and who is not of good moral standing, of good reputation, and of sound intellect," [16] academies retained their polemical function of dictating taste according to prevailing political moods. Royal academies continued to glorify the absolutist state, but their role as the sole authorized disseminators of officially sanctioned culture and public taste diminished as the ritualistic nature of academic pronouncements ceded to the propagation of knowledge.[17] Academies supported, in fact, the development of new forms of knowledge in the service of the state.

Academies' dissemination of knowledge in the eighteenth century blunted their earlier highly polemical function of exalting the monarchy's grandeur. Through them the Enlightenment expanded from the capital to the provinces, and in part because of them a more unified social body developed based on the widespread availability of knowledge. It is easy to understand how this was able to occur during the reign of Louis XV, since aristocrats were no longer faceless entities in the cast of hundreds whose sole purpose was to help the Sun King shine. After the latter's death, aristocrats scrambled to shake off the yoke of absolutism and to assert their own promi-

---

[16] This phrase, cited by Roche, p. 162, is part of the constitution of the Académie Française adopted in the seventeenth century.
[17] See Fogel, especially pp. 411–18.

nence in affairs of the state, even though many of them had no previous administrative experience; this led Montesquieu to compare the aristocrats of his century to those of the preceding one by noting that "a certain philosophy widespread today has it that our noblemen are more unprincipled, but that they are not so miserable." [18] If aristocratic virtue was a construction of history with little or no material evidence to support it, especially after Louis XIV relieved nobles of their traditional privilege of bearing arms for the state, more and more nobles were seeking administrative posts to underscore their worth to the nation. Particularly in the provinces, where large numbers of impoverished nobles required the monetary remuneration that filling such posts provided, aristocrats throughout France undertook offices and other administrative functions; this effectively denied the historical notion of privilege and abstract merit upon which their class was based.[19] That is, aristocrats who filled offices and performed administrative service for the state began to resemble the bourgeoisie and the *noblesse de robe*, whose noble pretensions had been the scourge of their existence less than a century earlier.

Accompanying the aristocrats' occupation of administrative posts was a concomitant redefinition of the ideology of nobility. As Guy Chaussinand-Nogaret has shown, fully 25 percent of the nobility in the eighteenth century joined the aristocratic ranks after 1700; by 1789, two-thirds of all aristocrats had achieved that status within the previous two centuries (30). The rapid social elevation of large numbers of people from the third estate, combined with a considerable percentage of hereditary nobles occupying the role of functionary, contributed to reshaping traditional aristocratic values. Recently ennobled individuals forswore all ties to their own cultural heritage; acceding to the ranks of the nobility involved assuming membership in an ideological complex that could not tolerate any traces of mean or base origins. Since, however, by far the greatest number of recently ennobled families were of middle-class urban origin, and because service to the king and to the nation constituted the new eighteenth-century aristocracy, bourgeois values encroached on the ancient concepts of *sang* and

---

[18] Montesquieu, *Mes pensées*, frag. 1300, in *Œuvres complètes*, vol. I, p. 1316.

[19] See Guy Chaussinand-Nogaret, *The French Nobility in the Eighteenth Century*, pp. 15–22.

vertu (blood and virtue) that had traditionally defined the aristocracy. Middle-class institutions confronted established aristocratic
values; a new noble ideology arose premised less on hereditary or
institutionalized virtue, and more on moral attitudes and the rendering of service.[20]

The newly developed ideology of aristocracy based on service and
moral worth enlarged the pool of people who could distinguish
themselves and rise to positions of institutional or literary recognition. The new elite were, according to R. Vierhaus, "neither aristocrats by birth, nor men of the cleric class, nor people belonging
to the proprietary classes; they were individuals belonging to
groups and exercising a function and often a directing role in an
institutional, political, or social system." [21] The new elite who were
an amalgamation of lesser nobility and people of the professional
middle class attended salons and in some cases funded and spon-
sored them. The demystifying powers of human reason and historical consciousness exemplified by the *philosophes* conferred on
them a skepticism toward received political and religious practices;
eager to justify their own newly acquired positions of power and
prestige in the government and at court, they readily identified with
the cynicism and mistrust that writers such as Bayle, Fénelon, Montesquieu, and Voltaire displayed toward tradition. In the *Esprit des
lois*, Montesquieu unveiled the corruption likely to occur in a monarchy supported by a hereditary aristocracy whose interests lay not
in justice and virtue but in power and self-aggrandizement: "The
monarchy is lost when the prince, bringing everything back to himself, calls the state to his capital, the capital to his court, and the
court to his person." [22] The spirit and values informing the predom-

[20] Chaussinand-Nogaret writes that "nobility was officially justified by ability and
merit, defining itself by middle class values" and that "the purest nobility is not
therefore of the blood, but takes its principle from moral worth and professional
ability" (p. 39). George Rudé concurs, and notes the blurring of the distinction
between aristocrats and bourgeois. "There was," he writes in *Europe in the Eighteenth Century,* "no clear dividing line between enlightened aristocrats and enlightened men of wealth" (p. 165). Rudé traces some of the political developments that
contributed to the blurring of the aristocratic/bourgeois distinction, and argues that
after the death of Louis XIV the Parlements assumed a greater role in the governing
of France. Particularly during the Regency, the Parlements carried out effective protests against legislation that would restrict their own power and that of the aristocracy (pp. 180–82).

[21] R. Vierhaus, *Elites et idéologie en Europe,* cited by Suratteau, p. 117.

[22] Montesquieu, *De l'esprit des lois,* Book VIII, chapter 6, in *Œuvres complètes,*
vol. II, p. 355.

inantly middle-class ideology that permeated France's administrative class derived from a demystification of arbitrary political power and its concomitant ideology; keen to legitimate their own executive, legislative, and intellectual situations, the new elite continued to question the values of traditional ideology, and began to promote the virtues underpinning their own political positions.

What I want to suggest is that the cultural changes I have briefly sketched out and which I am interested in charting specifically in the domain of fiction entailed modifications in both material life and the ways people perceived it and related to it. A concise synopsis of the manner in which practical and ideological concerns informed one another in the construction of bourgeois values might be in order here. Perhaps the most obvious manifestation of social transformation from a material perspective lies in the area of labor and production. In marked contrast to the preceding century, the dominant economic culture in the eighteenth century centered on work or service. Those who continued to live exclusively off the income their lands provided generally found themselves increasingly impoverished, since those yields remained fairly constant and prices were soaring. Alongside the necessity of working or performing a service for a living there developed the concomitant ideological investment in quantifying goods, services, ideas, and people. That is, in addition to standard economic treatises like Noël Chomel's *Dictionnaire œconomique* (1709), François Quesnay's *Tableau économique* (1758), and the *Dictionnaire portatif des arts et métiers* (1766), works purporting to catalog human history and geography appeared, most notably Barthélemy d'Herbelot's *Bibliothèque orientale* (1697), Bruzen de La Martinière's *Grand dictionnaire géographique et critique et historique* (1726–39), and Buffon's *Histoire naturelle* (1749–1804), of which the portion "Variétés dans l'espèce humaine" (Varieties in the human species) is particularly revelatory of the attempt to establish a general human equivalent—European—against which one might measure racial and ethnic traits.[23] The cataloging and the quantification of

[23] In the introductory paragraph to the essay, Buffon writes that "everything we have thus far said concerning the generation of man, his formation, development, state at different ages in his life, senses, and the structure of his body, such as we know it from anatomical dissection, only gives us the history of the individual. The history of the species requires a particular enumeration" (p. 223). When he describes the "savages of the north," Buffon includes a brief explanation of the custom in

knowledge reached their epitome, of course, in the *Encyclopédie*.
The point I would like to make here is that practical human knowledge and its political implications continued to be amassed, but
they generally remained subservient to an abstract notion of a
higher religious, social, or moral truth, heir to their Platonic and
Aristotelian conceptions. Human reason, and its progenitor education, consequently acquired the status of capital or of another
quantifiable commodity.[24]

The skepticism surrounding the received abstract models of political and moral truth thus found its home in the universalizing principles of Reason, which, as a quantifiable and concrete system, was
suited for accumulation and exchange. Formal coherence and ex-
perimental verification validated empiricism and materialism; if
philosophers recognized the social contingency of knowledge, they
also construed it as no longer an alienated entity composing a
"higher" realm of existence, but as a concrete and transmissible
component of daily life whose stability and regularity underpinned
the function of their society. Since the family occupied the seat of
bourgeois order, the values guaranteeing its preservation rapidly
accrued the status of general equivalent for society at large. Consequently, the symbol of bourgeois order and authority—the father—became the guarantor of social values;[25] sexual restraint,
particularly as it concerned women, formed the keystone of bourgeois order, since promiscuous feminine sexuality threatened the
stability of the family name and, consequently, its fortune. The co-

---

which men offered their wives to visitors. The idea originated, he writes, "because
they are aware of their own deformity and of the ugliness of their wives; they seem
to find the women whom foreigners have not disdained less ugly" (p. 227).

On the cataloging of human knowledge in the social and natural sciences, see in
particular Foucault, *Les Mots et les choses*, especially chapter V, "Classer."

[24] In *L'Eglise et la bourgeoisie*, Bernard Groethuysen notes that bourgeois were
well-disposed to believe that they had made their own lives: "He works and he saves,
he calculates and measures, reasons and predicts, and, creating order everywhere
and leaving nothing to chance, he will be able, by searching for a solid foundation
for his life in the moral and economic domains, to eliminate the powers of mystery"
(p. 172).

[25] In the *Encyclopédie*, in fact, political authority is expressly linked to patriarchy.
"No man has received from nature the power to command others. Freedom is a gift
from above, and each individual of the same species has the right to enjoy it as soon
as he accedes to reason. If nature has established some *authority*, it is paternal
power: but paternal power has its limits, and in the state of nature it would end as
soon as the children were able to take care of themselves. Any other *authority* comes
from an origin outside of nature" (article "Autorité politique," in *Encyclopédie*, ed.
John Lough and Jacques Proust, vol. I, p. 537).

hesive bourgeois family thus correlated the interwoven systems of reason, exchange, and social integrity.

If Truth remained an abstract ideal only imperfectly accessible through the application of bourgeois strains of reason, this in no way implies that it remained politically neutral. It remained above the level of quantifiable knowledge available through education and was, consequently, bereft of exchange value, yet Truth could easily be put into the ideological service of theorizing human freedom in its most negative, politically reactionary form: the freedom to be poor, ignorant, and economically enslaved. As Herbert Marcuse notes, since anyone could aspire to the spiritual heights that Plato promised in the realm of philosophical knowledge, "the freedom of the soul was used to excuse the poverty, martyrdom, and bondage of the body." [26] Vincent de Gournay's eighteenth-century maxim, "Laissez faire et laissez passer" (No interference, and complete freedom of movement), could thus be cynically applied to economic matters while in no way seeming to negate social and religious principles. The continued alienation of "higher" truths divorced from material reality served to validate the current social order as the perhaps imperfect but best available means to guarantee such intellectual flights. Reason and the concomitant values of family order and feminine sexual restraint secured the bourgeoisie's increasing dominance in intellectual and social endeavors.

In fiction, this translated into a rejection of the great globalizing narratives of the seventeenth century whose expressive causality directed readers' interpretation to a celebration of traditional aristocratic virtue. Early modern French fiction had begun, by the end of the seventeenth century, to unravel the thread of narrative conventions binding aristocratic ideology to the novel. Eighteenth-century fiction not only continued to abjure the overwrought and hackneyed conventions of its forebears but it radically altered the subjects, situations, and milieus novels depicted: *La Princesse de Clèves* initiated new subjects for fiction in its depiction of a married woman,[27] but the *Histoire de Gil Blas de Santillane, Le Paysan par-*

---

[26] Marcuse, "The Affirmative Character of Culture," p. 109.

[27] Furetière pointed out at the end of the first book of *Le Roman bourgeois* that novels never portray married women. Concluding the story of Nicodème and Lucrèce with their marriage, he writes that "if they lived happily together or not, you will only be able to learn about them if it becomes fashionable to write about the lives of married women" (p. 1024).

venu, and *Le Colporteur* portrayed rogues or bourgeois merchants in earthy, lawless, or scandalous settings. The near wholesale renunciation of aristocratic narrative paradigms filled the political function of challenging the outwardly monologic nature of contemporary French politics. By repudiating the expressive causality of heroic fiction, novelists implicitly impugned the discursive structure and ideology of knowledge that sustained power relations in the essentially feudalistic, top-to-bottom social configuration that had been mapped out centuries earlier. They introduced non-aristocratic principal characters—traditionally excluded from literary representation except to serve as the foil of ruling-class gentility—who, although frequently comic, sustained active, complex, and intelligent relationships to the movement of the plot.

The introduction of traditionally marginalized figures as main characters in novels effected significant and interrelated changes in novels' *histoires* and *récits*. Bourgeois or otherwise non-noble main characters fractured the usual vertical line of social relations by interjecting the representation of horizontal relationships among individuals and groups. Class opposition, particularly the variety that conferred value or identity on a group by juxtaposing it to the standards and practices of the dominant class, ceased to serve as the hallmark underpinning reader identification. Eighteenth-century novels highlighted instead philosophical and political difference. By way of illustration,we might note the radical dissimilarity in the subject positions allotted to non-noble characters who were generally objects of scorn or ridicule in works such as *Le Berger extravagant* or Scarron's *Roman comique*, and the positions assigned to similar non-noble characters in Lesage's *Gil Blas* or Marivaux's *Paysan parvenu*, in which comic effect is not necessarily contingent upon derision. In short, eighteenth-century novels discontinued the custom of alluding to aristocratic social and discursive practices as the touchstone for the representation of correct moral and political behavior.

Marginalized figures who served as main characters in fiction significantly altered narratives' *récits* because they had at best limited access to the conventions and traditions of the aristocratic way of life. As Furetière's *Roman bourgeois* aptly demonstrated, middle-class characters whose professional activities cause them to negotiate the complexities of two distinct realities—courtly and commercial—hypostatize social contradictions and appear ridiculous when they are depicted out of their element. Consequently, the standardized iconography and conventions of contemporary fiction simply broke down when they confronted the new professional middle class and lesser aristocracy of the eighteenth century.

The shift in emphasis away from the abstraction of aristocratic *vertu* toward the more practical considerations of service and material existence ultimately led to what has traditionally been labeled "realist fiction." As I mentioned above, two of the best-known books on eighteenth-century French fiction advance arguments that the development of true-to-life narrative arose from authors' attempts to flee critical attack. Vivienne Mylne and Georges May maintain that justifying the novel entailed causing it to appear either absolutely true or morally and aesthetically linked to earlier, sanctioned forms of literature.[28] I wholeheartedly agree with May's and Mylne's arguments that what is commonly referred to as "realism" developed in eighteenth-century fiction as an effect of moral and aesthetic exigencies; I would like to add, however, that the development of fiction that seemed better able to offer an adequation of real and represented events correlated the historical skepticism briefly outlined above. In addition, it offered an alternative to the production of ideologically laden signifying systems in which calculatedly dense artifice punctuated the interpretive mastery of aristocratic readers, and consequently excluded those dispossessed of the cultural capital required for its deciphering. In short, the development of "realistic" fiction, by which I mean sustained narrative works in prose that seemed to depict in less mediated fashion the world as most readers perceived it, is nothing short of a political phenomenon. Such a development represents not only the outright rejection of conventions traditionally associated with the dominant social group, but a determined effort to naturalize through literary representation the social practices of a heretofore marginalized group on its way to achieving political hegemony.

The development of realism in eighteenth-century fiction was

---

[28] See May, *Le Dilemme du roman*: "The evolution of the novel is effectively intelligible in this period only to the extent that it seems to adhere to novelists' preoccupation with justifying their works, either from an aesthetic or moral point of view, and to the extent that it seemed difficult if not impossible to satisfy the exigencies implied by these two systems of value at the same time and with the same works" (p. 15); and Mylne, *The Eighteenth-Century French Novel*, pp. 2–18.

consequently not a goal, as many critics seem given to believe, but an effect of the eradication of obtrusive and inappropriate or outmoded narrative convention. Critics and novelists alike in the eighteenth century were determined to demystify both the cultural requirements requisite to the interpretation of the literary text and the presuppositions concerning precisely who was reading works of literature. Writers and critics in the eighteenth century considered novels densely encoded works of literature, to be sure, but for all their complexity they still did not manifest the impenetrability of seventeenth-century fiction whose interpretation required possession of the cultural key. Indeed, novelists and critics alike called for the production of literary works easily accessible to a wide variety of readers. Formey, whose project was to help readers select books for their personal libraries, implicitly argued that educated people from any class could appreciate literary works when he wrote that "reading is generally appropriate for people of both sexes, as long as they have an education, an honorable birth, a modest fortune, and leisure time; in addition, they must desire to derive some benefit from all these advantages, and to enrich their lives with new appeals" (xxi). Formey's *Conseils* is directed at the newly ennobled or at those of the lesser nobility, as the qualities he attributes to potential readers reveal. The "bibliothèque peu nombreuse mais choisie" he advises them to acquire reflects an anxiety about accruing cultural capital on a limited intellectual and financial budget; the point of his essay is to smooth access to the ranks of the educated and the urbane. Argens' conception of readerships in the eighteenth century is similar to Formey's, but it is less ideologically slanted. He writes that "By the word 'reader' I mean a man of the world or a woman who has a taste for reading, and who, through natural good sense and some aptitude for reading well-written works, is able to judge them reasonably, and to appreciate the merit of an author who works more with charm and genius than with erudition" (50). Argens' "Discours sur les nouvelles" (Treatise on novellas) emphasizes not readers' possession of cultural capital or their capacity to disentangle the web of deliberate artifice, but the simple ability to recognize an abstractly defined artistic merit free of pedantic or arcane references. Argens' and Formey's failure or refusal to define the formal characteristics of literary merit reveals the extent to which they consider it a generally accessible feature of cultural life; readers with a modicum of education, urbanity, and judgment possess all that is required to appreciate refined literary works.

Argens' contemporary Marivaux put this theory of the general accessibility of culture into practice in his *Vie de Marianne*. In the fourth installment of the novel, which appeared just three years before Argens' essay, he introduces Marianne into the turbulent world of gracious society. Marianne, whose social status remains an enigma because she is an orphan of unidentified parents, passes as an intimate of Mme de Miran, a wealthy and urbane socialite. Brought to dine at the home of Mme Dorsin, Marianne discovers that her preconceptions of polite society were inaccurate. "Everything they said was proper and fitting, everything was harmonious, flowing, and gay. I had imagined the world completely different from what I saw there (and I was not so very far off); I had imagined it full of frivolous rules and small subtleties, full of serious and important frivolities difficult to understand, and which you had to know or risk appearing ridiculous, however ridiculous these frivolities were themselves."[29] Marianne explains her capacity to decipher the rules of polite society by noting, "I was born to have taste, and I understood what sort of people I was dining with" (204). Simultaneously demystifying the arcane rules informing behavior in works like *La Princesse de Clèves*, and affirming the relative ease with which outsiders could accede to urbane society, Marivaux's *Marianne* chronicles the adventures of a young woman who is adept at, in Ronald Rosbottom's words, "beating the establishment at its own game."[30] I would point out, however, that Marianne only beats the establishment to the extent that it allows her to—she has all the social and physical graces prized by the *honnêtes gens* of the mid-eighteenth century. She merely lacks, as many contemporary readers would have lacked, elevated aristocratic birth. Her relatively unobstructed rise in status to the venerated title of "Madame la comtesse de ***" might reassure readers of the administrative class that merit and virtue are not conferred at birth, but through the exercise of service and moral temperance.[31]

[29] Marivaux, *La Vie de Marianne*, p. 205.
[30] Rosbottom, *Marivaux's Novels*, pp. 145–46.
[31] Chesnaye Desbois drives home this point by remarking that "there is nothing unusual about a peasant falling in love; but it is indeed rare to find a person of a certain standing and of considerable fortune considering forming an alliance with a

Rosbottom and others have pointed out that Marianne is aware of the effect of her beauty and sincerity on others. For Marianne, entry into the world of polite society involves a studied imitation of their mannerisms and appearances. When Mme de Miran tells Marianne to dress for dinner and to neglect nothing in her appearance, Marianne reflects, "This order put my vanity at ease: I was going to be a coquette out of obedience" (202). Marianne understands the subtle semiotics of fashion; far from being a seductive siren, she clarifies her notion of coquettishness: "When I talk about coquettishness, I mean only that it is always involved when you dress yourself carefully—this is all I mean. I never strayed from the most austere decency" (202). Much of Marianne's life is devoted to projecting appearances and making an effect;[32] often admiring her own ability to move others with her sad tale ("I was so young, and consequently so captivating, that I think I made these women cry" [270]), Marianne realizes that her artful coquetry and underprivileged youth can work to her advantage: "I had no other recourse than to try to incite compassion" (235).[33] I will address below the significance of Marianne's seductive appeals; for the moment, however, we need to consider the studied artfulness in Marianne's story and in eighteenth-century fiction in general. The demystification of convention, which I will argue largely manifests itself in eighteenth-century fiction as either a complex seduction or as the laying bare of the formal scaffolding buttressing a work of art, was primarily responsible for articulating an ideological base supporting the aesthetic conventions that developed in fiction.

The relative ease with which Marianne penetrates aristocratic circles correlates the theories of Argens and Formey, who main-

---

peasant" (p. 32). Aubert was a fan of Marivaux and argued that *La Vie de Marianne* effectively portrayed virtue rewarded.

[32] In her book *Self-Imitation in the Eighteenth-Century Novel*, Marie-Paul Laden has also observed this phenomenon. Noting Marianne's refinement of her narrating abilities, Laden writes, "Marianne recounts her story several times to various audiences. The story may vary slightly according to the audience, but its impact is always the same; Marianne not only consistently wins over her listeners, she is also careful to note the effect of her tale as she tells it" (p. 102).

[33] Marivaux's Jacob has similar insights into his ability to spin an engaging tale: "I recall that in . . . speaking thus I felt nothing that would give the lie to my speech. Nevertheless, I confess that I strove to effect a touching appearance and the tone of a man who is crying; I wanted to adorn the truth. What is striking is that my intention took hold of me. I performed so well that I fooled myself, and I continued on without worrying about adding on to what I was feeling. It was thus a matter of the heart that had taken me over" (*Le Paysan parvenu*, p. 135).

tained that readers of any social class require only a particular level of refinement and judgment in order to appreciate a novel's literary merit. Pierre-Nicolas Desmolets, who defined the novel as a "mixture of fiction and history [*un mélange de la Fable & de l'Histoire*],"[34] also argues that readers require only keenness and sensitivity in order to apprehend fiction's worth; he isolates that worth, however, not merely in the utility or pleasure it can provide readers, but in the manner in which it allows them at once to perceive and ignore its self-conscious artifice. Desmolets puts forth a theory of fiction that seems to anticipate Marthe Robert's: recommending that readers both recognize and ignore narrative conventions, he nevertheless restricts the scope of his theory to middle-class audiences and their particular relationships to literature. After discussing different kinds of novels, Desmolets writes: "Those [novels] in which fiction dominates must hide much more art. Those in which the truth prevails could not conform too much to nature. Those which disguise the truth with allegory should only be obscure for people who lack penetration" (195). Like Argens and Formey, Desmolets refuses to ascribe a specific social class to those who might appreciate good fiction, but he does underscore the intellectual achievement required to understand its full scope. While critics like Jacquin claimed that novels were pernicious because they appealed only to sentimentality or sensualness ("The novelist seeks only to touch and to soften the heart" [20–21]), Desmolets continually emphasizes the tension they maintain between a seemingly direct representation of the real world and the opaque representation that calls attention to its own signifying process: "We love art," Desmolets writes, "but we find it painful to be too aware of its presence [*mais nous trouvons pénible de la sentir*]" (199). In other words, works that achieved the critical nod were those that forswore the opaque conventions characteristic of the previous generation's "high" art and promoted instead representation devoid of obtrusive and arcane conventions; at the same time, however, they allowed accomplished readers to perceive and appreciate their rhetorical turns.

Many novelists and critics attempted to expose the novel's traditional dependency on aesthetic convention and by that very fact

[34] Desmolets, *Continuation des Mémoires de littérature et d'histoire*, p. 193.

dismiss it as a valid literary genre. Guillaume Bougeant, for example, all but plagiarized Alluis' *L'Escole d'amour* in his *Voyage merveilleux du Prince Fan-Férédin dans la Romancie* (Prince Fan-Férédin's fantastic voyage in Novel Land), which appeared in 1735. Like Alluis' novel, Bougeant's work is a protracted satire of fiction's conventions, but unlike Alluis, Bougeant mocks the very nature of imaginative literature by implying that language without a concrete referent in the material world is extravagant and even unwise. His hero embarks on a quest for the Pays des Romans (Country of Novels) with the conviction that it must exist: "Because otherwise," he remarks, "if this country did not really exist, we would have to consider everything we read in novels nothing but ridiculous visions and childish fables." [35] Bougeant continually draws attention to the fact that he is inventing the most extravagant scenarios he can think of while ironically asserting, in the tradition of heroic fiction, that everything he relates is absolutely true. "But reflecting on the fact that it is not permitted to suppress the truth in order to avoid all suspicion of prevarication, I courageously take the position appropriate to any sincere historian to tell all the facts in their most precise truth" (21). In Bougeant's view of prose narrative, any description must have a corresponding philosophical or material theory supporting it. The language of fiction is incapable of constructing a world, he implicitly argues, but is able only to refer to an existing reality. For example, when the narrator touches a pile of rocks and finds them as soft as wool, he searches for an explanation from the body of received knowledge: "The day before, a most unhappy yet extremely eloquent lover had passed by, and he told the rocks of his troubles. His story was so touching, and his tone so sorrowful and pitiful, that the rocks were unable to resist, in spite of their natural hardness" (34).

Like Sorel, who censured the metaphoric and precious language of pastoral fiction in his *Berger extravagant* by depicting its breakdown in situations it was not accustomed to negotiating, Bougeant maligns literary language in prose narrative. His *Voyage merveilleux* closely follows the narrative paradigm of *L'Escole d'amour*, including a visit to Romancie, a fantasy world inhabited by Amadis de Gaule, King Arthur, Pharamond, and Cyrus. Like Alluis, Bou-

[35] Bougeant, pp. 6–7.

geant marvels at the fact that no one in heroic fiction ever eats or drinks, and also like Alluis he offers a school for the declaration of love. In addition, however, he includes a school for the language of fiction. Prince Zagaraph teaches the syntax of this language, which includes rules exhorting speakers "to express nothing simply, but always with exaggeration, figures, metaphor or allegory" (97); he reminds them "never to say a word without one or more epithets" (98). Bougeant creates a complex world that resembles Alluis' in nearly every respect. He imitates his predecessor by taking on the conventions of heroic fiction and demonstrating that they do not hold up under close scrutiny. Unlike Alluis, however, he condemns fiction's apparent ability to construct something out of nothing, and he continually expresses his dissatisfaction with novelists' appropriation of what had traditionally been the historians' and philosophers' prerogative. That is, the narrative and analytical discourses of history and philosophy were the only ones authorized to construct speculative worlds or domains; the privileging of these modes of discourse resulted, as Reiss has shown, from the practical effacement of the enunciating subject such that the knowledge it communicated appeared to be unquestioned "common sense."[36] Bougeant's Enfileurs, Souffleurs, Brodeurs, and Lanterniers are all workers—producers—inhabiting Romancie, and each of them is an allegory for a specific type of fiction; Bougeant condemns them because "they make a fat work out of matter that in itself is nothing" (191). To escape the charge, however, that his work is just another linguistic fabrication doing violence to history's and philosophy's traditional prerogative of creating their own objects, Bougeant concludes his work by having his narrator wake up from his nightmare.

While Sorel, Furetière, and Alluis had penned similar novels rid-

---

[36] See Reiss's *Discourse of Modernism*, p. 360: "The production of discourse, its objects, and its relation by the *I* of enunciation that originated it, in secret, in power, and with the complicity of a knowing elite, was gradually occulted: discourse became the common, transparent, and objective property of all, while the enunciating *I* was hypostatized as individual will. Discourse was infallible because it corresponded to 'common sense,' while will could control it only with the assent of all potential users." In *Marxism and Literary History*, John Frow comments on the constructed nature of any object of knowledge when he asserts that "knowledge . . . never confronts a 'pure' (real) object; it is neither a reflection nor a representation of the real but a structure of discourse which *constructs* its object through an ordered transformation of pre-theoretical values" (p. 24).

iculing the conventions of fiction, Bougeant's work is something of an anomaly in the eighteenth century. It is the only criticism of the novel I know of—with the possible exception of Jean Maillard's *Romans appréciés* (Novels appraised) (1756)—that takes the form of a novel for the express purpose of condemning the genre.[37] However, it effectively illustrates a crucial issue in the development of the eighteenth-century "realist" novel: language's capacity to create—and consequently to contest—narrative models of truth. Novelists' and philosophers' rejection of the globalizing narratives of the seventeenth century and the accompanying received models of religious and ontological truth constituted a nightmare for conservative thinkers who clung to tradition. Unwilling to cast off traditional conceptions of reality, they viewed as a frontal attack on contemporary political systems the new narrative models which failed to discriminate among readers on the basis of class. Fiction that required little or no access to the cultural paraphernalia native to the ruling classes seemed too egalitarian and, consequently, revolutionary in its political scope.[38]

Bougeant's parody of contemporary novels centered on their failure to respect received narrative models of truth and on their cavalier deployment of fashionable language to construct alternative versions of reality. In a somewhat bitter dismissal of novels and their superficial intellectual content, Bougeant's sympathizer Maillard scoffs at what he terms the fashionable contemporary maxim that "nothing is true about anything [*rien n'est vrai sur rien*]" (13). This trendy belief is responsible in Maillard's view for the proliferation of literary works, in particular novels, that fail to grapple with serious and timeless problems and settle instead for entertaining their readers. Because of their inability to negotiate complex

[37] The premise of Maillard's *Les Romans appréciés, ouvrage Qui n'est rien moins qu'un Roman* (Novels appraised: Work which is itself nothing less than a novel) involves the narrator's visit to a salon at which novels are discussed. Despite its rudimentary narrative construction, the work more closely resembles an essay than a novel.

[38] In *Story and History*, a book that appeared just as I was completing my own, William Ray investigates the complex relationship obtaining between personal or individual modes of narrating and the broader, legitimate or valorized modes authorized by a culture at large. Ray maintains that one can observe in both the French and the British traditions of prose fiction a strict association between personal identity and culturally determined styles of representation. Characters in eighteenth-century fiction, he argues, negotiate or contest their relationships to social hierarchies by appropriating for themselves particular forms of narrative.

philosophical and moral issues, Maillard believes novels to be so base that they are "worthy of being compared, not with the immortal works of the century of Augustus, but not even with the works of the most barbaric centuries" (90). Maillard rehearses many of the criticisms leveled against novels in the seventeenth century; he centers primarily on the fact that since they are not true and their authors adopt the modish position that truth is unattainable, they do not merit attention.[39]

The issue of truth's unattainability, however, frequently fueled arguments in favor of the novel. Ramsay began his defense of Fénelon's *Télémaque* with a neo-Platonic discussion of the manifestations of truth in literature reminiscent of similar seventeenth-century arguments,[40] and Maillard's contemporary Henri-François de La Solle argued in the preface to his *Mémoires de deux amis* that history and fiction are indistinguishable. Concurring with Bussy that history misleads readers because its globalizing narratives fail to account for conflicting interpretations, La Solle reminds his readers that "novels used to be history itself. This name was given to them because of the name of the language in which they were written, which we call Romance."[41] La Solle avers that since history and novels share a common origin they contain similar didactic value, with the crucial difference that the novelist has greater liberty to manipulate subject matter and consequently to offer more excellent examples of moral rectitude. He concludes his discussion by referring to Plato and the "fashionable" position that nothing is true: "Plato says that there is nothing real in the world, and that we only perceive shadows and phantoms in this life. Why, then, do we argue about the truth, if it doesn't exist? What difference could we find between history and fiction?" (xxxvi).

It is not entirely clear that La Solle's question is rhetorical. To insinuate that fact and fabrication share a common identity would

---

[39] Similar arguments abound throughout the eighteenth century and Georges May has assembled the most interesting and revealing of them. See his *Dilemme du roman*, especially pp. 106–38. See also Stewart, *Imitation and the Memoir-Novel*, especially pp. 169–93.

[40] "If we could savor unadorned truth, it would not seem to make itself loved through the ornaments that the imagination lends it. But pure and delicate light does not sufficiently flatter what is most sensitive in man; it requires the sort of attention which too often disturbs his natural inconstancy. To teach him you have to give him not only pure Ideas to enlighten him, but also concrete images to arrest him in fixed contemplation of truth" (pp. vii-viii).

[41] La Solle, p. xxv.

be quite a cavalier position to maintain, particularly in a work ostensibly dedicated to proving the moral superiority of fiction. La Solle takes great pains to demonstrate that contemporary criticisms of novels are unfounded and, moreover, that the impossible task history traditionally set itself of chronicling moral and political rectitude is more appropriately delegated to novels. "As far as the abuses and dangers resulting from reading novels filled with love are concerned, these dangers, it seems to me, are greater in history. Incest and adultery triumph there, and we see them abuse authority to commit any crime. . . . It is in [novels] that distributive justice is scrupulously observed. This justice does not depend on the whims of fortune, but on the spirit and rectitude of the author" (xxxiii). The answer to La Solle's question concerning the difference between history and novels thus seems clear: of the two forms of narrative, neither of which is able to offer the unadorned truth, novels retain the greater power to construct the sort of acceptable social image that a culture takes pride in displaying. The only way to distinguish between the two genres, in La Solle's view, is to discern which provides the more excellent example of moral probity—that one will be the novel.

By the middle years of the eighteenth century the idea that human knowledge was a socially contingent construction based in many ways upon the weight of political traditions and institutions was a commonplace. By 1772, Diderot had already begun his *Supplément au voyage de Bougainville*, in which he undertook a comparative analysis of, among other things, sexuality, property, and the law in European and foreign cultures. At the end of the century the marquis de Sade eloquently investigated the cultural limits of human reason in his *Justine* by pointing out that the human intellect is incapable of naming Providence and consequently unable to contain or control it. We will return to Sade in Chapter 9 in order to see where he understood ahistorical human rationalism to lead. Sade's libertines vehemently contest traditional political and moral positions; they articulate the view that most cultural institutions serve to empower the rich and keep the poor subservient. The demystification of political and religious institutions was a fundamental goal of Enlightenment philosophy, and *philosophes* such as d'Holbach, La Mettrie, and Montesquieu adhered to a materialist perspective that attempted to understand the origins and real social

effects of those institutions. Berkeley, Voltaire, and Diderot interrogated the relationship between perception and epistemology, and
each arrived at a specific conclusion of the general nature that physical perception lies at the heart of human knowledge; theories
about and observations of the blind contributed to formulating the
axiom that there is no inherent relationship among the human
senses. Consequently, since the interrelationships among the senses
need to be learned, one's perceptions and resulting apprehensions
of the world remain subjective, and so, too, does the idea of truth
informing one's affinity with reality.[42]

It is clearly beyond the scope of this study to analyze in detail the
principles of Enlightenment philosophy. It is important to emphasize, however, the empiricist thought that contributed to exposing
the irrationality underlying superstition, religious dogma, and political power in the eighteenth century. As early as 1682, when
Pierre Bayle published his *Pensées sur la comète* (Thoughts on the
comet), philosophers began to unpack the obfuscation of power
sustaining the oppressive religious, political, and economic regi-
mens of the day. Lucien Goldmann has sketched out the relationship between the bourgeois market economy of the eighteenth century and the series of philosophical abstractions contributing to
Enlightenment thought. Arguing that the production of goods for
market exchange—which he traces to the thirteenth century—radically altered human consciousness, Goldmann stresses the individual autonomy that inevitably arose as people perceived their specific relationships to generalized economic structures. The persis-
tent increase in individual autonomy, he maintains, gave rise to the
rationalism and empiricism dominating Enlightenment thought,
because both construed, to a greater or lesser extent, individual
consciousness as the origin of knowledge and truth.[43]

The Enlightenment's interest in exposing the tyranny of tradition
might have had more than a purely metaphysical dimension geared
to the philosophical autonomy of the individual. Economic condi-

---

[42] The texts that perhaps best illustrate the specific views of the authors men-
tioned are: Berkeley, *A Treatise concerning the Principles of Human Knowledge* and
New Theory of Vision; Voltaire, *Eléments de la philosophie de Newton*; Diderot,
Lettre sur les aveugles.

[43] Goldmann, *The Philosophy of the Enlightenment*, chapter 1. My schematic
treatment of the interrelationships between economics and Enlightenment philosophy that Goldmann outlines does justice neither to the complexity of the problem
nor to Goldmann's lucid handling of it.

tions, particularly in the early years of the eighteenth century, led
the wealthy to consider their financial autonomy as well. At the
death of Louis XIV, France was saddled with enormous debts because of Louis' aggressive military campaigns, and the nobility and
the financiers grew restless and rebellious. "Do not believe that this
momentous occasion brought about only moral reflections," Montesquieu's Usbek writes to Rhédi. "Each thought of his affairs and
of taking advantage of the turn of events." [44] Aristocratic opposition to absolutism appeared with a rejuvenated force; alliances between *robins* and the ancient nobility formed, especially over such
issues as the *taille* and the *dixième*, taxes levied to keep the government on its feet. Members of the privileged groups generally succeeded in finding shelters to avoid paying the taxes. The bourgeoisie, however, lacking the nobles' traditional exemption, were forced
to comply. Wealthy bourgeois forged alliances among themselves,
particularly after the death of Louis XV, and their mutual support
was strengthened when Turgot became comptroller general.
Closely allied with the middle classes and with the *philosophes*,
Turgot planned to levy direct taxes on all landowners regardless of
class, and abolish the *vingtième* and the *taille*. [45] By the middle
of the century, suspicious bourgeois ceased purchasing ennobling
offices and turned instead to profitable commercial investment.
Franklin Ford points out that the price of offices fell below those
charged in the 1660's and 1670's, and he attributes the bourgeois'
reluctance to purchase them both to the potential for a higher return on their money in industrial enterprises and, perhaps more
crucially, to a growing distrust of the monarchy. [46]

Philosophical skepticism and the emphasis on the autonomy of
individuals' perceptions within a specific historical and cultural
framework thus combined with economic alienation in the eighteenth century to render the middle classes and those of the lesser

[44] Montesquieu, *Les Lettres persanes*, lettre CXII, p. 151. Voltaire added that a
person reading memoirs of the first years of the reign of Louis XV "would only
notice in our nation softness, an extreme desire to become rich, and too much indifference for the rest" (*Histoire de Charles XII*, p. 32).

[45] See Lionel Gossman, *French Society and Culture*, pp. 62–63.

[46] Ford writes in his *Robe and Sword* that "doubtless the unpleasant recollection
of Louis XIV's bad faith in revoking provisions and his extortionate treatment of his
functionaries had also contributed to making public charges less attractive, though
this applied less to the sovereign courts than to the much-abused lower offices" (p.
149).

nobility suspicious of traditional models of truth. Even history, the immutable model of irrefutable truth, came under attack. Voltaire warned sovereigns in his *Histoire de Charles XII* that "history is a witness, not a flatterer" (32), and historians abandoned the narrative accounts of monarchs' grandeur, and attempted to isolate the general principles underlying human behavior. Nicolas Lenglet-Dufresnoy, for example, defined historical knowledge as follows: "To know [*savoir*] is to understand things through their principles; thus, to know history is to understand the men who furnish its material. It is to judge it rationally. To study history is to study men's intentions, opinions, and passions in order to penetrate all the ramifications . . . in a word, it is to learn to know oneself through others."[47] Dufresnoy exhorts historians to uncover the universal principles underlying human action and emotion; the ideal historical narrative should consequently communicate knowledge not only about the past, but about the present as well. Ernst Cassirer has written that the philosophy of history that developed during the course of the eighteenth century concerned itself less with narrative sequences of causality, and more with searching out the manifestations of human reason and its application to social and political life. He maintains that eighteenth-century history strove to show how reason "enters the stream of time and reveals there in gradually increasing purity and perfection its basic and original form."[48]

The privileging of reason at the expense of traditionally received models of thought translated into eighteenth-century fiction as the radical questioning of representations of reality. Novelists endeavored to show, as Maillard so cunningly put it, that "nothing is true about anything." They effectively turned ontological questions into political ones, and applied them to defenses of fiction. Correlatively, they endeavored to reveal art's capacity to create and structure a world according to a carefully controlled ideological point of view, and to show that the point of view adopted did not necessarily have to be an aristocratic one. Abandoning all attempts to

[47] Lenglet-Dufresnoy, *Méthode pour étudier l'histoire*, vol. I, pp. 2–3. Dufresnoy concludes his study of history by noting, "Although it is difficult to have facts that resemble one another in history . . . one can nevertheless draw rules for conduct from it by applying the temperance that prudence or judgment might suggest" (p. 565).
[48] Cassirer, *The Philosophy of the Enlightenment*, p. 221.

conform to the heroic models of *vraisemblance*, novelists opted to construct narrative accounts of the daily lives of ordinary individuals, and they attributed the lion's share of the creative process not to generic convention but to the author's genius. As La Solle notes, novels offer more penetrating examples of moral excellence that depend "not . . . on the whims of fortune, but on the spirit and rectitude of the author." In the eighteenth century, the issue of an accurate portrayal of reality became subservient to the question of works' formal coherence and authors' subjective mastery over their material. As Argens proclaimed, echoing Bussy, "Yet we do not grant the freedom to invent to whoever works in this style [i.e., fiction], except with the condition that he will only exercise his freedom to produce something more interesting than a completely unified reality [*un vrai tout uni*]" (33).

Eighteenth-century critics prevailed upon novelists to compose their works with an eye toward formal coherence and the irreproachableness of their morals. It was quite rare, however, for any of them to specify precisely what novels should advocate other than an abstract model of virtue based on sexual restraint. Jean-François Marmontel debated the question of truth and fiction in novels and history and arrived at the conclusion that "once the narration is unified [*d'accord avec elle-méme*], and *vraisemblable* in all its aspects, it is no longer a question of examining what it contains that is real in order to know what it contains that is useful."[49] The general reluctance to specify the particular moral or political stance novels should endorse suggests that novelists and critics were aware of their reading public's diversity; constructing a universally accepted didactic work must have seemed a daunting task indeed. Nevertheless, novelists could not give up the pretense that they were educating their readers without abandoning any claim to literary legitimacy.

May's and Mylne's work on techniques of realism in the eighteenth century, along with the work of English Showalter, seem to me to be beyond reproach. However, I would like to interrogate their conclusions, which have become axiomatic in the study of eighteenth-century French fiction, that realism developed as a result of harsh critical attack. A good many of the novels that claim for

[49] Marmontel, "Essai sur les romans, considérés du côté moral," in *Œuvres complètes*, vol. X, p. 359.

themselves either an unambiguous moral lesson or an absolute veracity generally reveal—in extremely subtle fashion, to be sure—
an equivocation underpinning their moral or truth; consequently,
it seems to me that what novels taught involved not the moral of
the narrative, but the narrative construction of morality. In other
words, eighteenth-century novels entertained the possibility that, as
Gossman argues, "literature itself might be considered the domain
of the possible—since nothing in it *need* be and anything can be
otherwise" (91). Fiction in the eighteenth-century continually
warned its readers not to accept as incontrovertible the reality that
traditional history and literature had portrayed. One of the novelist's principal goals was to undermine the hegemonic and fatuous
models of *vraisemblance* and represent the processes by which reality is constructed. What critics have traditionally identified as realism in eighteenth-century fiction manifests itself simply as the
repudiation of the generally obtrusive conventions associated with
seventeenth-century novels and history. These partisan representations of reality could no longer hold up under the eighteenth century's scrutiny. The point here is obviously not that eighteenth-
century novels were devoid of convention, but rather that as the
politically invested conventions of the previous century were cast
off, new narrative conventions were developing that could not yet
be recognized as such.[50] Consequently, for a brief but crucial moment in the development of the eighteenth-century novel, the form
was perceived as more true to life than its forebears because, failing
to discriminate against readers on the basis of class, it correlated
reigning sensibilities concerning skepticism and the narrative construction of reality. That a literary form which failed to respect the
politicized aesthetics of the dominant social group might come
under attack is hardly surprising—novels dared to replace the obtrusive narrative conventions of aristocratic fiction with sleeker,
more attenuated ones which responded to middle-class sensibilities.
We might consequently be justified in tampering a bit with May's

[50] This also explains why contemporary criticism normally points to the eighteenth century as the origin of the realist novel. The narrative conventions of the
eighteenth century have a greater affinity with modern notions of realistic fiction,
particularly as it is generally understood in the nineteenth century, than they did
with pastoral and heroic fiction. If one fails to consider the development of the novel
genre historically, one might indeed wind up with a mystified notion of realism that
identifies the mode as a goal, rather than an effect, of eighteenth-century literary
practice.

postulate that "novelists discovered the marvels of realism although their principal aim was to flee critical attack" (247). Realism did not, I might venture, result *from* moral and political critical attack—rather, it *produced* it.

One might cite two fundamental reasons for which eighteenth-century ("realistic") fiction brought down the wrath of conservative critics: on the one hand it was designed to appeal not to an elite circle of privileged readers whose socioeconomic circumstances empowered them to dictate literary taste in accordance with their own politics, but to a broad portion of the social spectrum well educated enough to appreciate its deft construction of alternative worlds. On the other hand, and closely related to the reason just mentioned, its extreme self-consciousness displaced emphasis away from the extratextual ideological concerns of the ruling classes and onto the process of mystification constituting fiction and, as these novels show, ideology itself. While a host of eighteenth-century critics condemn novels for these very reasons, none do so as eloquently as the abbé d'Irail: "[Novelists] sacrificed nature to art: they chose a metaphysics of sentiment and a frivolity heretofore unknown. They abandoned the great adventures, heroic programs, delicately woven plots, the play of noble passions, and their effects and implications. We no longer choose our heroes from the throne: now we find them everywhere, even among the dregs of the populace."[51] The last sentence betrays d'Irail's political stance, and it is significant that he links the representation of the populace with the sacrifice of nature to art: according to the ideology of *vraisemblance*, which sought to make its artifice seem to be the transhistorical and immutable reproduction of reality, conflicting political views were unnatural. Elevating the populace to the status of narrative protagonists could only be accomplished by sleight of hand. Novelists were casting aside venerated tradition and glorifying not received models of truth, but their own craftwork. They repudiated the ideological and aesthetic authority of the classical genres; by subtly revealing to readers the scaffolding supporting their own craft, a process I will analyze in detail in the following chapters, they provided readers not with trite moral lessons, but with valuable instruction on the political nature of the

[51] Irail, "Les Romans," in *Querelles littéraires*, vol. II, p. 343. Irail's critique is in effect a summary of Charles Porée's *De libris qui vulgo dicuntur Romanses* (1736).

literary text. No longer the slavish imitator of antiquity's formidable masters, the novelist became, as La Solle remarked, "the creator and master of his subject" (xxx).

One early example of the manner in which eighteenth-century novels ironically undermine traditional interpretive authority and uncover their own construction of conflicting analyses is Alain-René Lesage's *Histoire de Gil Blas de Santillane*. In the short preface entitled "Gil Blas au Lecteur" (Gil Blas to the reader), the narrator offers a brief epigraph ostensibly designed to help readers draw the most benefit from the work. The preface relates the story of a clever schoolboy rewarded for his ability to understand language's polysemantic richness. In the tale, two boys spy a stone upon which are inscribed the words "Here lies the soul of Master Pierre Garcias." [52] One of them scoffs at the inscription and departs; the other, however, "more judicious," digs up the ground and uncovers a purse containing 100 ducats and the message, "Be my inheritor, you who were wise enough to penetrate the sense of the inscription, and make better use of my money than I did." Roger Laufer reminds us that it was common to speak of the "*corps*" or "*âme*" (body or soul) of currency,[53] which emphasizes the clever boy's skill in comprehending the playful ambiguity of a linguistic pun. The tale's concluding paragraph warns readers that, like the schoolboy, they must remain attentive in order to grasp the work's "instructions morales" and to find, "according to Horace's precepts, the useful mingled in with the pleasing" (21).

Gil Blas' brief message to the reader offers more, however, than a simple allegory proclaiming the value of shrewd analysis. It also warns of the dangers of deception and of the duplicities of signs. Gil Blas tells his readers what happens after the boy finds the purse and the note: "Excited by his discovery [he] put the stone back the way it was before, and started back to Salamanca with the soul of the Master" (21). The boy's careful re-positioning of the stone casts the anecdote in an irony that goes beyond the pun on the word "*âme*" (soul) and extends to the moral the narrator offers. That is, anyone who later chanced across the stone might be clever enough to grasp the inscription's latent meaning; after digging and finding

---

[52] Lesage, p. 21.
[53] Laufer, editor of the Garnier-Flammarion text, also points out that Lesage borrowed this entire tale from the prologue to Vicente Espinel's *Marcos de Obregón*,

nothing, however, that person would interpret the epigraph quite differently than the boy had. The most logical interpretation would seem to be that the master's soul was empty, or that he did not have one. While the boy could attribute the epigraph and the implied "I" of the accompanying card as the voice of the master himself, his successor might likely assume that an embittered associate left the inscription on the stone as an ironic testimony to his friend's avarice or immorality. Oddly enough, then, this anecdote which ostensibly shows readers the importance of anagogic interpretation reveals instead how interpretations can inform, determine, and even undermine one another. In addition, it warns readers both not to accept literal interpretations and, perhaps most crucially, to accept with a grain of salt the ostensible moral that narrators, authors, or commentators attribute to works.

Lesage's prefatory moral offers an ironic lesson about the stability of interpretation, and it is emblematic of the remaining works I will consider. That is, his narrator constructs an apparently secure interpretive position for the reader by showing him or her the ostensibly optimum reading strategy to employ. Then, in sleight of hand he undermines that position by suggesting how and where it might lead the reader astray. In this case there might be, he seems to be suggesting, no value at all lying beneath the words. Like the boy who found the master's money, readers are inheritors, recipients of a specific literary heritage which, like a trust fund, traditionally stipulates the use to which it might be put. Lesage's brief tale is a caveat to readers that their heritage might be as empty as the master's tomb after the boy raided it. Eighteenth-century novels that seduce readers into believing that everything is laid bare for them and that they share the master's privileged stance continually undermine that position either by constantly erecting new frames of reference within the *récit*, or by privileging the non-constative registers of language in order to inhibit unequivocal interpretation. Frequently they employ as part of their duplicity a protagonist in the process of learning a new signifying system and who, like Mme de Clèves, seems vulnerable because of his or her putative naïveté.[54]

---

and that its theme derives from an early seventeenth-century book of maxims (p. 621 n. 2).

[54] Naomi Segal has shown in an engaging study of *Manon Lescaut* how Des Grieux learns the use and value of duplicitous language from Manon. See *The Unintended Reader*, pp. 21–27.

As I will show in the following chapters, this particular tactic creates a narrative irony that allows readers to believe they are exempt from the duplicity operating in this sign system because they are allowed to watch its effect on others. Narrators then appropriate the duplicity they depict in the *récit* and turn it on the unwary reader.

The following chapters offer detailed analyses of two novels from the middle and later years of the eighteenth century in which the processes outlined above are particularly evident. My principal aim in offering these readings of two canonical works is to demonstrate the degree to which the skeptical and modernist narrative modes, whose inferred realism correlates the political skepticism toward received discursive and epistemological models, overlay traditional narrative paradigms. The historical and theoretical discussion I have offered in this chapter of the social changes in the eighteenth century and their effects on fiction is in no way meant to imply any sort of neat and radical break with existing narrative modes—the widespread contradictions in social and political practice in the eighteenth century could never have tolerated any sort of clean rupture. Consequently, these works—like any modernist works— manifest an aesthetic disorder, since traditionally valorized narrative techniques and modes operate alongside the traits elaborated above.

The thematic device informing the following readings is that of seduction. I want to emphasize, however, that I have not chosen to underscore seduction because it readily affords a heuristic and synthetic link between *La Religieuse* and *Justine*, but because seduction plays an integral part in many, if not most, eighteenth-century novels. Canonical texts such as Prévost's *Manon Lescaut*, Marivaux's *La Vie de Marianne* and *Le Paysan parvenu*, Crébillon's *Egarements du cour et de l'esprit*, and Restif's *Paysanne pervertie*, as well as lesser-known works such as François-Antoine Chevrier's *Colporteur* and Crébillon's *Sopha*, have narratives that revolve around complex seductions. Even *La Princesse de Clèves* depends on a series of seductions, no doubt unconscious, since Mme de Clèves seduces the two men in her life by giving to each what the other desires. Pierre Saint-Amand has recently studied seduction in eighteenth-century French literature; he considers seduction primarily from a psychoanalytic perspective and, informed by the work of René Girard, he analyzes it within the context of mimetic desire. "Seductive mediation choreographs [an] active lure whose victims are the two partners. They return to each other the same desire," he writes.[55] When Saint-Amand studies the seductions operating in *Marianne*, *Manon Lescaut*, or *Le Paysan parvenu*, he is concerned primarily with the reversibility of seduction, the possibility that seducers are also always seduced. Showing, for example, that Marianne is a coquettish seductress whose charms play on a variety of people, Saint-Amand also reveals that Marianne is caught in her own trap: believing that she holds the secret to others' desire, she is unaware that all of her power is a social construction, since her specific brand of femininity was born of male desire (32–35).

While I agree with Saint-Amand that the unconscious effects of seduction always operate on both parties, I will focus on the conscious duplicity that specific characters undertake. That is, Suzanne Simonin deliberately performs a detailed seduction of the marquis de Croismare—she indicates this in the first paragraph of *La Religieuse* as well as in the postscriptum concluding her memoirs. Likewise, as I will show, Justine intentionally causes her listeners (and by extension readers of the novel) to inscribe marks of violence on her by deftly withholding part of her gruesome story. In both cases, the possibility that the heroines are lying cannot be dispelled, but this fact opens up issues far more complex than the simple questioning of the narrator's reliability. Suzanne and Justine play on language's self-referentiality; they attempt to deny it its constative function by foreclosing the question of whether their tales are true or false, specifying instead the perlocutionary force of their pitiful narratives. Bracketing the truth-value of their tales, they seek instead to construct engaging stories that will respond to their listeners' desires and cause them to act in their behalf. The novels seduce readers in turn by allowing them to believe that, since they are party to the seductions played out on characters within the works, they are immune to the duplicitous effects of language. Yet, these novels appropriate their protagonists' maneuvers and, undermining the position of mastery they allowed their readers initially to occupy, they reveal that this interpretive mastery is a fiction.

[55] Saint-Amand, *Séduire, ou la passion des lumières*, p. 17.

Revealing the interpretive mastery fabricated in the *récits* of history and fiction and the concomitant narrative construction of truth, however, is not by any means the same as advocating an ideological eclecticism for novels. Novelists like Furetière, Mme de Lafayette, and Lesage who had implicitly exposed the political biases underpinning traditional conceptions of verisimilitude contributed to the codification of new narrative conventions available to educated readers whose access to aristocratic cultural capital may have been limited. These conventions highlighted not the abstract worthiness and the social and economic hereditary privileges of a hegemonic group whose claim to ascendancy seemed increasingly arbitrary, but the accountable formation and exchange of goods, people, and ideas. Waning conceptions of *vraisemblance* were based on the authority of tradition; developing models, however, referred to the authority of value as it was fixed in currency, property, and, more abstractly, the convertibility of the human subject shaped to conform to bourgeois notions of property and propriety. Eighteenth-century novels of seduction highlight the duplicity of female protagonists, but they actuate more than simply a radical and free-floating skepticism about the narrative construction of truth. With the introduction of protagonists bearing unstable relationships to their social milieus, novels initiated a critique of the discursive practices constituting the subject. They refuted the belief in an essentialism based on birth, underscoring instead the learned nature of social identity. At the same time, they strengthened the foundation of bourgeois ideology with its emphasis on property and exchange by featuring the duplicitous seductress whose unimpeded ingress into the sanctuaries of the lesser nobility and the middle classes threatened the stability of the family name, wealth, and legitimacy.

Like Furetière's "amphibious" bourgeois characters, seductresses in eighteenth-century fiction are able to negotiate two or more radically disparate social milieus. Polyglots all, they speak the language native to the inhabitants of specific social circles—Marianne notes, for example, how easy it is to appeal to men once one knows what each kind wants: "For, with a strong desire to be to their liking, one has the key to all that they do to be to our liking, and there will never be any other quality in that than to be vain and coquettish" (89). The seductress's protean nature casts her as a member of whatever circle she happens to be in, and because she seems always able to respond to men's desire, she is a siren luring them away from their social obligations.

Perhaps the most obvious example of a seductress who corrupts men and leads them down the path to perdition is Manon Lescaut. Manon works her charms on the young Des Grieux who, as a chevalier, occupies the transitional pivot between noble and non-noble ranks. Prévost's novel depicts the young man as he is caught between the domains of hereditary wealth and commercial negotiation: after Des Grieux effectively renounces all claim to the family fortune, he must barter both for money and for honor, and he uses Manon herself as his currency. On at least two occasions he sells Manon's beauty to another man: "[M. de T.] will do something for a lovely young lady, even if only in the hope of obtaining her favors," Des Grieux plots;[56] more significantly, perhaps, he circulates her among other men as a mark of his own social success: "She embodied for me my honor, happiness, and fortune" (113). Once he meets up with Manon, Des Grieux abandons his plans to enter into the order of Malta, and takes up a nomadic existence on the streets and in the prisons and gambling houses of Paris. Manon, in other words, seduces Des Grieux, literally leading him astray from the social sphere to which by birth he was destined.

Manon herself is a figure far more complex than a simple medium of exchange, however. She dazzles Des Grieux with her beauty, to be sure, but more arresting still is her duplicity that seems to bring whatever she wants her way. Astonished by her capacity to manipulate appearances and the men who put stock in them, Des Grieux tells her, "You are an admirable chemist . . . you transform everything into gold" (176). Des Grieux attributes to Manon the ability to recast anything into a general equivalent—gold—and consequently to render it suitable for exchange. Manon's currency, however, is sexual desire, and she is adept at converting it into money and material goods. Des Grieux learns the power of desire from Manon, and during their first encounter at Amiens, in fact, he conspires with her without coaching to deceive her chaperone and spend the night with her. Segal notes that Des Grieux's duplicity awakens with the advent of sexual desire and that he learns to en-

---

[56] Prévost, *Histoire du chevalier Des Grieux et de Manon Lescaut*, p. 103.

dow language with the capacity to create surplus value beyond the simple reflection or representation of the real (25). Manon consequently represents pure convertibility: at once the means and the manipulator of material and linguistic exchange, she teaches Des Grieux the power of duplicity, and shows him that the instability of language can supplement, undermine, or take the place of monetary value. Indeed, Des Grieux's entire story is told to Renoncourt as a repayment for the money the latter had given him: "Monsieur . . . you treat me so nobly that I would reproach myself for the basest ingratitude if I held something back from you" (38).

Manon alienates Des Grieux from his legitimate inheritance because she awakens in him a sexual desire that extends beyond the confines imposed on it by bourgeois notions of virtue. That virtue consists in protecting the family name and fortune, and assuring its legitimate transfer from one generation to the next. Manon's capacity to convert everything into barterable merchandise, however, and her own nearly unlimited convertibility represent a danger to Des Grieux's family: her sexual promiscuity threatens the legitimacy of Des Grieux's name and, consequently, his lineage and the transmission of the family wealth. That is, Des Grieux falls for a woman not of his class and no amount of preaching from Tiberge, his father, or the authorities in Saint-Lazare can persuade him that the security of his family's property depends ultimately on a stable propriety dictating the rules for marriage and, ultimately, the transmission of the family's name and fortune.

It is appropriate at this point to make mention of the fact that seductions in eighteenth-century fiction are undertaken primarily by women. The female protagonist whose relationship to dominant models of virtue is compromised through the course of the novel served as the formal and ideological vehicle to communicate these truths. In his astoundingly detailed study of women in the eighteenth-century European novel, Pierre Fauchery suggests that if women played a key role in fiction, it was both because the novel's reading audience was composed principally of women and because women's traditional social positions kept them from the public arenas novels tended to depict.

In all times woman has been more contained, less active, or she has engaged in more restricted forms of activity: the gynaeceum and its precise work are in opposition to the vagabondage of the agora. Her

existence thus seems more concentrated, and easier to contain in a
single look; her passions—when she has any—easily invade the totality of her world. Her normal condition is not only "passive," it
seems to offer destiny a tempting and unarmed prey.[57]

If we disregard Fauchery's overly schematic depiction of feminine
domestic passivity, we can isolate a specifically formalist conception of narrative in his discussion of woman's relationship to destiny in the eighteenth-century novel. When he argues that woman
offers to destiny a tempting and available prey on which it can
wreak its destabilizing havoc, Fauchery is effectively describing
what the Russian formalists called the "defamiliarization" of reality in art.[58] That is, Fauchery calls destiny the overarching structure
that narrative provides when it is conscripted to account for the
way things are. Choosing woman as its object, narrational destiny
transforms her into something other and unfamiliar. As I mentioned earlier, eighteenth-century novels normally defamiliarize
women by depicting them in problematized or compromising relationships to virtue, generally encoded in the social regulation of
their sexuality and their bodies. Consequently, female protagonists
retain a measure of familiarity when they abide by the patriarchal
rules governing their sexuality. When they behave in ways that are
socially codified as unacceptable, it is the burden of the narrative
to account for their irregular position or activities and present them
as metamorphoses of the expected while maintaining plausibility.[59]

---

[57] Fauchery, *La Destinée féminine dans le roman européen du dix-huitième siècle*,
p. 14.

[58] Fauchery writes that "under the name of destiny, the portion assigned to
woman in human events is thus measured and adjusted by an adjudicating will, or
determined by a readable series of consequences. Here diverse morals, official or not
. . . could once again be invoked. They effectively furnish so many paradigms, the
choice of which depends, for the novelist as for the reader, on the lexicon in which
he is determined to transcribe the facts" (pp. 832–33).

Concerning the unfamiliar in art, Victor Shklovsky writes that "the technique of
art is to make objects 'unfamiliar,' to make forms difficult, to increase the difficulty
and length of perception because the process of perception is an aesthetic end in
itself and must be prolonged" ("Art as Technique," p. 12).

[59] See also Wallace Martin, who writes in *Recent Theories of Narrative* that "the
writer, beginning with the intention to create a story, must find plausibly realistic
explanations of the techniques he or she uses." Martin identifies three methods of
creating plausible defamiliarizations of reality. The first involves having characters
move about. Characters who travel encounter a variety of other characters, and as
long as authors meet the technical requirement of explaining why their characters
are traveling, they provide themselves with an acceptable manner of increasing their
tale's narrative repertory. The second method also involves movement, but it is social

However, since it is not self-evident that women as a group provided the most readily available means of constructing an engaging
and plausible defamiliarization of reality, we need to analyze the
particular function the female protagonist served for the novel. Historians of the novel generally explain the preponderance of female
protagonists by referring in cursory or dismissive fashion to the
ostensibly common but nevertheless unsubstantiated knowledge
that women read the majority of novels in eighteenth-century
France. This claim is generally supported by referring to catalogs
of libraries belonging to educated gentlemen—which tend to list
few works of fiction—or by alluding to the complaints of religious
authorities who feared that women were being corrupted by the
moral improprieties novels hawked. This purely circumstantial evidence, however, fails to negotiate adequately the anxiety surrounding women's perceived alienation from the canon of bourgeois religious, social, and sexual values. It proves not that women read
most of the novels being produced, but that educated men—like
Chapelain a century earlier—feared being caught reading them.
More significantly, however, it reveals the extent to which women's
perceived resistance to bourgeois ideology needed to be contained:
since female protagonists in eighteenth-century fiction either submitted to the patriarchal governing of their sexuality or were
harshly punished for their infractions, tales of their problematic
relationship to virtue reinforced bourgeois ideals as the lowest
common denominator of plausibility in fiction. Like the repeated
stories of lovers who were punished for forming socially incompatible alliances in seventeenth-century *histoires tragiques*, eighteenth-
century novels depicting the imposition of sexual virtue on women
construed the bourgeois order of paternal name, legitimacy, and
property as unquestionable and natural. Prose fiction in France
evolved as a literary practice that bolstered the hegemony of the
dominant social group while offering resistance to encroaching social forces; it seems safe, then, to propose that women were construed as representatives of a specific ideological opposition that
needed to be suppressed.

---

movement: characters such as servants or fallen aristocrats can inhabit more than
one social world. The third method of creating credible defamiliarization is to in-
corporate into fiction some non-literary mode of writing, such as correspondence
(pp. 48–49).

What I want to suggest, then, is that female protagonists in fiction often served an ideological purpose that parallels the proliferation of bourgeois subjects in seventeenth-century fiction. Late seventeenth-century fiction contested the narrative models and conventions of pastoral and heroic fiction either by revealing novels' inability to negotiate the new social configurations informing France's political and economic domains, or by incorporating class conflict into their narratives. Female protagonists in eighteenth-century fiction represented the bourgeois ideal when they were properly contained, since their bodies and desires were confined to the service of family, reproduction, property, and exchange. When they were unrestrained, however, women frequently embodied a sort of social dissipation that threatened to undo the legitimacy of property in both the private and public spheres.

Problematized feminine virtue in fiction ostensibly served simply as the most readily available illustration of the threats facing eighteenth-century French bourgeois culture, and it more deeply entrenched the ideological imperatives already inherent in dominant conceptions of *vraisemblance*. Because a favorite subject of eighteenth-century novels was the woman who surrendered her virtue or valiantly struggled to maintain it, what became codified as the rudimentary ground or nucleus of plausibility was the strict regulation of desire and sexuality appropriated as rigid obedience to bourgeois laws concerning property. Both Vera Lee and Ruth Thomas point out, however, that women of dubious morals populate eighteenth-century novels in order to arouse male interest.[60] Thomas argues that in many works, in particular Prévost's *Manon Lescaut* and Bernardin de Saint-Pierre's *Paul et Virginie*, women cannot live up to the male ideal of womanhood, and they consequently die. Their deaths, however, virtually always enable the man to preserve his dream (324). Nancy K. Miller refers to male authors writing "in female drag," which, she suggests, "allows the male 'I' not so much to please the Other—by subscribing or capitulating to women's 'taste'—as to become the Other . . . the better to be admired by and for himself."[61] Kristin Ross makes a similar point when she argues that Manon is continually construed as a mysterious and unavailable Other denied a material or social existence

---

[60] Lee, "The Edifying Example"; Thomas, "The Death of an Ideal."
[61] Miller, "'I's' in Drag: The Sex of Recollection," p. 49.

who helps Des Grieux accede to the paternal realm of wealth and property he shunned in taking up with her in the first place.[62] The point here is that female protagonists who either struggle to maintain their sexual integrity or wantonly flout the social conventions restricting it must assume an alienated concept of virtue as it is imposed on them from without. The lesson their stories impart consequently strengthens not a collective moral imperative applicable to all people in the culture, but the hegemonic force of middle-class males who stand to benefit, implicitly or explicitly, from the subjugation of women.

Leslie Rabine, however, offers a persuasive account of how the female character contributes to the construction of bourgeois ideology within the novel. Pointing out that Manon Lescaut is a character composed of contrary essences that the novel seeks to explain by hinting at a hidden nature supporting her eccentricity, Rabine shows that the birth of bourgeois individualism correlates capitalism's exclusion of women from socioeconomic independence. "The feminine is repressed . . . through the emergence of liberal ideological structures," she writes, "[and] also through their interplay with Renoncourt's disintegrating aristocratic structures."[63] Consequently, the novel is the site of ideological struggle between two opposing classes, and the figure of the woman, denied any real social substance, becomes a formal marker in the text articulating the conflict.[64]

The above discussion is clearly not by any means an exhaustive account of the complexities surrounding the female protagonist in eighteenth-century French fiction. I have merely attempted to isolate a portion of the political dimension women represented in novels, in particular the threat they seemed to pose to a burgeoning bourgeois culture. Eighteenth-century fiction construed women as

---

[62] Ross, "The Narrative of Fascination: Pathos and Repetition in *Manon Lescaut*."

[63] Rabine, "History, Ideology, and Femininity in *Manon Lescaut*," p. 83.

[64] In *Breaking the Chain*, Naomi Schor makes a similar claim for women in nineteenth-century novels. She maintains that "representation in its paradigmatic nineteenth-century form depends on the bondage of woman." Schor offers four reasons why this might be the case: women lost a great deal of power during the Revolution, a loss that was institutionalized under the Napoleonic Code; the disciplining of the female body that Michel Foucault theorized; the "fear of desire" Leo Bersani has observed; and the "increasing concern with entropy and the exhaustion of nonrenewable sources of energy" (p. 142).

either the seat of virtue or as its most dangerous threat; what is significant about this position—which, if it were true would be one of tremendous power, but which instead merely alienates and objectifies women as one more commodity—is that it is not indexed for class. Prévost's Manon, Restif's Ursule, Laclos' Mme de Merteuil, and Sade's Juliette represent the entire gamut of the social spectrum, and each is a menace to bourgeois morals. Consequently, the values these novels implicitly advance concerning the need to fortify the family name and fortune and regulate human and material commerce appear universally applicable. Unlike the fiction of the previous century, which was by and large aimed at a specific and restricted group, eighteenth-century novels cast their nets wide in their search for reading audiences. They had the difficult task of appropriating an aesthetic form that had evolved to express the interests of a politically antagonistic group and retooling it to promulgate what appeared to be more generalized concerns while preserving the form's generic structure. By featuring women as the saviors or annihilators of family and fortune, they found a formal vehicle able to transcend class boundaries and yet remain malleable enough to represent bourgeois concerns.

Maintaining the air of historical continuity in fiction was crucial in order to allow the novel to insinuate its ideology. Despite the novel's tenuous relationship to official or "high" culture, it was by the eighteenth century an established cultural form. The move to repudiate the overwrought conventions of the seventeenth century and cause novels to appear to represent the world directly thus correlated heroic fiction's effort to achieve moral—if not factual—*vraisemblance*. In addition, such a move not only contributed to warding off critical attack, but it also helped normalize the genre ideologically, since it could claim universal validity. Impugning the expressive causality that had marked earlier fiction, eighteenth-century novels of seduction radically questioned the narrative transmission of narrative models of truth, and this is precisely where fiction gained its most forceful political strength: acknowledging competing theories and interpretations in the device of seduction—which effectively hypostatizes the instability of language and the sign—fiction reappropriates instability into a culturally stable form by rehabilitating the seductress and controlling her as a cultural object subservient to the laws of value and property which mark bourgeois culture.

Ironically, then, we might view the critical discourse surrounding the proliferation of prose fiction in the eighteenth century as not only crucial to the novel's development but in many ways as supplemental to it. Menacing remarks like Jacquin's, who wrote that "once the mind is seduced and blinded, the heart readily adopts a doctrine too fitting its passions to seem illusory; and it is thus that we start out as feeble proselytes but soon become formidable Masters" (213), became part of the cultural framework theorizing the novel's continued development. In other words, Jacquin inadvertently described the manner in which the instability of an accomplished seduction can be reinserted into a broader discursive tradition which can consequently contain that instability by rewriting it and authorizing those seduced to speak for it. In this way, as the following readings of *La Religieuse* and *Justine* will show, the apparent volatility or eclecticism of interpretive practices aligns itself with the voice of a new master, one who is perhaps less obtrusive but for that reason all the more manipulative.

Chapter 8 "Burn the Letter!": *La Religieuse*

Behind the composition of Denis Diderot's *La Religieuse* lies a re-markable tale of deception and chicanery involving forged corre-spondence and blatant imposture on the part of the man who would later weep over the very fiction he himself contrived. It seems that Diderot and Grimm, along with several other conspirators, devised an elaborate hoax to lure one of their friends, the marquis de Croismare, back to Paris after the latter had retreated to his estates in Normandy. While away from the capital, M. de Crois-mare had taken an interest in the misfortunes that befell a young nun who tried to renounce her vows, and without even knowing her name he decided to intervene on her behalf, obtaining for her the help of several well-known lawyers. Suzanne Simonin, the nun in question, lost her trial and was ordered to remain in the convent. According to literary legend, however, Diderot perceived M. de Croismare's interest in the affair, and decided that she was the key to get him back to Paris. He concocted a tale in which she escaped from the convent, and he forged letters in her name asking M. de Croismare for his help and protection. The plot thickened as the counterfeiters required an address at which to receive Croismare's letters; they asked, Diderot tells us, a certain Mme Madin to receive and redirect all letters from Croismare. Employing another young woman to write Suzanne's letters, the band of pranksters carried on a correspondence with Croismare in which they tried to coax him to return to the capital to help the unfortunate nun. Things got out of hand, however, as the marquis fell for the joke hook, line, and sinker, so the group decided to kill off their fictional nun to prevent Croismare from getting more involved than he already was. The letter-writing campaign ostensibly lasted more than three months, and it was eight years before the entire plot was revealed to the victim, who supposedly took it all in good humor.[1]

According to the *préface-annexe*, Croismare was the dupe of a complicated scheme to get him to return to Paris. The scheme worked—or would have, had it been carried to its conclusion—primarily because Diderot and his friends knew him well enough to be able to write a story that would earn not only his belief but his pity as well. The group congratulated themselves on their ability to find just the right turn of phrase to pique the marquis' sympathies ("We spent our dinnertime laughing over letters meant to make our dear marquis cry" [850]) and they took great pride in their talent for directing their reader's responses ("and we read with just as much laughter the sincere responses of our worthy and generous friend" [850]). The pranksters had aimed their letters at what they knew to be Croismare's soft spot, and his inability to spot the letters' deft artifice amused them enormously. Above all they were happy that their victim was a sincere and trusting man like the marquis "who never for a moment suspected our perfidy" (850).

And why would Croismare suspect a hoax? After all, Diderot and company took great care to make the letters seem as realistic as possible to him, and their acquaintance with him facilitated their task. The success of their plan to seduce the marquis without arousing his suspicion depended on their ability to produce as duplicitous and transparent a narrative as possible—they needed to induce the marquis to read the letters for informational content, and not narrative form, and to concentrate on the letters' narrative signified and ignore the rhetorical strategy of the narrative signifier. Above all they had to be certain, as did Crébillon *fils* in his *Egarements du cour et de l'esprit*, that "the fact, artfully prepared, [be]

---

[1] The entire story of Diderot's forged letters to M. de Croismare as Diderot himself tells it can be found in the French edition in the *préface-annexe*. See the Classiques Garnier edition of Diderot's *Œuvres romanesques*, pp. 848–69. Future references to Diderot's *Religieuse* will be to Leonard Tancock's translation, *The Nun*; page numbers included in brackets for the convenience of readers more familiar with the work in French refer to the Classiques Garnier text. Since no readily available English translation still in print of *La Religieuse* includes the *préface-annexe*, page references to the *préface-annexe* are to the Classiques Garnier, my translation.

In addition, Georges May provides an exhaustive account of Marguerite Delamarre, a young nun whose story seems to have been the basis for Diderot's account of what became of Suzanne after escaping the convent. See his *Diderot et "La Religieuse"*, especially pp. 197–237.

delivered naturally." [2] Abiding by one of the fundamental precepts of the Western mimetic tradition, that of *ars celandi artem*, or art hiding art, their story had to appear true while minimizing the attention it called to itself as a fabricated artistic work. If we judge from the marquis' reactions to their story as they appear in the *préface-annexe*, we would have to admit that they succeeded admirably.

Diderot seemed to want to control the reader of his novel the same way he had controlled Croismare. In the *préface-annexe* we read that the letters were a "mystification [that] troubled the head of our friend" (850). Carol Blum is more direct when she says that "*La Religieuse*, at the time of its composition in 1760, was from the first page to the last an effort at seduction. . . . Sister Suzanne was created to ignite the imagination of the isolated Marquis, whose daydreams were no mystery to Diderot and his friends." [3] Yet, if it is relatively simple to explain the seduction's effectiveness on Croismare, it is not so easy to understand how Diderot intended to convert a personal correspondence directed at a particular individual into a novel accessible to a wide variety of readers and still keep intact its "mystification" or seductive appeal. How did Diderot plan to control his readers' reactions as well as he had controlled Croismare's? Perhaps keeping his friend's name as his heroine's *destinataire* gave Diderot the sense of control he was seeking: as Herbert Dieckmann points out, Diderot frequently wrote his philosophical and aesthetic criticisms with a particular reader in mind: "It is the reader, and not the public, that preoccupies Diderot." [4] Ignoring the reading public at large, Diderot most often tried to produce a particular effect or make a given point for a specific individual. [5]

But a novel is not a letter, nor do we generally think of it as a communication addressed to an individual. Diderot had seduced Croismare into believing that the fake letters were real ones. What,

[2] Crébillon, p. 42.

[3] Blum, *Diderot: The Virtue of a Philosopher*, pp. 70–71.

[4] Dieckmann, *Cinq leçons sur Diderot*, p. 18. Grimm, in fact, was Diderot's most frequent *destinataire*.

[5] See also Lefebvre, *Diderot, les affirmations fondamentales du matérialisme*, p. 45: "The public that read *Les Bijoux indiscrets* could not be exactly the same as that which devoured the 'Lettre sur les aveugles': with a prodigious suppleness, he responds, and responds to the precise expectations of each."

now, was his plan for the reader of *La Religieuse*? It is easy to see how forged letters might dupe a reader, since there is no formal, concrete distinction between a genuine letter and an artfully contrived or counterfeit one: the latter is an example of what Genette refers to as literary mimesis in that "the object signified (narrated) is itself language" (*Figures III*, 185). Without a frame of reference or a context that extends beyond the letter in question, one cannot distinguish between a genuine letter and a forged one. The same is not true, however, of novels. Novels purport to describe the real world, and they rely on language to represent non-linguistic realities. Thus, a novel always draws attention to itself as a work of art in that its deception of its readers, no matter how benign, is always apparent. Diderot thus had to find means to deceive, other than the imitation of genuine documents, in order to carry out his deception of *La Religieuse*'s reader.

In this chapter I will examine seduction in *La Religieuse*. First I will look at Suzanne's *mémoire*, a duplicitous, beguiling narrative designed to seduce her protector, the marquis de Croismare, into feeling omnipotent; then I will look at *La Religieuse* as a tightly controlled self-referential novel that undertakes a seduction of its own. We will see that *La Religieuse* is self-referential in two ways: on the one hand it draws attention to and exposes the narrative tools with which it is composed, and on the other hand the object of representation in the novel is not an external reality, but a text— the *mémoire* Suzanne writes to the marquis. Since *La Religieuse* is a framed narrative—Suzanne's *mémoire* is bracketed by her introduction and postscriptum—it allows the reader of the novel to see the context in which she undertook her seduction. Readers are thus induced to reflect critically on Suzanne's seductive strategy, and they are given to believe that they are part of the in-group, party to the hoax being carried out, and that all aspects of the work's fictive apparatus are laid bare for them.

Yet, the first thing to recognize, as Diderot obviously did, is that all aspects of a work's fictive apparatus can never be totally exposed, even by or for the author. In the hoax played on Croismare, for example, Diderot seemed to feel no more secure than his victim: would his attempted seduction backfire and return to him? Since the hoax consisted of exchanged letters, the marquis had the power of response; despite Diderot's attempts to control the situation by composing letters he knew would appeal to the marquis, he did not have complete control over either the letters' answers or his accomplices' covert activities. After receiving several of Croismare's responses to "Suzanne's" letters, Diderot, wary of his friends and afraid of being double-crossed, wrote to his friend Mme d'Epinay: "The marquis has responded; is it real? Is his heart mad? Is his head muddled? Is there not some sort of deception going on here? For I am quite suspicious of all of you." [6] Despite occupying the principal author's role in the project and governing the production of letters in the joke, Diderot seemed to realize that he could not be sure what happened to them after they left his hands. Had his friends diverted them and answered in place of the marquis, knowing the response Diderot wanted and ironically obliging him? Suddenly the possibility surged forth that these letters, like those he sent, were no more than artfully crafted documents designed to appear transparent. Diderot's authority in the hoax was being threatened, and he recognized that the nature of the letter-writing situation produced the threat. Since the dynamics of a correspondence go beyond the two individuals concerned, requiring the participation of others for the letters' delivery, Diderot realized that the detached and superior authorial position he wanted to occupy was untenable. Diderot's trepidation raises some interesting points: how can you assess the veracity or sincerity of a written communication, even when you are intimately acquainted with your correspondent? How do you avoid falling victim to your own joke? And, finally, how can you be sure the letters have not been misdirected, read, interpreted, and even answered by a third party?

These questions will form the basis of my reading of seduction in *La Religieuse* as I analyze both the *mémoire* Suzanne writes to her potential protector and the other letters exchanged in the novel. We will see that in all the correspondence transmitted, senders fear interception by a third party who, they presume, could "demystify" their motives and strategies. This third party would occupy the position of interpretive mastery, since he or she would not be subject to the dynamics of the exchange, and would be detached enough to see the whole story. Each writer connected with *La Religieuse* (whether Diderot, Suzanne, or Suzanne's correspondents) takes

---

[6] Letter of 10 February 1760 to Mme d'Epinay, in Georges Roth, ed., *Correspondance*, vol. III, p. 18.

special care to prevent the privileged role of interpretive mastery from being occupied. Each tries to ensure that only a specific *reader*, and not a reading *public*, will see his or her writing. Diderot in fact seems to have transferred his own insecurities about letters and their unsure circulation onto his title character, who repeatedly asks the marquis to burn the missive she sends him. I will argue that Suzanne's request reflects her anxiety that the marquis will not just read for the plot, but that he will analyze her tale too closely for veracity or sincerity, or that he will allow it to fall into the hands of another, better, reader who may not be so easily duped. Because her *mémoire* is an all-out attempt to seduce the marquis and has been written to appeal to his sensitivities, Suzanne realizes that the covert strategies and conventions she employs for his benefit might be obvious to a third party. Writing a *mémoire* to the marquis is Suzanne's only way of communicating with him, but she knows from experience that as written evidence, it can and will be used against her if it falls into the wrong hands: "So I wrote on a piece of paper (this fateful paper was preserved and it was used all too well against me)" (42–43) [255].

Suzanne wrote her *mémoire* to appear as uncontrived as possible. While repeatedly insisting that her story is true, she reveals in a postscriptum to herself, obviously not meant for him, that many of her techniques to achieve *vraisemblance* have little to do with the truth. This postscriptum, which I will examine below, shows Suzanne critically assessing her *mémoire*, wondering whether the strategies she has adopted in her attempt to seduce the marquis are good ones. Readers of *La Religieuse*, because they have access to the postscriptum the marquis will never see, enjoy the interpretive mastery described above because they have a wider frame of reference within which to interpret Suzanne's story. That is, since we read Suzanne's *mémoire* as well as her comments on her choice of rhetoric and her chances of success in her project to seduce the marquis, we can easily see that Suzanne is far more concerned with arousing the marquis' compassion than with depicting life in the convent. Because Suzanne's final words in *La Religieuse* concern not what she told but how she told it—"Do we count on its being easier to seduce [men] than to touch their hearts?" (189) [392]— we see Suzanne as a highly self-conscious narrator. Suddenly art no longer hides the fact that it is art. Suzanne's postscriptum erects a filtering screen between reader and story—unable to consider her tale transparent, we read her story of woe as much for form as for content, eager to discern, as the marquis presumably cannot, how she achieves her strong emotional effect.

Eighteenth-century novelists, particularly those employing the epistolary or memoir form, not infrequently prefaced their works by disavowing any knowledge concerning the truth of the tale to follow: they claimed to be interested in the way the tale was constructed. The ostensible editor in Laclos' *Les Liaisons dangereuses*, for example, claims to be interested in examining strategy over story when he writes, "It seems to me that at the very least it provides a service to morality to unveil the means employed by those who would corrupt the virtuous, and I believe that these letters can effectively lead to this end." [7] And, the marquis de Sade, whose *Justine* we will examine in Chapter 9, writes in the first sentence of that novel: "The very masterpiece of philosophy would be to develop the means Providence employs to arrive at the ends she designs for man." [8] In my reading of *La Religieuse* I will likewise focus not so much on the *histoire*, or narrative signified of Suzanne's *mémoire*, but on the situation in which it is written and the means Suzanne employs to induce Croismare to believe her and to act. In other words, I will emphasize not the faithful way in which Suzanne depicts reality, but the reasons for which she constructed the story the way she did. Then I will examine the novel's use of framed narratives and shifts in perspective to suggest for readers the possibility of being able to have the whole story, so to speak—to have, that is, the superior interpretive standpoint that would enable them to "demystify" the artfulness of even the most craftily constructed of the work's seductions.

Unlike many other eighteenth-century novels that employ the convention of found letters or memoirs to achieve *vraisemblance*, *La Religieuse* uses the convention to strip the work of any external referent. While most realist works purport to depict or represent the real world, as Mme de Lafayette claimed her novel did, *La Religieuse* represents not a world, but a text: Suzanne's *mémoire*. Bracketed by her own introduction and conclusion, which reveal

[7] Laclos, p. 17.
[8] Sade, *Justine*, p. 13.

that Suzanne never meant to send the marquis this version of her story, but a revision of it, Suzanne's *mémoire* as we read it is meant not to be believed but to be considered critically: as Blum observed, *La Religieuse* shows the *effort* at a seduction—the first sentence of the work reveals, however, that this seduction was still to be accomplished: "The Marquis de Croismare's reply, if he does reply, will serve as the opening lines of this tale" (21) [235]. Suzanne's *mémoire* must appear to Croismare to be a *récit*, the representation in narrative form of the events in her life. She must prevent him from realizing that her tale is not a description of real situations, but the attempt to incite him to act. Seductions differ from descriptions or depictions in that they are propositions or promises which, according to Shoshana Felman, cannot be judged "true or false, but only successful or aborted" (*Le Scandale*, 18). By considering Suzanne's *mémoire* a seduction, we limit our analysis of the tale to the narrative and rhetorical strategy with which it is composed. The *mémoire* must *appear* factual and uncontrived. This is what Felman calls "the trap of seduction": "The trap of seduction consists . . . of producing a *referential illusion* through an enunciation that is, better than any other, auto-referential: the illusion of a real or extra-linguistic act of engagement created by an enunciation that only refers to itself" (40). My analysis of seduction in *La Religieuse* will center around the differences Felman observes between texts that have an external referent, and those that are self-referential. I will examine the claims to accuracy in representation made in the various letters and *mémoires* of Diderot's novel, and, more importantly, the position defined for the reader of the work. The response demanded from readers of *La Religieuse* is a confusion of sympathy and admiration in that it is never clear whether one should identify with Suzanne and pity her, or admire the narrative craft she displays in trying to seduce the marquis. Do we occupy a position of interpretive superiority, since we are party to the tricks involved in the seduction of the marquis? The novel seems to present us with all the information necessary to demystify its duplicitous operation. Like *La Princesse de Clèves*, *La Religieuse* shows readers inappropriate or incorrect modes of reading, seeming to suggest that it lays bare the interpretive strategy best suited for it. Yet as we will see, despite its claims to the contrary, *La Religieuse* cannot demystify itself.

Before situating Suzanne's tale to the marquis within the complicated frame in which it appears, I want to analyze the tale itself as Suzanne's attempt to seduce the marquis de Croismare. Robert J. Ellrich has analyzed the rhetorical structure of Suzanne's story and he has found in it examples of classical persuasive rhetoric, including hyperbole, antithesis, anaphora, enumeration, and prolepsis.[9] While Ellrich's analysis of *La Religieuse* deals with the linguistic stratum of Suzanne's attempt to persuade the marquis to come to her aid, I will examine the way Suzanne arranges the events in her story in order to paint a convincing and pathetic scenario. It will be clear that Suzanne is extremely conscious not only of her prose, as Ellrich's observations would indicate, but of her ability to move her reader with the episodes she recounts as well.

Suzanne contends that her misfortunes originated before her birth in her mother's ill-fated decision to have an extramarital affair. The union resulted in Suzanne's birth, and the illegitimate girl was sent to live in a convent; Suzanne's experiences in the convent form the bulk of her story. There she is subject to a remarkable amount of cruelty at the hands of Sister Sainte-Christine, who attempts to impose strict discipline on the nuns, and later she is seduced by the unnamed superior at Saint-Eutrope who, taken with Suzanne's beauty and apparent innocence, lures her into bed and her first sexual experience. The superior dies and is replaced by Sister Thérèse, "elderly and full of ill-temper and superstition" (183) [388]. Thérèse accuses Suzanne of having bewitched her former superior, and when she is cruelly persecuted once again, Suzanne escapes from the convent, takes refuge in several houses of ill-repute, and closes her *mémoire* with the plea, "I do not know what fate has in store for me, but if I am obliged some day to go back into a convent I cannot answer for anything—there are wells everywhere. Sir, have pity on me, and do not lay up for yourself lasting regrets" (188) [392].

Suzanne's tale, which closes on a suicide threat, is composed of episodes of persecution and victimization that occur as a result of her marked distinction, a distinction that constantly troubles either paternal or religious order. Because Suzanne differs from her sisters in beauty, talent, and legitimacy, she is forced into the convent;

[9] Ellrich, p. 132.

because she alone refuses the discipline over and above that to which nuns submitted in taking their vows she is persecuted; because of her beauty and innocence surpassing those of the other nuns, she is seduced by the lesbian superior. Suzanne, aware that her distinguishing characteristics bring her nothing but misfortune, soberly observes that she would prefer to be like everybody else: "I would just have soon have met indifference or even insults" (22) [236].

It is worth noting that Suzanne's distinction, which she herself observes and laments, wreaks havoc in each and every house she inhabits, including her parents' house. Since she is presumed illegitimate, Suzanne threatens the Simonin household and M. Simonin's patriarchal authority because he fears that she will make a claim on his fortune: her parents force her into the convent to prevent her from making any such claim.[10] The instant Suzanne agrees to become a nun, the household returns to order, as the Simonins' servant reports: "As you only had one word to say to make your father and mother happy, as well as yourself, why did you wait so long before saying it? Monsieur and Madame look like I have never seen them do since I have been here" (43) [255]. Despite her wish noted above, however, to be assimilated into the order and remain as undistinguished as possible, Suzanne constantly makes waves. And it is particularly significant that in the story of her misery at home and in the three convents, Suzanne ceaselessly portrays herself as entirely guiltless—if her entrance into the convent resulted from her being scapegoated to atone for her mother's sin, she depicts herself as equally innocent of the causes of her subsequent misfortunes.

From her birth to her escape from the convent, Suzanne's life story is one of a constant scapegoat. Guiltlessly disturbing familial or convent order, she nevertheless suffers ruthless punishment. When her mother breaks her marriage vow of fidelity to her husband, it is Suzanne, and not her father, who becomes the victim of the transgression. Because Suzanne represents the constant reminder to her father that his wife betrayed him and that the purity

[10] In "Sacrifice and Innocence in *La Religieuse*," William F. Edmiston remarks, "Suzanne must be cast out of a family to which she belongs only by crime, not by laws. She has been disinherited from the family fortune to which she cannot legally lay claim. Parental authority is thus sanctioned by the laws" (p. 69).

of his lineage is no longer secure, the transgression of paternal law must be exorcised. Suzanne must pay for her mother's crime because to punish the mother would be to debase the father's supreme authority: no longer the solemn and omnipotent lawgiver, the father would appear threatened if he resorted to vengeance and retribution on Mme Simonin.[11] Paternal law must appear rational and wise, above the squabbles personal offenses occasion. Scapegoating Suzanne is a way of recognizing the sin of adultery and destroying the evidence, as it were, by hiding her away and making certain that, removed from the company of men, she is unable to reproduce the transgression and demonstrate, as did her mother, the arbitrary nature of paternal authority.

Such arbitrary authority, however, has far-reaching effects. Mme Simonin, subject to her husband's domination, is powerless to help her daughter. At once claiming her as her own ("My daughter— for such you are, whatever I do" (41) [254]), and manifesting concern for her ("If you survive me you will have no name, no money and no position. Tell me, wretched girl, what will become of you" (42) [254]), Mme Simonin also tells Suzanne that her first duty is to her husband: "I don't take advantage of my husband's openhandedness" (41) [253]; "Don't make me liable to commit an unwise act that would cause him to look upon me with hatred" (42) [254]. Finally, Suzanne's mother leads her to believe that unless she agrees to remain a nun, her mother will face the eternal wrath of God: "Reflect, my child, that your mother's destiny in the other world depends largely upon your behaviour in this one. God, who sees all, will in His justice mete out to me all the good and all the evil you do" (54) [265]. Mme Simonin's apparently willful abandoning of her daughter and masterly transplanting of guilt onto her reveal the extent to which maternal love is subservient to patriarchal authority. Whatever her feelings for her daughter, Mme Si-

---

[11] René Girard, who has written extensively on the subject of sacrifice, writes that one punishes not the perpetrator of a crime, but someone like the perpetrator because "if the gap between the victim and the community is allowed to grow too wide, all similarity will be destroyed. The victim will no longer be capable of attracting the violent impulses to itself; the sacrifice will cease to serve as a 'good conductor,' in the sense that metal is a good conductor of electricity. On the other hand, if there is *too much* continuity the violence will overflow its channels. 'Impure' violence will mingle with the 'sacred' violence of the rites, turning the latter into a scandalous accomplice in the process of pollution, even a kind of catalyst in the propagation of further impurity" (*Violence and the Sacred*, p. 39).

monin realizes that her own security depends on carrying out the will of her husband, so she readily condemns Suzanne to a life of woe in the convent.

Each of Suzanne's *directrices*, who also bear the title "mother," treat her in much the same fashion her own mother had, and this has led some critics to speculate that each of Suzanne's mother superiors is a surrogate mother for the poor parentless girl. Her relationship to each of her superiors parallels that to her mother, and if Suzanne attempts to find in them the love she missed at home, she finds instead women ready to make her repeat the role of sacrificial victim. Her first superior initially plays the role of Suzanne's advocate, appearing to be on her side in her attempt to break out of cloistered life. It does not take Suzanne long, however, to see through her guise: "Oh, Sir, you have no conception of the deceitful wiles of these Superiors of convents" (24) [238]; "A novice-mistress is always the most indulgent sister who can be found. Her object is to hide from you all the thorns of the vocation, she subjects you to a course of the most carefully calculated seduction" (26) [240]. Yet Suzanne finds even more troubling than the facade these nuns put forth the real object of their seduction: money.

> These women are well compensated for the trouble you give them, for one cannot suppose that they enjoy the hypocritical part they play and the nonsense they are forced to say over and over again. It all gets so repetitious and boring for them, but they face up to it for the sake of the thousand crowns their house makes out of it. That is the vital aim for which they spend a lifetime of deceit and prepare for innocent young girls forty or fifty years of despair and probably an eternity of suffering. (27) [240]

Repeating the role of Mme Simonin, who was willing to sacrifice her daughter for the financial security of the household, Suzanne's novice-mistress is not above condemning Suzanne to eternal damnation for the miserable dowry she brings to the convent.

Things are no better at Longchamp, Suzanne's second convent, for if she has found a superior who seems truly to love her, that superior is no less unable to help Suzanne break free from the rigorous confines that impose upon Suzanne's freedom. Despite her good intentions, Mme de Moni can only spout platitudes about cloistered life: "And don't other walks of life have their thorns also? We only feel our own. Come along, my child, let us kneel down and pray" (47) [259]. When the moment comes for Suzanne to pronounce her final vows, however, her superior seems to be at least as distraught as Suzanne: "Alas, I have never seen anybody enter the religious life without feeling anxiety for them, but never with any one of them have I felt so much worry as over you. I do so much want you to be happy" (50) [261].[12] At Saint-Eutrope, the last convent Suzanne inhabits, the relationship between Suzanne and her superior comes full circle, and mirrors what we might call the fundamentally erotic nature of the attachment Mme Simonin had for her daughter. It is the unnamed superior in this convent who seduces Suzanne, and Roger Lewinter believes that at the heart of Suzanne's search for a surrogate mother is her mother's frustrated desire to possess her daughter and Suzanne's desire to be possessed. He argues that the initial decision to put Suzanne into a convent, ostensibly to protect the family fortune, does not make logical sense, and it betrays Mme Simonin's overly intense attachment to her daughter.[13] Lewinter analyzes the erotic attachment underlying the mother/daughter relationship by observing that when Suzanne returns home after refusing to pronounce her noviatiate's vows, "the oedipal nature of the conflict emerges explicitly" (76). Remarking that Suzanne can only see and talk to her mother in her father's absence, Lewinter observes that M. Simonin frequently and obtrusively interrupts their interviews with unequivocal animosity. Seeming to view Suzanne as a rival for Mme Simon-

---

[12] Edmiston remarks that Mme de Moni's reactions to Suzanne's sacrifice parallel Mme Simonin's: "At Longchamp Suzanne finds a surrogate mother in Mme de Moni, who treats her with more tenderness but who is nonetheless powerless to resolve her dilemma. The prevailing authority demands a sacrifice to preserve order, and in the convent as in the family, this authority conceals financial interest disguised as religious piety. Both mothers, Mme Simonin and Mme de Moni, are emotionally troubled at the hour of Suzanne's sacrifice, yet neither is able to act against what seems to be an inexorable fate" (p. 72).

[13] Lewinter (p. 75) explains why Mme Simonin persuades Suzanne to enter the convent. He claims that the reason is not that bourgeois property laws would favor Suzanne's renunciation of her father's wealth, but that Mme Simonin's attachment to her daughter causes her to keep her out of reach of all other people. "The nature of the relations between Suzanne and Mme Simonin is immediately defined: when Suzanne announces to her mother that the suitor of one of her sisters desires her, her mother sends her to the convent. Logically, this action is absurd: neither the fact of her illegitimacy nor financial considerations explain it. Suzanne's illegitimacy should incite her mother to place her as soon as possible, so that she not be tempted to ask her father for anything. As far as her entry into the convent is concerned, this, too, requires a dowry. But affectively the action is clear: the mother does not want Suzanne to transfer her love to another; by removing her from the world, she keeps her for herself."

in's affections, M. Simonin surprises them in a private conversation; Suzanne describes the scene as follows: "At that moment Monsieur Simonin came in. He loved his wife, he saw the state she was in, he was a violent man. He stopped dead, gave me a terrible look and said: 'Leave this room!'" (42) [254].

Suzanne's relationship with each of her superiors consequently seems to be a reenactment of her familial situation. As we have seen, Mme Simonin imposed upon her daughter the responsibility of expiating her sin of adultery. Yet, her feelings for her daughter remain maddeningly equivocal, as her deathbed letter to Suzanne reveals: "Your birth is the one serious sin I have committed. Help me to expiate it. . . . Above all do not upset the peace of the family . . . I want you to remain in the religious life. The vision of you in the world with no help and support and so young, would be the final torment of my last moments" (54–55) [265–66]. Mme Simonin at once rejects her daughter and protects the patriarchal order while implicitly embracing Suzanne in the very last words she ever utters. Her sternness and concerned attachment for Suzanne are reproduced in Mme de Moni, Sainte-Christine, and the superior at Saint-Eutrope: each of Suzanne's mothers embraces her and rejects her, using the young woman for her own satisfaction (family stability, convent finances, sexual release) without letting her derive anything in return. Suzanne is always the obedient daughter who gives the mother what she wants.[14] Each of Suzanne's mothers provides the young nun with a dutiful daughter's role to fill, whether one of tender attachment, erotic affinity, or fearful subservience. Suzanne describes herself in her *mémoire* only as she plays the daughter's role to one of these mothers.

The analysis of Suzanne's filial relationships to a series of women has thus far been concerned only with other characters in her story. Yet, if Suzanne constantly plays the daughter's role it is not exclusively in relationship to a mother figure, nor is it exclusively for another character in her story. We must remember that Suzanne's *mémoire* is addressed to the marquis de Croismare, whom she de-

---

[14] Lewinter believes that Suzanne's constant repetition of the mother/daughter relationship underlies her quest for a coherent sense of self. He argues that Suzanne always represents herself as the dutiful daughter, and that her sense of self comes to her only as an effect produced by others. "[Suzanne] fixes the effect produced—others—in order that the producing cause—self—might be reconstituted, indefinitely, the same effect (re)producing logically the same cause" (p. 96).

scribes as "a man of the world [who] has had a distinguished military career, is elderly, a widower with a daughter and two sons whom he loves and who return his affection" (21) [235]; in short, he is a sort of good father figure. We must also remember that Suzanne's expressly stated purpose in writing her *mémoire* is to seduce the marquis into helping her. It seems clear, then, that if Suzanne constantly plays the daughter's role to a series of mother figures in the story she relates, she is also trying to fill the daughter's role for the man to whom she addresses her tale. Suzanne's plan is to incite the fatherly marquis to come to her aid, and in order to convince him of both her need of help and her disingenuousness in asking for it she asserts, "I am a woman, and weak in spirit like others of my sex" (99) [308]. The first step in Suzanne's seduction of the marquis is to disarm him, to convince him of her complete, uncalculating vulnerability. Marie-Claire Vallois, who affirms Lewinter's reading of *La Religieuse* as a reenactment of familial dynamics, writes of Suzanne's assertion of feminine weakness, "The fact of being a woman fixes here not only psychology but the very modalities of the heroine's discourse, a discourse that can only, in a certain sense, inscribe itself as a discourse of seduction." [15]

Vallois confirms my earlier claim that Suzanne attempts to seduce the marquis; because nearly the entire *récit* of *La Religieuse* is in Suzanne's own voice, we cannot separate the novel's narration from this feminine psychology of seduction. [16] Vallois also asserts that Suzanne attempts to seduce the marquis by adopting a blatantly helpless posture in an attempt to provide a father/daughter framework around the narratee/narrator relationship. Identifying along with Lewinter Suzanne's quest for suitable parent figures as a reenactment of the oedipal scenario, Vallois asserts that this scenario is "inscribed in implicit fashion in the novel, with Suzanne's drama being in effect that of a choice between her mothers and fathers in religion" (171).

As critically compelling as an analysis of Suzanne's family romance may be, however, such an analysis can only have meaning in the context of the narrator/narratee relationship of Suzanne's

---

[15] Vallois, "Politique du paradoxe: Tableau de mœurs / tableau familial dans *La Religieuse*," p. 169.
[16] I will discuss below the single brief incident in which a voice other than Suzanne's breaks into the *récit*.

seduction. That is, when we remember that Suzanne is writing her *mémoire* in order to incite the marquis to help her, we cannot rule out the possibility that she describes her dismal inability to find a suitable mother figure in order to increase her tale's pathos. We cannot be sure that Suzanne's description of her troubled relationship with her father is not merely a lure to incite the marquis to try to fill the father's role better. If she can make herself seem more abject owing to a lack of maternal love and familial identification, the marquis might be seduced and play his paternal role all the more effectively by coming to her rescue. In other words, we must consider not only the *récit* and the *histoire* of Suzanne's *mémoire*, but the *narration* ("the productive narrating act and, by extension, the complex real or fictive situation in which it takes place")[17] as well. Virtually none of the work on *La Religieuse* considers Suzanne's story in its context: a story told to procure for the narrator something she wants.[18] As though blinded to the context in which the story is told, owing to the compelling critical possibilities Suzanne's story offers, virtually all critics view the novel as a critique of cloistered life,[19] an examination of feminine sexuality in the Enlightenment,[20] or an experiment in realism.[21] It is as though each of these readers is seduced by Suzanne's story. We need to remember, however, as Ross Chambers reminds us, that "stories are produced by a storyteller for the benefit of a hearer, and it is agreements between those two that determine the relevance of a given story" (*Story and Situation*, 21). I now want to examine the *narration* of Suzanne's miseries—that is, the narrative act in which they are told—to determine how she tries to make the tale relevant to the marquis. I will show that the elements of Suzanne's story that most critics read as elements of the plot need to be seen, in fact, as part of the seduction.

As we have seen, Suzanne's seduction of Croismare involves playing the daughter's role to the marquis as good father figure. Now we need to look at the processes by which she attempts to control

[17] Genette, *Figures III*, p. 72.
[18] Two notable exceptions are Saint-Amand; and Philip Stewart, in *Half-Told Tales*.
[19] See Edmiston; Jean Catrysse, *Diderot et la mystification*; and Mylne, *The Eighteenth-Century French Novel*, especially chapter XI.
[20] See Mylne, "What Suzanne Knew: Lesbianism and *La Religieuse*"; and Rex, "Secrets from Suzanne."
[21] See Bremner, pp. 168–71; and May, *Diderot et "La Religieuse."*

his response to her *mémoire* by persuading him to be the missing father in her life. Luce Irigaray writes, concerning the daughter's seduction of the father: "The girl's only way to redeem her personal value, and value in general, would be to seduce the father, and persuade him to express, if not admit, some interest in her." [22] In order to extract from him some mark of interest on the most basic, humanitarian level, Suzanne closes her tale, as we have seen, with a suicide threat ("there are wells everywhere"). To make the marquis' sympathies for her more specifically paternal, she first tells him, "I had no father" (38) [251], and by disparaging the powers of the feminine mind ("I am . . . weak in spirit like others of my sex") she plays on his masculine identity. To indicate her need for a strong and guiding masculine force in her life, she narrates the heretofore total absence of such a force. She attempts to show him how sorely she needs paternal guidance, and this display takes the form of describing the corruption that arises when women are left in control. When, for example, she describes the lesbian superior's seduction, it is in terms of a rejection of paternity: both the lesbian superior's words and deeds, as well as Suzanne's reaction to them, imply the obviation of the paternal role and the signal importance of the maternal one. The lesbian superior forbids Suzanne from confessing her acts with her, denying that any wrong was committed and adding, "Who knows the importance that man may attach to it" (161) [366].

Suzanne submits to the superior's demands, and her obedience reflects the mother's subsuming of the father's authoritative role. Furthermore, Suzanne suggests not only that she accepts the mother's way of thinking, but that she is adopting her sexual preference as well. She describes how she felt during her sexual encounter with the lesbian superior as follows: "I don't know what was going on inside me, but I was seized with panic, and my own trembling and faintness justified the suspicion I had had that her trouble was contagious" (142) [348]. By revealing the calamity that results from the absence of the father, Suzanne hopes to provoke his response, and the strategy of suggesting an adoption of homosexuality implies a threat to the paternal order, a threat the marquis can fend off only by giving Suzanne what she wants. Irigaray believes that

[22] Irigaray, *Speculum of the Other Woman*, p. 87.

feminine homosexuality represents a threat to paternal authority because it repudiates the power of the phallus. The female homosexual is a problem, Irigaray writes, "because she refuses to allow herself to be seduced by the father quite as much as he refuses to become the surrogate object of her desire" (101). Thus, Suzanne tries to persuade the marquis to reassert paternal hegemony—to play the father's role—by extricating her from the circle of feminine homosexual desire. Claiming abandonment by M. Simonin and narrating her life gone awry since that time, Suzanne tries to show the marquis that she is a daughter desperately in need of adoption.

Up until now we have considered role-filling only as it relates to Suzanne, her mothers, and the potential father she tries to seduce. The question we now need to address is how *La Religieuse* employs the seductive strategy of Suzanne's *mémoire* to entice its reader to play a role or fill a position. Jay Caplan suggests that *La Religieuse* asks the reader to play two roles simultaneously: one is a "feminine" role that demands reader sympathy with Suzanne's predicament, and the other is a "masculine" role in which the reader is "invited to share . . . in the pleasure of making a female figure suffer and of occasionally suffering with her."[23] Caplan posits two diametrically opposed roles here, partially because he believes there is a narrative irony in *La Religieuse* that prohibits readers from knowing which role to take.[24] Caplan argues that the role the reader must take is forever undecidable, but he does not treat at any length the issue of the rhetorical frame in his analysis of *La Religieuse*. He does not explicitly address the fact that there is a distinction between the framed narrative (Suzanne's *mémoire*) and the framing one (Suzanne's introduction and postscriptum). It is easy to agree with Caplan, who contends that in reading the framed narrative one is enjoined to sympathize with Suzanne, since that is the whole point of her story—to evoke pity. This is what he terms the feminine role; the masculine role, however, is a bit more complex.

[23] Caplan, *Framed Narratives*, p. 55.
[24] The rest of Caplan's argument, which does not directly concern us here, has to do with "the necessity of distinguishing between the social position of the emergent novel's audience and the rhetorical position that it made available to that 'new reading public'" (p. 54). The phrase "new reading public" is Arnold Hauser's; in *The Social History of Art* he discusses bourgeois reactions to art in the eighteenth century.

Caplan identifies the masculine role as the "'phallic' position, the position of the missing part" (54); in Caplan's theory, Diderot's readers are induced to play the role of the missing member of a family. The reader in the phallic position "fills in" what is lacking in the family. If the marquis is meant to occupy the phallic role in the framed narrative (Suzanne's *mémoire*) by supplying what he thinks Suzanne wants and needs—a paternal figure to rescue her from her straits—the reader of *La Religieuse* occupies a similar phallic position. The occupier of the phallic position is presumed able to supply what is lacking. In this case, what Suzanne wants and needs from the person who reads her *mémoire* along with its introduction and postscriptum is the answer to her question concerning her narrative strategy. As we have already seen, Suzanne expresses trepidation that her strategy of appealing to the marquis' sense of vice rather than to his sense of virtue might not be a good idea ("do we count on its being easier to seduce [men] than to touch their hearts?"). The reader of *La Religieuse* is thus faced with the task of recognizing the pathos in Suzanne's tale (the feminine position) as well as the talent and the work that went into the production of such a finely crafted seduction. This is what Caplan calls "the 'masculine' pleasure of maintaining a critical detachment" (54). Thus "what is missing" is the role of the interpretant, the "masculine" reader who can remain critical and detached and synthesize the appeal to sentiment and pity in the framed narrative (the *mémoire*) and the cunning manipulation of narrative in the framing narration (Suzanne's introduction and postscriptum). The phallic reader of Suzanne's introduction, *mémoire*, and postscriptum would provide the definitive answer to Suzanne's question because he is detached enough not to be affected by the story. Suzanne's question is in effect addressed to the master, the person in control of language. Her question, which she extends by asking, "Could it be that we think men are less affected by a picture of our troubles than by a portrait of our charms?" (189) [392], is not, I believe, rhetorical. She experiences serious reservations about the believability of her tale, and what she needs is a direct answer to her query. Readers of *La Religieuse*, because they have the information provided in Suzanne's introduction and postscriptum, have a broader narrative perspective, and Suzanne's questions ask them to choose the narrative style she should adopt. Construed at the end of the novel as phallic readers, we are led to believe in the superiority, relative to the marquis', of our own interpretive skills.

Suzanne asks another question at the end of her postscriptum, one which caps off the reader's authoritative position: she asks for self-definition. "I am a woman," she writes, "and perhaps a bit coquettish, who can tell? But it is a result of our nature, and not of artifice on my part [*Mais c'est naturellement et sans artifice*]" (189) [393]. Here Suzanne refuses to define herself or to write a description of herself that will in any way reduce her to an easily recognizable type. Concluding with a contradiction in calling herself a natural coquette,[25] she leaves the task of defining what she is to readers who feel up to it.[26] Suzanne throws open to the readers of the work the question of her being, and she gives them the last word in interpreting her story and deciding what she is. Because they have information available to none of the readers depicted within *La Religieuse*, readers of the novel are enticed into believing in the authority and superiority of their own more broadly based interpretation. Suzanne's question about narrative technique and her leaving open the question of self-definition lead us to believe that we have the final answer, that we can give the solution that will round off her story. Construed as the best readers of her story, we become masters of the work.

The next task at hand involves demonstrating that the reader's position of interpretive mastery, like Mme de Chartres' mastery we saw in Chapter 6, is nothing but a fiction. It is true that Suzanne contextualizes for us her *mémoire* to the marquis by revealing that it is an attempt to seduce him—we read her introduction and postscriptum that tell us as much. We must take care, however, not to accept too readily the work's self-contextualizing, because frequently, as Chambers points out, the context a novel establishes for

[25] All of the Robert Dictionary's definitions of *coquette* insist either on the person's concentrated attempt to please the opposite sex or on his or her studied beautification.
[26] Baudrillard writes in *De la séduction* that the trap of seduction lies in soliciting interpretation: "If . . . [the seductress] tries to give herself reasons or guilty or cynical motivations, this is still a trap—and her last trap is to solicit interpretation by saying, 'Tell me who I am,' even though she is nothing, and indifferent toward what she is, immanent, immemorial and without history, and even though her power is precisely to be there, ironic and fleeting, blind with respect to her being but knowing perfectly all the mechanisms of reason and truth that the others need to protect themselves from seduction and in the shelter of which, if one arranges them, they will ceaselessly be seduced" (p. 120).

itself is part of the fiction itself: "One should not allow one's mode of reading to be determined exclusively by the text's situational self-reflexivity—that is, by the ideology of art to which the text happens to subscribe. On the contrary, by reading this self-situating as *part of the text*, one should free oneself to recontextualize it (that is, interpret it) along with the rest of the text" (27). As readers of *La Religieuse*, we must find some gap or opening in the fiction's apparent seamlessness and search out not only Suzanne's seduction of the marquis, but *La Religieuse*'s seduction of us. In other words, discovering that Suzanne charges her story with rich interpretive possibilities must not blind us to the fact that the novel itself attains a semantic richness precisely by allowing us to discover Suzanne's duplicity. We have seen that we are not the objects of Suzanne's seduction, and that she makes herself appear helpless in order to incite the marquis to occupy the phallic position, the missing position of power and authority. The marquis' paternal authority becomes his weakness, since Suzanne is directing the scene. "The strategy of seduction," Baudrillard writes, "consists in leading the other onto the terrain of your weakness, which will also be the other's weakness" (114). Now we need to discover how *La Religieuse*'s readers are seduced into feeling similar power and authority, and how this illusion of power constitutes a weakness.

Suzanne attempts to hide the mechanics of her seduction by preventing the marquis from examining the tale too closely: hence the importance of her plea "Burn the letter!" Since no reader of *La Religieuse* would take such a plea literally, the novel must employ other means to throw readers off the critical track. Locating a novel's duplicity, however, involves much more than simply determining whether or not it depicts real characters and situations—the stuff narrative purports to be "about." If it were simply a question of proving a novel's fictitiousness, we might agree with Clapiers de Vauvenargues, who wrote in 1746 that works without tangible referents in the real world do not hold up well under scrutiny and are worthless when analyzed: "Falsehood in and of itself wounds us and has nothing that can move us. What do you think people look for so avidly in fiction? The image of a living, passionate truth. . . . Falsehood . . . disgusts them the moment it reveals its presence. No one rereads a novel."[27] Vauvenargues' scathing critique of novels

[27] Vauvenargues, "Des romans," in *Introduction à la connaissance de l'esprit humain*, pp. 123–24.

implies that once one discovers that one is reading a novel, and not historical fact, further consideration of the work is unwarranted. His comments on the disgust self-conscious fiction provokes reveal his propensity to read for the plot or the work's external referent. Vauvenargues can find no value in a text that is not only false but admits it as well. He judges literary merit solely on the quality of the image (the narrative signified) produced with no concern for the means by which illusion is created. Yet, to read in such a way is to ignore the conditions a work establishes for its own reading, as well as to efface the author's signature from the work. Totally transparent art would be unidentifiable as art, and when a novel such as *La Religieuse* establishes one set of conditions in which it can be read as representation (the text of Suzanne's *mémoire*, for example), and another in which it must be read as self-referential (Suzanne's rhetoric exposed as seductive strategy), it attains a complexity unavailable to dominantly mimetic works. Readers must be aware that what they are reading is a literary and not a historical text. Chambers calls the tension between representational and self-referential narrative a "tug-of-war"; fiction, he argues, asks its readers both to recognize and to ignore its status as art.[28] We now need to analyze the "tug-of-war" between Suzanne's duplicitous narration, which would refer to her life in the convent, and her self-referential one, which refers to the art with which the tale is con-

---

[28] "If a text relies, for its point, on its artistic ('narrational') success, the transaction with the reader fails unless the narratee perceives that art is being produced. . . . But one of the more durable axioms of Western aesthetics has it that the greatest art lies in the concealment of art and that the production of art—and hence, the gain in narrational authority—is the greater when the art narrative is apparently nonart, that is, a form of communication concerned principally with its own referent. . . . Hence, there is a constant tug-of-war between conflicting strategies—between narrative *self-referentiality* whereby the story draws attention to its status as art and forms of narrative *duplicity* whereby the story pretends to be concerned only with its informational content and yet reveals in unobtrusive ways (usually by slight discrepancies) that this is not so" (pp. 52–53). Marthe Robert subscribes to Chambers' view that a novel's artistic success depends not on deception, but on the reader's noticing the literary craftwork involved. She believes that the most important characteristic of the novel is the "'as if' on which fiction survives exclusively—though it tries very hard to make us forget it" (p. 10). For Robert, the fictive text continually places between readers and the world it represents an implicit "as if," constantly inviting them to notice not so much the similarities between reality and fiction, but the differences. Yet, it simultaneously asks them to put enough stock in the world created that they can forget that everything they read is contingent upon this "as if." In "L'Histoire véritable dans la littérature romanesque du XVIIIe siècle français," Jacques Rustin sums up this conception of realist texts in a deceptively simple way: "The story is only 'true' through the sovereign decision of the author, and through the art by which it inserts the reader into its game" (p. 92).

structed. Only by examining the discrepancies between the real-world situations to which Suzanne's *mémoire* purportedly refers and the production of meaning gleaned from the palimpsestic layers of the novel can we hope to come up with some idea of how the novel, like Suzanne, attempts to seduce its reader.

I will devote the remainder of this chapter to that specific question. Of all the most frequently discussed of *La Religieuse*'s traits, the supposed errors Diderot committed in composing the novel are most often cited as the opening necessary to uncover the text's secrets. I will examine these so-called errors in order to discover what light they shed on the work. The *bévues*, as they have come to be called, are the clues that let readers see to what degree they are dealing with a skillfully crafted work of narrative art. In addition, I will treat in detail the claims to veracity Suzanne makes, implicitly in referring to her story as a *mémoire*, and explicitly in her assertions that despite appearances everything happened as she tells it. *La Religieuse* constantly demystifies its own *modus operandi*, the scaffolding supporting the fictive text, thus providing readers with the illusion of having the whole story as well as the most informed interpretation of it. Yet, because of its surreptitious erection of new frameworks, primarily in Suzanne's postscriptum and the tremendously complicated *préface-annexe* accompanying it, *La Religieuse* never quite lays its cards on the table; in the end it accomplishes a seduction that is surprisingly similar to Suzanne's.

Since at least as far back as 1915, when Paul Chaponnière published his short article "Une bévue de Diderot dans *La Religieuse*,"[29] readers have been fascinated with the problematic passage in which a letter Suzanne receives from her mother tells the story of its own transmission:

> They [Suzanne's sisters] have had suspicions, I don't know how, that I might have some money hidden between my mattresses, and there is nothing they have not had recourse to in order to make me get out of bed. And they succeeded, but fortunately the person to whom I am entrusting this money had come the day before, and I had given him this little package, with this letter which he has written to my dictation. Burn this letter. (54) [266]

[29] *Revue d'Histoire littéraire de la France*, 22 (1915), pp. 573–74.

Chaponnière's term *"bévue"*—a word that implies gross careless-
ness on Diderot's part—for this apparent authorial error has stuck.
Generations of scholars have gleefully gloated over Diderot's blun-
der which narrates an impossible situation: how could Mme Simonin have known, at the time she was writing the letter, that Suzanne's sisters were going to rifle through her mattress the
following day? Diderot, it seems, in the rush and excitement of
composition, overlooked this little glitch, a rather surprising fact
given that the manuscript in the Fonds Vandeul in the Bibliothèque
Nationale contains myriad corrections penned in Diderot's own
hand. Since Chaponnière's discovery of the *bévue*, people have
combed the work, tracking down more logical inconsistencies attesting to the work's *invraisemblance*, and a good half-dozen have
turned up, most of which are related to temporal sequence and
characters' ages.

Overlooking for the time being, however, the physical impossibility of such a letter, we can observe one thing for certain: by going
to such (impossible) extremes to ensure the confidentiality of her
deathbed communication, Mme Simonin demonstrates an acute
anxiety that her letter might fall into the wrong hands. Even if we
ignore the *bévue*, her insistence that Suzanne burn the letter makes
manifest this anxiety. Mme Simonin's wish that there be no trace
of her letter to her daughter comes as no surprise to us: Suzanne,
presumed illegitimate, is effectively cut out of her parents' will, and
Suzanne's greedy sisters would be outraged that their mother sent
a small sum of money to their bastard sister. By requiring her
daughter to destroy the evidence, Mme Simonin prevents her other
daughters not only from finding out by what underhanded means
she communicated with and sent money to Suzanne, but also from
learning that any exchange took place at all.

The problem with Mme Simonin's letter, of course, is that it
simply does not make sense. It is physically impossible that she
could have written such a thing. Yet, it makes perfect sense that
within the context of a seductive plea Suzanne would claim to have
received such a letter in her attempt to persuade the marquis of her
resourcelessness. It is in no way inconceivable that she would go to
great narrative lengths—even risking *invraisemblance*—to achieve
the desired effects. The scene's pathos is patent: Suzanne, as illegitimate daughter, has been abandoned by her family and forced into

a convent. Even her mother, her only living blood relative, cannot
communicate with her by any but the most clandestine means.
Mme Simonin has apparently risked a great deal in sending Suzanne the small sum of money, and she wants no trace of her communication with the shunned Suzanne to remain: she repudiates the
last letter she sends her daughter. Upon receipt of her dying mother's disavowed letter, Suzanne reaches the depths of loneliness and
abjection. Her only remaining possible advocate is gone.

As I have indicated, Suzanne's *mémoire* is full of supposed *bévues*: Suzanne narrates events she could not have witnessed ("[the
Superior] only rose when everybody had gone" (172) [377]); the
superior who seduced her is described as a woman of about forty
but Suzanne says that she had been at Port-Royal, which would
make her substantially older; and in a story that spans some nine
years, Suzanne ages fewer than three. In addition, when Suzanne
describes the help Sister Ursule gave her in sending a letter to her
lawyer, she writes the following blatant contradiction:

> This young person is still in the convent, Sir, her happiness is in your
> hands; if anyone should happen to find out what she did for me there
> is no describing the tortures she would be exposed to. I would not
> want to have opened the door of a prison cell for her, I would rather
> go back there myself. So burn these letters, Sir, for apart from the
> interest you are good enough to take in my fate they don't contain
> anything worth preserving.
>   That is what I told you then, but alas, she is no more, and I am left
> alone. (68) [278][30]

Suzanne aims for the greatest emotional effect possible in her *mémoire*, and if she sometimes needs to transgress the bounds of verisimilitude, she hopes the story is powerful enough that her reader
will not notice. Suzanne shares here the belief Diderot evinces in
his "Eloge de Richardson" that a moving story can make the reader
forget trivial matters concerning truth and verisimilitude: "Beaten
down with pain or enraptured with joy, you will no longer have the

---

[30] Henri Bénac proposes an ingenious way to resolve the apparent contradiction:
He contends that the section beginning with "This young person" up until "That is
what I told you then" is a citation of the consultation Suzanne addressed to her
lawyer. Concerned that the nun who transmitted the communication might be implicated, she asks the lawyer to burn the correspondence. Bénac does not indicate
why Suzanne would cite her own previous letter here, particularly without even
indicating that she is doing so. See Diderot, *Œuvres romanesques*, p. 872.

strength to hold back your tears . . . and say to yourself: *But perhaps this is not true*." [31]

If Suzanne can carry her illogical scenes off—if, that is, she can get the marquis to pity her abjection and loneliness without recognizing the absurdity of the scenes she has described—her seduction may succeed. Thus I would argue that we cannot legitimately call these episodes "*bévues*," since they perform a rhetorical function consistent with Suzanne's intentions throughout her *mémoire*: that of portraying herself as alone and as miserable as possible. To make certain, however, that the marquis does not have the chance to study the tale, including these "*bévues*," she asks him, as her mother did her, to burn the letter—ostensibly to protect both herself and him, but perhaps more probably because she fears being read by a less gullible reader.

Despite the logical inconsistencies in her *mémoire*, Suzanne still claims her tale is true. Like Mme de Lafayette, she calls her story a *mémoire*: "I have made up my mind to overcome my pride and reluctance and embark on these recollections [*mémoires*] in which I shall describe part of my misfortunes without talent or artifice, with the ingenuousness of a girl of my age and with my natural candour" (21) [235]. The use of the term *mémoire*, in both Suzanne's and Mme de Lafayette's case, implies the deliberate omission of obtrusive literary convention: Suzanne, in fact, insists on her own candid and uncalculating nature in the writing of her story. In a *mémoire*, the author was presumed to be telling the unmitigated truth, bypassing the mediation of conventional *vraisemblance* to get to the immediacy of the represented world. Suzanne's insistence that her story is true specifies a zero-grade narrative form: no special interpretive skills, other than the ability to read, are assumed. Although the *mémoire* was already a codified literary form, Suzanne uses it to claim that what she writes is the truth and nothing but the truth.

Both Mme de Lafayette and Suzanne use the term *mémoire* when referring to their stories, and each wants to emphasize the absence of codified narrative convention in her work. Mme de Lafayette wanted to stress the extent to which her work was unlike heroic fiction, which had relied extensively on improbable coincidence,

---

[31] "Eloge de Richardson," in *Œuvres philosophiques*, p. 35 (Diderot's emphasis).

implausible actions, and unabashed glorification of the old aristocracy. She indicates, as we saw in Chapter 6, that the word "novel"
evoked unrealistically stilted episodes and descriptions in readers'
minds. Suzanne calls her story sent to the marquis a *mémoire* as
well, but she is concerned not with demonstrating the inadequacy
of convention, but with proving to the marquis that her tale's informational content, and not its narrative structure, is what he
should concentrate on. She claims in addressing the marquis that
despite appearances to the contrary everything she relates really
happened: "I can hear you, Sir, and most of those who read these
memoirs, saying: 'So many horrors, so varied and so continuous!
A series of such calculated atrocities in religious souls! It defies all
probability.' I agree with you, but it is true, and I call on Heaven to
judge me with all its severity and condemn me to eternal flames if I
have allowed calumny to touch a single line of mine with its faintest
shadow!" (98–99) [307]. It is obvious that if Suzanne's seduction
of the marquis is to succeed she must never let him suspect that any
degree of calculation or insincerity went into the story. She attempts to forestall her reader's objection that the tale is not truthful, and since she writes to enlist his help she must be particularly
sensitive to his reactions. The fact that only *one* reader is the object
of her seduction facilitates her task somewhat and, as we have seen,
Suzanne tailors her account to appeal to what she presumes to be
the marquis' weak spots. Thus, when Suzanne states that her story
is true, she makes this claim not, as Dieckmann observed was the
case with Diderot's writings in general, to a *reading public*, but
merely to a particular *reader*.

When Mme de Lafayette and Suzanne use the term "*mémoire*"
they do so in order to claim faithful depictions of particular worlds,
but both Mme de Lafayette as novelist and Suzanne as memorialist
portray not just true-to-life worlds, but complex narrative strategies as well. That is, both Mme de Lafayette's and Suzanne's stories
can be read as transparent narratives (in that they imitate empirical
reality) as well as self-referential works that call attention to their
narrative craft. Both *La Princesse de Clèves* and *La Religieuse* derive part of their significance from the depiction of characters' attempts to cover up what they are really doing: courtiers try not to
be read, and Suzanne endeavors to seduce the marquis. These novels focus on the use of language to convey information (and misin-

formation), and they reveal to their readers the strategies that those attempting to mislead others employ.

Félix Martínez-Bonati argues that literary language generally represents or depicts real speech acts without, however, having linguistic signification of its own. He distinguishes between the "real authentic sentence," which he defines as a "perceptible product of a speaker's communicative action [that] effects communication by causing the listener (the addressee) to perceive and comprehend it as a communicative sign," and imaginary sentences.[32] The latter are "representatives of (absent) authentic sentences" (79), and the example he gives is reported speech. Martínez-Bonati contends that literature is a collection of imaginary sentences "iconically represented ... but imagined without any external determination of their communicative situation" (80). Literary language, he contends, does not represent the author's communicative action, since readers are addressees of imaginary sentences. Hence, he writes, "the author communicates to us not a particular situation (a communicated situation) by means of real linguistic signs but, rather, imaginary linguistic signs by means of nonlinguistic ones. In other words, the author himself does not communicate with us *by means of* language; instead he *communicates language* to us" (81). This is precisely what Mme de Lafayette accomplished when she depicted courtiers limiting their interpretations of others' behavior to the dictates of *vraisemblance* and *bienséance*: *La Princesse de Clèves* imitates not a world, but the language and interpretive processes of the court. Its self-referentiality is directed primarily at the very procedures of reading and interpreting its characters employ. *La Religieuse*, however, because of its framed narratives, is self-referential in far more complicated ways. If we read Suzanne's *mémoire* as she addressed it to the marquis, it is obvious that she attempts to communicate her misery in the convent *by means of* language, emphasizing narrative content. That is, she wants to appear, in her duplicitous narration, to give the marquis the most accurate account she can of how greatly she needs his help. Yet, on the other hand, if we read Suzanne's tale within its frame in *La Religieuse* we read not only Suzanne's attempt to seduce the marquis, but her admission that she is expressly endeavoring to accomplish a seduction. So,

---

[32] Martínez-Bonati, *Fictive Discourse and the Structures of Literature*, p. 78.

reading both first- and second-level narratives (Suzanne's *mémoire* and the frame in which it appears), we deal not so much with Suzanne's representation of convent life as with the contrived speech situation (the *mémoire*) she uses to carry out her seduction. In other words, the novel represents for us language tailored for a specific purpose. Thus, a duplicitous first-level narration is framed by the second-level, self-referential one.

Perhaps another way of viewing this problem is to put it in these terms: *La Religieuse* is effectively the story of an unfinished story. As it stands in its unedited format—that is, preceded and followed by Suzanne's comments on why she is writing and how well she thinks she did—the *récit* contains not Suzanne's *mémoire* to the marquis, but her first draft. The final paragraph of the novel—Suzanne's postscriptum—reveals her critical assessment of her work:

> I have noticed that without the slightest intention I had shown myself in every line, certainly as unhappy as I was, but much more attractive than I am. Could it be that we think men are less affected by a picture of our troubles than by a portrait of our charms? And do we count on its being easier to seduce them than to touch their hearts? I have too little experience of them, and I have not studied them sufficiently to know. And yet supposing the Marquis, who is reputed to be the most delicate of men, were to persuade himself that I am addressing myself not to his charity but to his lust, what would he think of me? (189) [393]

Suzanne considers her work critically, wondering whether her strategy of appealing to her reader's sense of vice rather than to his sense of virtue will pay off. She fears, in addition, that this strategy might be too apparent. In other words, with the question, "Supposing the Marquis . . . were to persuade himself that I am addressing myself not to his charity but to his lust, what would he think of me?" Suzanne worries that the *modus operandi* of her text—the "as if" in Robert's terms—is too evident, and hence that the marquis will all too easily dismiss it, much as Vauvenargues claimed readers who discover the lie can dismiss novels. As though to dissuade him from critically examining the tale as she has just done, she entreats him, as we have seen, to burn the text: "You will burn this letter, and I promise to burn your answers" (22) [236].

Because *La Religieuse* incorporates two tales, one of a nun's experiences and the other of the nun's writing, it deftly plays duplicitous and self-referential narratives off one another. The first-level story—Suzanne's experiences—appears real enough, since obtrusively imposing literary conventions are lacking. Taken in the context, however, of a framed narrative, the realist internal narrative assumes a role subservient to the frame: it is no longer possible to ask whether Suzanne's story is true or false, as Felman suggests is the case with all seductions, only whether it might accomplish the goal of seduction the frame reveals.[33] If Diderot claimed to be writing a referential novel that would expose the evils of religious life, one might question his motive for including the postscriptum, in which Suzanne's calculating, deceptive nature is revealed. No longer the innocent and unwilling victim, Suzanne is unmasked at the end of the work to be a conniving, scheming fabricator. Yet, much of the ambiguity we find in *La Religieuse* stems from Diderot's own uncertainties about his work. Should he call it a novel? An "unformed draft [*ébauche informe*]"? Memoirs? Given the frequency with which he interchanges these words when referring to the work in his correspondence, Diderot seems unable to classify the text. No longer simply putting into play the antithetical natures of truth and fiction, testing the *vraisemblance* of the memoir novel and the complex discursive modes of *La Religieuse*, Diderot mobilizes the oppositions between narrative self-referentiality and duplicity on the one hand, and story and context on the other.

Characters in *La Religieuse* implicitly oppose the same issues in their own letters, as each correspondent in the novel fears having her story come to light. Suzanne learned this the hard way when, on two separate occasions, her own letters were misdirected: "So I wrote on a piece of paper (this fateful paper was preserved and it

---

[33] Herbert Josephs points out in "Diderot's *La Religieuse*: Libertinism and the Dark Cave of the Soul" that this novel eschews a narration that would place it squarely either in the camp of realist fiction, polemical condemnation of monasticism, or conventional memoir. Josephs believes that the addition of Suzanne's postscriptum as well as the *préface-annexe* continually confounds our attempts at interpretation: "*La Religieuse* implies more than it says and its subtlety as a work of fiction, while increasing the novel's effectiveness as an instrument of polemics, succeeds at the same time in blurring the distinctions on which its more direct humanitarian appeals depended. Diderot's own ambivalence with regard to Suzanne's story can be observed in his hesitations over the narrative structure—autobiographical letter or memoirs—best suited for the novel, and in the addition of the *préface-annexe*, effecting a sudden reversal of sympathies and underscoring a psychological uncertainty that testifies to the duality of inspiration at the heart of the work" (p. 734).

was used all too well against me" (42–43) [255]; and "how did it come about that that letter, which should have remained in the Mother Superior's possession, passed later into that of my brothers-in-law?" (44) [256]. Sister Ursule, Suzanne's one friend in the convent, fears similar exposure from the making public of her letters. Consigning a packet of her own old letters to Suzanne, she says, "I have never been able to make up my mind to part with [them], though it was dangerous to keep them and upsetting to read them. Alas, they are almost blotted out by my tears. When I am no more you must burn them" (115) [323]. Correspondents in *La Religieuse* fear a demystification—to use the opposite of Diderot's term for the hoax played on Croismare—of their life stories, and each tries to ensure that her story not come to light.

If demystification is what letter writers fear in *La Religieuse*, it is precisely what the *préface-annexe* accompanying the novel purportedly attempts to achieve. The *préface-annexe* ostensibly provides the letters between Diderot and Croismare that culminated in the composition of *La Religieuse*. Its rather contradictory title indicates something that comes before and yet is added on to a text. In fact, as Dieckmann has shown, this rather accurately describes how the *préface-annexe* came to be written. In his article "The Preface-annexe of *La Religieuse*," Dieckmann shows, from a reading of extant manuscripts, that the composition of the novel was actually concurrent with Diderot's mischievous correspondence. Because Diderot made several additions and corrections to the *préface-annexe*, Dieckmann believes that contrary to the way it appears in the autograph manuscript, the novel was intended to be published along with it.

If Dieckmann is correct in believing that the *préface-annexe* was always meant to form part of *La Religieuse*, this complicates significantly the already problematic relationship between duplicitous and self-referential narrative in *La Religieuse*. The *préface-annexe* raises the question of demystification, and by that I mean the laying bare of the work's mechanics or fictive apparatus. It exposes the art and craftwork that went into the novel's composition. Early readers of Diderot's novel, in particular Devaines and Naigeon, complained that publishing the *préface-annexe* along with Suzanne's story drastically undermined a serious piece of social criticism, not to mention the fact that it ruined the reader's pleasure of getting lost in the illusion of fiction.[34] This reproach, which echoes Vauvenargues' and seems to anticipate Robert's use of the "as if," implies that once the author's technique is visible and the illusion of realism is gone, the pleasure or utility one can derive from a work is destroyed. Naigeon believed that including the *préface-annexe* vitiated reader interest, as well as "this aspect of truth so difficult to obtain in all the arts of imitation, and which particularly distinguishes this work of Diderot's."[35] Devaines, Dieckmann reports, believed that a work of fiction is like a building, and "once the building is erected the scaffolding has to be removed" (21).

The attitude that fiction's conventions must always remain invisible if a work is to survive was not uncommon. In 1774 one of Diderot's contemporaries, Baculard d'Arnaud, wrote: "As soon as the lie betrays itself, it loses its seduction; the interest it had excited fades, and reason, restored to all the severity of its judgment, critiques and pronounces in some fashion against the pleasure of sentiment: once the illusion is destroyed, the author completely misses his object."[36] Arnaud believes that novelists only retain power over their readers as long as their works seem to refer to an external reality. Once it becomes clear that novels deal in lies—that is, fiction—they lose their appeal. This attitude betrays a fundamental belief that fictional texts must at all costs hide their fictitiousness if they are to survive. Novelists in the eighteenth century went to great lengths, as we have seen, to claim veracity for their works, and criticisms like Arnaud's and Devaines' show the belief that one should valiantly struggle to maintain what was so hard won. When authors insist on including in their novels the proof of their fictitiousness, this argument goes, they cannot expect to be taken seriously.

Diderot obviously wanted to be taken seriously, but it seems he also desired to ensure his readers' appreciation of his craftwork. That is, he wished to display his narrative skills, but he also hoped to avoid the sort of dismissal of his work that Arnaud's critique of self-conscious narrative called for. Thus, Diderot's novel is caught in the conflict between narrative duplicity and narrative self-

[34] See Dieckmann, "The Preface-annexe," p. 21.
[35] *Œuvres de Denis Diderot*, ed. J.-A. Naigeon, vol. XII, pp. 285–96, cited by Dieckmann, "The Preface-annexe," p. 21.
[36] Arnaud, *Nouvelles historiques*, pp. i-ii.

referentiality. We can see Diderot's conflicting ideas on what novelistic representation should accomplish in his "Eloge de Richardson," in which he praises the author of *Clarissa* and *Pamela* for his ability to depict in a strikingly accurate manner the world about him. Diderot recognized that the word "novel" carried with it the baggage of seventeenth-century fiction and thus unfavorably predisposed readers toward the genre; he believed, as did Mme de Lafayette before him, that a new word was needed. "By novel, we have up until now understood a fabric of chimerical and frivolous events, the reading of which is dangerous for one's taste and for one's morals. I would like us to find another word for Richardson's works, which elevate the spirit, touch the soul, express the love of goodness, and which we also call novels" (29). There was nothing wrong, in Diderot's opinion, with novels—the problem was that they had a bad reputation. In his praise for the English writer he attempts to palliate the offense of writing novels by showing how valuable they can be when well written. Diderot admits to turning to Richardson's novels for technical instruction, but the Englishman's craftwork was so minutely refined that Diderot lost sight of it, just as Arnaud might have wished: "Several times I began reading *Clarissa* for my own instruction; but just as often I forgot my intention by the twentieth page" (40). In the midst of his praise for Richardson and his ability to depict reality in a seemingly unmediated manner, however, is Diderot's admission that reading Richardson's technically perfect novels stymied him:

> Richardson's genius has completely stifled any that I might have had. His illusions incessantly wander in my imagination; if I want to write, I hear Clementine's appeal; the shadow of Clarissa appears before me . . . dear Miss Howe, while I converse with you, the years of labor and the harvest of laurels pass; and I proceed toward the last term, without attempting anything that might recommend me to the future. (48)

Richardson's genius frustrates Diderot's attempts to write. Unable to locate the source of Richardson's literary skills in a host of novels that seem to efface the craftsmanship from which they are composed, Diderot confesses his inability to imitate Richardson.

If Richardson's inimitable narrative style thwarted Diderot's attempt to produce similarly seamless mimetic works, the publication of the *préface-annexe* seems to represent Diderot's effort to inspire his readers not to be fooled by his narrative mimesis, but to recognize his genius and craftsmanship. As if to suggest that he worked too hard on the novel to have his efforts go unappreciated, Diderot appears to unmask the fiction designed by his own admission to captivate the audience. By including the *préface-annexe*, Diderot pretends to bare the origin of *La Religieuse*'s fictitiousness; he reveals that he, and not some external reality, lies at the heart of the work's composition. Unwilling to admit, however, that in stripping the work of its referential function he destroys its seductive appeal, Diderot claims to have been totally enthralled by *La Religieuse*. In a letter to Mme d'Epinay, he wrote: "I began to work on *La Religieuse*, and I was still at it at three o'clock in the morning. I am flying through it. It is no longer a letter, it's a book."[37] One particularly famous incident is frequently cited to illustrate Diderot's involvement with his tale. In an episode recorded in the *préface-annexe*, M d'Alainville, a friend of Diderot's, reported that he visited Diderot in his home one day and found him "plunged in sorrow and his face flooded with tears." When he asked what the matter was, Diderot responded: "I am devastated over a story I am writing" (852).

This brief incident seems to suggest that even a tale with absolutely no duplicity left can still move its readers. That is, even the author of this story, who presumably understood its narrative strategy better than anyone else, found it touching. Before we risk falling dupe to another of Diderot's hoaxes, however, we must realize that it was not actually Grimm who reported the d'Alainville incident, but Diderot himself. Diderot merely attributed the story to his friend. This situation, in which author becomes reader reading himself, applies not only to Diderot but, as we have seen, to the merry band of pranksters who gathered at dinner to laugh over their letters to Croismare; it also applies to Suzanne addressing herself in the postscriptum. In each case the author unveils the craft of inventing, yet the unveiling does not, as those who criticized the publication of the *préface-annexe* claimed, nullify the artistic creation; instead, it draws attention to the work *as fiction*. While one might refer to the *préface-annexe* as a demystification of the seduction of Diderot's fiction, as Julie C. Hayes does, this demystification

[37] Letter of November(?) 1760, in Diderot's *Correspondance*, vol. III, p. 221.

does not destroy the fiction; it merely makes readers aware of its artifice. Hayes writes: "The *Préface* presents itself as demystification very much as Suzanne presents herself as wholly true; true or not, it accomplishes at least the goal of throwing the entire previous recital of her woes into yet another different light. By so doing, it continues the process already begun, forcing the realization that what one has read is not what one thought."[38] The *préface-annexe* shows that even with its referentiality refuted and its artifice exposed, a well-wrought piece of fiction can still stand on its own.[39] Each time we see the fabricators of fictions connected with *La Religieuse* reading and commenting on their own work, we are led to believe that since the illusion they are creating is destroyed we can see the conventions on which the fictions rely stripped bare. Yet, although Vauvenargues argues that the destruction of a work's artifice calls for its dismissal, it makes more sense to suggest that such a destruction of artifice calls merely for a reconsideration of the work.

In addition to calling for a reconsideration of their functions and veracity, however, both the *préface-annexe* and Suzanne's postscriptum, like the bizarre letter Suzanne received from her mother, tell the story of the coming-into-being of the text of which they form a part. It is difficult to imagine a tale more self-conscious than one that narrates its own history, but this is precisely what Mme Simonin's letter and the *préface-annexe* purport to do. The *préface-annexe*, as we have seen, relates the hoax at the heart of its existence. In some respects, the *préface-annexe* is merely a chronicle of the hoax played on Croismare. Yet the hoax was not merely that played on the marquis; it extends to any reader of the *préface-annexe* as well. I have already pointed out Diderot's deliberate deception of the preface's reader in his inclusion of the anecdote, supposedly reported by Grimm, that he was found weeping over his own story. The preface's "*mystification*" is more profound than this, however: the concluding remarks of the *préface-annexe* ex-

---

[38] Hayes, "Retrospection and Contradiction in Diderot's *La Religieuse*," p. 240.
[39] In fact, Diderot himself seems to have worried little that his works would be destroyed even by such demystification. In *Jacques le fataliste* we read: "It is quite clear that I am not writing a novel, since I neglect what a novelist would not fail to include. He who takes what I write as the truth would perhaps be less mistaken than he who took it as fiction" (*Œuvres romanesques*, p. 505).

plain why the group of counterfeiters decided to kill Suzanne. Diderot and company had received word that the marquis was preparing an apartment in his château for his daughter who was to leave the convent shortly; in addition, a "maid, who was at the same time to play the role of the young person's governess" (867) was to accompany her. The tricksters presumed this was none other than their Suzanne. The *préface-annexe* continues:

> These thoughts left us no choice concerning the path we had to take; and neither the youth, beauty, nor innocence of Sister Suzanne, nor her sweet and tender soul, able to touch those hearts least inclined toward compassion, could save her from certain death. But since we all shared Mme Madin's feelings for this charming creature, the regrets her death caused us were scarcely any less painful than those of her respectful protector. (867–68)

One can see once again, in his compassion and regrets for Suzanne, the extent to which Diderot seems to have been moved by his fictitious nun. Yet there is one more troubling aspect about this passage, in addition to the fact that Diderot seems to have become perhaps a little too attached to his Suzanne: Mme Madin, with whom everyone presumably agreed and who was supposed to redirect all of Croismare's letters, was as fictional as the nun. No such person ever existed; she was invented for the express purpose of increasing the verisimilitude of the *préface-annexe*.[40] The *préface-annexe*, condemned for demystifying a beautiful and powerful work of fiction, lays bare, finally, absolutely nothing because it contains elements of fiction as well.

Finally, the concluding paragraph of the *préface-annexe* contains a rather troubling statement that casts further doubt on the document's demystifying capabilities. While we had been led to believe that the *préface-annexe* contained the letters that prompted the writing of *La Religieuse*, we read that "if it happens that there are some minor contradictions between the *récit* and the *mémoires*, this is because most of the letters were written after the novel" (868). If this is true, then the entire *préface-annexe*, like the campaign to seduce Croismare, is a hoax as well. It explains nothing at all about the inception of the novel it purports to demystify. The *préface-*

---

[40] See Dieckmann, "The Preface-annexe," p. 34.

annexe, so condemned by Diderot's contemporaries because they felt it unmasked the beauty and utility of the novel it accompanied, is no more firmly rooted in reality than any other fiction.[41]

The *préface-annexe* confronts readers with the illusion that all of the narrative duplicity in the preceding novel has been debunked and laid out in front of them. *La Religieuse* (and I am considering the *préface-annexe* part of the novel) seems to perform an auto-analysis. Yet, for all its ostensible debunking and demystifying of the fiction it caps off, the *préface-annexe*, like Suzanne's *mémoire*, concludes on a rather unstable, irresolute question:

QUESTION FOR PEOPLE OF LETTERS

M. Diderot, after having spent several mornings composing letters that were well written, well thought-out, pathetic, and befitting a novel [*bien romanesques*], spent his days ruining them by deleting, on the advice of his wife and of his partners in crime, everything they contained that was striking, exaggerated, or contrary to extreme simplicity and to exact *vraisemblance*. The result was that if you had picked up the first sort in the street, you would have said, "This is beautiful, quite beautiful," and if you had picked up the others you would have said, "This is quite true." Which are the good letters? Are they those that would perhaps have received our admiration? Or those that would certainly have produced an illusion? (868)

It is highly ironic that the question of truth versus fiction which closes the *préface-annexe* should occur in a document that eschews the difference between (in Dieckmann's words) "the 'real' story and the work of art." By closing *La Religieuse* with a question, challenging readers to identify the difference between the work of art and the real thing, Diderot accomplishes two things. On the one hand he establishes a categorical distinction between letters that are "well written, well thought-out, pathetic, and befitting a novel," and those bereft of "everything they contained that was striking, exaggerated, or contrary to extreme simplicity and to exact *vrai-*

---

[41] Dieckmann remarks: "The *préface-annexe* can no longer be considered as a document which gives the biographical and historical background of *La Religieuse*, the 'true story' behind the 'fiction' of the novel, and it certainly is not a scaffolding which Diderot ought to have removed according to Devaines and Naigeon. . . . The *préface-annexe* is part of the novel, it is as much invention and fable as the novel itself. Diderot subjected it to the same 'literary' revision to which he subjected *La Religieuse*. . . . To be sure, the preface still gives the immediate occasion for the novel, its origin in a trick played on a real person. But soon the trick became part of the overall invention and . . . the line could no longer be drawn between the 'real' story and the work of art" (p. 31).

semblance." Diderot's challenge to readers to distinguish between fact and fiction is ironic not only because it appears in a document which is itself impossible to pin down: the two groups of letters, which the unsuspecting reader would identify as either beautiful or true, were both concocted by the same man in the same context. The letters deemed "true" were produced simply by removing everything that was pathetic or exaggerated from the beautiful letters. The true letters are nothing more than derivations of the beautiful ones. Neither group of letters is more firmly rooted in fact than the other.

On the other hand, the novel's concluding question, like Suzanne's query at the end of her postscriptum, solicits the reader's response to the issue of self-definition. To answer the question is to assume the role of interpretive mastery, to presume to be able to pin the novel down and locate its fictitiousness securely in the camp of either representational or self-referential art. To answer the question "Which are the good letters?" is, then, precisely to miss its point. Posed within the framework of an ironic text that is neither fact nor fiction but an admixture of both, the question is not meant to be taken literally or rhetorically: it is a challenge to readers like Vauvenargues or Arnaud who think there is a flatly determinate difference between the truthful, representational text and the artful, self-referential one. Without further contextual information, trying to decipher fact from fiction in *La Religieuse* is as fruitless as trying to decide whether Suzanne's *mémoire* is true or false. Reading for referentiality instead of contextual self-situation—that is, the conditions narrative establishes for itself—is in this case quite pointless.

To conclude my reading of *La Religieuse*, I will look at the contexts the fictions connected with the novel establish for themselves and the explanations of meaning and the origins framing narrations provide for the narratives framed. We have seen that each narrative the novel relates—whether the hoax played on Croismare, Suzanne's seduction of the marquis, or the demystification of the *préface-annexe*—seems to be exposed by the narrative frame immediately superior to it, and we will see that *La Religieuse*, like the *préface-annexe*, closes on a question. This is because the novel, unlike the letter Suzanne received from her mother, cannot explain its own origins. There is one larger frame of reference, one context which is missing in *La Religieuse*, and if Diderot cannot ask his readers to burn the letter, as his letter writers did to prevent scrutiny of their writing, at least he can mystify them once again with a final destabilizing element.

We have seen that both Suzanne's *mémoire* and the *préface-annexe* close with questions directed to a reader. Suzanne asks whether she is a coquette and whether it is a good idea to try to seduce the marquis, and the final lines of the *préface-annexe* ask whether representational or self-referential narrative is preferable. Both questions reveal the self-referentiality of the narratives in which they occur, and both deal with the power of narrative—that is, the circumstances in which it is most effective in obtaining the desired response. Keeping in mind Dieckmann's discovery that the *préface-annexe* is part of the fictive *récit* of *La Religieuse*, we can see that both questions, in addition, are self-reflective in that they ask whether their own narrative techniques were wisely chosen and put into practice. Suzanne's narrative and the *préface-annexe* exercise the power to theorize themselves and to define themselves—each explains the premises on which it is based, and each interrogates its own internal workings. The powers of fiction to theorize itself and to define itself are two of the three powers Chambers attributes to fiction. The third, he maintains, is fiction's power to specify its own impact.[42] We have seen that the point of *La Religieuse* is the seduction of Croismare—to that end, it is not the veracity of the episodes Suzanne recounts that has interested us, but the effectiveness of her discourse, the means of persuasion at her disposal to convince the marquis of her helplessness. Suzanne's story can only have the desired impact on her reader if she specifies the context in which the tale is to be read; she does this, as we have seen, by calling it a *mémoire* and by inviting the marquis to play the role of the fatherly reader who will recognize the threat to pa-

---

[42] Chambers writes: "But whereas the power of a text to theorize itself and the power of self-definition are analytic powers, the claim to seductive power is a claim of perlocutionary force, another *kind* of power. It is not self-directed but other-directed; and it is definable as the power to achieve authority and to produce involvement (the authority of the storyteller, the involvement of the narratee) within a situation from which power is itself absent. If such power can be called the power of seduction, it is because seduction is, by definition, a phenomenon of persuasion: it cannot rely on force or institutional authority ('power'), for it is, precisely, a means of achieving mastery in the absence of such means of control" (pp. 211–12).

ternity Suzanne's humiliations represent. Yet, how can we determine the perlocutionary force of her *mémoire* on another reader? How can anyone—Suzanne included—ever predict with absolute certainty a reader's response to a text?

The only means at our disposal of answering that question involve analyzing the context she provides in which the marquis is supposed to read her *mémoire*. The context here is that of authority and mastery, and Suzanne attempts to seduce the marquis by depicting a threat to the patriarchy, the structure of authority with which she assumes he identifies. Suzanne provides the marquis, in effect, with the frame of reference in which to read her story. As disinterested, detached readers, we can see the formation of that context or frame of reference because our point of view is broader than the marquis'—we read, that is, both framed and framing narratives, Suzanne's *mémoire* and her introduction and postscriptum, and we are quickly led to believe in the superiority of our own point of view. As we have seen, each framed narrative in *La Religieuse* is meant to be read as a transparent narrative by the intended narratee, and each framing narrative reveals how the narrative it brackets can and should be read self-referentially. Diderot's original letters to Croismare, for example, were duplicitous missives meant to fool him, but the explanatory narrative bracketing these letters asks us to appreciate the art with which they were composed. Each narrative level in *La Religieuse* provides the context and the reading strategies for the level it embraces.

By situating the context in which its various narratives need to be read, *La Religieuse* accomplishes a seduction of its readers in precisely the same way that Suzanne planned to seduce the marquis. Ironically, it is by putting the marquis in the position of authority that she can gain power over him, and the seduction *La Religieuse* undertakes of its readers operates in a parallel fashion. Because readers see all the contexts in which the various narratives in the novel are produced, their own interpretive mastery, relative to that of the novel's internal readers, seems assured. In addition, the questions with which both Suzanne's *mémoire* and the *préface-annexe* close elicit the reader's masterful interpretation; they wait for him or her to give the last word on what they are and how they work. In both seductions accomplished in *La Religieuse*, the victim or object is seduced by being led to believe in the power and authority of the masterful position occupied. The reader's response is controlled by dictating the context in which the tales are to be read.

Both the position of power in which *La Religieuse* places its readers and the interpretive mastery it allows them to feel remain in effect as long as they are provided with the re-contextualization of each of the novel's framed narratives. Each such re-contextualization consists of a reduplication of the language in which the framed narrative was originally related. For example, the frame that Suzanne's introduction and postscriptum provide for her *mémoire* reproduces verbatim the framed narrative—the *mémoire* itself. Likewise, the frame represented by the *préface-annexe* provides a word-for-word transcription of the letters that were originally supposed to have been sent to the real Croismare. Unlike many framed narratives, such as Bernardin de Saint-Pierre's *Paul et Virginie*, in which the framed narrative is reported in indirect discourse by the frame's narrator, in *La Religieuse* narrators in framing narratives reduplicate the language of the narratives they frame. The various narrative levels in *La Religieuse* consist essentially of narrators directly quoting other narrators as part of their own narratives.

It is important to consider the reduplication and representation of language in *La Religieuse* because of the constant demystifications the novel purports to undertake. Each demystification consists in causing the reader to view an originally referential, transparent narrative as a self-referential one in which the *récit*, and not the *histoire*, is emphasized. To this end, then, *La Religieuse*, like *La Princesse de Clèves*, highlights readers' interpretive possibilities, and the point of the work becomes not the representation of some external reality, but the situations in which narrators tell stories and readers interpret them. Yet, if each of *La Religieuse*'s framing narrations—Suzanne's introduction and postscriptum, as well as the *préface-annexe*—reveals its own origins by demystifying the narratives framed, there is still a demystification missing, the one that would explain how Suzanne's *mémoire* was detoured to appear in the form in which we read it. As Michel Foucault points out, "One could say . . . that one letter is missing in *La Religieuse* (the one in which should be told the story of the letter that would no longer have to tell of its own adventures)."[43]

Foucault is concerned with narrative reproducing both the language and the conditions in which tales are told, what he calls "the very opening of language on its system of auto-representation" (47). Reduplication of language occurs in two ways in *La Religieuse*: the first is the transcription of a framed narrative by a framing one, as we have just seen, and the second is in the duplication of letters transmitted by characters in Suzanne's *mémoire*. Concentrating on the letter Suzanne receives from her mother that narrates its own transmission, Foucault considers this episode not a *bévue*, but a "sign, above all a sign that language tells its own story: that the letter is not the letter, but the language that redoubles it in the same system of reality (since this language speaks at the same time as the letter and it uses the same words and it has the identical body: it is the letter itself in flesh and blood)" (47).[44] Foucault is describing representation that imitates its object directly because it is language turning back on itself. This is precisely what each framing narrative in *La Religieuse* does with respect to the narrative it frames. The only difference between a text and a replication of that text is imperceptible, Foucault indicates; if the difference does become apparent, he continues, it is only through a snag (*accroc*) of language, a snag that would somehow indicate to readers that they are reading not an original document, but a mere copy. The linguistic doubling to which Foucault refers produces an exact replica of the imitated model, differing only if a snag in the language can be perceived. We can only perceive such a snag if there is a recontextualization of the narrative's situational self-referentiality. That is, we need a larger context or framework in which to consider the tale in question.

---

[43] Foucault, "Le Langage à l'infini," p. 47.

[44] Foucault continues: "And yet it is absent, but not through the effect of this sovereignty we afford the writer; this language absents itself, rather, by crossing the virtual space in which language makes itself an image for itself and crosses the limit of death through a redoubling in the mirror. Diderot's '*bévue*' is not due to an overly pressing authorial intervention, but to the very opening of language on its system of auto-representation: the letter in *La Religieuse* is only the analogon of the letter, similar to it in all aspects save one: it is its double, but imperceptibly temporarily displaced (a displacement becoming visible only through a snag [*accroc*] in language)" (p. 47).

The access we have to each narrative's context makes visible the snags Foucault describes. By taking a duplicitous narrative (one meant to lure the narratee into belief) and making it self-referential (one that calls attention to its artistry) the larger narrative contexts provided for each seduction in *La Religieuse* rob the embedded narrative of duplicity and make obvious its rhetorical function. The apparent transparency of the language is destroyed, and a narrative that communicated *by means of* language now represents instead *language* itself. This is how *La Religieuse* attempts to specify its own impact: by identifying for readers the context in which their interpretation is superior to that of the seduction's *destinataire*.

Each demystification connected with *La Religieuse* purports to reveal the reality behind appearances. "Any discourse concerned with meaning attempts to bring appearances to an end—this is its lure and its imposture," Baudrillard writes (78). Putting an end to appearances is a lure, however, precisely because each narrative can always be re-contextualized. The final recontextualization in *La Religieuse* we need to consider occurs almost imperceptibly, but it radically shifts the work's narrative frame of reference. Each of the victims seduced by the letters he receives feels confident that he has been given the complete story. It is only because we read letters unavailable to the victims that we can spot where they went wrong. What we do not see is the information others may have to which we are not party. But, near the end of the novel there occurs an interruption in Suzanne's *mémoire*. We cannot positively identify the voice that interrupts, but the interruption accomplishes, as did Suzanne's postscriptum and the *préface-annexe*, a radical shift in the narrative perspective because it reveals that there remains information unavailable to us. "Here the memoirs of Sister Suzanne become disconnected, and what follows is only notes for what apparently she meant to use in the rest of her tale. It seems that the Superior went mad, and the fragments I am about to transcribe must refer to her unhappy state" (179) [384]. The third person who breaks into Suzanne's story calls what Suzanne had written *mémoires*. This verifies the original premise of *La Religieuse*, that a young nun is writing to the marquis for help and protection. However, the role of this new voice is not merely one of verification. Rather, this external narrator showing itself for the first time at the very end of *La Religieuse* forces a reconsideration of the relationship between narrator and character. Up until this moment in the novel, we had been led to believe that the narrator and the principal character were one and the same person. What had appeared to be the framing narration, Suzanne's brief introduction in which she explains why she is writing and her postscriptum in which she reconsiders her work, is now revealed to be itself a framed narration, bracketed by the external narrator's commentary. Narrator and principal character are now radically separated, and we realize that this new narrator tells more than any of the characters in the narrative knows.[45] What the external narrator tells, however, is not without problems, and like the *préface-annexe* it actually problematizes more than it clarifies.

Besides verifying that Suzanne's tale is indeed a *mémoire*, the external narrator also acknowledges that Suzanne had planned to write a *récit* later on. In other words, his phrase "what follows is only notes for what apparently she meant to use in the rest of her tale" refers back to Suzanne's introduction ("The Marquis de Croismare's reply, if he does reply, will serve as the opening lines of this tale. . . . I thought that the summary [*abrégé*] at the end, as well as the profound impression I shall keep as long as I live, would suffice to bring [the events] back to my mind with accuracy" (21) [235]). Here we have a narrator who is doing no more than reading and commenting on the text he has brought to our attention. However, the last line of his interjection—"and the fragments I am about to transcribe must refer to her unhappy state"—raises some extremely problematic questions. Who is the "I"? Are the fragments he is transcribing exactly the same as the *abrégé* Suzanne had indicated terminates her *mémoire*?

They cannot be. If they were, the external narrator's interruption would be completely pointless. Suzanne had mentioned in her introduction that an *abrégé* would conclude her *mémoire*; thus, unless the fragments transcribed by the third-person narrator differ in some meaningful way from the ones Suzanne wrote, the external narrator's interruption accomplishes nothing, save indicate his very presence. The presence of this particular bracketing narrator differs from every other one we saw, however, because it is not clear whether he, like they, reduplicates the exact language of the framed narrative. With his concluding remark, "It seems that the Superior went mad, and the fragments I am about to transcribe must refer to her unhappy state," a structuring intentionality completely divorced from the dynamics of the original *mémoire* appears. That is, the narrator admits that the fragments he transcribes *seem* to provide the link to Suzanne's "unhappy state"; it is unclear whether he transcribed everything as he received it, or whether he selected from among many fragments only those that would form the link to Suzanne's unhappiness, giving the story a rounded totality because it makes sense. Before his interruption we might have expected a time, after the accomplishment of Suzanne's *récit*, when story would join telling. That is, the marquis' response to Suzanne's *mémoire*, included in Suzanne's *récit*, would bridge the temporal gap between Suzanne's writing for help and her receiving it.[46] The rhetorical effectiveness of Suzanne's tale would be manifest. Now, however, with the intervention of an external narrator, we see that such a joining is impossible. The movement of the tale from Suzanne to the marquis and back to Suzanne has been short-circuited, and we have no idea whether Suzanne's tale has merely been reframed and re-contextualized, or rewritten for this narrator's own unexplained purposes.

In fact, it seems logical to suggest that the "I" who interrupts Suzanne's memoir is none other than Grimm—or Diderot's rewriting of Grimm—since the only other "I" in the work outside of the memoir belongs to him ("This remarkable bit of mischief took a completely different turn, as you will see in the correspondence that I will place before your eyes" [850]). If this is so, not only does this brief intervention fracture the integrity of Suzanne's memoir, but it causes the ostensible provenance of the novel—the attempt to get the real Croismare back to Paris—to erupt into the novel's *récit*. Consequently, the tension between mimetic language and self-conscious literary language seeps out of the *préface-annexe* and into the text of Suzanne's memoir; now, however, it is no longer a question of Suzanne's indecision concerning which strategy to em-

---

[46] This is a not uncommon characteristic in eighteenth-century fiction, particularly in framed narratives. The narrator closes the story by tying it to the situation in which it is being told. Lesage's *Gil Blas* closes in this way, as does perhaps the best-known example of this phenomenon, *Manon Lescaut*. Des Grieux begins his story by describing his youth, and finishes at that point, elaborated by the framing narrator, at which he met the latter and began his tale.

ploy. Rather, the authoritative voice of the "I" reminds readers both that the entire text is a seduction and that the work is incomplete. As one might expect, however, the suggestion that the work is incomplete also finds its contradiction in the *préface-annexe*:

> But this novel only ever existed in fragments, and there it remained: it is lost, just like an infinity of other productions of a rare man, who would have immortalized himself with twenty masterpieces if, had he used his time better, he had not abandoned it to a thousand indiscreet people whom I summon to the last judgment, where they will respond before God and man for the crime of which they are guilty. (And I, who know M. Diderot, would simply add that he finished this novel and that these are the memoirs themselves that you have just read, where you must have witnessed how important it is to be suspicious of friends' praises. (851)

The novel only ever existed as fragments but this is how Diderot designed it and carried it out: to be an ambivalent and equivocal narrative representation that eschews classification as either a literary or an exegetical text, as well as one that undermines traditional notions of narrative completion or closure.

The point of *La Religieuse* is not to train readers how to distinguish between these different kinds of discourse. Rather, it is to expose the fruitlessness of the effort to make such arbitrary distinctions. The frequent calls for reader reconsideration which occur in Suzanne's postscriptum, the *préface-annexe*, and the external narrative voice that creeps in near the end of Suzanne's *mémoire* admonish readers to interrogate both the teller and the told, the narrative's self-contextualizing as well as what it claims to be about. Thomas Kavanagh asks the pointed question, "How can a novel be about something, how can telling a story be about anything other than the very act of its telling?"[47] *La Religieuse* is about readers reading and tellers telling. Cautioning readers, as did *La Princesse de Clèves*, to be wary of the dulling effects of relying on narrative convention, *La Religieuse* offers readers strategies for reading itself, continually seeking out and constantly muting the voice that might unite all levels of its signification.

The seduction that Suzanne's memoir is designed to perform on her reader mobilizes the threats to religious and social authority I

---

[47] Kavanagh, *The Vacant Mirror*, p. 155.

described in Chapter 7. Her duplicity draws attention to one of the most unstable elements in the bourgeois patriarchal order—its ability to control feminine sexuality and, consequently, to protect the bequeathing of name and fortune. In addition, the hardships she describes having undergone make manifest some of the fundamental contradictions in the bourgeois social regime: Suzanne's presumed illegitimacy and her repeated attempts to leave the convent reveal the tenuous stability of a patriarchal order based on the verifiable legitimacy of progeny. Everywhere in *La Religieuse* moral issues become economic or political ones. Nuns in charge of her turn religion into venality as they battle for the money in her dowry; and, as a commodified and disposable object of exchange, Suzanne has a specific value for each of the maternal figures as she is sacrificed for the domestic stability of the Simonin family, the financial viability of each of the convents she inhabits, and the sexual gratification of the unnamed superior. Suzanne is, however, both an embarrassment and a disruption; because she has no rightful or formally recognized position in society, she generates a tension disarticulating the bourgeois order's economic, social, and moral codes. Effectively outside of the bourgeois family structure, divorced from conventional forms of labor or production, and removed from traditional conceptions of sexuality and morality, Suzanne remains exterior to bourgeois patriarchy's modes of subjection and, consequently, the forms of subjectivity it authorizes. She depicts herself subject not to the law of the father, but to a dissolute feminine economy on the periphery of the dominant economic and religious orders. Thus, her deliberately contrived seduction places the marquis in the position of having to defend the bourgeois patriarchal order by assuming a protective fatherly stance in order to deliver her from people and institutions that threaten not only her but the entire social fabric.

Yet, the novel's demystification of Suzanne's seduction as well as of its own origins recontains Suzanne and returns interpretive control to the very social order her tale threatens to destabilize. This is because the process of demystification—showing the origins and the strategies of seduction—automatically refers readers to a hermeneutic tradition dictating how texts acquire meaning and legitimacy. Demystification, in other words, translates ambivalent or unstable literary language into an analytical discourse reflecting contemporary theories and practices of literature and its interpretation. The framing narratives of *La Religieuse* mobilize the distinction between duplicitous or mimetic language and exegetical or analytic language; this situates the work squarely in the middle of the debate concerning the political and moral advisability of allowing literary works to lead unsuspecting and impressionable readers away from received truths. At the same time, framing narratives that explain the origins and operations of seduction replace duplicity with elucidative reason, objectifying previously transparent conventions of *vraisemblance* as opaque rhetorical strategies. By providing readers with the means to appreciate the craftwork involved in Suzanne's and the novel's seduction, the work effectively expands its own general accessibility and it makes the literary text available as an object of cultural exchange by firmly anchoring it to contemporary aesthetic values.

More crucial than translating the specific literary ambivalences of *La Religieuse* into the material of contemporary aesthetic debates, however, is the manner in which the novel reaffirms the philosophical and ideological currents prevalent in the mid-eighteenth century. By continually enlarging the contexts in which its different framed narratives can be read, up to and including that established by the unidentified "I" who interrupts Suzanne's memoir, the work eschews any conception of truth not immediately rooted in a specific context. Effectively illustrating Maillard's maxim that "nothing is true about anything," Diderot's novel adopts the materialist position, built by Enlightenment philosophers and his forebears in fiction alike, that reality is quantifiable and subject to taxonomic description which different types of rhetoric and discourse can provide. By the same token, however, if *La Religieuse* investigates the conditions of meaning, it also provides the specific ideological context for establishing the validity of meaning. By continually exhorting a contextual specificity requisite to the interpretation of each successive framed narrative and consequently the truth it contains, demystification aligns itself with existing hermeneutic practices. Since the demystified truth always appears available if a valid context is specified, its earlier alienation abates, and it assumes a transmissible and readily accessible form, producing a continuum with bourgeois material and ideological culture.[48]

---

[48] In their book *Dialectic of Enlightenment,* Max Horkheimer and Theodor Adorno theorize the relationship between reason and ideology by noting that "the technical process, into which the subject has objectified itself after being removed

La Religieuse reasserts the hegemony of the social order Suzanne implicitly attacks by causing bourgeois patriarchal ideology to serve as the normalizing discourse demystifying the heroine's seduction. Affirming the universality of virtues contingent upon contained or confined feminine sexuality, the novel abstracts women as a social force contesting the validity of those virtues and consequently the legitimacy of the dominant social order. In its continued demonstration that truth requires a social context in order to be valid and socially useful, the work eschews any suggestion of a transcendental subject of knowledge or interpretation, demolishing the last vestige of such a possibility by falsifying the ostensibly historical account of how the novel itself came to be. *La Religieuse* allows its title character temporarily to disarticulate the moral codes of religion and feminine chastity from the economic order of legitimate patriarchal bequest of property; the demystification of its own fictitiousness, however, reintegrates the fragmented moral, political, and economic discourses into an apparently seamless language whose purpose lies in reaffirming the bourgeois social order "naturellement et sans artifice."

---

from the consciousness, is free of ambiguity of mythic thought as of all meaning altogether, because reason itself has become the mere instrument of the all-inclusive economic apparatus" (p. 30).

Chapter 9

Justine and the Discourse of the
(Other) Master

In the preceding chapters we saw two heroines engaged in processes
of seduction that were also processes of self-definition. Mme de
Clèves seduced both her husband and her would-be lover and kept
them at a distance, striving resolutely to conform to her mother's
image of her while trying to recapture the security her mother's
stories promised her. Suzanne Simonin attempted a verbal representation of herself that would induce Croismare to come to her aid,
but uncertain that her narrative tactics would work, she calls in her
postscriptum for an interpretation of who or what she really is.
Mme de Clèves and Suzanne Simonin attempt to seduce by projecting images of themselves. Learning efficacious discursive strategies
from the people around them, they try to appear other than they
really are, and in the process they question the reliability of the
discursive structures that provide stability to their social milieus. In
the marquis de Sade's *Justine ou les malheurs de la vertu* we will
see another protagonist employ the discursive mode she learns from
others. She not only represents herself with the express intent to
seduce, but she threatens the security of bourgeois patriarchy's system of values.

Since Suzanne Simonin's *mémoire* contains a host of illogical or
impossible events that nevertheless contribute to her tale's pathos,
she asks the recipient of the document to burn it after reading it. In
a letter to Marc Antoine Reynaud, who had written against many
of the *philosophes*, most notably d'Alembert, the marquis de Sade
makes a similar request: "They are currently printing one of my
novels, one which is far too immoral to be sent to a man as wise,
pious, and decent as yourself. I needed money, and my editor asked

me to write something really spicy, so I made it capable of defiling the devil. It's called *Justine ou les malheurs de la vertu*. Burn it, and do not read it if by chance it falls into your hands. I disavow it."[1] Unlike Suzanne, Sade is not worried that his correspondent will discover his narrative tricks; rather, he is ashamed of this work written in haste when he needed money.[2] But Sade was not alone in calling for the burning of his books. Virtually all his contemporaries except Restif de la Bretonne—who wrote his share of scandalous works—demanded the incineration of his work, and the authors of the *Tribunal d'Apollon*, an eighteenth-century periodical, were torn between demanding the burning of the books and the burning of the author himself.[3] The *Journal général de France* recommended that mature men read *Justine* to see how far human imagination could go, and burn it immediately after: "You, mature men, whom experience and the calming of all passions have placed above danger, read it in order to see just how far the delirium of human imagination can go; but immediately afterwards, throw it into the fire. This is advice you will give yourselves if you have the strength to read the book completely [*entièrement*]."[4]

Sade's contemporaries condemned him for having depicted everything, even the most hideous crimes. Fearing that the portrayal of acts never before seen in novels would lead to their widespread acceptance, people called for the censoring of *Justine*, a novel "in which nothing had been spared."[5] Interestingly enough, Sade's critics frequently gave plot synopses and summaries of the offensive scenes in their reviews, which suggests that it was not the acts that should be censored, but the specific narrative style used to describe them.[6] That narrative style evokes contemporary standards of *vraisemblance*, and as I will argue in more detail below, much of *Justine*'s rhetorical power derives from the contradiction between its naturalistic, first-person narrative style, and the preposterous ex-

[1] Sade, *Œuvres complètes*, vol. XII, p. 488.
[2] In 1797, in the preface to *La Nouvelle Justine*, Sade denied authorship of *Justine*, claiming that a foppish friend to whom he had given the larger manuscript made excerpts and published them in the form of a novel, calling it *Justine*.
[3] *Tribunal d'Apollon*, 2, no. 10 (1799), pp. 193–97. See also Françoise Laugaa-Traut, *Lectures de Sade*, pp. 53–55.
[4] Cited in *Œuvres complètes*, vol. II, p. 481.
[5] *Journal des Arts, des Sciences et de Littérature*, no. 79, 19 Aug. 1800, p. 114, cited by Laugaa-Traut, p. 56.
[6] See Laugaa-Traut, p. 55.

periences its principal narrator undergoes. Sade's unfettered and luxuriant use of language and narrative and the response they generated consequently provide us with a working definition of pornography in the late eighteenth century. Pornography is the representation of that which should not be represented; it either contradicts the expressed moral and political positions of the dominant social group—which is not the same thing as contradicting the actual or lived positions of that group—or it articulates the site of intense social and political conflict within a social structure. Pornography is, thus, always *invraisemblable* to the extent that it never portrays things as the discursively dominant class expressly states they should be. Pornography attempts to leave nothing to the imagination; it tries to tell everything. The one thing it must not reveal, however, is its own tenuous relationship to truth. Pornography ostensibly bares all and gives its readers a glimpse of the naked truth. If, unlike ideologically invested representation, it does not attempt to suppress information, in claiming to tell the truth it hides the fact that truth is a social and linguistic construct. As I intend to show, the principal discursive strategies delineated in *Justine*, strategies attributed to the logic of vice and to the logic of virtue, both claim for themselves privileged access to truth.

Unlike the novels examined in the previous chapters, *Justine* ostensibly hides nothing. It is based on the idea that telling everything is the best policy. The conventions of fiction, including but not limited to *vraisemblance*, were clearly too constraining for Sade in his attempt to expose everything. Yet, the only means at his disposal to convey his message was the language of the day. Sade used the novel form in his attempt to tell the truth, and despite his wish to break with previous modes of representation, he was still subject to the genre's formal limitations.[7] As we will see, the people who torment Justine try to tell everything as well. In their quest for liberation from the conventions restricting their pleasures, they attempt to conflate word and deed, language and referent. Since, as we will see, their pleasure depends on violation, they need to ensure their victims' complete understanding of all aspects of their

[7] In *Sade romancier*, Alice Laborde writes that "all the while attempting to show the limits of the literary conventions his predecessors employed, [Sade] nevertheless borrows from the French and British fictive patrimony some tried and true techniques: dialogues, portraits, and description, which he systematically exploits" (p. 9).

transgressions, including the philosophical aspects. It is for this reason that they attempt to explain everything before they act. If something remains unsaid, violation might be incomplete. They, too,
however, are constrained by the formal limitations of the language
they use. Despite their claims to escape the constraints of conventional morality, they remain as bound by it as are the victims they
abuse. When it is her turn to tell the story of her life, Justine reproduces in minute detail everything ever said or done to her, and she
does so using the rhetoric employed by the people who abused her.
Unlike her tormentors, however, Justine refuses to tell everything.
She indicates to her audience that some portion of her tale remains
unsaid, and by holding back some aspects of her tale, Justine attains a narrative mastery the significance of which I will address
below.

Despite critics' claims that *Justine* is a novel "in which nothing
has been spared," the narrator who opens the work before handing
narrative responsibility over to Justine implicitly addresses the possibility of achieving narrative mastery, the complete discursive control over the articulation and interpretation of texts. In the first
sentence of the novel, he disavows the feasibility of representing
the world completely.

> The very masterpiece of philosophy would be to develop the means
> Providence employs to arrive at the ends she designs for man, and
> from this construction to deduce some rules of conduct acquainting
> this two-footed individual with the manner wherein he must proceed
> along life's thorny way, forewarned of the strange caprices of that
> fatality they denominate by twenty different titles, and all unavail-
> ingly, for it has not yet been scanned nor defined.[8]

It is impossible, the narrator states, to represent everything. People
might be better off if they could understand and explain nature and
thus avoid the "strange caprices" that befall them; so far, however,
no one has succeeded in domesticating nature, or in giving it a
name whereby one could know and comprehend its system. If there
were a masterpiece of philosophy—but the narrator reveals his
skepticism in his use of the conditional mood—it would reveal na-

---

[8] Sade, *Justine ou les malheurs de la vertu* translated as *Justine, or Good Conduct
Well Chastised* in *Three Complete Novels*, p. 457. For the convenience of readers
more familiar with the work in French, page numbers in brackets will refer to the
10/18 edition [p. 13].

ture as final cause, and demonstrate the system according to which it deals with people. The paradox here is that articulating that which escapes naming might make us feel more secure, but even with twenty different names the mysteries of nature still elude our understanding. Naming unveils and simultaneously dissimulates because it establishes specific discursive structures not only as adequate or realistic representations of actual social practice, but also, as we will see, as substitutes for those practices themselves.[9]

In this chapter we will see a series of cruel and vicious people explain in intricate detail their philosophies of life and nature. Justine, their captive audience, resists every word they pronounce. Despite her protests, however, we will see that she learned more than she lets on about their beliefs. Justine appears to be seduced by her captors' discursive practice, so much so that she imitates it, apparently in order to seduce two people into helping her escape the cycle of debauchery into which she has fallen. In the novels we have examined up until now, readers are generally provided with a framework or set of internal narratives that furnish them with more information than any of the work's characters, especially the putatively innocent heroine; readers are led to believe in their own interpretive superiority, relative to that of the work's internal readers. *Justine* purports to be a didactic work intended to teach readers the benefits of virtue and the horrors of vice. Readers begin the work on firm moral footing, instructed by the narrator that the same principles of virtue to which they ostensibly subscribe will be exemplified in the work. It contains, for instance, "examples of afflicted virtue" that can "restore the spirit" of even the hardiest of miscreants (458) [14]. Reader identification with Justine is thus quickly established. Justine's virtue is repeatedly put to the test, and she says that she will never abandon its precepts. By analyzing Justine's virtue, however, and the discourse she uses to describe it, we will see its ambiguous nature as well as the ambivalent position in which the reader of the novel is placed.

[9] The introduction to *La Nouvelle Justine* is slightly less equivocal concerning the restricting properties of naming. Nearly identical to the first paragraph of *Justine*, the first paragraph of the later novel concludes: "The bizarre caprices of this fortune that people have alternately named Destiny, God, Providence, Fate, and Chance, all of which are defective denominations, each as deprived of good sense as the others, and each communicating to the mind only vague and purely subjective ideas" (I, 25).

In his "Idée sur les romans" (Idea on novels), Sade offers advice to budding novelists. Recommending that they keep their prose natural and avoid grandiloquent moralizing statements, he suggests that if the needs of the story require a character to pronounce a philosophical oration, the author should write the philosophy "without affectation, and without the pretension of [philosophizing]. The author should never moralize; this is better left to the characters." [10] Continuing his advice, Sade tells novelists to adhere to the principles of *vraisemblance*, and to avoid boring readers with repetitive or digressive narratives. "Let your episodes always be born in the depths of the subject [*fond du sujet*], and let them return there," he warns (18). Anyone familiar with Sade's fiction might accuse him of hypocrisy. Few eighteenth-century French novels have characters who philosophize as much or as pretentiously as Sade's. Scarcely any narrate episodes as repetitive as Sade's. Excluding fantastic fiction such as Lesage's *Diable boiteux* or Crébillon's *Le Sopha*, it is hard to think of a novel with a situation less plausible than Justine's living to tell of the tortures she underwent.

Yet, Sade at least followed his own advice concerning the "depths of the subject." *Justine* describes its title character's valiant attempt to retain her virtue—the only quality by which she defines herself—while those around her endeavor to procure pleasure by depriving her of it. In this respect, the novel is about personal autonomy, that of the evil-doers and of Justine herself, as the former seek to dominate all others in their affirmation of self, and the latter tries to retain some vestige of her individuality despite others' repeated attempts to annihilate her. We might gloss Sade's use of the word "*sujet*," then, not as "subject matter," but as "individual." That is, the subject we will be concerned with in this reading of Sade is the speaking subject. The speaking subjects in *Justine* attempt to represent or depict themselves completely. They try to find the verbal representation of self that is so comprehensive and accurate that it fully expresses their reality. They want to define themselves so perfectly that their representation of self will be received by their *destinataires* exactly as they intend. They attempt, in other words, to produce a master discourse of truth and stability. Like the master

---

[10] *Œuvres complètes*, vol. X, p. 18.

discourse we saw in seventeenth-century heroic fiction, the master discourse Sade's characters strive to produce is endowed with an expressive causality. This discursive mode would purport to express the profoundly integrated totality of non-contradictory being the various antagonistic characters experience, but, as we will see, such a discourse *constitutes* a political reality more than it *expresses* one. Strikingly enough, despite the radically antagonistic nature of the relationships in *Justine*, each speaking subject employs the same discursive strategy, one that would reveal in all its splendor the autonomy of the bourgeois individual as eighteenth-century materialist philosophy construed it. I will begin my analysis of the master discourse and the attempt to attain personal autonomy by studying the actions and philosophies of the people who abuse Justine.

The plot of *Justine* begins with a third-person account of the death of the parents of two young girls, Justine and her sister Juliette. The girls are ejected from the convent in which they had been living, and while Juliette decides to make the best of her beauty and follow the road of crime, infamy, and prostitution, Justine prefers to follow the precepts of virtue that had been inculcated in her in the convent. Years pass and Juliette goes on to become rich and famous; her sister's lot is not so easy. For thirteen years she wanders across the countryside looking for someone to take her in and give her respectable work, but each person she meets abuses her physically and emotionally. One day, a certain Mme de Lorsange and her lover, M. de Corville, find themselves watching prisoners being unloaded from a coach. They notice one particularly beautiful young woman, and engage her to tell them the story of how she got to where she was. That young woman, of course, is Justine. Taking over the novel's narration, and under the pseudonym Thérèse, she tells of how in her travels she was systematically and horrendously abused by each person she met. All Justine ever asked for was honest work, shelter perhaps, and a little food, in exchange for her meager services. All she really wanted was to keep her virtue. Yet all the people she met, people whom she calls *libertins*, seemed not only interested in violating her in as unspeakable a manner possible, but in shaking her dogged adherence to the principles of virtue as well. After Justine finishes her long story, all the while having referred to herself as Thérèse, Mme de Lorsange is revealed to be Juliette, the two sisters recognize one another, there is a happy reunion, and they go off to Juliette's château. There Justine is coddled and cared for, receiving the rightful recompense she—and we—had been led to believe awaited unfailing virtue. Then she is struck by lightning and horribly disfigured.

The word Justine uses to denote the perverted villains she encounters is "*libertin*," and before we examine in detail these characters' philosophies, it might be helpful to look briefly at the history of libertinism. In the sixteenth century, the word "*libertin*" denoted a person who did not follow, either in practice or in belief, the laws of religion; it was synonymous with "impious," "unbelieving," and "irreligious." It also connoted a free man, one who submits to no authority. Early in the seventeenth century it came to refer to a "strong spirit, freethinker," and not until the end of the seventeenth century did it come to have the designation Justine uses of a person who is completely unregulated and unchecked in his or her morals or conduct and who does whatever necessary to procure pleasure.

In the early years of the seventeenth century when a *libertin* was still a freethinker, there were various forms of *libertinage*: *scandaleux*, *érudit*, *subtil* and *secret*. The characteristic common to all *libertins* in the early years of the seventeenth century was their aggressive atheism. All *libertins* denied the existence of the deity contemporary organized religions worshiped. If these early *libertins* did not believe in God or in any sort of spiritual tradition, however, most believed in some sort of destiny which organized the universe and continued to exercise some control over it. In 1622, Père Garasse published his *Doctrine curieuse des beaux esprits de ce temps* (Curious tenet of today's cultivated thinkers), and in it we read the *libertins*' articles of faith concerning their disbelief in God and the supreme force they did believe in:

> II. Cultivated individuals do not believe in God except for reasons of *bienséance* and when ordered by the state. . . .
> IV. All things are driven and governed by Fate [*le Destin*], which is irrevocable, infallible, immutable, necessary, eternal, and inevitable for all men, whatever they may do. . . .
> VI. There is no other divinity or sovereign power in the world than NATURE, which we must satisfy in all things without refusing anything to our bodies or to our senses in the exercise of their natural powers and faculties.[11]

[11] Cited by Adam in his *Libertins*, pp. 41–42.

These *libertins érudits* were thinkers and philosophers; they chose not to adhere to organized religion because they found too many contradictions in it. They debated issues such as how an infinite being could limit itself by taking human form, how a supreme goodness could allow itself to punish people with unceasing torture in hell, and how an unchanging being could change its mind by taking into account prayers people addressed to it. These problems are raised in an early text called "Quatrains of a Deist," penned by an unknown hand.[12] The *libertins* saw in organized religion an attempt to form synthetic links among human beings, links that served not to unite them and make their lives richer and easier, but to control them. They believed that religion regulated conduct in a way that was not self-evidently beneficial to the majority of people.

Later on, in 1639, Gabriel Naudé wrote his *Considérations politiques sur les Coups d'Estat*, in which he invited readers to interpret the facts of political and religious life by examining the ideologies upon which each was based. Naudé found that religious beliefs, when sanctioned by political structures, encouraged an insidious form of oppression that played on peoples' fears and ignorance. He believed that by exposing the ideology that maintained the ruling class in power he could subvert it and help liberate the downtrodden. He cites Romulus, Clovis, and Mohammad as the most blatant examples of oppressors of the people. Naudé believed that there was "no other God than nature, no other life than this one, no other hell than prison"[13] and that the kind of superstition encouraged by organized religion established an absolute tyranny over peoples' capacity to reason.

Although they professed no belief in the God of Catholicism, and for this reason called themselves atheists, it is perhaps more appropriate to refer to the *libertins* as theists because of their belief in a cosmic force of Nature. The *libertins* insisted they did not believe in God, and they cited as their reason the impossibility of knowing whether or not a supreme being exists. The early libertines did not object to the belief in God so much as the use of religion combined with politics to keep the disenfranchised out of power, primarily

---

[12] Quatrain 12 (cited by Adam, *Libertins*, p. 92), for example, poses the following question: "Can one conceive of an infinite torment/To please the Eternal One and content his ire/Without supposing Him infinitely cruel/And worse than our own worst tyrants?"

[13] Cited by Adam, *Libertins*, p. 127.

through fear. They criticized occulted political ideologies, the exposure of which they believed would lead to the downfall of extant power structures. They attempted, through their own theorizing, to expose official ideology for the oppressive system they believed it was. Critical thought was one of the major components of the early forms of libertinism and because of their politically unpopular beliefs, *libertins* occupied tight-knit, closed circles.

Later forms of libertinism evolved along the lines of epicureanism. Since the lot of human beings seemed to be sadness and pain, libertines directed their attentions to amusement and pleasure. Unlike their predecessors, these later libertines saw no value in exalting human reason and turned instead to ridiculing it. Since human beings could know nothing, they believed, why waste one's time even bothering with reason? These libertines, whose beliefs were extremely unpopular, avoided any sort of publicity of their philosophy or way of life. Since the libertines felt themselves united in a common front, Joan DeJean writes, "friendship was the most sacred of all values for those fortunate enough to be among the initiate, and the hospitality of this friendship was freely extended to all individuals persecuted because of their intellectual beliefs. By reason of this persecution alone, they won admission to the inner circle." [14]

In the inner circles of *libertinage*, critical thinking and reasoning reigned supreme. Early libertines were readers and interpreters, intent on exposing the dominant ideologies of the day as oppressive. The ties created among people served the reigning political forces, and the *libertins* wanted to break these synthetic ties to allow more natural, essential human bonds to develop. Libertines wanted to profess their strategies and points of view, but were constrained by a political climate that did not favor publication of subversive ideas. *Libertins* took pleasure in thought and reason, and if they wanted their beliefs known it was not because they desired to be imitated and admired, but because they wanted to encourage others to think about the same or similar issues. René Pintard sums up the situation of these *libres penseurs*: "They want to remain themselves, but they fear being imitated; they want to have confidants, but as few disciples as possible. They are astonishing researchers

[14] DeJean, *Libertine Strategies*, p. 16.

who hasten to cover up half of their discoveries. Each one is a sort of Prometheus embarrassed at his audacity; each extinguishes the fire he stole from the gods before transmitting it to others." [15]

The closed and hermetic circle of Sade's libertines resembles that of the previous century in many ways. Sade's libertines usually live in small groups with people of similar mind. They are atheists who believe in some sort of cosmic force of nature, and they disdain societal organization of any sort, especially religion. They believe that the ties uniting people are sterile and constraining, and that only fools agree to be bound by oppressive, confining human law. They want first and foremost to retain or establish their personal autonomy. Sade's libertines differ from seventeenth-century free-thinkers in one significant respect, however: if they do transmit their spark of knowledge concerning political oppression, it is not to further the cause of learning and philosophy, but in order to oppress others and affirm their own authority. Sade's libertines use knowledge and philosophy for antagonistic pleasurable ends. If seventeenth-century epicureans felt that human reason was impotent, the libertines who torment Justine use reason as a very powerful weapon.

Libertine pleasure in *Justine* is an extremely complex matter involving crime, violence, and the articulation of the philosophy informing the pleasurable act. The libertine pleasurable act, however, is not a simple moment of enjoyment or a brief diverting activity. When performed and experienced correctly, that act would annihilate the object of violence and allow libertine subjects complete self-absorption. The perfect or ideal libertine pleasurable act would eradicate the object so completely that not a trace would remain, not even a vestige of the difference between the libertine subject and its object. Libertine pleasure, for which orgasm is merely a woefully inadequate substitute, has its roots in the antagonism defining the polarities "subject" and "object." Its consummation entails not necessarily sexual release, but the annihilation of all personal and political ties that constitute the victim as the libertines' other and which, consequently, block libertines from attaining full subjectivity. As long as there is an other, libertines lack integrity and plenitude, and each crime they commit is an attempt to capture these

[15] Pintard, *Le Libertinage érudit dans la première moitié du dix-septième siècle*, p. 54.

things. La Dubois delivers a cogent treatise on libertine philosophy after she murders three people.

> One must never appraise value save in terms of our own interests. The cessation of the victims' existences is as nothing compared to the continuation of ours, not a mite does it matter to us whether any individual is alive or in the grave; consequently, if one of the two cases involves what in the smallest way affects our welfare, we must, with perfect unremorse, determine the thing in our own favor; for in a completely indifferent matter we should, if we have any wits and are master of the situation, undoubtedly act so as to turn it to the profitable side, entirely neglecting whatever may befall our adversary; for there is no rational commensuration between what affects us and what affects others; the first we sense physically, the other only touches us morally, and moral feelings are made to deceive; none but physical sensations are authentic . . . . But every strong and healthy individual, endowed with an energetically organized mind, who preferring himself to others, as he must, will know how to weigh their interests in the balance against his own, will laugh God and mankind to the devil, will brave death and mock at the law, fully aware that it is to himself he must be faithful, that by himself all must be measured, will sense that the vastest multitude of wrongs inflicted upon others cannot offset the least enjoyment lost to himself or be as important as his slightest pleasure purchased by an unheard-of host of villainies. (491–92) [50–51]

La Dubois claims that others are significant only to the extent that they are tools for libertine pleasure. Devoid of all value save a use value from which libertines can extract pleasure, they are objects of consumption libertines dispose of at will. La Dubois explains that the libertines strive to destroy every vestige of a moral or sentimental link between themselves and other human beings, retaining only the ability to feel the pleasure that arises from making others suffer.[16] La Dubois' speech raises three significant issues that we now have to pursue in our analysis of libertinism: the libertines' need to work violence, their commitment to transgress their victims and dissolve their ties to other people, and the obligation they feel to explain their beliefs in detail to those they violate.

Explanations of their beliefs nearly always precede libertine acts of violence. Sade's libertines tell Justine that they see no logical reason to abide by the precepts of organized religion or community

---

[16] See also Laborde: "The sadistic criminal act, when perpetrated, entails the undeniable alienation of the victim and his or her executioner" (p. 160).

custom, because such precepts stand between them and pleasure. Each libertine Justine meets enthusiastically explains why he engages in the practices he does.[17] All of them try to show Justine the logic of their beliefs and the senselessness of virtue, which, they normally point out, is a specifically political, and not a moral code of behavior. The comte de Bressac, for example, disdains Christianity because it prohibits homosexuality, his sole source of pleasure; he tells Justine that Christianity is simply a collection of "mysteries which cause reason to shudder, dogmas which outrage Nature, grotesque ceremonies which simply inspire derision and disgust" (514) [74]. La Dubois explains to Justine that most social conventions are inequitable because they are based on harsh economic realities designed to keep the rich in power and the poor subservient. Illegal, transgressive acts, she says, are more egalitarian and righteous than legitimate ones. What is more, she continues, the oppressiveness of the wealthy compels the poor to break the law: "The callousness of the Rich legitimates the bad conduct of the Poor; let them open their purse to our needs, let humaneness reign in their hearts and virtues will take root in ours; but as long as our misfortune, our patient endurance of it, our good faith, our abjection only serves to double the weight of our chains, our crimes will be their doing" (481) [39].[18] Despite libertine eloquence, Justine remains steadfast in her choice to remain virtuous. After each explanation of libertine philosophy, Justine sums up her own beliefs by contradicting everything her interlocutor said. When we return to a detailed discussion of Justine and the philosophy of virtue, we will see that Justine has no theories of her own, and that she defines virtue simply as the other of libertinism.

On the face of things, it would appear that the libertines explain their philosophies to Justine in order to persuade her to free herself from the bonds of oppressive virtue and join them in their un-

[17] I am using the masculine pronoun advisedly here. With the possible exception of La Dubois, all of the libertines in *Justine* are male. La Dubois, at the time of her first meeting with Justine, is only an aspiring libertine, and does not yet have the power and the finances requisite for full libertine status.

[18] See also Roland's similar speech: "Learn that though civilization may overthrow the principles of Nature, it cannot however divest her of her rights; in the beginning she wrought strong beings and weak and intended that the lowly should be forever subordinated to the great; human skill and intelligence made various the positions of individuals, it was no longer physical force alone that determined rank, 'twas gold" (p. 668) [239].

bridled quest for pleasure and satisfaction. Nothing, however, could be further from the truth. Libertines explain their philosophies to their victims to articulate the gap separating them: attempting to demonstrate their differences at the most basic level, libertines explain to their victims that the beliefs the latter take for granted as fundamental to the human species are erroneous. Using traditional philosophic language to explicate their beliefs, libertines begin their acts of violation by upsetting the stable grounds of logic and reason on which their victims think they stand. In *Sade mon prochain*, Pierre Klossowski comments on the libertine use of reason and logic, noting that the libertines begin with a description of their crimes, and then continue with a moral explanation of the act. Klossowski argues that libertines use crime as a sort of expressive causality in that they cause each act to express their ideology and way of thinking. Consequently, their violence is always regulated by normative reason.[19] Klossowski separates libertine thoughts and feelings [*intériorité*] from violence and reason [*extériorité*]. He maintains that the libertine act of communicating or of self-expression is effected by both violent actions and philosophical explanations. By showing victims that the acts they undergo are not examples of random violence, but carefully pondered deeds, libertines transgress them not only physically, but intellectually as well. By revealing to them that logic and reason can be tools to promote vice as well as virtue, they disarticulate the bourgeois social order from the language traditionally used both to describe it and to sustain it. Libertines disassemble an entire moral and political fabric by pointing to the tenuousness of its discursive foundation; they undo their victims' identities by pointing to the ideological instability of the political and discursive practices informing their subjectivities.

Physical violence performed on a victim does not consequently suffice in the libertines' quest for autonomy. They need to demonstrate their total disdain for any force greater than their own, and

[19] Klossowski writes (p. 23): "Thus [the libertine] establishes between the perverse way of feeling and the perverse way of acting the double relationship which the expression of his *interiority* proper entertains on the one hand with *the exteriority of the aberrant act* and with the *exteriority of normative reason* on the other. The result is that the distinction between *premeditated sadism and the unpremeditated act* can never be brought about save through the mediation of normative reason. What results is an indissoluble totality in which the tangible (or experience proper to Sade) is obscured all the while discourse justifies the act."

their logical explanations are designed to show that nothing will keep them from exercising their own wills. No power or authority can constrain their desire, and nothing will prohibit them from doing whatever they must for pleasure. Klossowski remarks that the libertine use of reason is logically connected to their atheism because it radically alters their own sense of autonomy. Organized religion is arbitrary and consequently perverse, and Klossowski points out that libertines believe that only individual autonomy can maintain the norms of the human race (20). Reason and atheism are intimately linked because both establish libertine autonomy by denying the existence of anything superior that could inhibit them in their quest for pleasure. In addition to showing Justine that virtue is not natural—that it is based, in other words, on a particular logically explicable political ideology—the libertines show her that they recognize no authority greater than their own and hence feel free to commit any act, no matter how criminal or outrageous others may consider it.

If the libertines use reason and philosophy to demonstrate their ascendancy over any other authority, they also use them to ensure total violation of their victims. Since the violation of others leads to libertine autonomy, they need to explain to their victims each and every aspect of their crimes; if their victims do not understand how they are being violated—if, that is, they retain some of their beliefs and individuality—the libertine cannot achieve total mastery. So, they show their victims that nothing restrains them in their quest for pleasure. Nature itself, they aver, authorizes and encourages their acts. All of the libertines explain to Justine that everything is natural; it is absurd, in their view, to claim that a particular act or belief violates nature's plans, because nature would never allow the existence of any act or belief that was not in accordance with its principles. Humans have the power to change the form of things nature has created, but the power to create and destroy is reserved to nature itself. The comte de Bressac explains to Justine that "man has not been accorded the power to destroy; he has at best the capacity to alter forms, but lacks that required to annihilate them: well, every form is of equal worth in Nature's view" (518) [80]. Thus, murder is not a crime, merely a change in form. The count contends that "it is man's pride alone [that] erects murder as a crime" (519) [81]. The monks at the Benedictine monastery of Sainte-Marie-des-Bois make certain, to ensure total violation of Justine's religious beliefs, that she understands each aspect of Roman Catholic dogma being violated before they force her participation in the mock apparition of the Virgin Mary they stage to inspire people to give alms. Roland the vivisector, after tricking Justine into thinking he wanted her near him so that he could feel the presence of virtue in his household, tells her:

> Do not believe . . . that the kind of deference I showed to the virtue in you proves that I either esteem virtue or have the desire to favor it over vice. Think nothing of the sort, Thérèse, 'twould be to deceive yourself; on the basis of what I have done in your regard, anyone who was to maintain, as consequential to my behavior, the importance or the necessity of virtue would fall into the very largest error, and sorry I would be were you to fancy that such is my fashion of thinking. (544) [107]

Libertines need to dominate the victim in every way, and by explaining their entire ideology to him or her, they can ensure maximum transgression of the victim's body and belief structure. For the libertines, the language of violence is as important as acts of violence.

Klossowski indicates that the libertines attempt to achieve autonomy by annihilating others; he is primarily concerned with the libertines' use of reason to prove to their victims how insignificant they are. Maurice Blanchot agrees that each libertine attempts to become autonomous: "To be Unique, unique in one's class, is the sign of sovereignty." [20] While Klossowski analyzes the libertines' use of reason, Blanchot examines the libertines' need to commit crimes. Early in his study of Sade he makes a statement a libertine might make: "What difference does it make if I have to purchase the most feeble of pleasures with an outrageous collection of crimes? Pleasure satisfies me, it is in me, but the effect of the crime does not touch me—it is outside of me" (19).[21]

Both Klossowski and Blanchot establish a distinction between the libertines' interiority and their exteriority: Blanchot's "pleasure . . . is in me" and Klossowski's "perverse way of feeling" are the libertines' interiority, while the effect of the crimes the libertines commit and the explanations of them are their exteriority. Both Klossowski

[20] Blanchot, *Lautréamont et Sade*, p. 31.
[21] Although he does not indicate so, Blanchot is paraphrasing a statement La Dubois makes in *Justine* (p. 492) [51].

and Blanchot recognize the libertines' paradoxical need for an other in order to be autonomous; for Klossowski that other occupies the role of *destinataire* in the libertine philosophical explanation, and for Blanchot that other is the object of the crime, the recipient of physical violence. In Blanchot's reading of Sade, physical violence performed on the other must be recognized as a crime in order to give the libertines pleasure, and they will do anything for pleasure regardless of the effect it has on others.

Libertine pleasure increases in direct proportion to the havoc they wreak on their victims' minds and bodies. Usually their pleasure comes from inflicting pain on others: "All the while my murderer frolics joyfully," Justine narrates, "his mouth glued to mine, he seems to inhale my pain in order that it may magnify his pleasures" (732) [307]. Roland the counterfeiter tells Justine: "if pleasure-taking is seasoned by a criminal flavoring, crime, dissociated from this pleasure, may become a joy in itself; there will then be a certain delight in naked crime" (680) [252]. Clément, one of the perverted men of the cloth whom Justine encounters at Sainte-Marie-des-Bois, tells her: "Ah, dear girl! you have no idea to what lengths this depravity leads us, you cannot imagine the drunkenness into which it plunges us, the violent commotion in the electrical fluid which results from the irritation produced by the suffering of the object that serves our passions; how one is needled by its agonies! The desire to increase them . . ." (598) [165].

Not infrequently, however, the libertines enjoy having pain inflicted on themselves. After Séverino spanks one of the women in the monastery, for example, Justine says that "armed with a handful of nettles, the eldest woman retaliates upon him for what he has a moment ago done to the child; 'tis in the depths of painful titillations the libertine's transports are born" (573–74) [138]. Libertine pleasure increases in proportion to the harm inflicted, and Blanchot goes so far as to remark that it does not matter to the libertines who undergoes the harm: "For the complete man [*l'homme intégral*], which is the totality of man, no harm can come. If he inflicts pain on others, what voluptuousness! If others inflict pain on him, what pleasure!" [22] Libertines derive pleasure from inflicting pain on others or from causing others to inflict pain

[22] Blanchot continues: "Virtue causes him pleasure because it is weak and he can crush it; vice causes him pleasure because he derives satisfaction from the disorder that results, even if it is at his expense" (pp. 30–31).

on them. It seems, then, that what the libertines call physical pleasure we might more generally call sensation. Clément, no doubt the
most loquacious of all the libertines, explicitly reveals this in his
tirade concerning *les goûts cruels*: "What is the aim of the man who
takes pleasure? is it not to give his senses all the irritation of which
they are susceptible in order, by this means, better and more
warmly to reach the ultimate crisis . . . the precious crisis which
characterizes the enjoyment as good or bad, depending upon the
greater or lesser activity which occurs during the crisis?" (603,
translation modified) [170].

Libertines continually strive to increase the quantity and the intensity of their physical sensations, and because their sensations
frequently include painful ones, it makes sense perhaps to speak
not of libertine pleasure, but of *jouissance*. *Jouissance* is a psychoanalytic term that refers to the pleasure or satisfaction obtained in
the sensation of momentary plenitude or union with an other.
Jouissance is not necessarily pleasurable, in the sense that its effects
are not synonymous with orgasm. *Jouissance* is a kind of gratification experienced with the reduction of tension and the concomitant
annihilation of difference. It can be an unpleasurable gratification
that nevertheless provides the subject with a certain satisfaction—
neurotic symptoms, for example, typically fall into this category.[23]
The subject who experiences *jouissance* sustains a temporary suspension of difference and what Ellie Ragland-Sullivan has called "a
narcissistic pleasure rediscovered in the other." [24]

The difference that *jouissance* annihilates, particularly as it relates to *Justine*, is the complex of psycho-historical characteristics
that represent the subject. I would argue, then, that libertine *jouissance* entails an annihilation of subjectivity, but it is first and foremost the subjectivity of the victim that must be eradicated. Libertine *jouissance* is contingent upon the expunction of any specificity
conferring personal identity on the victim. Once that subjectivity is

[23] In "The Analytic Experience: Means, Ends, and Results," Jacques-Alain Miller
writes of the symptom and its relation to *jouissance*: "It is because you may think
that in spite of suffering from your symptom, in spite of not being satisfied by your
symptom, you may well be satisfied by it without knowing it. And if you lend yourself to interpretation, it is because you already suspect that this satisfaction can be
known, deciphered. This secret satisfaction hidden in unsatisfaction, in displeasure,
is what Lacan has called *jouissance* as distinct from pleasure, distinct from pleasure
because it may be realized as displeasure" (pp. 85–86).

[24] Ragland-Sullivan, *Jacques Lacan and the Philosophy of Psychoanalysis*, p. 303.

identified and extinguished, libertines can indulge in the fleeting narcissistic pleasure of wholeness from which is temporarily absent the necessary dialectical dimension of the other. Libertine *jouissance* is, in other words, the radical obliteration of difference; it is the total denial of any trace linking the subject to a dialectical or constituting other.

The libertines' need to annihilate the other's subjectivity occupies all of their time, but their work is made easier by the fact that the eponymous victim in *Justine* subscribes completely to bourgeois patriarchy's moral code for women. The specifically sexual violence the libertines inflict on her threatens her value to the culture, since her capacity to produce legitimate progeny is endangered; consequently, the sexual violence Justine undergoes is not only physically painful, it dismantles her subjectivity. Raised in a convent and taught to guard her honor with her life, Justine begs not to be deflowered, promising anything if she can keep her virginity. Her training has taught her to prize this one immaterial part of herself above everything else: when she finally does lose her virginity, she says that the man responsible "snatches away what is most dear to me" (502) [62]. The libertines violate not just Justine's body, then, but the entire corpus of virtue inculcated in her by her culture. Omphale, in fact, reveals that libertine pleasure is physical as well as mental. The *idea* of transgression, the feeling of violating the victim's own sense of self, cannot be divorced from inflicting physical pain:

> Their extreme caution protects them against everything. They do not absolutely confine themselves to virgins: a girl who has been seduced already or a married woman may prove equally pleasing, but a forcible abduction has got to take place, rape must be involved, and it must be definitely verified; this circumstance arouses them; they wish to be certain their crimes cost tears; they would send away any girl who was to come here voluntarily; had you not made a prodigious defense, had they not recognized a veritable fund of virtue in you, and, consequently, the possibility of crime, they would not have kept you twenty-four hours. (587) [153]

Libertines employ pain and transgression in order to distance themselves as much as possible from their victims. They strive, in their philosophical diatribes, to show the logical fallacies of virtue and its political nature. Each libertine undertakes to explain his philosophy to Justine, and each explanation is different, but they all share one thing in common: in the rare instances in which Justine poses a question or raises an objection, the libertine has an answer, and he takes special care to prove Justine wrong in whatever point she makes. Thus, libertine philosophy is not a positive philosophy, because there seem to be no principles or beliefs peculiar to all libertines. It is a philosophy of the moment, premised on negating the beliefs of the victim. Libertine philosophy is little more than the contradiction of virtue; it is based on locating victims' area of greatest philosophical resistance and bludgeoning them with sophistry. Physically or philosophically, libertines always take the path of greatest resistance. Simone de Beauvoir writes that resistance and crime are important to the libertine because his definition of self is contingent upon distancing himself from the rest of humanity: "Through crime the libertine refuses any complicity with the horrors of the elemental, of which the masses are only the passive—and consequently abject—reflection; he prevents society from dozing in injustice and he creates an apocalyptic state which forces all individuals to assume in a continual tension their separation, and thus their truth."[25] De Beauvoir concludes that libertines need an other, a victim, to violate, but that it is absurd to claim the libertines have nothing in common with them, no matter how hard they try to distance themselves. If they had nothing in common, she writes, there could be no pleasure. What they contest, she avers, "is the a priori existence of a relation between myself and the other on which my conduct should abstractly base itself" (76).

Blanchot, Klossowski, and de Beauvoir each show the libertines' need for an other in their project to attain personal autonomy, and each in his or her way shows that the libertines distance themselves from any preconceived notions of humanity by negating the other. Yet, another of Sade's readers finds the simple negation of the other insufficient. Geoffrey Bennington claims that pleasure and pain are but two of the sensations that interest the libertines. Bennington agrees with Klossowski's and Blanchot's interpretations of the uses of reason and crime in Sade, but he goes one step further in defining libertine desire. Noting that libertine pleasure is always coupled

<hr />

[25] De Beauvoir, *Faut-il brûler Sade?*, p. 75.

with philosophical debate, Bennington believes that pleasure, "ir-ritation," "crisis," and even the *idea* of crime fall short of their true goal: the libertines are driven, he writes, "by the desire to experi-ence *everything*, and the philosophical whole will be determined as excess with respect to conventional totalizations" (180). Libertines aim for total sensory experience, and this includes a fullness or plenitude of awareness that would make every nerve and every or-gan alive with stimulation. With one's sense organs constantly fir-ing at full capacity and relaying information incessantly, one would be able to experience a communion with nature limited only by the capacity of human sense organs. In Bennington's reading of Sade, experiencing *everything*, since it is linked to the "philosophical whole," is not limited to physical sensation but extends to human knowledge and understanding as well. Desiring to experience *everything*, libertines strive, in their quest for autonomy, to be like nature. In their ambitious pursuit of individualism they want to be alone and unique with all sensation and knowledge present to them. In an archtypical Enlightenment formulation, in fact, Cœur-de-Fer tells Justine that "Nature sufficeth unto herself" (496) [56], and libertines strive to imitate nature, to be complete in and of themselves.

Bennington points out that the libertines find in nature a totality of being in that nature contains everything and nothing exists out-side of it. Nature and natural law are the only authoritative and stable entities that exist. If nature spoke, Clément believes, this is what it would say:

> Be advised that there is nothing in you which is not my own, nothing
> I did not place in you for reasons it is not fitting you be acquainted
> with; know that the most abominable of your deeds is, like the most
> virtuous of some other, but one of the manners of serving me. So do
> not restrain yourself, flout your laws, a fig for your social conventions
> and your Gods; listen to me and to none other, and believe that if
> there exists a crime to be committed against me it is the resistance
> you oppose, in the forms of stubbornness or casuistries, to what I
> inspire in you. (609) [176]

Nature's discourse is truth, unchanging and eternal. What nature says simply is, for nature *is* first, last, and always. If nature could speak and humans could understand it, the discourse would be lit-eral and unambiguous; word and referent would coincide. Believing that nature is the totality of being and that its language alone is stable, the libertines use their own language and reason, Bennington states, to destabilize the linguistic order Justine recognizes. Bennington argues that the libertines only use language to prove to their victims how tenuous and unstable it is. The symbolic order is one more system the libertines strive to dismantle, one more connection among people they endeavor to break in order to dislodge victims' sense of security and self. Bennington writes that libertines strive to smash the foundations of language in order to destroy the link it establishes among people. "The *libertin*," he writes, "must contest language and the stability of reference if he is to become the 'souverain'" (208). Bennington thus adds to the libertine activities already described the destabilization of language. Sensation does not suffice to make the libertines self-present in their need for prescience and awareness: only by explaining to their victims in clear and logical language their philosophies of nature and by dislodging victims' footing in the world can the libertines ensure total transgression and hence complete pleasure and self-presence.

The use and abuse of language, in fact, is what some have isolated as the single most important libertine characteristic. Both Roland Barthes and Philippe Sollers believe that it is not the taking of pleasure or the inflicting of pain that defines the libertine, but the use of logical language. Barthes defines the libertine as the master of language. Only one trait, he argues, distinguishes the libertines from their victims, and that is speech. He writes that "the master is the one who speaks, who disposes of language in its entirety; the object is the one who remains silent, separate, through a mutilation more absolute than any erotic torture, from any access to speech, since he does not even have the right to *receive* the master's speech."[26] Barthes equates murder and language, which is appropriate particularly in light of Bressac's remarks concerning that crime. Bressac referred to murder as a simple mutation, a change of form; the murderer disposes of the victim at will in order to take pleasure. The libertine, Barthes writes, "disposes of language"; he mutilates or manipulates it according to his need in order to make his victim aware of all aspects of the violence he or she will undergo. Libertine use of language keeps the victim separate. The

[26] Barthes, "L'Arbre du crime," p. 32.

body of the victim and the body of language are intimately connected here, since libertines are the masters of both. Mutilating the victim's body is a simple matter, given the large repertory of tools of torture the libertines possess; violating the body of language is equally simple, and the tools the libertines use are primarily those of sophistry. All they need do is demonstrate to their victims the instability of the linguistic order to which they cling. The libertines frequently use either extremely broad definitions of words to make their points,[27] or they completely shift the grounds of the discussion so that their points seem stronger. La Dubois does a complete about-face, for example, when she argues that people were all created equal. First she maintains that sheer chance destroyed the equilibrium; later she attributes the disturbance to money and power (481) [39–40]. Libertines "dispose of language," then, to the extent that they twist and turn it for their own purposes. Victims who fail to recognize the intimate connections between the tenuous ideology of virtue and the apparent stability of language are extremely susceptible to this kind of abuse.

Philippe Sollers agrees with Barthes that the definition of the libertine depends explicitly on the use of language. Sollers writes that the libertine "is he who says what he does and does what he says, and *never anything else.*"[28] Both Sollers and Barthes emphasize the linguistic component of *libertinage*; Sollers adds to Barthes' notion of the intermingling of crime and language the idea of literalness. Sollers reads the libertines' discourse as the instantiation or the near perfect verbal representation of their crimes. Saying equals doing in his treatment of the libertines, who can both ensure a one-to-one correspondence between word and referent and halt the metonymic slippage of signifiers signifying other signifiers. In short, the libertines are in control of truth. According to Sollers, the libertine monster is the master in control of the signifier, and Sollers avers that in libertine ideology "what is at stake, . . . veiled by speech but already fully active, is a relation not to thought as cause of language, but to language without cause, to the very writing of the signifier as effect" (39).

---

[27] See, for example, Rodin's argument on the cultural dependency of the word "virtue" (pp. 543–44) [106–7], or Bressac's canny interchanging of the words "détruire" and "varier" (pp. 518–19) [79–80].

[28] Sollers, "Sade dans le texte," p. 43 (Sollers' emphasis).

If libertine *jouissance* entails the annihilation of the body and the subjectivity of the hapless victim, herein lies the paradox of the pleasure seekers' activities. They require an other in order to effect their radical independence from it. They need an other, that is, so that they may dispense with it and achieve the pleasure of unity. Unlike nature, which "sufficeth unto herself," however, libertines can neither approach nor sustain the narcissistic state they seem to require except by articulating their desires and by impugning received cultural truths in order better to violate their victim. This is why libertine activity couples speech with sexual violence. Were libertinism merely synonymous with sadism, there would be no pressing need to be concerned with the victim's identity. In the situation Justine narrates, however, speech serves to define the victim. Not only does speech prepare the ground for continued violation by representing the specific sorts of violence about to occur, it specifies the victim as victim by delineating the zones of moral and ideological contention that characterize the antagonism in *Justine*.

The victim-libertine relationship as Justine narrates it is consequently one of antagonism, in that the constitution of an other implies a fundamental inadequacy or incompletion on the part of the subject in question. This is because the subject not only acts upon the other, but is in turn acted on by it. In the very gesture of constituting an other or in recognizing an other as such, the subject invests the other with a portion of its being even if that portion is only one of negation. In *Justine* the victim provides the libertines with a dialectically situated other that they must destroy in order to achieve *jouissance*; paradoxically, however, in recognizing the need to destroy the other, the libertines circumvent the possibility of narcissistic self-identity. The victim-libertine antagonism, then, functions in a dialectical relation constituting identity, but more importantly, each of the polar opposites blocks the other from achieving self-identity.[29]

[29] That the recognition of an other blocks the full identity of the subject is clear when one considers what is generally *not* construed as other. Furniture, animals, or anonymous people do not normally figure the other. Consequently, the other is linked to the subject by a trace specifying in what subjectively crucial way the other informs the subject and represents for it specific, often failed aspects of its subjectivity. For an interesting linking of psychoanalytic and political readings of the other and antagonism, see Ernesto Laclau and Chantal Mouffe, *Hegemony and Socialist Strategy*, especially pp. 122–34; and Laclau, *New Reflections on the Revolution of Our Time*, especially pp. 3–39.

Now that we have seen the libertines' need for an other and for language to reach that other, we can understand Bennington's claim that the libertines' "philosophical whole will be determined as excess with respect to conventional totalizations." Libertines must say everything or they will not be assured complete transgression and the possibility of experiencing everything, yet as we have seen, speaking the truth about their philosophy renders them dependent on their victims and hence not autonomous. It frustrates their desire. Bennington writes that "it now seems possible to say that [the] various pretences of speaking the truth about perversion, to present 'perversion' as the truth of nature . . . always already constitute a perversion of speaking the truth. . . . Sententious propositions in Sade come to have the status of simulacra of truth, which functions as a fictional *frein* to the progress of . . . desire" (207). Libertine destabilization of language thwarts their own desire to be absolutely other. It reveals that the language of vice is as tenuous as that of virtue. By demonstrating their mastery through their control of language, their ability to mutilate and manipulate it, libertines try to show their victims that the stability of language is only an appearance, that virtue and reason are social and political constructs—the same discursive frameworks of which they are composed can be used to promote vice. Unable to become absolutely other, the best the libertines can do is *say* that they are other, and in so doing they reveal that their position is not selfsame and unique, but part of a binary opposition requiring the participation of an other.

Barthes calls Justine an "ambiguous victim endowed with narrating speech" (32). Justine is the victim of a great many violent crimes, which certainly makes her seem a victim, but because she speaks she possesses what we have determined to be a very significant libertine characteristic: the manipulation of language. In fact, Justine's use of language is remarkably similar to the libertines'. "The master is the one who speaks, who disposes of language in its entirety," Barthes wrote. For three hundred pages, almost the entire *récit* of the novel, Justine is in control—she narrates, and she controls the scene. Not only is she the novel's principal narrator, but every time she meets a libertine she narrates the story of her life thus far: "And then I told in detail all of my ills" (469) [26]; "[the first president judge] heard with interest the tale of my misfortunes" (509) [69]; "I relate the horrors whereof I was simultaneously an observer and object" (709) [283]. If libertines are those who speak and those who take pleasure in all sorts of sensation, Justine is indeed an ambiguous victim; in fact, as I will show, she looks very much like a libertine. If Justine does not derive some sort of benefit from the sensations the libertines evoke in her, it is hard to imagine why, after having learned the consequences, she continues to tell her tale.

Since the libertines can only occupy the master's position by opposing the principles of virtue and defining themselves against an other, it seems logical to ask whether Justine defines herself in opposition to the libertines. As she tells her tale, Justine takes no positions and she has no philosophies of virtue; she only ever contradicts libertine sophistry. If she is virtuous, then, it is to the extent that she attempts to be the other of vice. Yet, Justine rarely, if ever, resists the libertines. She *says* that she is virtuous, but her actions belie her words. Situations frequently arise in which Justine has the power to escape her tormentors' clutches, but more often than not she passes them by. When she attempts to flee the château of Gernande, the mad blood-letter, she succeeds in getting as far as the courtyard, but there she finds herself trapped. She narrates the rest of the scene as follows:

> The sun rose at last; merciful Heaven! the first object to present itself to me . . . is the Count himself: it had been frightfully warm during the night, he had stepped out to take a breath of air. He believes he is in error, he supposes this a specter, he recoils, rarely is courage a traitor's virtue: I get trembling to my feet, I fling myself at his knees.
> "Thérèse! What are you doing here?" he demands.
> "Oh, Monsieur, punish me," I reply, "I am guilty and have nothing to answer you." (652) [221]

In similar fashion, when Roland the counterfeiter places his life in Justine's hands by giving her the end of the rope he uses to hang himself while masturbating, she never seems to realize what power she wields over him. After he performs the act he passes out. Justine concludes the episode: "When 'tis all shot out without any assistance whatsoever from me, I rush to cut him down, he falls, unconscious, but thanks to my ministrations he quickly recovers his senses" (687–88) [260]. After she awakens him, he tries to murder her. Justine reveals the ambiguous nature of her status as victim that Barthes noted in her mindless obedience to the libertines and in her hesitation to escape even when the occasions arise. People tell her they are her master and she believes them. At the conclusion of the Roland episode cited above, Justine simply remarks, "What possibility of hesitation had I? Was he not my master?" (687) [259].

Justine knows only one way to be virtuous, and that is to tell people that she is. She rarely performs or takes responsibility for a selfless virtuous act: in most instances in which Justine helps another it is for the benefits she can reap.[30] In fact, she remarks early in the novel that "people are not esteemed save in reason of the aid and benefits one imagines may be had of them" (461) [17], and Justine herself seems to subscribe to this platitude. After Rodin burns the brand of the thief on Justine's shoulder and thus prevents her from turning him in to the authorities, Justine flees, leaving poor Rosalie, Rodin's daughter, to be vivisected.

> Anyone else might have been little impressed by the menace; what would I have to fear as soon as I found the means to prove that what I had just suffered had been the work not of a tribunal but of criminals? But my weakness, my natural timidity, the frightful memory of what I had undergone at Paris and recollections of the château de Bressac—it all stunned me, terrified me; I thought only of flight, and was far more stirred by anguish at having to abandon an innocent victim to those two villains, who were without doubt ready to immolate her, than I was touched by my own ills. (557) [120]

Underscoring how unlike anyone else she is, Justine says that leaving Rosalie aggrieves her but she makes no move to help her; the only action she foresees is *proving*—that is, telling or explaining—her innocence.

Justine's most protracted attempt to tell of her innocence is the novel's *récit* itself. Except for fifteen paragraphs, the novel is composed of Justine's narrative to Corville and Lorsange. Justine en-

---

[30] One of Justine's rare efforts to help another ends in disaster when she attempts to save a baby from a burning building. Justine stumbles in the confusion and winds up heaving the infant into the flames: "I advance along a half-consumed beam, miss my footing, instinctively thrust out my hands, this natural reflex forces me to release the precious burden in my arms . . . it slips from my grasp and the unlucky child falls into the inferno before its own mother's eyes" (712) [286]. Disclaiming responsibility, Justine blames nature for the mishap.

counters Corville and Lorsange when on her way to Paris for the confirmation of the death penalty she received in Lyon for having killed the baby in the fire. Lorsange and Corville ask her to tell them the story of her life, and since they appear rich and influential, Justine decides to oblige them. Attempting to charge her tale with all the pathos and abjection she can, Justine begins. Calling herself Thérèse in order to defend her family's honor, she prefaces her story with a disclaimer, informing her listeners that her narrative is transgressive: "'To recount you the story of my life, Madame . . . is to offer you the most striking example of innocence oppressed, is to accuse the hand of Heaven, is to bear complaint against the Supreme Being's will, is, in a sense, to rebel against His sacred designs. . . . I dare not. . . .' Tears gathered in this interesting girl's eyes and, after having given vent to them for a moment, she began her recitation in these terms" (468) [25]. From the very beginning of Justine's narrative we can see some of the tricks she picked up from libertine narration. Barthes and Sollers showed that the libertine use of language went beyond simple representation, and actually became criminal itself: as Sollers showed, telling became an act, the accomplishing of a crime. In the first sentences she utters, Justine accomplishes a transgression merely by her use of language: she claims that to recount equals to accuse and to bear complaint; to tell her story, she says, is to rebel against God's will. She turns a speech situation into a speech act because narrating her story, she avers, perpetrates an offense. Pausing only a moment to let the transgressive elements of her tale register with her audience, she plunges enthusiastically into the story.

Justine pauses a half-dozen or so times during her narrative, punctuating the *récit* with reminders that telling the story is transgressive: "Oh, Madame, I shall not attempt to represent the infamies of which I was at once victim and witness" (709) [282]. With a little encouragement, however, she narrates the libertines' attempt to inscribe their marks of violence on Thérèse, the principal character in Justine's story. Justine's hesitations accomplish more than simply signaling to her audience that the tale is violent and that the very telling is blameworthy, however. Perhaps realizing that repeated description of events can cause her listeners' attention to wander, Justine incites them, through her hesitations, to inscribe their own marks of violence on her heroine Thérèse: "You will permit me, Madame, ... to conceal a part of the obscene details of this odious ritual; allow your imagination to figure all that debauch can dictate to villains in such instances ... and indeed it still will not have but a faint idea of what was done in those initial orgies" (569) [133]. Justine gives them all the material they need to complete the story, but cannily telling them that what really happened is far worse than what she narrates, she gets them to supply for themselves the erotic details and to write their own endings to the story she begins. To keep her listeners actively involved, she frequently breaks her tale off: "But how can I abuse your patience by relating these new horrors? Have I not already more than soiled your imagination with infamous recitations? Dare I hazard additional ones? 'Yes, Thérèse,' Monsieur de Corville put in, 'yes, we insist upon these details'" (670) [241]. Justine's narrative strategies here resemble the libertines' to the extent that she informs her listeners that transgression is about to occur, and also to the extent that she redefines herself as victim by inciting her listeners to violate her mentally as they imagine scenes of violence she must have undergone.

Justine's use of language is equivalent to that of the libertines. The libertines, unable to achieve their goal of self-affirmation and plenitude, need language to define themselves over and against an other. The same is true of Justine. In order to assure maximum reaction from their addressees, the libertines describe the violence about to occur. The same is true of Justine, who hesitates before telling her audience the explicit aspects of her tale, and who reveals that even narrating her story is an affront to God. The libertines proceed by describing their acts of violence to Justine, and then inscribing their marks on her. The same is true of Justine, who incites her listeners to perform mental violence on her as she sets up a scene and then leaves the conclusion to them. But while the libertines use language as a means to *jouissance* and the concomitant narcissistic unity, Justine's narrative, despite making her seem the epitome of virtue and integrity, actually effects a radical split in her subjectivity. If the image of virtue she presents to her listeners seems designed to evoke their pity and provoke them to help her—which they finally do—the reality of Justine, the woman behind the image, is more complex and elusive than her representation of herself would suggest. Justine portrays herself, in the figure of Thérèse, as absolutely other to vice and libertinism, but as we will now see, Justine and Thérèse are not simply different names for the same woman: the two are radically different in their otherness and resistance to libertinism.

Klossowski argues that Justine is the paradigm of virtue and that her function in the novel is to throw the libertines into relief. Maintaining that she is no more complex than the image of virtue that the libertines and Corville and Lorsange receive from her narrative, he claims that the libertines manage to reach her in the deepest recesses of her being. He argues that Sade portrays Justine as "always equal to herself" and that Sade exploits the distress "of a consciousness reduced to its last defenses at the point at which it sees its inviolate self-possession threatened, in the representation that the self has of its own integrity, while consciousness always remains inseparable from the body lost to its eyes" (157). Yet, I would have to argue that Justine cannot be "equal to herself," because she depicts herself as a text, a collection of episodes, indeed a *récit*. Her complexity arises from the disjunction separating her life from the representation of it. Using the pseudonym Thérèse, she constructs a narrative other that necessarily differs substantially from her reality. She only describes episodes that cause her to appear virtuous because she is the other of libertinism. Her ordeals last more than thirteen years, and enough certainly happens to Justine over the course of these years to give her material for her tale. But Justine tells not "the story of [her] life," which is what she claims to be doing; she only tells the story of her troubles and of her resistance to the libertines. On at least four occasions Justine collapses periods of up to four years into one sentence ("I had remained four years in this household unrelentingly persecuted by the same sorrows" (517) [78]), and she never tells any episode in her thirteen-year journey unless it is hideously violent and morally degrading. She admits that some amusing anecdotes exist in her repertory, but the necessity of detailing her misfortunes takes precedence: "Were my cruel situation to permit me to amuse you for an instant, Madame, when I must think of nothing but gaining your compassion, I should dare describe some of the symptoms of avarice I witnessed while in that house" (476) [33]. By her own admission events occurred in Justine's life that do not contribute to the image she tries to project. Her narrative self does not correspond to her reality; Justine constructs her narrated self—Thérèse—with a very particular point in mind: to move her listeners to pity (*attendrir*). Justine is not, consequently, portrayed "equal to herself," as Klossowski claims, and Thérèse becomes an alienated, textual manifestation of Justine.

Like Suzanne Simonin, Justine is concerned with the perlocutionary force of her tale, and she seems never to worry that her story might appear exaggerated or untrue. Justine strives to move her audience to pity, and the strategy she has chosen for doing so involves portraying Thérèse, her narrated self, as the incarnation of virtue. Thérèse is the undauntable other of libertinism whose spirit the libertines never succeed in breaking. Her story consists of nothing but repeated episodes of violence, and her virtue appears greater with each encounter because she never ceases to offer resistance. Justine and Thérèse differ in one significant respect, however. The more violence Thérèse suffers in Justine's story, the greater her virtue and her resistance to corruption seem to be. The real woman Justine, however, the narrator who lived through these ordeals, had an entirely different kind of resistance, one essential to the pathos of the story she constructs. That resistance is a specifically physical resistance. If we look closely at Justine's encounters with the libertines, we see that she is repeatedly violated because she offers strong moral *and* physical resistance. That is, everyone who meets Justine is taken with her remarkable beauty, and one of the reasons why the libertines find her so attractive as a victim is that her body appears fresh and virginal, and hence ripe for transgression. Even after repeated scenes of violence, even after being raped, branded, beaten, and infibulated, Justine's body is none the worse for wear. All marks on Justine's body mysteriously disappear—even her hymen grows back (557) [121]. At the end of her ordeals Justine is still described as a woman with "the loveliest figure imaginable, the most noble, the most agreeable, the most interesting visage, in brief, there were there all the charms of a sort to please" (467) [24].

The significance of Justine's inability to retain a trace of the marks of violence inscribed on her is paramount if she is to appear as the quintessence of virtue. Since the strength of her virtue is in direct proportion to the amount of violence she undergoes, it figures that Justine must be violated as often as possible if she is to appear the other of libertinism. Yet, if her body showed signs of wear, the transgression involved in each violation would be less, particularly since the libertines violate whatever offers greatest resistance. The narrated, textual Thérèse thus differs from Justine in its ability to retain the marks or memory of violence. By creating the textual Thérèse, Justine constitutes a means by which the traces of violence she underwent can be recorded and inscribed in the memory of her audience. The more violence they hear she underwent, the more they construe her as the apotheosis of virtue. Justine's description of her resistance to vice in the figure of Thérèse in this way makes virtue—as we saw was the case with libertine vice—a specifically discursive phenomenon.

Consequently, Justine's story of Thérèse foregrounds a form of *vraisemblance*. Despite the fact that it is physically impossible for anyone to have lived through the ordeals Justine describes, much less to remain beautiful and innocent to boot, the tale retains an affective and ideological register clearly endorsing bourgeois patriarchy's conception of feminine sexuality and, consequently, moral rectitude. The story of Thérèse is not realistic in any traditional sense, but it is *vraisemblable*, since in the abstract and globalizing conception of virtue it highlights a determined political vision of the way things ought to be. Strikingly, then, Justine's version of virtue, which depends on the narrative construction of Thérèse as the unrealistic yet ideologically plausible apotheosis of virtue, is rhetorically equivalent to libertine vice. It is a discursive construction with no sound philosophical or moral basis, and it exists solely as the negation of its other.[31]

Justine and her libertine tormentors are engaged in a dialectical struggle in which neither virtue nor vice has any positive character-

---

[31] Jacques Lacan has noticed that the victim in Sade survives all means of torture and violence, and in *L'Ethique de la psychanalyse* he writes that "it seems that everything that happens to the subject is incapable of altering the image in question, even by erosion. But Sade, who is of another nature than those who pose us these riddles, goes further since we see profiled in the horizon of his work the idea of an eternal torture" (p. 238). Picking up on this idea, Slavoj Zizek writes in *The Sublime Object of Ideology* that there are two deaths in Sade. "This difference between the two deaths can be linked with the Sadeian fantasy revealed by the fact that in his work his victim is, in a certain sense, indestructible: she can be endlessly tortured and can survive it; she can endure any torment and still retain her beauty. It is as though, above and beyond her natural body (a part of the cycle of generation and corruption), and thus above and beyond her natural death, she possessed another body, a body composed of some other substance, one excepted from the vital cycle—a sublime body" (p. 134).

istics. Each exists solely as the negation of its other, and each requires the support of a discursive representation in order to smooth
over the gaps implicit in its logical and ideological composition.
Both Justine and the libertines depend on the narrated figure
Thérèse to fill in the holes in their philosophical narratives. The
libertines need to inscribe their violence on Thérèse in order to annihilate her and approach the consummation of their own *jouissance*, and Justine must mark Thérèse so that her tale will attain
the level of *vraisemblance* required to convey the pathos she specifies early on. Justine and the libertines are consequently engaged in
a rhetorical struggle, one concerned less with the ideology of virtue
and more with the narrative structure of ideology.

Justine and the libertines compete in telling different stories about
Thérèse. The novel could go on forever, like *Le Roman bourgeois*,
except for the *deus ex machina* that terminates Justine's life. Up
until the moment of Justine's death, the novel is a battle of conflicting philosophies, with each side sharpening and refining its point
of view with no possible resolution in sight. Justine's narrative
winds down to the point at which she met Mme de Lorsange and
M. de Corville when, as in a labyrinthine heroic novel, she discovers that Mme de Lorsange is her sister Juliette. Justine and Juliette
retire to the latter's château, where Justine receives all the loving
attention she ever wanted. One day a storm appears.

> Lightning glitters, shakes, hail slashes down, winds blow wrathfully,
> heaven's fire convulses the clouds, in the most hideous manner makes
> them to seethe; it seems as if Nature were wearied out of patience
> with what she has wrought, as if she were ready to confound all the
> elements that she might wrench new forms from them. Terrified, Ma-
> dame de Lorsange begs her sister to make all haste and close the shut-
> ters; anxious to calm her, Thérèse dashes to the windows which are
> already being broken; she would do battle with the wind, she gives a
> minute's flight, is driven back and at that instant a blazing thunder-
> bolt reaches her where she stands in the middle of the room; at that
> moment a burst of lightning lays her flat in the middle of the room.
> . . . The unhappy Thérèse has been struck in such wise hope itself
> can no longer subsist for her; the lightning entered her right breast,
> found the heart, and after having consumed her chest and face, burst
> out through her belly. (741–42, translation modified) [316]

Where no mortal had succeeded in reaching Justine and leaving a
trace on her virginal body, in a flash nature inscribes its mark on

her and annihilates her, thus putting to an end in as random a fashion possible the antagonistic relationship she entertained with the libertines.

The arbitrary conclusion to Justine's life represents more than simply Sade's only way out of the impossibly antagonistic relationship he had created, however. The final inscription of violence on the victim's body is a literal and metaphoric dis-figurement of the character Justine. The lightning permanently deforms the beautiful young woman, thus accomplishing the feat Justine's antagonists failed to perform. Correlatively and more importantly, however, the marks left on Justine's body by a non-intentional, indeliberate force obliterate her figurative incarnation in the form of the narrated Thérèse: eliminating the discrepancy between the woman and her self-representation, the force of nature that marks and kills her immediately extricates her from the dialectical and antagonistic relationship with vice.

In concert with the opening paragraph of *Justine*, then, the title character's death shows nature as final cause. Indeterminate because it lies outside of any discursive configuration capable of containing it, nature as a force of the Real lacks any ideological dimension. Yet, the conclusion of *Justine* underscores the determinate work of interpretation that ascribes to any act a meaningful and finite sense: Juliette reads the marks on her sister Justine's body, and she inserts the woman's life into the narrative and ideological paradigm that the tale's *vraisemblance* was designed to construe. "The miserable thing was hideous to look upon; Monsieur de Corville orders that she be borne away. . . .'No,' says Madame de Lorsange, getting to her feet with the utmost calm; 'no, leave her here before my eyes, Monsieur, I have got to contemplate her in order to be confirmed in the resolves I have just taken'" (742) [316]. Juliette contemplates her sister's disfigured body, and reads in the hideous marks the unambiguous proof that nature demands people's adherence to the principles of virtue. Her interpretation of her sister's gruesome death is that straying from the path of virtue might provide one with a few chimeric rewards here on earth, but the true road to felicity lies in austere virtue. Juliette goes off to become a Carmelite, and the horrible example of her sister's death leads her to become "the example of order and edification, as much by her great piety as by the wisdom of her mind and the regularity of her manners" (743, translation modified) [318].

The conclusion of Justine's pitiful life strikes Juliette as too significant not to be meaningful. The story seems to close on a highly charged, resolute note: the miscreant Juliette sees the light and reforms her life. She thinks she recognizes the will of nature in the marks it inscribed on Justine's body, and as she contemplates the corpse, she pronounces these final words:

> The unheard-of sufferings this luckless creature has experienced although she has always respected her duties, have something about them which is too extraordinary for me not to open my eyes upon my own self; think not I am blinded by that false-gleaming felicity which, in the course of Thérèse's adventures, we have seen enjoyed by the villains who battened upon her. These caprices of Heaven's hand are enigmas it is not for us to sound, but which ought never seduce us. (742) [317]

Juliette abandons vice and embraces virtue, it seems, solely because of the natural phenomenon that disfigured and killed her sister. She interprets the definitive marks left on Justine by the bolt of lightning as the unequivocal proof that the moral of her sister's story unambiguously advocated virtue, and furthermore that this moral represents a divine will. In addition, Juliette continues to refer to Justine as Thérèse, even though she knows her true identity, as if to emphasize the discursively constructed nature of both her life and her virtue. Juliette observes the bizarre yet nevertheless natural phenomenon of her sister's untimely death, and forces it into one of the narrative paradigms that Justine's tale offers.

Juliette's interpretation of Justine's story matches the one prescribed by the novel's external narrator. This narrator, who opens the novel and who assumes control after Justine's death near its conclusion, apologizes for having written a didactic work whose lesson may be difficult to absorb:

> Doubtless it is cruel to have to describe, on the one hand, a host of ills overwhelming a sweet-tempered and sensitive woman who, as best she is able, respects virtue, and, on the other, the affluence of prosperity of those who crush and mortify this same woman. But were there nevertheless some good engendered of the demonstration, would one have to repent of making it? Ought one be sorry for having established a fact whence there resulted, for the wise man who reads

to some purpose, so useful a lesson of submission to providential decrees and the fateful warning that it is often to recall us to our duties that Heaven strikes down beside us the person who seems to us best to have fulfilled his own? (458) [14]

The opening paragraphs of the work situate the novel within the didactic critical tradition that had evolved to shield fiction against charges of illegitimacy or moral indecency. In addition, the unequivocal interpretation concerning bourgeois virtue's moral and political superiority that the narrator's posturing intimates all reasonable readers will advocate situates the novel in the tradition of heroic fiction's master narratives. Juliette's interpretation of her sister's life, sanctioned by the novel's external narrator, strips Justine of her personal specificity and makes of her a purely abstract, emblematic figure of bourgeois conceptions of virtue.

The conclusion of *Justine* highlights the hermeneutic processes implicated by the story Justine tells and by the tradition of the moral exemplum to which the work belongs. Juliette insists on seeing a moral significance in her sister's natural death, and she inscribes the young woman's life in the ideology of bourgeois patriarchal virtue. *Justine* consequently resembles *La Princesse de Clèves* and *La Religieuse* to the extent that it objectifies a valorized interpretive practice and underscores the limits of its ability to negotiate contemporary political and moral reality. Where *La Princesse de Clèves* and *La Religieuse* foreground the failure of literary convention and the concomitant demystification of fiction's mechanisms, however, *Justine* undertakes a dismantling of the politics supporting a privileged model of *vraisemblance*. It uncovers the resilience of a determinate ideological system to appear natural even when the narrative episodes it contains could scarcely be more preposterous.

Unlike many of his predecessors who ceaselessly repeated that their narratives were true, Sade never claims that *Justine* is referentially accurate. He ironically maintains, rather, that the violent narrative episodes he relates are essential to impart the moral lesson that virtue is better than vice.[32] However, Sade never depicts any actions in *Justine* that might be construed as virtuous—except,

---

[32] For a more detailed account of the question of truth in Sade and its political and psychosexual dimensions, see Josué Harari's *Scenarios of the Imaginary: Theorizing the French Enlightenment*, pp. 139–50.

perhaps, the heroine's resistance to libertine sophistry. Since we have seen, however, that libertine vice and Justine's virtue constitute themselves exclusively through the negation of their other, it is equally possible to interpret vice as the libertine attempt to resist the oppressive ideology of bourgeois notions of virtue, a class-based political philosophy designed to keep the disenfranchised powerless. *Justine* unsettles the traditional bourgeois conception of virtue, a conception based primarily on sexual restraint and the respect of property, and it demonstrates the extent to which an individual's body and his or her access to pleasure have become a marketable commodity and, consequently, a form of property whose circulation can be rigidly controlled. Sade's libertines strive to break free from the politically determined apprehension of their own bodies and of the pleasures that traverse them; their failure to achieve unmediated access to the complete repertory of their own sensations, however, rehearses the narrator's early warning that all attempts to erect self-contained and self-present systems are doomed to failure. Sade's libertines rely on narrative constructions to transgress their victims and increase their own pleasure; their own access to the truth they propound is consequently restricted to language's capacity to represent the ideological systems they strive to breach.[33] The idea of truth in *Justine* is not only relational and contingent upon the dialectic between vice and virtue, but it is constructed at every step of the way, from the philosophical explana-

---

[33] In parallel fashion, the amount of pain Sade's libertines can inflict never escapes the bounds of representation. In *The Body in Pain*, Elaine Scarry has written that one of the dimensions of physical pain "is its ability to destroy language, the power of verbal objectification, a major source of our self-extension, a vehicle through which the pain could be lifted out into the world and eliminated. Before destroying language, it first monopolizes language, becomes its only subject: complaint, in many ways the nonpolitical equivalent of confession, becomes the exclusive mode of speech. Eventually the pain so deepens that the coherence of complaint is displaced by the sounds anterior to learned language. The tendency of pain not simply to resist expression but to destroy the capacity for speech is in torture reenacted in overt, exaggerated form. Even where the torturers do not permanently eliminate the voice through mutilation or murder, they mime the work of pain by temporarily breaking off the voice, making it their own, making it speak their words, making it cry out when they want it to cry, be silent when they want its silence, turning it on and off, using its sound to abuse the one whose voice it is as well as other prisoners" (p. 54). Sade, however, never allows Justine's pain to transcend her capacity to represent it. Giving her complete control to harness in linguistic fashion the experience her body undergoes, he consequently restricts libertine transgression and the concomitant pleasure it procures them to quantifiable increments of a man-made system.

tions of transgression to the physical mutilation of Justine's body, uniquely through narrative.

Sade's novel depicts individualism as it is constructed only through the transgression of existing social laws. His libertines strive to upset their victims' sense of virtue by disfiguring the stability of the philosophical language used to support it and consequently wrenching them free of the social bonds uniting them to their fellow humans. Paradoxically, delivery from social bonds constitutes both the source of *jouissance* for the libertines, who strive to become absolutely unique, and the epitome of torture for Thérèse, who requires a sense of identity with her fellow human beings in order for her conception of virtue to make sense. Libertines can only accomplish optimum transgression and retain the linguistic and physical mastery that ensues by expounding their philosophies and by narrating the scenes to transpire; in addition, their mastery relies on a disfiguring of language. Consequently, their quest for pleasure and mastery depends on a dual dialectic linking the opposition between the individual and the social to that opposing mimetic and poetic uses of language. That is, libertines first establish themselves as the masters of language by deploying standard tools of rhetoric and sophistry in order to upset their victims' stable conceptions of truth, a process that disconnects their victims from their own social realities. Demonstrating that language can shape and re-form reality as much as it can refer to it, they isolate their victims and strip them of all social identity. The ensuing physical mutilation pits consecrated individuals against one another. The victims inevitably lose the battle because they define themselves as victims: not to do so would rob them of the only sense of identity remaining to them.

Justine, however, retains her identity throughout these horrendous ordeals and it is primarily because she has appropriated libertine mastery of language. Telling her story to each of the libertines she meets, she constructs a narrated persona on whom she heaps the repeated scenes of abuse that contribute to construing her as the apotheosis of virtue. Thérèse consequently seduces the libertines because she presents an unsounded depth of material ripe for transgression. Justine as narrator enjoys a mastery of language similar to the libertines' because she remains in control of discourse's constative function by directing her audience to inscribe their own marks of violence on Thérèse. The pathetic figure that emerges is purely an effect of language. Destabilizing narrative's referential capacity, Justine avers in the very first words she speaks to Corville and Lorsange that her story is, in fact, a blasphemous speech act that questions God's sacred intentions. Thus, Justine's language reproduces the libertines' in its dual dialectical construction. Seducing her listeners into believing that her narrative contains a truth-value joining her to the social construction of virtue, she nevertheless withholds the information that reveals her individualistic and poetic use of language.

Justine's tale is a protracted seduction designed to project to her listeners an image corresponding to their desire, and she obfuscates the crucial difference on which her narrative depends between telling the truth and constructing it. That is, the story must appear referentially accurate if her virtue is to appear intact, but the tale derives its rhetorical strength by liberating itself from a purely constative register so that the play of language may construct a pathetic figure based not on truth but on listeners' desire. *Justine* consequently hypostatizes the representational indeterminacy characteristic of eighteenth-century French fiction: it sketches out the zone of conflict between ideologically incompatible positions, and situates its narrative at the precise juncture where their epistemological preconditions meet. Vice and virtue in *Justine* are discursively formulated, both depending on the logic of the narrative in which they appear. Neither enjoys an a priori preeminence, and both are shown to be truths constructed through a poetic use of language in which the constative dimension is overshadowed by language's power to construct meaning in the social world it putatively describes. The work's narrative, from which the external narrator indicates readers should draw their own conclusions about the benefits of virtue, consequently establishes a polemical tension between the competing ideologies it puts forth, as well as a continuing ambivalence concerning its own truth-value. Its title character imitates and subsequently appropriates libertine mastery of language in an attempt to direct reader response toward her own putative virtue. Justine's attempt to speak an unequivocal master discourse bereft of a figurative dimension open to interpretation is thwarted, however, at the novel's close. The bolt of lightning that disfigures her and the call for interpretation of her life that it seems to issue refigure her language, effectively summoning a reevaluation of her story and the ostensible stability of the master's language.

Justine flirts with the possibility of an unequivocal, master discourse of narrative and philosophy whose stable referentiality would reproduce in unmediated fashion the truth of the events or analytic systems to which it refers. The work's random and nonsensical conclusion, however, renders the master's position untenable, and it consequently contests the putatively natural ascendancy of any of its ideological positions. Although *Justine* claims to follow in the tradition of the didactic tale whose self-evident moral promotes reigning conceptions of virtue, it ironically undermines that claim by highlighting its immaterial basis. Projecting to different classes of readers the lesson they have been historically and culturally conditioned to recognize, the novel deftly skirts the issue of political or moral absolutism by allowing the traditional moral reading to coincide with the philosophically and politically more astute one. Those associated with this latter reading receive the author's sardonic nod of approval for recognizing that political or moral truth is a construction of received narrative traditions, and they can claim for that very reason the privileged position of interpretive superiority—at least temporarily. Sade's novel incites the critically astute to assert their own smug attitude of "political correctness" by pointing out the obfuscated operations of political hegemony on the unknowing folks who blindly respect its teachings.

This last position is a difficult one to escape, however, even if it is easy to criticize. Clearly my own account of Sade's fiction, to say nothing of the historical narrative of the development of the novel in France I have erected, cannot escape similar charges of critical and political blindness. To bracket a specific interpretation and reveal its shortcomings is, of course, to attempt to occupy the master's position. To assert the legitimacy of one's own historical narrative—be it of a literary genre, the history of interpretation, or the sociopolitical events constituting war or revolution—is to attempt to foreclose interpretation and to privilege an expressive causality that one simply "found" in the raw data analyzed. The master's position, as must by now be all too clear, is an untenable one. As Diderot's *Religieuse* demonstrates, each tale and every history can always be re-framed and re-contextualized. The position of mastery is always a resolutely political one, since it strives to make its own accounts and claims appear natural and unconstructed. Readers of *Justine* who understand that its truth extends beyond the level of its narrative and is constituted instead on the level of its discourse—where the very notion of truth is constructed in the first place—are those who come closest to reading the work "entièrement."

I have argued against May, Mylne, and others that realist fiction did not result from critical attack, but rather produced it. Eighteenth-century fiction typically forsook the depiction of noble or aristocratic characters engaging in verisimilar grandiose actions in favor of less conventionally encoded narratives that revealed the ideological missions of canonical texts. Fiction began to appear "realistic" not because it somehow more accurately or completely coincided with referential reality, but because it rejected fiction's existing conventions and the ideological baggage associated with them. The less obtrusive conventions became, the more narrative appeared to offer unmediated accounts of reality.[34] Clearly there is nothing inherently political in the attempt to represent more accurately than one's ancestors had the real world; consequently, I would argue, eighteenth-century fiction's ostensible "realism" might more properly be labeled a bourgeois representational revolution. Unlike the attempts wealthy bourgeois made to imitate the iconographic trappings of the aristocracy in the seventeenth century, eighteenth-century prose fiction strove to rid itself not only of the overwrought and obtrusive conventions obtaining in earlier works, but the exclusionary ideology that made the literary text available only to those who possessed the cultural capital required to decode it as well. By depicting characters and situations with which more readers would be familiar, and by proposing alternative reading strategies that interrogated the ostensible stability

[34] Wallace Martin writes in *Recent Theories of Narrative* that "in the context of reading, 'realism' appears to be that broad area of narrative without any identifiable conventions, one in which literary artifice has disappeared and everything happens as it would in life. . . . In the best realistic narratives, we are startled into awareness of the real: we would never have imagined the revelation that came just after we turned the page, but after it appears, we realize that it was inevitable—it captures a truth of experience that we knew, however dimly, all along" (p. 58).

of earlier fiction's expressive causality, novelists liberated themselves from deferential imitation of the ancient masters. They put narrative to work not only in exposing the hegemonic and constructed nature of received models of truth, but in demonstrating that it is the storyteller who is master.

Afterword

The axiom that the novel appeared with the bourgeoisie and correlated its rise to predominance has long been unquestioned in the
study of European fiction. Realism is generally the hero of the story
of the novel's rise, and in most narratives about early fiction it enters the scene sometime during the eighteenth century, conquering
all contenders in order to achieve ascendancy. I have tried to propose an alternative scenario by showing that the development of
the novel in France, and particularly the realist novel, was not the
inevitable historical phenomenon that many literary historians
make it out to be. Early French prose fiction, I have claimed, responded to a dynamic tension between the aesthetic and political
domains. It registered the conflict between dominant political
groups in different periods during the seventeenth and eighteenth
centuries, and constituted itself as the literature of resistance
against encroaching hegemony. Prose fiction became popular in
France when groups of aristocrats felt their traditional ascendancy
in political and social life threatened both by infiltrating bourgeois
participation in government and by growing monarchic absolutism. The novel in France was at its earliest stages of popularity a
type of resistance literature in which authors and readers attempted
to reassert the importance of the aristocratic values that they feared
were headed for antiquation. Although the novel was quickly mobilized to articulate bourgeois political concerns, it remained a literature of resistance. Throughout the eighteenth century, prose fiction interrogated the beliefs and practices commonly held to be
universal and transhistorical, and it undermined the literary conventions generally deployed to sustain them.

In my account of the aesthetic and political tensions informing

the development of the novel in France in the seventeenth and eighteenth centuries I have attempted to articulate some of the effects
that literary and social practice had on one another. I have sought
to separate some of the many and heterogeneous strands of literary
and ideological discourse that form the knot of the homogeneous
abstraction we call the novel. Clearly, however, I have overlooked—in some cases deliberately—many of the crucial dialectical tensions that contributed to the shaping of the novel as a canonized genre in France. Many of these tensions suggest themselves
plainly in the texts I have discussed: considerations of female authorship, sexuality, philosophical discourse, the commodification
of the body, the significance of colonialism, and the issue of race
are but a few of the concerns that pose themselves. I have also
ignored some texts which might be considered crucial in the development of fiction in France. Nevertheless, as I stated in my Introduction, my aim has been neither to catalog the canon nor to rehearse the modern discovery of realism in prose fiction. Rather, I
have tried to suggest avenues for disarticulating two forms of social
practice I consider crucial in the development of the genre: the aesthetic and the ideological. My narrative of the development of
prose fiction in France privileges specific literary and historical
structures in order to account for the particular ideological and
formal configurations fiction assumed. I am aware that I have narrated this story in the realist mode and that I have excavated a
narrative causality which, by implication, I simply "found" in the
historical and literary sources I consulted. With this brief caveat
concerning the restrictive nature of our own historical and literary
tools for understanding the intricate links between literature and
politics, I make no claims for mastery. I would only hope that, like
the schoolboy in Lesage's prefatory remarks to *Gil Blas*, I have not
been duped by the apparent stability of the material I have analyzed, and that I have remained aware of how greatly previous interpretations and accounts have structured my own.

Reference Matter

Works Cited

Adam, Antoine. *Les Libertins au XVIIe siècle*. Paris: Buchet, 1964.
———, ed. *Romanciers du XVIIe siècle*. Paris: Bibliothèque de la Pleiade, 1958.
Addison, Joseph, and Richard Steele. *The Tatler. Complete in One Volume.* London: Jones, 1829.
Alluis, Jacques. *L'Escole d'amour ou les heros docteurs*. Grenoble: Robert Philippes, 1665.
Althusser, Louis. *Lire le capital*. Paris: Maspero, 1967.
Anderson, Perry. "Modernism and Revolution." In *Marxism and the Interpretation of Culture*, ed. Cary Nelson and Lawrence Grossberg. Urbana: University of Illinois Press, 1988.
Apostolidès, Jean-Marie. *Le roi-machine*. Paris: Minuit, 1981.
Argens, Jean-Baptiste de Boyer d'. *Lectures amusantes, ou les délassements de l'esprit*. The Hague: Adrien Moetjens, 1739.
Aristotle. *The Poetics*. Trans. G. M. A. Grube. Indianapolis, Ind.: Bobbs-Merrill, 1958.
———. *The Politics*. Trans. Carnes Lord. Chicago: University of Chicago Press, 1984.
Arnaud, François Thomas Marie de Baculard d'. *Nouvelles historiques*. Paris: Delalain, 1774.
Austin, J. L. *How to Do Things with Words*. Cambridge, Mass.: Harvard University Press, 1975.
Bakhtin, Mikhail. *The Dialogic Imagination*. Trans. Caryl Emerson and Michael Holquist. Austin: University of Texas Press, 1983.
Bannister, Mark. *Privileged Mortals: The French Heroic Novel, 1630–1660*. Oxford: Oxford University Press, 1983.
Barthes, Roland. "L'Arbre du crime," *Tel Quel*, no. 28 (Winter 1967).
Bary, René. *La Rhétorique françoise, ou l'on trouve de nouveaux exemples sur les Passions & sur les Figures*. Paris: Pierre le Petit, 1659.
Baudrillard, Jean. *De la séduction*. Paris: Galilée, 1979.
Bayle, Pierre. *Dictionnaire historique et critique*. Rotterdam: Michel Bohm, 1720.

Belleforest de Comingeois, François de. *L'Histoire des Neuf Roys Charles.* Paris: Olivier de P. L'Huillier, 1568.

Bennington, Geoffrey. *Sententiousness and the Novel.* Cambridge: Cambridge University Press, 1985.

Bernstein, J. M. *The Philosophy of the Novel.* Minneapolis: University of Minnesota Press, 1984.

Berteaud, Madeleine. "De *L'Astrée* au *Polexandre,* pourquoi mourir?," *Travaux de linguistique et de littérature,* 22, no. 2 (1982).

——. *L'Astrée et Polexandre: Du roman pastoral au roman héroïque.* Geneva: Droz, 1986.

Bitton, Davis. *The French Nobility in Crisis.* Stanford: Stanford University Press, 1969.

Blanchot, Maurice. *Lautréamont et Sade.* Paris: Minuit, 1963.

Blum, Carol. *Diderot: The Virtue of a Philosopher.* New York: Viking, 1974.

Boaistuau, Pierre. *Histoires tragiques.* Paris: Champion, 1977.

Boileau-Despréaux, Nicolas. *Œuvres.* Ed. G. Mongrédien. Paris: Garnier, 1961.

Boisrobert, François Le Metel de. *Histoire indienne d'Anaxandre et d'Orazie.* Paris: F. Poneray, 1629.

Bougeant, Guillaume Hyacinthe. *Voyage merveilleux du Prince Fan-Férédin dans la Romancie.* Paris: LeMercier, 1735.

Bourdieu, Pierre. *La Distinction: Critique sociale du jugement.* Paris: Minuit, 1979.

Boursault, Edme. *Le Prince de Condé, nouvelle historique.* Paris: Guignard, 1681.

Bray, René. *La Formation de la doctrine classique en France.* Paris: Nizet, 1963.

Bremner, Geoffrey. *Order and Chance: The Pattern of Diderot's Thought.* Cambridge: Cambridge University Press, 1983.

Brenkman, John. *Culture and Domination.* Ithaca, N.Y.: Cornell University Press, 1987.

Brownlee, Kevin, and Marina Scordilis Brownlee. *Romance: Generic Transformation from Chrétien de Troyes to Cervantes.* Hanover, N.H.: University Press of New England, 1985.

Buffon, Georges-Louis Leclerc, comte de. *De l'homme.* Paris: Maspero, 1971.

Bussy, Roger de Rabutin, comte de. *Les Mémoires de Messire Roger de Rabutin, Comte de Bussy.* Paris: J. Anisson, 1696.

Calinescu, Matei. *Five Faces of Modernity.* Durham, N.C.: Duke University Press, 1987.

Camus, Jean-Pierre. *Les entretiens historiques.* Paris: Bertault, 1639.

——. *Les spectacles d'horreur.* Paris: André Soubron, 1630.

Caplan, Jay. *Framed Narratives*. Minneapolis: University of Minnesota Press, 1985.

Carter, Angela. *The Sadeian Woman*. London: Virago, 1979.

Cassirer, Ernst. *The Philosophy of the Enlightenment*. Trans. Fritz Koelln and James Pettegrove. Princeton, N.J.: Princeton University Press, 1951.

Castiglione, Baldasare. *Le Courtisan*. Paris: N. Bonfons, 1585.

Catrysse, Jean. *Diderot et la mystification*. Paris: Nizet, 1970.

Cervantes, Miguel de. *Don Quixote*. Trans. John Ormsby and ed. Joseph R. Jones and Kenneth Douglas. New York: Norton, 1981.

Chabert, Nicole. "L'Amour du discours dans *L'Astrée*," *Dix-septième siècle*, 133, no. 4 (Oct./Dec. 1981).

Chaitlin, Gilbert. "Psychoanalysis and Narrative Action: The Primal Scene of the French Novel," *Style*, 18, no. 3 (Summer 1984).

Chambers, Ross. *Story and Situation*. Minneapolis: University of Minnesota Press, 1984.

Chapelain, Jean. "De la lecture des vieux romans" in Pierre-Daniel Huet's *Lettre-traité sur l'origine des romans*. Ed. Fabienne Gégou. Paris: Nizet, 1971 [1646].

———. "Lettre ou discours du Monsieur Chapelain à Monsieur Favereau Conseiller du Roi en sa cour des Aides, portant son opinion sur le poème d'*Adonis* du Chevalier Marino," [1623] in his *Opuscules critiques*. Paris: Droz, 1936.

———. *Ode à Monseigneur le Cardinal duc de Richelieu*. Paris: Jean Camusat, 1633.

Chaponnière, Paul. "Une Bévue de Diderot dans *La Religieuse*," *Revue d'Histoire littéraire de la France*, 22 (1915).

Charnes, Jean-Antoine de. *Conversations sur la critique de La Princesse de Clèves*. Paris: Claude Barbin, 1679.

Chartier, Roger, Marie-Madeleine Compère, and Dominique Julia. *L'Education en France du XVIe au XVIIIe siècle*. Paris: Sedes, 1976.

Chaussinand-Nogaret, Guy. *The French Nobility in the Eighteenth Century*. Trans. William Doyle. Cambridge: Cambridge University Press, 1985.

Chaytor, H. J. *From Script to Print: An Introduction to Medieval Literature*. Cambridge: Cambridge University Press, 1945.

Chesnaye Desbois, François-Alexandre Aubert de la. *Lettres amusantes et critiques sur les romans en general*. Paris: Gissey, 1743.

Clark, G. N. *The Seventeenth Century*. Oxford: Clarendon Press, 1947.

Clarke, D. R. "Corneille's Differences with the Seventeenth-Century Doctrinaires over the Moral Authority of the Poet," *Modern Language Review*, 80, no. 3 (July 1985).

Clorinde. Paris: Augustin Courbé, 1654.

Collas, Georges, ed. *Les Sentimens de L'Académie Françoise sur la tragi-comédie du Cid.* Paris: Picard et fils, 1912.

Constant, Jean-Marie. *La Vie quotidienne de la noblesse française au XVIe–XVIIe siècles.* Paris: Hachette, 1985.

Corbin, Jacques. *Les Amours de Philocaste, où par mille beaux et rares accidens il se voit que les variables hazards de la fortune ne peuvent rien sur la constance d'amour.* Paris: Jean Gesselin, 1601.

Corneille, Pierre. *Œuvres complètes.* Paris: Seuil, 1963.

Coulet, Henri. *Le Roman jusqu'à la Révolution.* Paris: Colin, 1967.

———. "Un siècle, un genre?," *Revue d'Histoire littéraire de la France*, 77, no. 3–4 (May/Aug. 1977).

Courtilz de Sandraz, Gatien de. *Mémoires de M.L.C.D.R.* The Hague: Henry van Bulderon, 1713 [1687].

Crébillon, Claude Prosper Jolyot de. *Les Egarements du cœur et de l'esprit.* Paris: Gallimard, 1977.

Cuthbertson, Gilbert. *Political Myth and the Epic.* East Lansing: Michigan State University Press, 1975.

Damisch, Hubert. "L'Ecriture sans mesures," *Tel Quel*, no. 28 (Winter 1967).

Danto, Arthur C. *Narration and Knowledge.* New York: Columbia University Press, 1985.

Davis, Lennard. *Factual Fictions.* New York: Columbia University Press, 1983.

———. *Resisting Novels.* New York: Methuen, 1987.

Debaisieux, Martine. *Le Procès du roman.* Saratoga, Calif.: Anma Libri, 1989.

de Beauvoir, Simone. *Faut-il brûler Sade?* Paris: Gallimard, 1955.

DeJean, Joan. *Libertine Strategies.* Columbus: Ohio State University Press, 1981.

Della Valle, Daniella. "Le Thème et la structure de l'"echo' dans la pastorale dramatique française au XVIIe siècle." In *Le Genre pastoral en Europe du XVe au XVIIe siècle*, ed. Claude Longeon. Saint-Etienne: Publications de l'Université de Saint-Etienne, 1980.

de Man, Paul. *Blindness and Insight.* Minneapolis: University of Minnesota Press, 1983.

Desmaretz de Saint-Sorlin. *Rosane, histoire tirée de celles des Romains et des Perses.* Paris: H. Le Gras, 1639.

Desmolets, Pierre-Nicolas. *Continuation des Mémoires de littérature et d'histoire.* Paris: Simart, 1728.

Diderot, Denis. *Œuvres.* Ed. J.-A. Naigeon. Paris: Desray et Deterville, 1798.

———. *Correspondance.* Ed. Georges Roth. Paris: Minuit, 1957.

———. *Œuvres philosophiques.* Paris: Classiques Garnier, 1959.

———. *Œuvres romanesques.* Paris: Classiques Garnier, 1962.

————. *The Nun.* Trans. Leonard Tancock. New York: Penguin, 1972.

Dieckmann, Herbert. *Cinq leçons sur Diderot.* Geneva: Droz, 1959.

————. "The Preface-annexe of *La Religieuse*," *Diderot Studies* II (1952).

Doutrepont, Georges. *Les Mises en prose des epopées et des romans chevaleresques du XIVe au XVIe siècle.* Brussels: Palais des Académies, 1939.

Du Bellay, Joachim. *La Deffence et illustration de la langue francoyse.* Ed.

Du Bellay, Joachim. *La Deffence et illustration de la langue francoyse.* Ed. Henri Chamard. Paris: Marcel Didier, 1970.

Du Chesne, André. *Les Antiquitez et recherches de la grandeur & majesté des Roys de France.* Paris: Jean Petit-Pas, 1609.

Duchet, Claude. "Une écriture de la socialité," *Poétique,* 16 (1973).

DuPlaisir. *Sentimens sur les lettres et sur l'histoire.* Paris: C. Blageart, 1683.

Dupont, J. B. *Le Miroir des dames, où les effects d'une saincte amitié sont en vif représentés.* Lyon, 1605.

d'Urfé, Honoré. *L'Astrée.* Lyon: Pierre Masson, 1926.

Eagleton, Terry. *Criticism and Ideology.* London: Verso, 1978.

Edmiston, William F. "Sacrifice and Innocence in *La Religieuse*," *Diderot Studies* XIX (1978).

Ehrard, Jean, and Guy Palmade. *L'Histoire.* Paris: Colin, 1964.

Ehrmann, Jacques. *L'Amour et l'illusion dans "L'Astrée."* Paris: PUF, 1963.

Ellrich, Robert J. "The Rhetoric of *La Religieuse* and Eighteenth-Century Forensic Rhetoric," *Diderot Studies* III (1961).

Fauchery, Pierre. *La Destinée féminine dans le roman européen du dix-huitième siècle.* Paris: Colin, 1972.

Felman, Shoshana. "Henry James: Madness and Interpretation," *Yale French Studies,* 55/56 (1978).

————. *Le Scandale du corps parlant.* Paris: Seuil, 1980.

Fénelon, François de Salignac de la Motte de. *Les Aventures de Télémaque.* Paris: Classiques Garnier, 1987.

Fogel, Michèle. *Les Cérémonies de l'information dans la France du XVIe au XVIIIe siècle.* Paris: Fayard, 1989.

Ford, Franklin. *Robe and Sword.* New York: Harper and Row, 1965.

Formey, Jean Henri Samuel. *Conseils pour former une Bibliothèque peu nombreuse mais choisie.* Berlin: Haude et Spener, 1755 [1746].

Foucault, Michel. "Le Langage à l'infini," *Tel Quel,* no. 15 (1963).

————. *Les Mots et les choses.* Paris: Gallimard, 1966.

Freud, Sigmund. *Complete Psychological Works: Standard Edition.* Trans. and ed. J. Strachey. New York: Norton, 1976.

Frow, John. *Marxism and Literary History.* Cambridge, Mass.: Harvard University Press, 1986.

Frye, Northrop. *Anatomy of Criticism.* Princeton, N.J.: Princeton University Press, 1971.

Furetière, Antoine. *Le Roman bourgeois*. In *Romanciers du XVIIe siècle*, ed. Antoine Adam. Paris: Bibliothèque de la Pléiade, 1958.

Gallop, Jane. *Intersections*. Lincoln: University of Nebraska Press, 1982.

———. *The Daughter's Seduction*. Ithaca, N.Y.: Cornell University Press, 1982.

Genette, Gérard. *Figures II*. Paris: Seuil, 1969.

———. *Figures III*. Paris: Seuil, 1972.

Gerzan, François du Soucy. *L'Histoire afriquaine de Cléomède et de Sophonisbe*. Paris: C. Morlot, 1627.

Girard, René. *Violence and the Sacred*. Baltimore, Md.: Johns Hopkins University Press, 1977.

Glotz, Marguerite, and Madeleine Maire. *Salons du XVIIIe siècle*. Paris: Nouvelles Editions Latines, 1949.

Godenne, René. *Histoire de la nouvelle française aux XVIIe et XVIIIe siècles*. Geneva: Droz, 1970.

Godzich, Wlad, and Jeffrey Kittay. *The Emergence of Prose*. Minneapolis: University of Minnesota Press, 1987.

Goldmann, Lucien. *The Philosophy of the Enlightenment*. Cambridge, Mass.: MIT Press, 1973.

Gomberville, Marin Le Roy de. *Polexandre*. Paris: Augustin Courbé, 1641.

Gossman, Lionel. *French Society and Culture*. Englewood Cliffs, N.J.: Prentice-Hall, 1972.

Gournay, Marie de Jars de. *L'Ombre de la damoiselle de Gournay*. Paris: Jean Libert, 1626.

Greenberg, Caren. "The World of Prose and Female Self-Inscription: Scudéry's *Les Femmes illustres*," *L'Esprit créateur*, 23, no. 2 (1983).

Grente, Georges, ed. *Dictionnaire des lettres*. Paris: Fayard, 1954.

Groethuysen, Bernard. *L'Eglise et la bourgeoisie*. Paris: Gallimard, 1956.

Harari, Josué. *Scenarios of the Imaginary: Theorizing the French Enlightenment*. Ithaca, N.Y.: Cornell University Press, 1987.

Harth, Erica. *Ideology and Culture in Seventeenth-Century France*. Ithaca, N.Y.: Cornell University Press, 1983.

Hauser, Arnold. *The Social History of Art*. New York: Vintage Books, n.d.

Hayes, Julie C. "Retrospection and Contradiction in Diderot's *La Religieuse*," *Romanic Review*, 77, no. 3 (May 1986).

Hayman, David. *Re-Forming the Narrative: Toward a Mechanics of Modernist Fiction*. Ithaca, N.Y.: Cornell University Press, 1987.

Hazard, Paul. *La Crise de la conscience européenne, 1680–1715*. Paris: Fayard, 1961.

Heller, Agnes. *Lukács Reappraised*. New York: Columbia University Press, 1983.

Herodotus. *The Histories*. Trans. Aubrey de Sélincourt. New York: Penguin, 1983.

Hipp, Marie-Thérèse. *Mythes et réalités: Enquête sur le roman et les mémoires (1660–1700)*. Paris: Klincksieck, 1976.

Hirsch, Marianne. "A Mother's Discourse: Incorporation and Repetition in *La Princesse de Clèves*," *Yale French Studies*, no. 62 (1981).

Hollander, John. *The Figure of Echo*. Berkeley: University of California Press, 1981.

Holton, R. J. *The Transition from Feudalism to Capitalism*. New York: St. Martin's, 1985.

Homer. *The Iliad of Homer*. Trans. Richmond Lattimore. Chicago: University of Chicago Press, 1974.

Horkheimer, Max, and Theodor Adorno. *Dialectic of Enlightenment*. New York: Continuum, 1987.

Huet, Pierre-Daniel. *Lettre-traité sur l'origine des romans*. Ed. Fabienne Gégou. Paris: Nizet, 1971 [1669].

Irail, Saint-Simon-Augustin, abbé d'. *Querelles littéraires, ou Mémoires Pour servir à l'Histoire des Révolutions de la République des Lettres, depuis Homère jusqu'à nos jours*. Paris: Durand, 1761.

Irigaray, Luce. *Speculum of the Other Woman*. Trans. Gillian Gill. Ithaca, N.Y.: Cornell University Press, 1985.

Jacquin, Armand-Pierre. *Entretiens sur les romans: Ouvrage moral et critique*. Paris: Duchesne, 1755.

Jameson, Fredric. *Marxism and Form*. Princeton, N.J.: Princeton University Press, 1971.

———. *The Political Unconscious*. Ithaca, N.Y.: Cornell University Press, 1982.

Josephs, Herbert. "Diderot's *La Religieuse*: Libertinism and the Dark Cave of the Soul," *MLN*, 91, no. 4 (May 1976).

Judovitz, Dalia. "The Aesthetics of Implausibility: *La Princesse de Clèves*," *MLN*, 99, no. 5 (Dec. 1984).

Kamuf, Peggy. *Fictions of Feminine Desire*. Lincoln: University of Nebraska Press, 1982.

Kavanagh, Thomas. *The Vacant Mirror. Studies on Voltaire and the Eighteenth Century*, 104 (1973).

Kearns, Edward John. *Ideas in Seventeenth-Century France*. Manchester, Eng.: Manchester University Press, 1979.

Kettering, Sharon. *Patrons, Brokers and Clients in Seventeenth-Century France*. New York: Oxford University Press, 1986.

Klaits, Joseph. *Printed Propaganda under Louis XIV: Absolute Monarchy and Public Opinion*. Princeton, N.J.: Princeton University Press, 1976.

Klossowski, Pierre. *Sade mon prochain*. Paris: Seuil, 1967.

Laborde, Alice. *Sade romancier*. Neuchâtel: Baconnière, 1974.

Lacan, Jacques. *L'Ethique de la psychanalyse: Le séminaire, livre VII*. Paris: Seuil, 1986.

Laclau, Ernesto. *New Reflections on the Revolution of Our Time*. London: Verso, 1990.

Laclau, Ernesto, and Chantal Mouffe. *Hegemony and Socialist Strategy*. London: Verso, 1985.

Laclos, Pierre Choderlos de. *Les Liaisons dangereuses*. Paris: Garnier-Flammarion, 1964.

Laden, Marie-Paul. *Self-Imitation in the Eighteenth-Century Novel*. Princeton, N.J.: Princeton University Press, 1987.

Lafayette, Marie-Madeleine, comtesse de. *Correspondance de Madame de Lafayette*. Ed. André Beaunier. Paris: Gallimard, 1942.

———. *Romans et nouvelles*. Paris: Classiques Garnier, 1970.

———. *The Princesse de Clèves*. Trans. Nancy Mitford. New York: Penguin, 1978.

La Martinière, Antoine Augustin Bruzen de. *Introduction générale à l'étude des sciences et des belles lettres en faveur des personnes qui ne savent que le François*. The Hague: Beauregard, 1731.

La Mesnardière, Hippolyte-Jules Pilet de. *La Poétique*. Paris: Antoine de Sommaville, 1639.

La Mothe le Vayer, François de. *Œuvres*. Paris: Augustin Courbé, 1662.

La Solle, Henri-François de. *Memoires de deux amis*. London, 1754.

Lattimore, Richmond. "Preface" to his translation of *The Iliad of Homer*. Chicago: University of Chicago Press, 1974.

Laugaa, Maurice. *Lectures de Madame de Lafayette*. Paris: Colin, 1971.

———. "Pour une poétique de la négation," *Revue des sciences humaines*, 41, no. 164 (1976).

Laugaa-Traut, Françoise. *Lectures de Sade*. Paris: Colin, 1973.

Lee, Vera G. "The Edifying Example." In *French Women and the Age of Enlightenment*, ed. Samia I. Spencer. Bloomington: Indiana University Press, 1984.

Lefebvre, Henri. *Diderot, les affirmations fondamentales du matérialisme*. Paris: L'Arche, 1983.

Leiner, Wolfgang. "Mars et Minerve: sur le statut des écrivains." In *L'Age d'or du mécénat, 1598–1661*, ed. Roland Mousnier and Jean Mesnard. Paris: Editions du CNRS, 1985.

Lely, Gilbert. *Vie du marquis de Sade*. Paris: Garnier Frères, 1982.

Lenglet-Dufresnoy, Nicolas. *Méthode pour étudier l'histoire*. Paris: Pierre Gandouin, 1729.

Lesage, Alain-René. *Histoire de Gil Blas de Santillane*. Paris: Garnier-Flammarion, 1977.

Les tragiques amours du fidel' Yrion et de la belle Parithée, où se voit combien peut un'amour honorablement et sainctement poursuivie et comme se termine celle qui a ses intentions impudiques. Paris: Canut et Mareschel, 1601.

Levenson, Michael H. *A Genealogy of Modernism: A Study of English*

Literary Doctrine, 1908–1922. Cambridge: Cambridge University Press, 1984.

Lever, Maurice. *Le Roman français au XVIIe siècle.* Paris: PUF, 1981.

———. "Le Statut de la critique dans 'Le Berger extravagant'," *Revue d'Histoire littéraire de la France,* 77, no. 3–4 (May/Aug. 1977).

Levron, Jacques. *La Vie quotidienne à la cour de Versailles aux XVIIe–XVIIIe siècles.* Paris: Hachette, 1978.

Lewinter, Roger. *Diderot ou les mots de l'absence.* Paris: Champ Libre, 1976.

L'Extraordinaire du Mercure Galant. Apr. 1678.

l'Hermite, François. *Page disgracié.* Paris: Stock, 1946.

Lord, Albert. *The Singer of Tales.* Cambridge: Harvard University Press, 1960.

Lord, George deForest. *Trials of the Self: Heroic Ordeals in the Epic Tradition.* Hamden, Conn.: Archon Books, 1983.

Lorris, Pierre-Georges. *La Fronde.* Paris: Editions Albin Michel, 1961.

Lotringer, Sylvère. "La Structuration romanesque," *Critique,* 26 (1970).

Lougee, Carolyn C. *Le Paradis des Femmes: Women, Salons, and Social Stratification in Seventeenth-Century France.* Princeton, N.J.: Princeton University Press, 1976.

Lough, John, and Jacques Proust, eds. *Encyclopédie.* Paris: Hermann, 1976.

Lukács, Georg. *The Theory of the Novel.* Trans. Anna Bostock. Cambridge, Mass.: MIT Press, 1968.

Lyons, John D. "Narrative, Interpretation and Paradox: *La Princesse de Clèves,*" *Romanic Review,* 72, no. 4 (Nov. 1981).

Maillard, Jean. *Les Romans appréciés, ouvrage Qui n'est rien moins qu'un Roman.* Amsterdam: Neaulme & Gosse, 1756.

Malherbe, François de. *Œuvres.* Ed. Antoine Adam. Paris: Bibliothèque de la Pléiade, 1971.

Mandrou, Robert. *Des humanistes aux hommes de sciences.* Paris: Seuil, 1973.

Marcuse, Herbert. "The Affirmative Character of Culture," in his *Negations: Essays in Critical Theory.* Trans. Jeremy J. Shapiro. London: Free Association Books, 1988.

Marivaux, Pierre Carlet de Chamblain de. *La Vie de Marianne.* Paris: Garnier-Flammarion, 1978.

———. *Le Paysan parvenu.* Paris: Gallimard, 1981.

Marmontel, Jean-François. *Œuvres complètes de Marmontel.* Paris: Verdière, 1819 [1787].

Martin, Henri-Jean. *Livre, pouvoirs, et société à Paris au XVIIe siècle.* Geneva: Droz, 1969.

Martin, Wallace. *Recent Theories of Narrative.* Ithaca, N.Y.: Cornell University Press, 1986.

Martínez-Bonati, Félix. *Fictive Discourse and the Structures of Literature.* Ithaca, N.Y.: Cornell University Press, 1981.

May, Georges. *Diderot et "La Religieuse."* Paris: PUF, 1954.

———. *Le Dilemme du roman au XVIIIe siècle.* Paris: PUF, 1963.

McKeon, Michael. *The Origins of the English Novel, 1600–1740.* Baltimore, Md.: Johns Hopkins University Press, 1987.

Mézeray, François Eudes de. *Abrégé chronologique de l'histoire de France.* Amsterdam: Abraham Wolfgang, 1682.

———. *Histoire de France depuis Faramond jusqu'à maintenant.* Paris: Mathieu Guillemot, 1643–51.

Miller, Jacques-Alain. "The Analytic Experience: Means, Ends, and Results." In *Lacan and the Subject of Language,* ed. Ellie Ragland-Sullivan and Mark Bracher. New York: Routledge, 1991.

Miller, Nancy K. "Emphasis Added: Plots and Plausibilities in Women's Fiction," *PMLA,* 26, no. 1 (Jan. 1981).

———. "'I's' in Drag: The Sex of Recollection," *The Eighteenth Century,* 22, no. 1 (1981).

Molière, Jean Baptiste Poquelin. *Œuvres complètes.* Paris: Garnier, 1962.

———. *The High-Brow Ladies.* New York: Modern Library.

Montesquieu, Charles-Louis de Secondat. *Les Lettres persanes.* Paris: Garnier-Flammarion, 1964.

———. *Œuvres complètes.* Paris: Bibliothèque de la Pléiade, 1949.

Moriarty, Michael. *Taste and Ideology in Seventeenth-Century France.* Cambridge: Cambridge University Press, 1988.

Mortimer, Armine Kotin. *La Clôture narrative.* Paris: Corti, 1985.

Mouligneau, Geneviève. *Madame de Lafayette romancière?* Brussels: Editions de l'Université de Bruxelles, 1980.

Mueller, Marlies. *Les Idées politiques dans le roman héroïque de 1630 à 1670.* Lexington, Ky.: French Forum Publishers, 1984.

Murray, Timothy. *Theatrical Legitimation.* New York: Oxford University Press, 1987.

Mylne, Vivienne. *The Eighteenth-Century French Novel: Techniques of Illusion.* Cambridge: Cambridge University Press, 1981.

———. "What Suzanne Knew: Lesbianism and *La Religieuse,*" *Studies on Voltaire and the Eighteenth Century,* 208 (1982).

Nagle, Jean. "Furetière entre la magistrature et les bénéfices: Autour du Livre Second du *Roman bourgeois,*" *Dix-septième siècle,* no. 128 (July/Sept. 1980).

Navarre, Marguerite d'Angoulême de. *L'Heptaméron.* Paris: Garnier, 1967.

Nicole, Pierre. *Les Imaginaires et les Visionnaires.* Cologne: Pierre Marteau, 1683.

Niderst, Alain. *La Princesse de Clèves: Le roman paradoxal.* Paris: Larousse, 1973.

Nohrnberg, James. "The *Iliad.*" In *Homer to Brecht: The European Epic and Dramatic Traditions*, ed. Michael Seidel and Edward Mendelson. New Haven, Conn.: Yale University Press, 1977.

Pavel, Thomas. *Fictional Worlds.* Cambridge: Harvard University Press, 1986.

Perrault, Charles. *Paralelle des anciens et des modernes, en ce qui regarde les arts et les sciences.* Paris: Coignard, 1688.

Picard, Roger. *Les Salons littéraires et la société française.* New York: Brentano, 1943.

Pintard, René. *Le Libertinage érudit dans la première moitié du dix-septième siècle.* Paris: Boivin, 1943.

Plato. *The Republic.* Trans. G. M. A. Grube. Indianapolis, Ind.: Hackett, 1974.

Pleynet, Marcelin. "La Poésie doit avoir pour but. . . ." In *Théorie d'ensemble*, ed. Michel Foucault, Roland Barthes, and Jacques Derrida. Paris: Seuil, 1968.

Pottinger, David T. *The French Book Trade in the Ancien Régime, 1500–1791.* Cambridge: Harvard University Press, 1958.

Prévost, Antoine-François. *Histoire du chevalier Des Grieux et de Manon Lescaut.* Paris: Garnier-Flammarion, 1967.

Rabelais, François. *Œuvres complètes.* Paris: Garnier, 1962.

Rabine, Leslie. "History, Ideology, and Femininity in *Manon Lescaut*," *Stanford French Review*, 5, no. 1 (Spring 1981).

Racine, Jean. *Théâtre complet.* Paris: Garnier-Flammarion, 1965.

Ragland-Sullivan, Ellie. *Jacques Lacan and the Philosophy of Psychoanalysis.* Urbana: University of Illinois Press, 1987.

Ramsay, André-Michel. "Discours de la Poesie epique et de l'excellence du poeme de Telemaque." In François de Salignac de la Motte de Fénelon, *Les Avantures de Telemaque.* Paris: Florentin Delaulne, 1717.

Rapin, René. *Réflexions sur la poétique de ce temps, et sur les ouvrages des Poètes anciens & modernes.* Geneva: Droz, 1970 [1675].

Ray, William. *Story and History.* Cambridge, Mass.: Basil Blackwell, 1990.

Reichler, Claude. *La Diabolie.* Paris: Minuit, 1979.

Reiss, Timothy J. *The Discourse of Modernism.* Ithaca, N.Y.: Cornell University Press, 1982.

Restif de la Bretonne, Nicolas-Edme. *La Paysanne pervertie.* Paris: Garnier-Flammarion, 1972 [1776].

Rex, Walter E. "Secrets from Suzanne: The Tangled Motives of *La Religieuse*," *The Eighteenth Century*, 24, no. 3 (Spring 1983).

Reynier, Gustave. *Le Roman sentimental avant L'Astrée.* Paris: Armand Colin, 1908.

Robert, Marthe. *Origins of the Novel.* Bloomington: Indiana University Press, 1980.

Roche, Daniel. *Les Républicains des lettres*. Paris: Fayard, 1988.

Rosbottom, Ronald C. *Marivaux's Novels: Theme and Function in Early Eighteenth-Century Narrative*. Cranbury, N.J.: Fairleigh Dickinson University Press, 1974.

Rosmarin, Adena. *The Power of Genre*. Minneapolis: University of Minnesota Press, 1984.

Ross, Kristin. "The Narrative of Fascination: Pathos and Repetition in *Manon Lescaut*," *The Eighteenth Century*, 24, no. 3 (Spring 1983).

Rousset, Jean. *La Littérature de l'age baroque en France*. Paris: Corti, 1953.

Rudé, George. *Europe in the Eighteenth Century*. Cambridge, Mass.: Harvard University Press, 1985.

Rustin, Jacques. "L'Histoire véritable dans la littérature romanesque du XVIIIe siècle français," *Cahiers de l'Association Internationale des Etudes Françaises*, 18 (1966).

Ryding, William W. *Structure in Medieval Narrative*. The Hague: Mouton, 1971.

Sade, Donatien-Alphonse-François, marquis de. *Justine ou les malheurs de la vertu*. Paris: 10/18, 1969.

———. *La Nouvelle Justine*. Paris: 10/18, 1978.

———. *Œuvres complètes*. Paris: Cercle du livre précieux, 1967.

———. *Three Complete Novels*. Trans. Richard Seaver and Austryn Wainhouse. New York: Grove Press, 1965.

Saint-Amand, Pierre. *Séduire, ou la passion des lumières*. Paris: Klincksieck, 1987.

Saint-Réal, César, abbé de. *Dom Carlos*. Amsterdam: Gaspar Commelin, 1672.

Scarry, Elaine. *The Body in Pain: The Making and Unmaking of the World*. New York: Oxford University Press, 1985.

Schor, Naomi. *Breaking the Chain*. New York: Columbia University Press, 1985.

Scudéry, Madeleine de. *Artamène ou le Grand Cyrus*. Paris: Augustin Courbé, 1650.

———. *Ibrahim ou l'Illustre Bassa*. Paris: Antoine de Sommaville, 1641.

Segal, Naomi. *The Unintended Reader*. Cambridge: Cambridge University Press, 1986.

Serroy, Jean. *Roman et réalité*. Paris: Minard, 1981.

Sfez, Fabien. "Le Roman polylexique du XVIIe siècle: La parole sur le texte e(s)t la parole du texte," *Littérature*, no. 13 (Feb. 1974).

Shklovsky, Victor. "Art as Technique." In *Russian Formalist Criticism*, ed. Lee T. Lemon and Marin J. Reis. Lincoln: University of Nebraska Press, 1965.

Showalter, English. *The Evolution of the French Novel, 1641–1782*. Princeton, N.J.: Princeton University Press, 1972.

Sollers, Philippe. "Sade dans le texte," *Tel Quel*, no. 28 (Winter 1967).

Solnon, Jean-François. *La Cour de France*. Paris: Fayard, 1987.

Sorel, Charles. *De la connoissance des bons livres, ou examen de plusieurs auteurs*. Ed. Lucia Moretti Cenerini. Rome: Bulzoni, 1974.

———. *Histoire comique de Francion*. In *Romanciers du XVIIe siècle*, ed. Antoine Adam. Paris: Bibliothèque de la Pléiade, 1958.

———. *La Bibliothèque françoise*. Paris: Compagnie des Libraires du Palais, 1667.

———. *Le Berger extravagant. Ou parmy des fantaisies amoureuses on void les impertinences des Romans & de Poësie*. Paris: Toussainct du Bray, 1627.

———. *L'Orphise de Chrysante*. Paris: Toussainct du Bray, 1623.

———. *Polyandre, histoire comique*. Paris: Chez la veuve Nicolas Cercy, 1648.

Stegmann, André. "L'Ambiguïté du concept héroïque dans la littérature morale en France sous Louis XIII." In *Héroïsme et création littéraire sous les règnes d'Henri IV et de Louis XIII*, ed. Noémie Hepp and Georges Livet. Paris: Klincksieck, 1974.

Stewart, Philip. *Half-Told Tales*. Chapel Hill: North Carolina Studies in the Romance Languages and Literatures, 1987.

———. *Imitation and Illusion in the French Memoir-Novel, 1700–1750: The Art of Make-Believe*. New Haven, Conn.: Yale University Press, 1969.

———. *Rereadings: Eight Early French Novels*. Birmingham, Ala.: Summa, 1984.

Stone, Lawrence. *The Crisis of the Aristocracy*. Oxford: Oxford University Press, 1967.

Suleiman, Susan. *Authoritarian Fictions: The Ideological Novel as a Literary Genre*. New York: Columbia University Press, 1983.

Suozo, Andrew G., Jr. *The Comic Novels of Charles Sorel*. Lexington, Ky.: French Forum Publishers, 1982.

Suratteau, Jean. "De la bourgeoisie de province à la bourgeoisie nationale: Renouvellement des élites?" In *Bourgeoisies de province et révolution*, ed. Michel Vovelle. Grenoble: Presses Universitaires de Grenoble, 1987.

Tans, J. A. G. "Un Sterne français: Antoine Furetière, la fonction du *Roman bourgeois*," *Dix-septième siècle*, no. 128 (July-Sept. 1980).

Tapié, Victor. *France in the Age of Louis XIII and Richelieu*. Trans. and ed. D. Lockie. Cambridge: Cambridge University Press, 1984.

Thomas, Ruth P. "The Death of an Ideal: Female Suicides in the Eighteenth-Century French Novel." In *French Women and the Age of Enlightenment*, ed. Samia I. Spencer. Bloomington: Indiana University Press, 1984.

Todorov, Tzvetan. *Introduction à la littérature fantastique*. Paris: Seuil, 1970.

Turk, Edward Baron. *Baroque Fiction-Making: A Study of Gomberville's Polexandre.* Chapel Hill: University of North Carolina Press, 1978.

Valincour, Jean-Henri du Trousset de. *Lettres à Madame la Marquise *** sur le sujet de La Princesse de Clèves.* Ed. Albert Cazes. Paris: Blossard, 1925.

Vallois, Marie-Claire. "Politique du paradoxe: Tableau de moeurs / tableau familial dans *La Religieuse*," *Romanic Review*, 76, no. 2 (Mar. 1985).

Varga, Kibédi. "La Vraisemblance—Problèmes de terminologie, problèmes de poétique." In *Critique et création littéraires en France au XVIIe siècle*, ed. Marc Fumaroli. Paris: Editions du CNRS, 1977.

Vauvenargues, Luc de Clapiers, marquis de. *Introduction à la connaissance de l'esprit humain.* Paris: Garnier-Flammarion, 1981 [1746].

Veins du Coudray, Aymar de. *Les Amours de Charitene et Amandus.* Paris: A. du Brueil, 1597.

Verdier, Gabrielle. *Charles Sorel.* Boston: Twayne, 1984.

Veyne, Paul. *Comment on écrit l'histoire: Essai d'épistémologie.* Paris: Seuil, 1971.

Viala, Alain. *Naissance de l'écrivain.* Paris: Minuit, 1985.

Villiers, Pierre de. *Réflexions sur les défauts d'autruy.* Paris: Claude Barbin, 1690.

Voltaire, François Marie Arouet. *Histoire de Charles XII.* Paris: Garnier-Flammarion, 1968.

von Wartburg, W. *Evolution et structure de la langue française.* Bern: A. Francke, 1969.

Watt, Ian. *The Rise of the Novel.* Berkeley: University of California Press, 1967.

Weber, Max. *The Methodology of the Social Sciences.* Trans. Edward A. Shils and Henry A. Finch. Glencoe, Ill.: Free Press, 1949.

White, Hayden. "The Value of Narrativity in the Representation of Reality." In *On Narrative*, ed. W. J. T. Mitchell. Chicago: University of Chicago Press, 1981.

Williams, Ioan. *The Idea of the Novel in Europe, 1600–1800.* New York: NYU Press, 1979.

Wine, Kathleen. "Furetière's *Roman bourgeois*: The Triumph of Process," *L'Esprit créateur*, 19, no. 1 (1979).

Young, Robert. *White Mythologies: Writing History and the West.* London: Verso, 1990.

Zizek, Slavoj. *The Sublime Object of Ideology.* London: Verso, 1989.

Index

In this index an "f" after a number indicates a separate reference on the next page, and an "ff" indicates separate references on the next two pages. A continuous discussion over two or more pages is indicated by a span of page numbers, e.g., "pp. 57–58." *Passim* is used for a cluster of references in close but not consecutive sequence.

Library of Congress Cataloging-in-Publication Data

DiPiero, Thomas, 1956-
  Dangerous truths and criminal passions: the evolution of the French novel,
1569–1791 / Thomas DiPiero.
     p.   cm.
Includes bibliographical references.
ISBN 0–8047–1999–3 (alk. paper):
  1. French fiction—17th century—History and criticism. 2. French fiction—
18th century—History and criticism. 3. French fiction—16th century—History and criticism. 4. Crimes of passion in literature. 5. Politics and literature—France. 6. Literature and society—France. 7. Social classes in literature.
8. Aristocracy in literature.   I. Title.
PQ645.D5   1992
843.009'358—dc20
91–40396
   CIP

⊗ This book is printed on acid-free paper.

DATE DUE

NOV 0 9 2009			